The Political Economy of Poverty, Equity, and Growth

Series editors
Deepak Lal and Hla Myint

A World Bank
Comparative Study

*The Political
Economy of Poverty,
Equity, and Growth*

*Five
Small Open
Economies*

**Edited by
Ronald Findlay
Stanislaw Wellisz**

Published for the World Bank
Oxford University Press

Oxford University Press

OXFORD NEW YORK TORONTO
DELHI BOMBAY CALCUTTA MADRAS KARACHI
KUALA LUMPUR SINGAPORE HONG KONG TOKYO
NAIROBI DAR ES SALAAM CAPE TOWN
MELBOURNE AUCKLAND
and associated companies in
BERLIN IBADAN

Published by Oxford University Press, Inc.
200 Madison Avenue, New York, N.Y. 10016

Oxford is a registered trademark of Oxford University Press.

Manufactured in the United States of America
First printing June 1993

Library of Congress Cataloging-in-Publication Data

Five small open economies / edited by Ronald Findlay, Stanislaw
Wellisz.
    p. cm.—(A World Bank comparative study. The Political
economy of poverty, equity, and growth.)
    Includes bibliographical references (p.   ) and index.
    ISBN 0-19-520880-3
    1. Poor—Developing countries—Case studies. 2. Developing
countries—Economic conditions—Case studies. 3. Developing
countries—Economic policy—Case studies. I. Findlay, Ronald.
II. Wellisz, Stanislaw. III. Series: World Bank comparative
studies. Political economy of poverty, equity, and growth.
HC59.72.P6F58 1993
330.9172′4—dc20   93-4390
                                                                    CIP

Foreword

This volume is the sixth of several emerging from the comparative study "The Political Economy of Poverty, Equity, and Growth," sponsored by the World Bank. The study was done to provide a critical evaluation of the economic history of selected developing countries in 1950–85. It explores the *processes* that yielded different levels of growth, poverty, and equity in these countries, depending on each country's initial resource endowment and economic structure, national institutions and forms of economic organization, and economic policies (including those that might have been undertaken).

The Scope of the Comparative Study

The basic building block of the project is a coherent story of the growth and income distribution experiences of each country, based on the methods of what may be termed "analytical economic history" (see Collier and Lal 1986) and "political economy." Each country study provides both a historical narrative and a deeper explanation of how and why things happened. Each study also seeks to identify the role of ideology and interest groups in shaping policy.

Our comparative approach involved pairing (or, in the present case, grouping) countries whose initial conditions or policies seemed to be either significantly similar or significantly different. Although initial impressions of similarity or difference may not have been borne out on closer inspection, this binary approach offered a novel and promising way of reconciling in-depth case studies with a broader comparative method of analysis.

To provide this in-depth study of individual cases, a smaller number of countries was selected than is conventional in comparative *statistical* studies. We have serious doubts about the validity of inferences drawn from such cross-sectional regression studies about historical processes (see Hicks 1979). Therefore this project, by combining qualitative with quantitative analysis, has tried instead to interpret the nature and significance of the usual quantifiable variables for each country in its historical and institutional context.

To provide some unifying elements to the project, we presented the authors of the country studies with several provisional hypotheses to be considered in the course of their work. These concern the determinants of growth, the importance of historical and organizational factors in determining alternative feasible paths of growth to redress poverty, and the relative roles of ideas, interests, and ideology in influencing decisionmaking.

The following list of the country studies and their principal authors suggests the range of the overall comparative study:

Malawi and Madagascar	Frederic L. Pryor
Egypt and Turkey	Bent Hansen
Sri Lanka and Malaysia	Henry Bruton
Indonesia and Nigeria	David Bevan, Paul Collier, and Jan Gunning
Thailand and Ghana	Oey A. Meesook, Douglas Rimmer, and Gus Edgren
Brazil and Mexico	Angus Maddison and Associates
Costa Rica and Uruguay	Simon Rottenberg
Colombia and Peru	Antonio Urdinola, Mauricio Carrizosa Serrano, and Richard Webb
Five Small Open Economies: Hong Kong, Singapore, Malta, Jamaica, and Mauritius	Ronald Findlay and Stanislaw Wellisz

Several of these volumes have been or will be published in this series by Oxford University Press. In addition, a volume of special studies on related topics has been published (Psacharopoulos 1991).

This Volume

Unlike all other volumes in this series, each of which analyzes a pair of countries on a comparative basis, this volume involves a comparison of five small open economies. All five are islands with small populations (the largest being Hong Kong, with a little more than 5 million people), and all have long been connected with the United Kingdom as former or, in the case of Hong Kong, present colonies. This status gives them a similar political and institutional background and a common dependence on external markets for their development.

This volume consists of five case studies, preceded by an introduction that describes the similarities and differences among the five cases and the methodology followed in conducting the research. The concluding chapter analyzes the outcomes in a comparative manner.

Despite the similarity in initial conditions, reflected in a relatively narrow dispersion of per capita incomes in 1960, the economic status of the five economies today is vastly different. The economies of Hong Kong and Singapore have grown at spectacular rates, exceeding those of most countries in the world over the same period, while Jamaica, despite having the best natural resource endowment of the five, has performed disappointingly. Malta places a respectable third in economic growth, followed by Mauritius, which has done quite well overall, especially in recent years.

Thus it is the three "barren" islands, whose only natural resources have been their harbors and favorable locations, that have done the best, while the two better-endowed plantation- and mineral-based economies, especially Jamaica, have faltered. As indicated in the studies, the struggle among domestic groups over rents from natural resources tends to engender policies that fail to promote the export of manufactures to expanding world markets.

Although Hong Kong and Singapore are often linked as East Asian export-oriented "miracle" economies, the study shows how different the development strategies have been beneath the surface. Only Hong Kong approximates the laissez-faire ideal, but even here there has been extensive government control of land use and provision of public housing. The Singaporean government, by contrast, has intervened extensively to promote domestic saving and to channel investment (largely by foreign multinational companies) into certain sectors, while providing generous physical and social infrastructure to induce this direct foreign investment, which is the mainstay of production and exports. Malta, unlike both Hong Kong and Singapore, has not had a liberal trade policy, but it has nevertheless done well in manufacturing, production, and export growth.

In light of recent tragic events in other parts of the world, it is encouraging to note that three of the islands—Mauritius in particular but also Singapore and Jamaica—have delicate ethnic balances to contend with in their political economy and that all have done so remarkably well.

Another important finding is that growth has not occurred at the expense of equity. Both Hong Kong and Singapore have experienced no deterioration in income distribution despite their extremely rapid growth. In fact, it is export growth that has raised wages and so served as an engine of redistribution as well as of growth. It is slowest-growing Jamaica that has experienced the greatest decline of equity, because it has lacked a vigorous mechanism for providing jobs and incomes for poor people. In Mauritius the wealthy Franco-Mauritian planters, with their sugar profits taxed heavily by the Hindu majority government, have invested actively in the export processing zone and thus provided a more dynamic source of employment and wage growth.

Taken together, the experience of the five small open economies vindicates the general wisdom of outward-looking policies.

Deepak Lal and Hla Myint
Series editors

References

Collier, Paul, and Deepak Lal. 1986. *Labour and Poverty in Kenya, 1900–1980.* Oxford, U.K.: Clarendon Press.

Hicks, J. R. 1979. *Causality in Economics.* Oxford, U.K.: Blackwell.

Psacharopoulos, George, ed. 1991. *Essays on Poverty, Equity, and Growth.* Elmsford, N.Y.: Pergamon.

Contents

1 Introduction

Ronald Findlay
Stanislaw Wellisz

This book presents a comparative study of the political economy of trade and development in five small open economies. It is one of eight volumes to emerge from the comprehensive study "The Political Economy of Poverty, Equity, and Growth," directed by Deepak Lal and Hla Myint, and, like the project as a whole, its purpose is to shed light on the determinants of growth and equity in developing countries. Although we do not eschew the standard analytical methods employed by growth models and trade theory, we believe that a deeper understanding of development can be gained through a study of a country's political economy—particularly the relations between a country's resources, its political conditions at independence, and its economic policies. The structure of the polity, in addition to that of the economy, can provide considerable insight into the interests and objectives that governing regimes and pressure groups in society contribute to economic policy.

These social and political variables, usually considered strictly exogenous in standard economic analysis, are themselves strongly influenced by such things as trade patterns and economic change in general. At the same time, they react to the economic policies pursued by the regime, whether because of the prospect of support for, or the threat of opposition to, the "passions and the interests" of the various segments of the polity. The intellectual tools needed to study development in this broader fashion are provided by analytical economic history and the "new" political economy.

Background and Methodology

Our "sample" consists of five small island economies, all of them former British colonies—Hong Kong, Singapore, Jamaica, Mauritius, and Malta. They are all small not only in the physical sense of area and population but also in the technical sense of being price takers in world commodity and capital markets. That is to say, they are severely limited in the extent

1

to which they can influence their terms and conditions of trade. Other common features are that they inherited similar institutions from their British colonial past and are equally exposed to the opportunities and the vicissitudes of world markets.

They differ notably in the natural resources they possess, in the ethnic variation in their populations, and in the nature of their polities. Hong Kong, Singapore, and Malta have no natural resources other than their excellent harbors, while Jamaica and Mauritius depend on their land and climate to support their plantation economies. Jamaica, in addition, is well endowed with a valuable mineral, bauxite. As for ethnic composition, the population of Hong Kong is almost entirely Chinese; Singapore's is predominantly so, but with substantial Indian and Malay communities; Malta is homogeneous; and Jamaica and particularly Mauritius have a diverse mixture of descendants of African slaves, Indian and Chinese indentured workers, and European planters. Politically, Jamaica, Mauritius, and Malta have democratic governments with active and open competition among their political parties; Hong Kong is governed by British civil servants and Singapore by a single dominant party and an elite bureaucracy. This rich mixture of economic structures and sociopolitical characteristics provides an interesting field for a comparative study of the political economy of trade and development.

Of these societies, only Malta has an indigenous population descended from its earliest inhabitants. Jamaica's native Arawaks were killed off by the Spaniards at the time of discovery; Mauritius was uninhabited when taken over by its first owners, the Dutch. Jamaica and Mauritius were subsequently acquired by the British and the French, respectively, who developed sugar plantations with the aid of imported African and Indian labor. Hong Kong and Singapore were more or less deserted islands until they were developed as ports and trading stations by the British in the nineteenth century with labor imported from the Chinese mainland. Although each had an important role to play in the vast machine of the British Empire, their status after World War II was highly problematic. The British military withdrawal after the Suez crisis of 1956 caused consternation in both Malta and Singapore, which at the time greatly depended on the expenditures of the British naval establishment. Mauritius, too, faced bleak prospects, with its growing population, scarcity of land, and soft markets for sugar. The situation in Jamaica was not much better, despite a larger and more diverse resource base. And Hong Kong saw its hopes for continuing as an entrepôt dashed when the Communists took over the mainland in 1948 and a flood of refugees poured into its territory.

The conditions of the postcolonial world were indeed harsh for these small economies, which found themselves struggling to maintain their viability in the face of dwindling options for attacking their problems. The outlook for Malta had grown so dismal that a United Nations report recommended mass emigration as the only feasible solution in the long run. But emigration was actually contributing to the problem, since those who departed tended to be the ones with skills, capital, and an entrepreneurial spirit. Even political integration with larger entities—such as Malaya in the case of Singapore, or a Caribbean federation in the case of Jamaica—proved undesirable or unfeasible.

Not only did these societies face an uncertain economic future, but they had to deal with urgent questions of social justice and redistribution, which also affected the means they chose for linking up with the world economy. These issues were of particular concern in Mauritius and Jamaica, where ethnic minorities (of French descent in the former and English descent in the latter) owned or operated the sugar estates; furthermore, multinational enterprises had firm control of the bauxite deposits in Jamaica. Militant labor movements, which had already been organized during the colonial period in both economies, were able to press for higher wages and other redistributive measures all the more strongly after independence, under ruling parties with close links to the trade unions. The implications for employment, production, investment, exports, and growth of measures taken in this regard were of the utmost importance for the future of these countries. In Hong Kong and Singapore the basic national resource was the skill and enterprise of the population, which quickly recognized that the margin for taxation, even of direct foreign investment in manufacturing, was limited by the mobility of foreign capital. Malta's strategic location also acted as a natural resource. The rents that other countries paid to gain access to the region allowed Malta to undertake extensive social welfare measures, particularly under labor-oriented governments. Thus the presence or absence of natural resources governed the approach to redistribution and growth in each island.

Up to now, much of the development literature has assumed that the choice of development strategy and the nature and extent of income redistribution have been guided by some abstract "social welfare function" that governments or policymakers wished to implement in the national interest. These decisionmakers were thought to be completely disinterested and benign entities whose job was to weigh only such abstract issues as present against future consumption, equality against efficiency, and so on. The position taken in this volume, in keeping with that of the project as a whole, is that policymakers do not make their choices in this manner. Rather, their choices are greatly influenced by the interests and concerns of the various groups in the government and the polity, such as the bureaucracy, organized labor, landowners, and others. Policy choices are therefore believed to have an endogenous dimension in that they are based on sectional interests, including those of a possibly "autonomous" state.

The extent to which this idea applies to conditions in developing countries can be determined by examining the links between the politics of interest groups and the patterns of factor endowment reflected in the distribution of income, as influenced by policy variables such as tariff rates and levels of government expenditure (see Findlay and Wellisz 1982; Findlay and Wilson 1987; Wellisz and Findlay 1988; and Findlay 1988, 1990). This method of analysis makes it possible to view the political economy of countries in the framework of simple stylized models of the familiar trade theory type, but with historical and political dimensions added by making economic policies endogenous to the extent that this is reasonable. Ultimately, of course, a degree of autonomy and independence is provided by the influence of personality and other forces that defy any attempt at complete historical determinism within a fully closed system.

Each of the islands examined in this study can be regarded as a politico-economic entity embedded in and interacting with a world politico-economic system. Each has a distinctive government, economy, and polity. The polity is made up of various social classes and interest groups such as entrepreneurs, landowners, the urban middle class, peasants, workers, and so on. The government is made up of the state's formal executive, legislative, and judicial institutions. And the economy, of course, refers to the economic system as conventionally understood. Schematically, each island can be analyzed in terms of the way these three components interact with each other and the way the three together interact with the external political and economic system of the world. This last includes not only the world market in the usual sense of where the prices of tradable goods are determined but also government negotiations on market access and foreign aid and the policies of relevant international institutions such as the International Monetary Fund (IMF). The interdependence of these various conceptual entities is depicted in figure 1-1.

In conventional economic analysis, the economy, E, responds to the policies and parameters set by the government, G, and the rest of the world, W. The polity, P, in the sense defined, has no role to play in the analysis. A diagram of this situation would have causal arrows going only from G to E, in the form of tax rates, tariff structures, and the like, and from W to E, in the form of tradable goods prices, interest rates, and so on. The term "political economy" as we understand it, however, refers not only to these kinds of interactions but also to attempts to make government policies endogenous by considering how they may be determined by the structure of various interests in the polity—including the ideological groups represented in the government, G. We must therefore include a causal arrow from the polity, P, to the government, G, along with a weaker causal arrow, indicated by a broken line, from G to W, to indicate that the government can also influence, within limits, the terms and conditions that it faces in the outside world. Market access for exports and the level of foreign aid are mutually determined by the government and the world through the foreign economic policy that the government adopts.

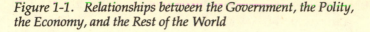

Figure 1-1. Relationships between the Government, the Polity, the Economy, and the Rest of the World

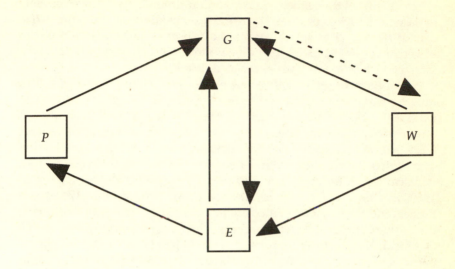

It is even more important to include an arrow going directly from the world to the government to signify the constraints placed on the government's actions not only by major foreign powers but also by international institutions such as the World Bank and the IMF. These constraints become particularly acute at times of crisis, when a state is in urgent need of credit and financial assistance.

An arrow from *E* to *G* indicates that the government greatly depends on revenue, which in turn depends on the performance of the economy. It is the flow of revenue that determines whether the government will be able to satisfy the various claims that are made on it. Another important part of the system can be depicted by an arrow going from the economy to the polity. It signifies that the performance of the economy directly affects social classes and interest groups through the distribution of income, unemployment, inflation, and so on. Changes in the condition of the polity again affect the government, which must adapt its policy instruments and objectives in response. Thus the system as a whole keeps moving in a dynamic sequence of interactions among interdependent parts. Particularly sharp crises in the economy will transmit themselves to the polity and lead to changes in government, as in the case of the transitions in Jamaica from the regime of Michael Manley's People's National party (PNP) to that of Edward Seaga and the Jamaica Labor party (JLP) and back again to Manley.

In our scheme, exogenous shocks come from the world, in the form of fluctuations in general activity or in particular commodity markets.

Although the polity is influenced by the economy, we do not maintain any rigid hypothesis of "economic determinism," according to which any change in politics or the social order must be due to influences emanating from the economic system. Certain important developments in the polity, such as the sharp turn to the left in Jamaica during the 1970s, cannot be traced to purely economic causes. Exogenous changes in ideology and other social forces also play a role, although these forces interact with economic influences at all levels.

Per capita incomes in our five economies were all fairly similar in 1960, ranging from about US$1,700 in Singapore and Hong Kong to about US$1,000 in Mauritius, a disparity of only 70 percent. By 1985, however, the disparity was enormous. Singapore and Hong Kong, at more than US$9,000, were essentially at the level of developed countries, having quintupled their per capita income over the twenty-five-year period. Jamaica, which had been quite close to Hong Kong and Singapore in 1960, was now at the bottom, at only US$11,725—a mere 17 percent higher over the two and a half decades. These figures reflect a dramatic disparity between the performance of the East Asian city-state, on the one hand, and a primary exporting country like Jamaica, on the other— perhaps the widest gap in performance in the entire developing world. Malta came in a respectable third, while Mauritius, last in 1960, did considerably better than Jamaica (see table 7-1).

Accounting for this huge variation in outcomes is essentially the main task of this study. Chapters 2–6 are devoted to analytical narratives of the experience of Hong Kong, Singapore, Jamaica, Mauritius, and Malta, in that order. Chapter 7 undertakes a comparative study of the relative successes and failures of the five small open economies as a function of their national endowments, social structures, and political systems, as well as internal and external shocks. We attempt not only to analyze which policies succeeded and which failed but also, wherever possible, to account for the political determinants of those policy decisions.

Hong Kong

Hong Kong is widely considered to exemplify the success of laissez-faire economic policy. Many analyses attribute this success to the lack of government intervention and assume that the free unfolding of market forces sufficiently explains the dynamism of the economy. Such a simplistic analysis has at least two flaws. First, history shows that laissez-faire capitalism is a fairly short-lived phenomenon inasmuch as the development of economic interest groups and the expansion of state power invariably cause the state to intervene more and more in the economic arena. Second, there is no reason to assume that a laissez-faire policy automatically leads to a dynamic, highly competitive economy. Even in the absence of government intervention, firms may exert market power, rigidities can develop in the labor market as the result of labor organization, entrepreneurship may be lacking, and so on.

The chapter on Hong Kong explains how a variety of economic, political, social, and geographic factors have interacted in a systemic fashion to sustain laissez-faire and competitive markets in Hong Kong. Principal among these factors are (a) the political and economic behavior of the immigrants, who have weakened the labor movement, provided a ready body of entrepreneurs, and reduced social and political pressures on the government, and (b) the government's peculiar form of colonial laissez-faire—showing extreme resistance to economic pressure groups but considerable sensitivity on social issues.

Because of these interacting factors, Hong Kong has, for the most part, remained a highly competitive economy, with an efficient allocation of resources at all times, full employment of labor, and high levels of capacity utilization. Not only is it efficient in the usual static sense, but it has also been able to shift resources rapidly from one sector to another in response to changes in world demand. This has allowed it to sustain rapid and steady growth in the face of severe external shocks.

Although there is no a priori reason that a free-market equilibrium should be either equitable or inequitable, Hong Kong's income distribution has been fairly equitable over the years and, at least until the early 1980s, improved over time. Rapid growth has benefited all economic groups, and the rapid rise in wages and employment has greatly alleviated the problem of poverty. As a consequence, by 1976 the poorest 20 percent of the population had an average annual household income of US$1,300, which is well above the per capita income of most developing countries.

Singapore

Singapore was another outstanding success story of economic development in the post–World War II era, along with Hong Kong and the other newly industrializing economies of East Asia. Since 1960 it has done as well as, if not better than, the other members of that select company in the category of per capita income growth. By 1985 it had overtaken economies such as Italy and New Zealand and was even close on the heels of its colonial creator, the United Kingdom.

Chapter 3 examines the nature and outcome of the strategies that made this achievement possible, as well as the social and political circumstances under which these strategies emerged. Although Singapore's development strategy has clearly been outward oriented, with almost no trade restrictions or capital controls, it cannot be considered a laissez-faire policy. The state has played a central and crucial role in the development of Singapore. How has it done this?

The state in Singapore has played the role of an intermediary between foreign multinational corporations, on the one hand, and the domestic labor force, on the other. It has encouraged multinationals to locate in Singapore by providing (a) an extensive infrastructure that offers prompt and efficient services and facilities of all kinds and (b) a system of labor relations that ensures employers the freedom to hire and fire as they deem necessary without fear of strikes and other labor disruptions. Wage negotiations are overseen by the tripartite National Wages Council, which is dominated by the government. Although the council's guidelines are not mandatory, they are considered to have an effect. Consequently the government attempts to influence the structure of industry by manipulating the rate of increase in nominal wages.

The main institution that the government has used to intervene in the economy is the Central Provident Fund, to which both workers and employers make mandatory contributions. Since the early 1980s these contributions have amounted to 25 percent of wages each, thus creating a massive fund with a net inflow of about 30 percent of domestic savings, or (since domestic savings constitute about 40 percent of national income) no less than 12 percent of national income. In comparison with other successful export-oriented economies, such as Hong Kong, Singapore has experienced much higher rates of savings and investment, and therefore significantly higher incremental capital-output ratios, since growth rates are comparable. Furthermore, it has relied more on direct foreign investment. The foreign component of gross domestic product (GDP), representing mainly profits of multinational firms earned in Singapore, rose from about 10 percent in 1966 to about 25 percent in the early 1980s.

The key feature of Singapore's political economy has been the ability of the ruling People's Action party to dominate the political scene, despite technically free elections. As a result, the government has been able to pursue long-term national objectives without making concessions to special interest groups. The ruling party appears to have been given this autonomy in the policymaking sphere as part of an implicit social contract making it responsible for "delivering the goods" in the form of rising living standards for the majority of citizens (which it certainly has done), in return for the support of the people at the ballot box.

Jamaica

From its colonial past Jamaica inherited a Westminster-type constitution and a plantation economy centered on sugarcane. Militant labor is another historical legacy. Before emancipation in 1839 there were several slave revolts; since then, workers have frequently resorted to direct action. Universal suffrage, gained in 1944, brought the workers political power, and their votes have come to be vital to both of the parties that dominate Jamaican politics—the Jamaican Labour party (JLP), which is the more conservative, and the People's National party (PNP), which is more left-leaning. Both parties espouse populism, however, and act as patronage-dispensing machines.

Jamaica's economy developed slowly in the postwar period until 1952, when commercial exploitation of the island's bauxite deposits sparked rapid growth. In the 1960s the expansion of tourism also contributed to prosperity. As is typical of "Dutch disease" situations, the production of other tradables, notably agricultural export crops, stagnated, while non-tradables such as construction boomed. This shift toward nontradables was magnified by the expansion of the government bureaucracy and of government-sponsored social service schemes. Growth in manufacturing has been largely confined to sheltered import-substituting industries.

The bauxite boom came to an end in 1973, and a seven-year decline in national income followed. The collapse was precipitated by a conjunction of exogenous factors and government policies. On the one hand, the demand for bauxite leveled off because of the world recession; on the other, the 1973 and 1979 rises in fuel prices put Caribbean mines at a disadvantage in relation to major producers in other parts of the world. The situation was aggravated by the attempts of the PNP—which, under Michael Manley, came into power in 1972 after ten years of moderate JLP rule—to restructure the country along democratic socialist lines. It adopted a costly social welfare program and nationalized a number of enterprises, causing the flight of financial and human capital. To balance its growing budget, the government imposed a bauxite levy that accelerated the decline of the industry. The legacy of this period was a heavily indebted economy, saddled with inefficient government enterprises and shackled by import, price, and credit controls.

The moderate JLP government that came into power in 1980 undertook to revitalize the economy and to put it on a sound financial footing. Initially the government counted on the revival of the bauxite industry, and it hoped that liberalization would stimulate other productive sectors, thus obviating the need for retrenchment measures, such as devaluation and public employment reduction, that might cost it labor support. This strategy proved to be flawed. Bauxite production remained low because of world demand and the emergence of cheaper sources of supply. Moreover, the reform measures met with limited response on the part of other productive sectors. Public debt mounted, and the government had to impose increasingly severe fiscal restraints that delayed recovery.

Why did the reforms have only a limited effect? Liberalization does not automatically lead to harmonious labor relations. The structure of the Jamaican polity favors government intervention in economic life. Hence the lack of confidence in the permanence of a policy of nonintervention. Under such circumstances, laissez-faire meets with limited success, which strengthens the cause of advocates of a government-led economy.

Mauritius

In 1960 Mauritius was an overcrowded sugar plantation economy. Except for its fertile land, virtually all of which was under cultivation, the island had no natural resources. Given rapid population growth (close to 3 percent a year in the late 1950s), its prospects seemed bleak. The social situation was potentially explosive: wealth was concentrated in the hands of a small Franco-Mauritian planters' elite, while the Hindu majority competed for jobs with the sizable Muslim, Créole (mixed Afro-European), and Chinese minorities.

During the 1960s the government attempted to diversify the economy by taxing sugar exports while protecting import-substituting industries. This strategy met with little success. The few manufacturing establishments that were created had high operating costs and generated few jobs. The economy remained dependent on the sugar sector, and gross national product (GNP) grew, on average, by only 1.6 percent a year.

The situation changed drastically in the mid-1970s. Although Mauritius suffered the consequences of the 1973 oil shock, it benefited from a sugar boom, with its terms of trade rising from a base of 100 in 1970 to 215 in 1975. Part of the windfall accrued to the government in the form of taxes and led to a rapid (and, as it turned out, unsustainable) increase in public services, and part went to raise the wages of sugar workers. The plantation owners also benefited, however, and they invested heavily in export-oriented manufacturing, made attractive by the 1971 Export Processing Zone (EPZ) law, which gave virtually free-trade status to production for export.

The sugar boom collapsed in 1976, and the terms of trade declined to 79 by 1977, causing a decline in GNP and necessitating a retrenchment in government expenditures. Although the export-oriented sector survived, it too stagnated during the general recession of the early 1980s. Since 1983, the export-oriented industries have expanded again at a rapid pace, aided by further relaxation of controls and the infusion of capital from Hong Kong, mainly into the clothing industry, which accounts for 70 percent of the jobs and 80 percent of the EPZ export earnings.

The establishment of the EPZ transformed the island's economy. In 1984, thirteen years after the scheme had been introduced, EPZ firms employed 70,000 workers (about 28 percent of the total labor force), generated a third of total export earnings, and accounted for approximately 7 percent of GDP. Export-oriented enterprises and, to a lesser extent, tourism are the main engines of growth.

The progress of the economy, given its initial conditions, has been remarkable. Between 1965 and 1980 GDP increased, on average, by 4.9 percent a year. The rate of growth between 1980 and 1985 was slower (3.9 percent a year), but it compared favorably with the 2.1 percent growth rate of the middle-income countries with which Mauritius is classified.

The story of Mauritius demonstrates the possibilities of constructive compromise within a pluralistic, democratic society. The government, in response to popular pressures, followed a pro-labor policy (minimum wages, high degree of workers' protection, and so on) but not to the point of discouraging private enterprise. Large planters were taxed heavily, but not to the point of confiscation, and their capital and administrative talents found a fruitful outlet in the industrial field. When the import substitution strategy failed, emphasis shifted to export manufacturing, although firms oriented to the local market continued to benefit from protection. Population pressure was eased through the widespread dissemination of family planning information. The improvement in economic conditions reduced socioethnic conflicts, which were also eased through the application of a complex system that ensures all ethnic groups a voice.

Malta

As already mentioned, the economy of Malta has revolved around the island's strategic location in the central Mediterranean. In 1530 the Holy Roman Emperor Charles V ceded the island to the Knights of St. John, who fortified and defended it against the Ottoman Turks. The British formally took over its administration in 1814, holding it until independence in 1964. During that time Britain maintained a naval base and military installations that in 1961 accounted for 15,000 jobs out of a total labor force of 85,000, while manufacturing industries employed only 10,000 workers. British withdrawal in 1971 reduced base-related employment to 6,000—by which time the labor force had grown to more than 100,000. The island was faced with an adjustment problem of major proportions, to which emigration seemed the only feasible solution.

Contrary to the dire predictions of the experts, Malta succeeded in developing alternative sources of employment through manufactures for export and tourism. Manufacturing employment reached about 20,000 in 1971 and surpassed 30,000 by the early 1980s, when it accounted for about 30 percent of total employment. Tourist arrivals rose fourfold over the 1970s, and GNP per capita rose at a rate of 8.1 percent a year from 1965 to 1985. Although data on income distribution are scarce, the society shows a remarkable absence of outward signs of inequality.

Economic policy was marked by extensive state intervention. There was a comprehensive national health and welfare system. Despite the minuscule domestic market, tariffs and trade controls operated through a bulk-buying scheme. Industries that produced light consumer goods were protected. Today, there is considerable state ownership of banking, transport, and heavy industries such as shipbuilding and naval repair facilities. Many government enterprises are cofinanced by foreign governments (Libya, for one) and produce for sheltered foreign markets, which may explain why the apparent distortions in resource allocation do not seem to damage the economy. Another element of strength lies in the conservative budgeting and balance of payments policy followed by the successive governments.

Malta has two political parties that are evenly balanced: the Labour party, which draws its support from the dockyard workers and other blue-collar occupations, and the Nationalist party, which is connected more with the middle classes and white-collar unions. The Labour party, led for most of the period by the charismatic and forceful Dom Mintoff, was in power from 1971 until 1987, when it was narrowly defeated by the Nationalists (in power from 1964 to 1971).

The Comparative Study

Among the five economies considered in this volume Hong Kong and Singapore, the two manufacturing city-states, obviously form one well-defined pair, while Jamaica and Mauritius, the two relatively resource-abundant primary exporters, form another. These two sets of "twins" provide ample possibilities for comparative analysis. Two intragroup comparisons can be made within manufacturers and primary exporters, and then an intergroup comparison can be made of the two different kinds of small open economy. Malta is in many ways more similar to Hong Kong and Singapore than to Jamaica and Mauritius, except for the fact that its rentier income from its naval and dockyard facilities, combined with its strategic location, has put the island into the resource-abundant category. Consequently it has not been compelled to promote outward-oriented manufacturing to the same extent as the two city-states.

The comparative study concentrates on the following issues:

GOVERNMENT INTERVENTION. How have the pattern and composition of production, resource allocation, and trade been affected by government intervention in Singapore, and to what extent has this intervention been either beneficial or harmful in comparison with the hands-off stance of the authorities in Hong Kong?

FOREIGN PARTICIPATION. Foreign multinational corporations have played a dominant role in Singapore, whereas local entrepreneurs, using small plants, have been the driving force in Hong Kong's manufacturing growth. What government strategies have produced these two out-comes, and what have been the consequences of each?

LABOR. What, if any, economic or political differences can be attributed to the labor markets in Singapore and Hong Kong because of govern-ment wage regulations in the former and the considerable influx of labor from the mainland into the latter?

FREE TRADE. Has Malta paid a discernible price in growth and efficiency for not following a free trade policy?

THE POLITICAL SYSTEM. What do these countries tell us about the nature of the state and its relation to the polity, or civil society? Hong Kong has been governed by a small group of British colonial admin-istrators who appear to embody the disinterested characteristics of the Platonic "guardians" of the Greek city-state and to be just as aloof from the concerns of the multitude. They do not seem to serve British interests in any recognizable way, and during Labour party regimes their style of administration has differed sharply from that of the mother country. Singapore has had a popularly elected independent government since the early 1960s, but the ruling party has been so overwhelmingly predominant that this is another instance of rule by a group akin to Plato's guardians—in this case the British-educated lawyers and technocrats of Lee Kuan Yew's People's Action party (PAP). The PAP government does not tolerate any direct pressures from local interest groups, and it formulates policies and programs that appear to serve broad national goals.

In contrast, Malta, Jamaica, and Mauritius have genuine pluralistic multiparty systems, and all have undergone changes in government as a result of national elections. The parties are clearly responsive to trade unions, business groups, ethnic minorities, and the gamut of special interests. Trade restrictions and redistributive measures have been adopted by governments in response to, or in anticipation of, these pressures.

The relations depicted in figure 1-1 suggest that the government in each of the two city-states tends to be autonomous in relation to the polity. Hence the arrow from the polity (*P*) to the government (*G*) is faint and broken. In the case of the pluralistic democracies, however, the arrow is solid. Politics tends to become administration in Hong Kong and Singapore, whereas it is intense and volatile in Jamaica, Mauritius, and Malta. The consequences for the relationship of the government to the polity will be a central concern of the comparative study.

NATURAL RESOURCES. What has been the role of natural resource rents in the group as a whole? It is clear from the record that the barren "rocks" of Singapore, Hong Kong, and even Malta have done better than the well-endowed islands of Jamaica and Mauritius. It seems that good endowments of natural resources can inhibit manufacturing production and exports through a variety of channels, of which the following are but a few:

- The natural resource sector draws labor and other scarce domestic resources away from other uses, including manufacturing.
- Foreign exchange earnings during international commodity booms appreciate the domestic real exchange rate, stimulating construction and other nontraded sectors but discouraging the export of manufactures and other nontraditional exports (the familiar "Dutch disease" story).
- The natural resource sector can be dominated by a privileged social class that uses its wealth and status to influence the government and the society at large in a manner that makes it difficult for more modern or progressive forms of private or public enterprise to emerge.
- The rents from natural resource booms can flood the coffers of the government, leading to wasteful public expenditures and a bloated bureaucracy that cannot be cut back once the boom is over. Other sectors, including manufacturing, then have to bear the increased burden in the form of additional taxation or reduced availability of capital, raw materials, and other imported inputs.
- The natural resources may be exploited by foreign multinational corporations that have no other interest in the economy and will thus fail to develop potential forward and backward links.
- The availability of natural resource rents, either directly or through the government, makes rent-seeking a more lucrative occupation than the mundane task of finding and developing genuinely productive activities.

The extent to which these factors have influenced the experience of the five countries under consideration is investigated in the concluding chapter.

References

Findlay, Ronald. 1988. "Trade, Development and the State." In Gustav Ranis and T. Paul Schultz, eds., *The State of Development Economics*. Oxford, U.K.: Blackwell.

———. 1990. "The New Political Economy: Its Explanatory Power for LDCs." *Economics and Politics* 2(2):193–221.

Findlay, Ronald, and Stanislaw Wellisz. 1982. "Endogenous Tariffs, the Political Economy of Trade Restrictions and Welfare." In Jagdish N. Bhagwati, ed., *Import Competition and Response*. Chicago, Ill.: University of Chicago Press.

Findlay, Ronald, and J. D. Wilson. 1987. "The Political Economy of Leviathan." In Azzaf Razin and Efraim Sadka, eds., *Economic Policy in Theory and Practice*. New York: Macmillan.

Wellisz, Stanislaw, and Ronald Findlay. 1988. "The State and the Invisible Hand." *World Bank Research Observer* 3(1):59–80.

2 *Hong Kong*

Ronald Findlay
Stanislaw Wellisz

Hong Kong, a British colony of about 421 square miles located on the southeastern coast of China, is widely regarded as the prime example of a successful laissez-faire economic policy.[1] At the macroeconomic level, neither taxation nor government expenditure has ever been used in a countercyclical fashion.[2] There are no tariffs, quotas, or other trade barriers and no controls on the movement of capital in and out of the colony. There is no central bank, and the currency, issued by two private banks, has always been strongly backed by foreign assets or precious metals, except in the period between 1972 and 1983.[3]

At the microeconomic level, government intervention has been moderate in comparison with that in other countries. Until the postwar era, the government was involved only in the reclamation and sale of land, the provision of infrastructure, and the granting and regulation of public utility monopolies. In the 1950s it developed an extensive public housing scheme and in the 1960s enacted labor legislation covering items such as severance pay and child labor and the regulation of the banking system. In the next two decades it began granting cheap land to investors who would diversify Hong Kong's industrial structure. Under this noninterventionist government policy, GDP per capita increased more than fourfold between 1960 and 1985, despite a doubling of the population.

This chapter is a summary by the editors of a much longer study on Hong Kong prepared for this project by Alwyn Young in 1987. Because of the pressure of other commitments, he was unfortunately not able to summarize and revise the study himself, in time for publication in this volume, in line with his current views on Hong Kong. These views are expressed, for example, in Alwyn Young, "A Tale of Two Cities: Factor Accumulation and Technical Change in Hong Kong and Singapore," NBER *Macroeconomics Annual: 1992*, edited by Stanley Fischer and Olivier Blanchard (Cambridge, Mass.: MIT Press). Full responsibility for all statements in this chapter is taken by the editors alone, with the full consent of Alwyn Young.

Many analyses of the economic success of Hong Kong point out the lack of government intervention and stop there, assuming that the free unfolding of market forces sufficiently explains the dynamism of the economy. History has shown, however, that laissez-faire capitalism is actually a short-lived phenomenon because as soon as economic interest groups develop and state power expands, the government is bound to intervene in the economic arena. This process began in Hong Kong in the 1950s and has continued slowly since then, giving rise to various kinds of microeconomic intervention. The question is, why has this process been so slow in developing, why has it taken the particular form it has, and has this form aided or hindered the performance of the economy?

It is also important to recognize that a laissez-faire policy does not automatically lead to a dynamic and highly competitive economy. Even in the absence of government intervention, firms might exert market power, rigidities could develop in the labor market as a result of labor organization, entrepreneurship might be lacking, and so on. Thus, there are differing degrees to which an economy may become competitive under a laissez-faire regime.

Another notable feature of the economy of Hong Kong is the rapidity with which productive resources are reallocated in response to shifts in demand. This chapter examines the economic, political, and social factors that make for such a high degree of flexibility. The story begins with Hong Kong's postwar economic history.

Economic Development since World War II

Before World War II and immediately afterward, Hong Kong functioned primarily as an entrepôt economy that processed trade between China and the rest of the world but had little manufacturing activity of its own. In May 1951 the United Nations imposed an embargo on the export of strategic materials to China, and the United States imposed a total embargo on imports from China. As a result, China's share of Hong Kong's total exports fell from 39 percent (HK$1,604 million) in 1951 to a mere 4 percent (HK$136 million) in 1956. It has been estimated that the trade embargo on China reduced Hong Kong's national income by a third (Woronoff 1980: 187). This economic shock was compounded by the flow of Chinese returning to Hong Kong following the Japanese surrender in 1945 and an additional flow of refugees following the Communist victory on the mainland in 1949, which together raised the population from 600,000 in 1945 to more than 2 million in 1951 and created serious shortages of housing, food, clothing, and other necessities (Woronoff 1980: 80).[4] Hong Kong was surely the last place one would expect an economic miracle to occur.

Amazingly, the Hong Kong economy recovered. A number of Shanghai entrepreneurs who had fled mainland China in 1949 brought their own machinery and foremen and in many cases rerouted machinery orders to Hong Kong (Woronoff 1980: 164). Using the informational links of Hong Kong's many trading companies, which had previously handled trade with the mainland, these entrepreneurs began exporting textile products to the United Kingdom and other industrial economies. From 1955 on, entrepôt trade once again thrived as Hong Kong's trading companies began to purchase goods from Japan and the United States for redistribution in Southeast Asia (Woronoff 1980: 187). Slowly, the economy recovered, and by 1963 total exports reached US$873 million, finally surpassing their 1951 level of US$780 million. The 1961 census listed only 0.7 percent of the population as unemployed (Woronoff 1980: 81).

Since the early 1960s, Hong Kong has experienced rapid, if not always steady, growth (see figure 2-1). Between 1960 and 1985 real GDP rose by 8.9 percent on average, and per capita GDP in that period increased more than fourfold. Growth slowed significantly during 1967–68, 1974–75, and 1982. Annual growth rates have varied considerably, ranging from

Figure 2-1. GDP at Market Prices, Hong Kong, 1960–85

Billions of constant Hong Kong dollars

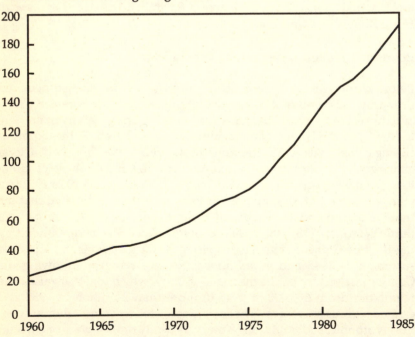

Source: World Bank data.

highs of 17 to 18 percent to lows of 0 to 2 percent. Downturns, allowed by the government to go unchecked, have almost always been followed by spectacular recoveries.

Manufacturing and Exports

Hong Kong's commodity exports have grown faster than its GDP; the two are clearly closely related, although the export series shows greater variation. Because of heavy net capital inflows, Hong Kong has never had a positive trade balance. When China reemerged in the international arena in the 1970s, reexports began to recapture some of their prewar importance in Hong Kong's trade, and their share of total exports rose from 19 percent in 1970 to 37.7 percent in 1984 (figure 2-2).

The aggregate data conceal rapid changes in the composition of exports. As mentioned earlier, textile entrepreneurs from Shanghai, and their exports, helped Hong Kong recover from the disasters of the early 1950s. By 1958, however, the United Kingdom was imposing "voluntary" quotas on imports of cotton textiles from Hong Kong. The United

Figure 2-2. Commodity Trade, Hong Kong, 1950–84

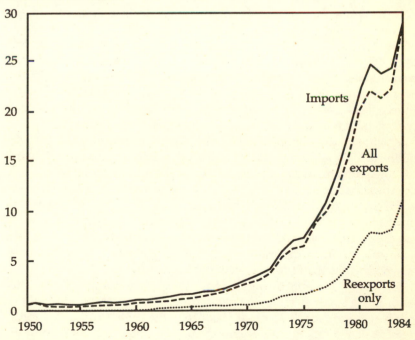

Billions of U.S. dollars

Source: World Bank data.

States instituted similar restraints in 1961 (Woronoff 1980: 165–66). Throughout the 1960s and 1970s one country after another imposed increasingly comprehensive quantitative restraints on imports of all textile goods from Hong Kong (Lin 1979: 307), and the share of textiles in total exports fell from 19 percent in 1960 to 7 percent in 1979 (Woronoff 1980: 166). The share of textiles in total manufacturing employment fell from a high of 22.6 percent in 1963 to 14.6 percent in 1977 (Lethbridge 1980: 25–26). The Hong Kong economy had run into a barrier to growth.

Hong Kong's entrepreneurs responded to the export restrictions on textiles by moving into the manufacture of finished clothing products. Although success in this area also generated various trade barriers, the great degree of product differentiation in the clothing industry allowed Hong Kong producers to change their specifications constantly and thus to circumvent specific barriers. Even when this was not possible, Hong Kong clothing exporters successfully upgraded the quality, and consequently the value, of clothing exports. By the 1970s Hong Kong was producing products with the labels of famous designers such as Cardin and Gucci and holding its own in international fashion shows (Woronoff 1980: 166). Between 1959 and 1975 clothing's share of total exports grew from 34.8 to 44.6 percent, and its share of total manufacturing employment increased from 17.8 to 33.5 percent (Lethbridge 1980: 25–26). By the late 1970s, however, the clothing industry had begun to play a smaller role in the national economy as new industries appeared on the scene.

In response to quota restrictions, Hong Kong entrepreneurs also moved into the plastics and toy industries. Whereas in 1959 plastics accounted for 5.1 percent of total manufacturing employment, by 1970 their share had increased to 12.6 percent. During the same period, their share of total exports rose from 7 to 11 percent (Lethbridge 1980: 25–26). More remarkable is the growth of toys within the plastics industry. Emerging as a separate industry in the late 1950s, toys accounted for 7.9 percent of exports by 1970 (or more than half of total plastics exports). The value of toy exports rose from HK$100 million in 1960 to HK$3 billion in 1977. Although the toy industry initially subcontracted mainly for foreigners or copied foreign designs, it soon began turning out its own designs and even produced and exported molds. By 1979, with sales of HK$5,156 million, Hong Kong had become by far the biggest toy producer in the world (Woronoff 1980: 168–69). Although plastics and toy production continued to grow, their relative importance in the local economy began to decline in the 1970s as more and more resources moved into electronics and watch manufacturing.

Electronics manufacturing, aided by foreign investment, expanded from three small firms assembling transistor radios, in 1961, into a full-blown industry (Woronoff 1980: 169). By 1974 it accounted for 9.1 percent of manufacturing employment, after starting out at only 0.4 percent in 1963. In addition, the electronics industry's share of domestic exports increased from 2.4 percent in 1964 to 12.0 percent in 1974

(Lethbridge 1980: 25–26). Gradually, a number of former employees of foreign-owned firms began to set up their own firms, operating as independent subcontractors, manufacturing their own components, and even developing their own brand names (Woronoff 1980: 170).

The growth of the domestic electronics industry indirectly generated phenomenal growth in the watch industry. Until the late 1960s Hong Kong imported sophisticated Swiss movements to put into locally manufactured cases. The highly trained labor necessary for the manufacture of high-quality movements was simply unavailable in Hong Kong. With the development of electronic digital quartz watches, however, Hong Kong watch entrepreneurs found a new avenue for growth. Many of the necessary components were already being produced by the local electronics factories, which soon became major suppliers of the Hong Kong watch industry. Thus the industry's share of exports increased from 0.2 percent in 1965 to 7.8 percent in 1979. During this time sales rose from HK$7.7 million to HK$4,354 million, a 565-fold increase! In quantity, if not value, Hong Kong had become the world's biggest exporter of watches (Woronoff 1980: 180).

The quick rise and equally quick decline of the wig industry illustrates another important characteristic of Hong Kong's entrepreneurs—their flexibility. In 1961 only one factory in Hong Kong was making wigs (Woronoff 1980: 181). As wigs became more fashionable, so grew the wig industry, armed with the competitive advantage of Chinese hair—which is considered particularly suitable for wig production because it is coarse and thus holds a set well. By 1970 the wig industry was employing 39,000 people (more than 5 percent of manufacturing employment at the time) and accounted for 8 percent of domestic exports. Then in 1970–71 world fashion shifted from wigs made with human hair to wigs made of synthetic fibers. In 1971 Hong Kong wig exports fell by 44 percent. Hong Kong's wig industry tried to meet the changing demand but was hampered by a shortage of synthetic fibers (Riedel 1974: 32). In addition, in the early 1970s world demand for all kinds of wigs fell sharply. By 1977 the Hong Kong wig industry had only fifty-nine employees (Lethbridge 1980: 78).

In most economies, such a catastrophic industrial decline would generate long-term unemployment, cause growth to slow down, and create a morass of government subsidies and protectionist measures. In the case of Hong Kong, resources moved quickly into other productive endeavors with a minimum of economic and social dislocation. Exports and manufacturing employment continued to grow as former wig laborers relocated to other industries. As for the entrepreneurs who had opened the wig factories, many of them found that the machinery used in wig production was particularly suitable for scaling fish. As a result, the growth rate of both GDP and exports in 1971 (7.3 and 14.2 percent, respectively) was only slightly below the average for the postwar era.

This rapid structural change was marked not only by intra-manufacturing shifts but also by a rapid rise and decline in whole economic sectors. Manufacturing jumped from only 8.8 percent of GDP in 1950 to 26.5 percent in 1960, then dropped from 29.0 percent in 1970 to 26.5 percent in 1976, and moved back up to 30.4 percent in 1980. In contrast, transport and communications slid from 15.6 percent of GDP in 1950 to a mere 6.9 percent in 1980. At the same time, financial and commercial services grew from 14.5 to 18.8 percent of GDP between 1970 and 1976. By 1976 Hong Kong's International Standard Industrial Classification (ISIC) sectors 8 (financial and commercial services) and 9 (community, social, and personal services) accounted for 36 percent of GDP, which exceeded the comparable figure for the United Kingdom, the Federal Republic of Germany, Japan, and Singapore (Lethbridge 1980: 78). Although manufacturing continues to be a dominant component of the Hong Kong economy, its importance in relation to financial services and retail trade, among other services, is declining (see table 2-1).

The rapid pace with which industries adapted to shifts in demand is reflected in the stability of the aggregate value of exports. As table 2-2 shows, the coefficients of variation remained at one-half to one-quarter those of Singapore, the Republic of Korea, and Taiwan (China), all of which are highly successful export-oriented economies.[5]

Poverty and Equity

Estimates of Hong Kong's postwar income distribution vary to a surprising degree, even though almost all are based on the same data (see table 2-3). As Chow and Papanek (1981) have noted, the data are riddled with inaccuracies, particularly before 1971, when the government began to collect better information.[6] Nevertheless, several clear trends emerge. To begin with, between 1957 and 1966 income distribution remained constant and fairly unequal, with a Gini coefficient close to 0.5. The income share of the poorest 40 percent fell from 15.4 to 13.4 percent during the period, whereas that of the top 10 percent rose from 42.0 to 45.5 percent. The data for this early period are fairly poor, however, and not too much emphasis should be put on these relatively small changes.

During the 1970s income distribution improved steadily and by the end of the decade had attained a fairly equitable Gini coefficient of 0.37 to 0.4. Between 1966 and 1979–80 the income share of the top 20 percent fell from 57.7 to 46.5 percent, with the fourth, third, and second quintiles showing gains of 4.8, 2.7, and 2.8 percent, respectively. The poorest 20 percent appear to have gained only marginally from this improved income distribution; their share of income rose from 5.3 to 6.2 percent, and the increase took place entirely in the late 1970s. In absolute terms, Hong Kong's rapid economic growth raised the income of all groups (table 2-4), with the middle 60 percent of the

Table 2-1. GDP, by Industrial Origin, Selected Years, 1950–80
(millions of Hong Kong dollars)

Industry	1950[a]		1960[a]		1970[b]		1980[b]	
	GDP	Percent	GDP	Percent	GDP	Percent	GDP	Percent
Agriculture and mining	104	3.5	217	4.0	687	2.9	615	1.0
Manufacturing	258	8.8	1,441	26.5	6,948	29.0	18,643	30.4
Construction	181	6.2	557	10.2	1,223	5.1	3,668	6.0
Electricity, gas, and water	48	1.6	103	1.9	423	1.8	503	0.8
Transport and communication	460	15.6	785	14.4	1,864	7.8	4,240	6.9
Trade and finance	392	30.3	2,295	42.2	*	*	*	*
Other branches	997	33.9	41	0.8	12,811	53.5		
GDP at factor cost	2,940	100.0	5,439	100.0	23,956	100.0		

* Included in other branches.
a. At current prices.
b. At constant 1973 prices.
Source: World Bank 1984.

Table 2-2. Coefficients of Variation for Exports, Hong Kong and Selected Economies

Coefficient	Hong Kong	Singapore	Korea, Republic of	Taiwan (China)
Regression 1				
Standard error	0.162	0.345	0.405	0.112
Mean[a]	9.51	8.86	4.86	3.83
Coefficient of variation	0.017	0.039	0.083	0.029
Regression 2				
Standard error	0.143	0.345	0.319	0.114
Mean[a]	9.51	8.86	4.86	3.83
Coefficient of variation	0.015	0.039	0.066	0.030

Note: The regression equations are as follows:

Regression 1

Hong Kong:	$LHKEXP = C + B^1(T) + B^2(P \times T)$
Singapore:	$LSIEXP = C + B^1(T) + B^2(P \times T)$
Korea:	$LSKEXP = C + B^1(T) + B^2(P \times T)$
Taiwan (China):	$LTWEXP = C + B^1(T) + B^2(P \times T)$

Regression 2

Hong Kong:	$LHKEXP = C + B^1(T) + B^2(P \times T) + B^3(PRC \times T)$
Singapore:	$LSIEXP = C + B^1(T) + B^2(P \times T)$
Korea:	$LSKEXP = C + B^1(T) + B^2(P \times T) + B^3(SKXP \times T)$
Taiwan (China):	$LTWEXP = C + B^1(T) + B^2(P \times T) + B^3(TWXP \times T)$

The dependent variable is always the logarithm of the economy's exports; C is a constant; T is time running from a value of 1 in 1955 to a value of 28 in 1982; P is price, the inflation dummy variable that has a value of 0 before 1970 and a value of 1 from 1970 on; PRC is the dummy variable for Hong Kong's trade normalization with China and has a value of 0 before 1973 and a value of 1 from 1973 on; $SKXP$ is the dummy variable for Korea's shift to export promotion and has a value of 0 before 1963 and a value of 1 from 1963 on; and $TWXP$ is the dummy variable for Taiwan's shift to export promotion and has a value of 0 before 1961 and a value of 1 from 1961 on.

population benefiting the most, as indicated above. By 1976 the poorest 20 percent, with an average household income of US$1,300, were "way above any poverty index established for any Asian country" (Chow and Papanek 1981: 474).

Between 1979 and 1981 income distribution deteriorated. The Gini coefficient rose to 0.45–0.48. The share of the top 20 percent posted an impressive 6.4 percent gain, but that of the poorest 20 percent fell by almost half, to 3.7 percent (table 2-3).[7]

One of the most important determinants of income distribution in Hong Kong has been the repeated waves of immigration from mainland China (discussed below). The tripling of Hong Kong's population between 1945 and 1948 must have greatly depressed the return to labor in relation to that of capital. The 1949–50 wave of immigration, although

Table 2-3. Income Distribution Estimates for Hong Kong, Selected Years, 1957–81

Income group	1957[a]	1963–64[b]	1966[c]	1971[c]	1973–74[b]	1976[c]	1979–80	1981
Share of total income (percent)								
Bottom 10 percent	1.8	1.7	1.3	1.5	1.2	1.5	—	—
Bottom 20 percent	5.7	4.4	5.3	5.3	4.1	5.1	6.2	3.7
Second 20 percent	9.7	8.9	8.1	10.1	10.9	9.5	10.9	8.5
Third 20 percent	11.7	12.2	12.4	13.7	15.9	13.9	15.1	14.1
Fourth 20 percent	16.7	17.8	16.5	18.3	22.1	21.2	21.3	20.9
Top 20 percent	56.2	56.7	57.7	52.6	47.0	50.3	46.5	52.9
Top 10 percent	42.0	42.2	45.5	37.4	31.3	37.0	—	—
Top 5 percent	30.0	30.7	32.6	27.6	20.6	24.4	—	—
Gini coefficient, by source								
Lin (1985)	0.470	0.462	0.467	0.409	0.398	0.409	0.373	0.453
Chau (1984)	0.48	0.50	0.487	0.439	0.24[d]	0.435	0.4	0.481
Chow (1981)	0.48	0.50	0.50	0.45	0.42	0.44	..	..
Cheng (1985)	..	..	0.50	0.43	..	0.425	..	0.46
Ho (1979)	..	..	..	0.405	..	..	..	..

— Not available.
.. Not given.
a. Based on Household Expenditure Surveys and various supplementary surveys. Hence, estimates use expenditure data. All other sources use income data. The 1963–64 sample accounted for 82 percent of personal income, the 1973–74 sample for 87 percent of personal income.
b. Based on two housing surveys, covering 79 percent of national income.
c. Based on census data: 1966 did not require income information and therefore covers only 64.3 percent of households; 1971 contains complete enumeration; in 1976, 4.7 percent of households did not report income
d. The figure as quoted in source appears anomalous.
Source: Percentages of total income up through 1976 from Chow and Papanek (1981). Percentages for 1979–80 and 1981 from Lin 1985. Chau 1984 listed in Lin 1985. Chow 1981 from Chow and Papanek 1981. All other data as indicated.

Table 2-4. Household Income of Different Income Groups, Selected Years, 1957–76
(constant 1966 Hong Kong dollars per year)

Income group	1957	1963–64	1966	1971	1973–74	1976	Change (percent), 1966–76	Change (percent), 1957–76
Bottom 10 percent	918	1,866	1,100	1,924	2,081	2,363	115	157
Bottom 20 percent	1,472	2,292	2,242	2,821	3,009	3,225	44	119
Second 20 percent	2,013	3,581	3,000	4,798	7,772	6,777	126	237
Third 20 percent	2,161	6,331	5,231	6,710	11,126	9,936	90	360
Fourth 20 percent	4,084	7,786	6,846	9,589	15,442	13,802	102	238
Top 20 percent	13,549	23,646	24,227	25,682	33,348	34,035	40	151
Top 10 percent	20,161	35,444	38,560	37,287	44,355	47,191	22	134
Top 5 percent	28,696	53,088	48,000	54,716	59,599	54,587	14	90

Source: Chow and Papanek 1981: table 5, p. 473.

accompanied by massive capital inflows, led to a fall in the real wage which, being followed by the 1951 United Nations embargo on trade with China, was fairly long lived (table 2-5). Not until 1960 did the real wages of semiskilled and unskilled workers, who made up the vast majority of laborers at the time, recover to their 1948 levels. Large waves

Table 2-5. *Average Daily Wage in Manufacturing, 1948–81*
(constant 1948 Hong Kong dollars)

Year	Unskilled	Semiskilled	Skilled	Index numbers of average real wage		
				(a)	(b)	(c)
1948	3.75	5.2	6.75	100		
1949	3.35	4.64	6.03	89		
1950	3.63	4.91	5.98	95		
1951	3.35	4.53	5.71	88		
1952	3.29	4.46	5.62	87		
1953	3.27	4.42	5.58	86		
1954	3.15	4.53	5.71	84		
1955	3.25	4.67	5.89	86		
1956	3.15	5.12	5.71	86		
1957	3.52	4.69	7.42	92		
1958	3.37	4.76	7.54	90		
1959	3.13	4.96	9.19	89		
1960	3.85	5.19	11.15	105		
1961	3.82	5.15	11.07	104		
1962	3.88	6.51	11.24	110		
1963	5.42	8.37	11.06	145		
1964	5.22	8.07	12.63	142	100	
1965	6.01	7.89	13.21	157	109	
1966	5.69	9.20	12.33	154	113	
1967	6.17	8.96	12.66	162	119	
1968	6.42	9.56	13.61	170	117	
1969	6.28	9.30	12.90	165	122	
1970	6.38	9.10	13.36	167	134	
1971	6.48	9.64	13.09	171	146	
1972	7.54	10.95	16.18	199	157	
1973	7.93	10.84	14.57	203	160	
1974	7.25	9.64	13.74	185	141	
1975	7.59	9.98	14.87	194	135	96
1976	7.55	9.82	15.24	193	152	107
1977	8.57	11.32	16.20	219	160	113
1978	—	—	—			123
1979	—	—	—			137
1980	—	—	—			134
1981	—	—	—			136

— Not available.

Note: Column (b), real wages "excluding fringe benefits" (Lethbridge 1980); column (c), real wages "including fringe benefits," July 1973–June 1974 = 100 (Cheng 1985).

Source: Unless otherwise noted, Chow and Papanek 1981.

of immigration during 1961–62 and 1978–80 appear to have slowed the rate of increase in wages during periods of relative prosperity, and the immigration between 1973 and 1974, combined with the world recession, led to a sharp decline in real wages.[8]

The movements in real wages outlined above have clear implications for Hong Kong's income distribution. A sudden increase in the supply of labor followed by a fall in the real wage and a concomitant increase in the return to capital would lower the per capita income accruing to labor and increase the per capita income of owners of capital, whose numbers remain fairly fixed, in the short run. Hence, income distribution would deteriorate, as occurred in Hong Kong in the late 1950s (table 2-3) following the massive labor force increases at the end of the war. In view of the United Nations embargo, which may have hurt the return to capital as much as it did labor, it is difficult to say whether the deterioration in the real wage in the early 1950s worsened income distribution. In the late 1960s and early 1970s the growth of labor fell back and income distribution began to improve.[9] Thus the sudden deterioration in income distribution between 1979 and 1981 could have been partly a result of the inflow of labor during this period.

In any case, since World War II Hong Kong has displayed an unusual ability to overcome obstacles and to achieve rapid growth and a reasonable degree of equity. The colony's resiliency can be attributed to a number of social and political factors, which are discussed in the sections that follow.

Labor and Labor Relations

Economic flexibility has a great deal to do with the structure of the labor force and the nature of labor organization. Since young workers are much more mobile than older workers, the rate of job change generally declines with age, as does the frequency of intersectoral shifts. In view of the labor shifts in Hong Kong, an important question is whether its labor force is exceptionally young.

Skill, too, affects mobility. On the one hand, a broader education enables a worker to handle a greater range of tasks (although the worker may then become more selective about the kinds of jobs he or she is willing to take). On the other hand, training in a specific area makes workers less mobile, as does on-the-job training—which is one of the reasons why mobility decreases with age.[10]

Between 1961 and 1981 Hong Kong's labor force grew at an average rate of 3.8 percent a year—much faster than in the United States or Japan and as fast as, if not faster than, in most developing countries (table 2-6). During this period changes in the participation rate accounted for 13.8 percent of the labor force increase, while population growth was responsible for 86.2 percent.

Table 2-6. *Growth of the Economically Active Population, 1961–81*

Year	Economically active (number)	Annual change (percent)
1961	1,211,999[a]	
1966	1,454,730[a]	3.7
1971	1,654,907[b]	2.6
1976	1,952,000[c]	3.4
1981	2,567,700[d]	5.6
1961–81	n.a.	3.8

n.a. Not applicable.
a. *Hong Kong Statistics 1947–67*, 23.
b. *Hong Kong Population and Housing Census 1971*, 17.
c. *Hong Kong 1976 By-Census*, 21.
d. *Hong Kong Monthly Digest of Statistics* (December 1981: 84).

Hong Kong's natural rate of population growth was 3 percent a year in the 1950s, but it plummeted in the 1960s and by 1982 stood at 1.2 percent a year. Even so, the colony's population grew an average 8.1 percent a year over the 1947–86 period as a result of immigration.

From 1925 to 1947 immigration accounted for a staggering 97 percent of population growth, but the share slipped to 45 percent in 1947–57, 16 percent in 1957–67, 26 percent in 1967–77, and 60 percent in 1977–82. For the 1945–82 period as a whole, immigration accounted for 50.8 percent of Hong Kong's population growth.

Data from the 1961 census on the age structure of recent immigrants to Hong Kong show arrivals concentrated in the prime working-age category, ages 15–54, with immigrant age averaging approximately twenty-seven years (table 2-7).[11] That half of the colony's 3.1 percent annual population growth was associated with twenty-seven-year-old entrants has been of considerable importance to the economic development of Hong Kong because the number of economically active workers has grown but there has not been the long period of high dependency ratios experienced by most developing countries.

The average age of Hong Kong's labor force remained at about thirty-five during the period 1961–82 (table 2-8). Although this is somewhat below the average age of labor in industrial countries such as Japan and the United States, it is fairly high for a developing country. Hence, even though Hong Kong, unlike Japan, has so far been spared the problem of a rapidly aging labor force, the age of its working population cannot account for its flexibility.[12] Note, too, that since 1961 immigration has not greatly affected the average age of Hong Kong's population in general, as the average age of immigrants appears to have been quite close to that of the existing population.

Table 2-7.   Age Structure of Recent Immigrants, 1961
(percentage in each category)

Age group	Males	Females	Total
0–14	13.62	10.38	24.00
15–24	16.54	11.40	27.94
25–34	10.38	10.47	20.85
35–44	4.63	7.28	11.91
45–54	2.52	5.40	7.92
55–64	1.25	4.04	5.29
65 and older	0.56	1.53	2.09

Source: Fan Shu-ching 1974: 41.

Pattern and Causes of Chinese Immigration to Hong Kong

Since the end of World War II, Hong Kong has received several waves of immigrants, primarily from mainland China. The largest wave arrived between 1945 and 1947 with the return at the end of the war of former Hong Kong residents, most of whom had first come to Hong Kong as refugees in the 1930s to escape the civil wars of the warlords and the Japanese invasion of the mainland (Davis 1977: 90–92). Approximately 1.2 million Chinese came in this initial wave. The next wave occurred in 1949 and 1950, when close to 340,000 mainlanders fled Communist forces advancing south; almost three-fourths of these returned to the mainland the following year. The third wave of immigration occurred in 1961–62, when China allowed 130,000 mainlanders to cross the border into Hong Kong because it was unable to feed its population after the disasters of the Great Leap Forward and was faced with mounting discontent. A fourth wave, numbering 150,000 Chinese, came in 1973–74 when China opened up following the turmoil of the Cultural Revolution. Again, emigration to Hong Kong may have been used as a means of dealing with discontent. Finally, in the late 1970s, the fall of the "Gang of Four" and a new period of political and economic liberalization in China

Table 2-8.   Average Age of the Economically Active Population, 1960, 1970, and 1982
(years)

Year	Hong Kong	Japan	United States
1960	35.8[a]	36.6	40.0
1970	35.4[b]	38.1	39.0
1982	35.3	40.8	36.6

a. 1961.
b. 1971.
Source: Computed from International Labour Organisation statistics, 1966–83.

generated a new wave of about 400,000 mainland Chinese. In between these large waves, there has been a smaller continuous stream of immigrants from the mainland. Hong Kong has readily attracted immigrants, no doubt because of the economic opportunities there and, perhaps to a lesser extent, because of the political stability and personal freedom available in the colony.

These surges of immigration were largely the result of exogenous conditions on the mainland beyond the control of the Hong Kong authorities. Thus it is not surprising that more than 50 percent of the 891,923 Chinese immigrants who arrived in Hong Kong between 1961 and 1979 entered illegally (Sit 1981b: 5). In fact, until 1980 the Hong Kong government encouraged illegal immigration with its "touch-base" policy, under which any illegal entrant who managed to make his or her way to the urban areas needed only to report to the appropriate authorities to be duly registered and given an identity card.

In October 1980 the government, faced with the prospect of more illegal immigrants into the already congested colony, revised its policy. Now any illegal entrant caught by the authorities must be repatriated, and employers are prohibited from hiring anyone without proper identification (Sit 1981b: 8). To date, this policy appears to have been quite successful in discouraging attempts at illegal immigration: the number of illegal entrants repatriated fell from 82,125 in 1980 to 8,680 in 1982 (*Hong Kong Annual Report* 1983: 138). Thus it appears that although events on the mainland were the catalyst for immigration into Hong Kong, the government's lenient policy before 1980 was responsible, at least in part, for the magnitude of the flow.

Indeed, the influx was so great that until the early 1960s more than half of Hong Kong's population was born outside the colony (Sit 1981b: 12), and even as late as 1981 this share had only fallen to 42.8 percent of the population (*1981 Census*). In other words, Hong Kong was and to a large degree remains an immigrant society. As we shall see in the sections below, this fact has had enormous consequences for the colony's economic and political development.

The Nature of Labor Organization

Hong Kong's labor force is only weakly unionized. Unionization increased from 10 percent of the labor force to 17.3 percent between 1961 and 1976 but fell sharply in the early 1980s (table 2-9).[13] Even allowing for the low level of unionization, Hong Kong has had an unusual record of industrial peace, as shown in table 2-10. Among seven economies for which data are available from 1968 through 1976, Hong Kong had by far the least number of working days lost per 1,000 employees as a result of industrial disputes, and in most years it lost fewer working days per 1,000 employees than Germany or Sweden, both of which have had unusual records of industrial peace.

Table 2-9. Share of the Labor Force Unionized, Selected Years, 1961–81

Year	Percent
1961	10.0
1966	11.8[a]
1971	14.0[b]
1976	17.3
1980	16.9[b]
1981	14.5[b]

a. 1967 declared union membership projected against 1966 labor force; likely to be an overestimate.

b. Based on membership as declared by the unions but likely to be an overestimate; see table 2-11.

Source: Number of union members drawn from data presented in table 2-11; size of the labor force from *Hong Kong Statistics 1947–67*, 23; *Hong Kong Population and Housing Census 1971*, 74; *Hong Kong Monthly Digest of Statistics*, December 1981: 84.

Surprisingly, manufacturing, which is the backbone of most labor movements, is the least unionized aspect of Hong Kong's economy (table 2-11). In fact, most of the increase in unionization shown in table 2-9 is attributable to the growth of white-collar unions. Of the 108 white-collar unions in existence in 1979, about two-thirds were founded in the 1970s (Woronoff 1980: 95).[14] Those representing teachers, government clerks, and typists are reputedly the most vociferous and combative and are probably among the fastest growing (Woronoff 1980: 95; Lethbridge 1980: 97). Twenty-one of the forty-seven new unions formed between 1960 and 1969 were in the public sector (Hopkins 1971: 239–40), as were forty-eight of the seventy formed between 1979 and 1982 (*Hong Kong Annual Report* 1980–83). In contrast, two-thirds of the ninety-five manufacturing unions registered in 1977 had been around since before 1953 (Woronoff 1980: 95)—a startling fact considering that all of Hong Kong's principal manufacturing industries, apart from some textile operations, developed after that date.

Politically, Hong Kong's trade union movement is divided into two main competing factions: those unions affiliated with the Communist-leaning Hong Kong Federation of Trade Unions (FTU) and those affiliated with the pro-Taiwanese Hong Kong and Kowloon Trades Union Council (TUC). A third faction consists of the politically uncommitted independent unions. In 1961 the FTU-affiliated unions claimed 64 percent of the total declared membership and the TUC-affiliated unions 14 percent. The remaining 22 percent was claimed by unaffiliated pro-FTU and pro-TUC unions and by independent unions. By 1981 FTU membership had declined to 52 percent of the total and TUC membership to 10 percent, with independent unaffiliated unions accounting for 28 percent and unaffiliated pro-FTU and pro-TUC unions for the remaining 10 percent.

The Hong Kong labor union movement is also divided along the lines of craft, industry, occupation, employer, geographic location in Hong

Table 2-10. Number of Working Days Lost because of Industrial Disputes per 1,000 People Employed, Selected Years, 1964–76

Economy	1964–66	1968	1969	1970	1971	1972	1973	1974	1975	1976	1968–76
Hong Kong	89	7	32	37	20	31	40	7	12	3	21
Australia	400	460	860	1,040	1,300	880	1,080	2,670	1,390	1,490	1,241
Belgium	—	230	100	830	720	190	520	340	340	—	—
Canada	970	1,670	2,550	2,190	800	1,420	1,660	2,550	2,750	2,270	1,984
Germany, Fed. Rep. of	—	—	20	10	340	10	40	60	10	40	—
France	—	—	200	180	440	300	330	250	390	420	—
India	—	1,150	1,270	1,440	1,100	1,300	1,330	2,480	1,430	—	—
Italy	—	930	4,160	1,730	1,060	1,670	2,470	1,800	1,640	2,200	1,962
Japan	240	160	200	200	310	270	210	450	390	150	260
Sweden	40	—	30	40	240	10	10	30	20	10	—
United Kingdom	190	370	520	740	1,190	2,160	570	1,270	540	300	851
United States	870	1,590	1,390	2,210	1,600	860	750	1,480	990	1,190	1,340

— Not available.

Source: Lethbridge 1980: 96; 1964–66 data from Hopkins 1971: 210.

Table 2-11. Extent of Unionism, by Major Economic Sector, 1966, 1971, and 1976
(percent)

Sector	1966	1971	1976
Transport and communications	53.1	61	64
Public utilities	64.3	100	47
Mining and quarrying	9.6	7	25
Community service	14.4	19	22
Commerce	6.5	16	18
Construction	7.4	6	16
Manufacturing	6.5	9	11

Note: Figures show percentage of economically active industrial group claimed as trade union members.
Source: Hopkins 1971: 238; Lethbridge 1980: 94.

Kong, and origin (in China) or dialect of the work force (Hopkins 1971: 241). As Lethbridge explains:

It [the labor movement] is highly fragmented, split not only between the two often duplicating yet opposing political factions, but also containing many very small and highly specialized unions (e.g. the Hong Kong Edible Bird's Nest Workers Unions with twenty-one members; the Hong Kong Prosthetists and Orthodontists Association with seventeen members; and the Hong Kong and Kowloon Camphor Wood Trunk Workers Union with fourteen members).... There would appear to be considerable duplication (e.g. two Sharks' Fin Associations; four restaurant unions, each beginning with "Hong Kong and Kowloon ..." and ending "... Workers General Union." The middle words are either "Cafe," "Tea-House," "Restaurant and Cafe," or "Eating Shop." There are separate unions for Hong Kong taxi drivers and for Kowloon taxi drivers; there is a catering union only for migrants from the Chiu Chow area, one for migrants from the Shanghai and Ningpo area (sea navigation), while others are for persons only from Shanghai. (Lethbridge 1980: 93)

Although most of the unions are affiliated with politically opposed factions, politics is not a primary concern of organized labor. Since World War II there have only been two brief periods of disruptive political activity. In the late 1940s, during the final phase of the civil war in China, the FTU and the TUC engaged in competitive strikes, hoping to win workers to their side, and in 1967 the leftist unions agitated in support of China's Cultural Revolution.

During these disturbances the Hong Kong police raided the offices of the militant unions in search of weapons and explosives and arrested and prosecuted union leaders on criminal charges. Surprisingly, membership in the leftist FTU dropped from 96,735 to 95,408, or by 1.4 percent, after these riots. Apparently this activity did not win the FTU any additional support from either its own membership or the population at large. If anything, the political riots "shed a general stigma on the whole labor movement," and the total number of unionized workers declined by 3.5 percent, from 171,620 to 165,670 (Lethbridge 1980: 89). The population seems to have reacted negatively to the idea of labor union involvement in politics in general.

Unions that have no interest in politics might be expected to concentrate on wages and conditions of work. But this is not the case in Hong Kong. Although 49 percent of union secretaries say that higher wages and better working conditions are their first priority, they devote more attention to keeping up general correspondence, carrying out financial work, attending meetings, handling benefit claims and paying out benefits, and writing up the minutes of meetings.

Perhaps the strongest indication of the lack of a genuine drive for higher wages is that the unions had few resources for launching a strike. In the late 1960s only one of the non-Communist unions was thought to have a strike fund (Hopkins 1971: 246)!

Another notable characteristic of Hong Kong unions is that they show little interest in boosting membership. In a survey of trade union secretaries carried out in the mid-1960s, only 1 percent saw the "largest possible union membership" as a top priority (table 2-12). And when asked about obstacles to union growth, 52 percent of them responded "not applicable" (Hopkins 1971: 244). Considering that Hong Kong labor unions have managed to recruit only a minority of the labor force, this attitude seems surprising.

The most important union activity is to provide services for workers outside the workplace.[15] As of March 1969, registered unions ran a total of 70 schools, 56 clinics, and 156 business undertakings (such as dormitories, cooperative stores, and cemeteries).[16] Union welfare services also

Table 2-12. Priorities of Trade Unions according to Trade Union Secretaries

Aim	Percentage of secretaries
Higher wages and better working conditions	49
Helping members with their individual problems	24
Better union-provided welfare benefits	17
Creating unity between all workers in Hong Kong	4
Effective consultation with management	3
Urging government to protect workers by legislation	3
Striving for largest possible union membership	1
Total	101

Note: Number of observations, 71.
Source: Hopkins 1971: 246.

included cash benefits for unemployment, sickness, accidents, marriage, maternity care, and proper funerals. The amount spent on death gratuities in 1968 approached HK$600,000, which was twice the amount spent on all other cash benefits (Hopkins 1971: 245).

Passivity of the Hong Kong Labor Movement

Hong Kong's labor law does not actively seek to promote collective bargaining. But such a "passive" legal approach cannot be held responsible for the weakness of organized labor. British practice up to the 1960s was similar, but it certainly did not limit unionization in the United Kingdom. The freedom of Hong Kong trade unions to strike and picket is guaranteed by the Trade Union Registration Ordinance of 1961.

Although it is true that the 1949 Illegal Strikes and Lockouts Ordinance prohibits strikes "calculated to coerce the government either directly or by inflicting hardship upon the community" (Hopkins 1971: 218) and that many trade union activities might be considered illegal under the Public Order Ordinance of 1967, neither law has ever been enforced. The Trade Disputes Ordinance of 1948, based on British labor law, empowers the governor to refer trade disputes to arbitration, with the agreement of both parties, but this right has been exercised only once, in the dairy farm dispute of 1950 (Hopkins 1971: 219). Thus, the weakness of the trade union movement in Hong Kong cannot be ascribed to government policy.

Why then do the unions in Hong Kong avoid collective action in the workplace? Riedel (1974) has suggested that Hong Kong unions have concentrated on the provision of services to win workers over to their ideological point of view. This argument makes little sense. To begin with, workers might respond equally enthusiastically to better wages and working conditions as to welfare benefits. In addition, welfare benefits alone, with no concomitant political orientation in the organization, do not win workers over to a particular ideology. The recruitment of members and a service clientele is indeed a frequent first step in political mobilization. To be effective, however, it must be followed up with some form of political indoctrination—which Hong Kong's unions have failed to do.

Lethbridge (1980) has argued that China's economic interests have "always been placed first." The implication is that the possible benefits to be gained through political action by the Communist unions are far outweighed by the damage political instability might inflict on Hong Kong's economic prosperity and, consequently, on China's foreign exchange earnings and access to sensitive modern technology (via "backdoor" illegal transfer through Hong Kong) and the profitability of Chinese-owned firms in Hong Kong (Lethbridge 1980: 88–89). Another point to note is that when China was isolated internationally, it had a political interest in maintaining as good a relationship as possible with the United Kingdom. Similarly, the passivity of the rightist unions might be explained by the need of Taiwan (China), in its struggle for recognition with China, to maintain equally good relations with the British.

Still another possible reason for union passivity is that it is what the members want. Surveys indicate that the immigrant population in Hong Kong is extremely apathetic politically and even resists political involvement (Young forthcoming). Furthermore, as will be discussed in later sections, the people of Hong Kong, particularly the immigrants, are achievement oriented and have a high propensity to change jobs or start their own firms. In a sense, they are economic individualists. Collective bargaining and long-term group benefits and wage increases are of little interest to them. Thus, if Hong Kong's politically affiliated unions focus on providing various types of welfare services, it is because attempts at political or economic action will drive away rather than attract potential members.

In that case, there should be a correlation between the proportion of immigrants in different sectors and the degree and militancy of union organization. Although immigrants constituted 72 percent of the economically active population in 1966, they accounted for only 61.9 percent of senior government personnel, 49.8 percent of lower-level government functionaries, 62.4 percent of technicians, and 65.4 percent of professionals; the last three groups are all part of the more aggressive and well-organized white-collar unions.[17] These aggregate data probably conceal much higher native-born concentrations in militant professions such as teaching and medicine. The percentages of immigrants in different economic sectors increases fairly steadily in inverse relation to the degree of unionization (table 2-13). A rank correlation yielded a coefficient of 0.821, which is significant at the 5 percent level, with a probability value close to 2 percent. Thus, the above argument would appear to have some validity.

That is not to say that the sole, or even principal, determinant of unionization rates in Hong Kong is the presence of immigrants. Indeed, research has shown that unionization depends on (a) how long estab-

Table 2-13. Proportion of Immigrants, by Economic Sector, 1966

Sector	Percentage
Public utilities	61.7
Transport and communications	64.5
Community service	71.3
Mining and quarrying	78.1
Construction	82.8
Commerce	78.3
Manufacturing	74.3
Total economically active	72.0

Source: Hong Kong 1966 By-Census, table 160, p. 129.

lished the sector is, (b) whether the sector provides services, and (c) the proportion of skilled male labor (see Young forthcoming). Note, too, that most Hong Kong industries do not possess monopoly power, and hence there is no monopoly rent for labor to squeeze out of capitalists. This might explain why the public sector unions—whose employer, the government, can extract a surplus from the remainder of the economy—are so vociferous. It does not explain, however, why other unions in monopoly industries, such as public utilities, are so passive. Although traditional economic factors are an important determinant of the strength of the union movement in Hong Kong (as in other countries), the low level of unionization in general and the political and economic quiescence of Hong Kong's blue-collar unions in particular, in sharp contrast to the well-organized militancy of its white-collar unions, can be attributed to the large number of immigrants in the economy as a whole and to their concentration in the weakly unionized sectors.[18]

The United Kingdom has argued that Hong Kong trade unions are in many cases simply "friendly societies" that "provide the power necessary for bargaining" but in some cases are "really associations of people who have joined together for recreational and social reasons"—parties, dinners, picnics, and so on—and are registered as trade unions rather than societies merely to avoid the police surveillance to which the latter are more likely to be subjected (cited in Young forthcoming: 74–76).

The politically indifferent and individualistic immigrants who move from job to job in the quest for greater material gain have no interest in collective bargaining for political or economic objectives, but they do approve of friendly recreational societies. Unions concentrate on providing services because this is the only thing that will attract paying members.

In fact, the mutual aid component of Hong Kong trade unions appears to resemble the traditional friendly societies that existed in China before the revolution. Those societies were also divided on the basis of dialect or region of origin. Many, such as the Tung Wah and Po Leung Kok, which continue today in Hong Kong (Lethbridge 1978: 52–103), functioned as mutual aid societies within a particular region. Others were essentially travelers' aid groups that would offer a place to stay to people who spoke the same dialect or came from the same region as their members. Thus, there exists a cultural precedence for Hong Kong's friendly trade union societies.

Work and Entrepreneurship

If there is one distinguishing characteristic of the people of Hong Kong, it is that they work extremely hard. A 1968 survey found that 87 percent of those employed worked Saturdays and 73 percent worked Sundays. Only 12 percent worked eight hours or less per day whereas 42 percent worked eleven hours or more (Hopkins 1971: 208). Although the official workweek in 1971 was forty-eight hours, 50.2 percent of the labor force put in more than fifty-four hours a week, and 11.4 percent put in more than seventy-five hours (*1971 Census*). Indeed,

> there are many workers who voluntarily rush off to a second job, or a third, after putting in a full day at their regular job. Some who are employees during the day retire to their home-cum-office and act as employers or are self-employed in some tiny enterprise. It is not surprising to find professionals, either teachers, lawyers or accountants, "moonlighting." Shops during the day are turned into miniature factories at night, your friendly grocer producing little packets of tissues while his wife weaves baskets. A mother may come home with a bundle full of toys to assemble, with everyone working together in the living room. When they are not working, many are studying to pass exams, learning a new skill, or getting ahead in some way. (Woronoff 1980: 84)

This can hardly be classified as exploitation by employers, however, because they work as hard as their employees—up to 31 percent are known to work between ten and sixteen hours a day (Woronoff 1980: 135).[19]

Some might argue that people work these long hours simply because they are poor. Comparative data suggest that this is not necessarily the case. In 1968, 52 percent of the workers surveyed in Hong Kong worked ten hours or more a day and 58 percent worked seven days a week, whereas in Singapore, an economy with a similar per capita national income, the figures were 20 and 21 percent, respectively (Hopkins 1971: 208). On average, Hong Kong persons in manufacturing in 1971 worked 6.5 more hours than their equally wealthy counterparts in Singapore, 4 hours more than the considerably poorer Koreans, and 18.4 hours more than the wealthy and somewhat sedentary Americans (table 2-14). Note, however, that the average hours of work in manufacturing declined

Table 2-14. *Average Hours of Work per Week in Manufacturing, Hong Kong and Selected Economies, 1971 and 1976*

Economy	1971	1976
Hong Kong	55.9	50.5
Japan	42.6	40.2
Korea, Republic of	51.9	52.5
Singapore	49.4	48.4
United Kingdom	43.6	43.5
United States	37.5	37.2

Source: Hong Kong calculated from midpoints in census data, with a midpoint of 80 assigned to the 75 plus hours a week category. *Hong Kong Population and Housing Census 1971*, basic tables, p. 29; *Hong Kong 1976 By-Census*, basic tables, p. 33. Other countries from United Nations data.

rapidly during the 1970s and by 1980 had fallen to 48.6 (*1981 Census*: 25). Similarly, the average hours of work in the entire economy fell from 55.5 hours in 1971 to 51.6 in 1976 and 49.9 in 1981 (*Population and Housing Census 1971; 1976 By-Census; 1981 Census*).

Focus on Material Gain

A 1969 study of shopworkers in Hong Kong found that job satisfaction was strongly associated with salary and supplementary benefits such as overtime pay, bonuses, and tips and was little affected by regularity of working hours, monthly holidays, fixed meal breaks, or the kind of shop. Of those planning to look for a job elsewhere, 67 percent mentioned improved wages as their reason for moving. Only 19 percent mentioned working hours, and a mere 6 percent said they were looking for a more interesting job. Thus, the source of job satisfaction and the primary motivation for changing jobs was the employee's take-home pay, with little thought to working conditions.

At least until recently, the people of Hong Kong did not attach prestige and status to class background or education but simply to the acquisition of wealth. Thus, until 1980 or so, the government conferred the prestigious nonsalaried positions in the Legislative and Executive councils only on extremely wealthy private individuals (Jarvie 1969: 188). Gossip in Hong Kong rarely focuses on political figures. Rather, who has made how much money and how it was done is the perennial topic of conversation. Hong Kong is indeed a "capitalist paradise" and "callous colony" (from titles cited in Woronoff 1980). In recent years, with the development of a large native-born and well-educated white-collar class, these values have been partly supplanted by the more conventional respect for educational, civic, and bureaucratic (organizational) achievement.

In general, then, the people of Hong Kong engage in highly entrepreneurial activity in the pursuit of material gain, and this helps keep markets strongly competitive.

The Economic Character of the Population

Since almost the entire population of Hong Kong is Chinese, many observers have attributed the economic behavior of its residents to the Chinese propensity for hard work, frugality, risk-taking, and general business acumen. The outstanding entrepreneurial success of the Chinese in countries as disparate as Malaysia, Mozambique, and the United States is frequently cited as evidence in support of this argument. Some say it is the "Confucian work ethic" that has motivated economic growth in Hong Kong, as in Japan, Singapore, the Republic of Korea, and Taiwan (China).

Ironically, however, traditional Chinese society discouraged entrepreneurship and a drive for material gain. As Marjorie Topley explains,

In the homeland certain institutional arrangements and values worked together to discourage a number of activities aimed at maximizing gain. The family system put checks on the means of acquiring greater wealth. It discouraged movement into occupations bringing greater income but placing the individual outside family control. The system of inheritance led to continual division of family fortunes. . . . The class system allotted a low social status to the tradesman and tended to discourage individuals from entering commerce on a permanent basis. External factors such as poor communications, lack of opportunities elsewhere and sometimes absence of law and order again tended to inhibit emigration into more productive forms of employment. (cited in Jarvie 1969: 180–85)

Because educators stressed personal qualities rather than expertise, many scholars had little regard for technical ability or practical affairs and thus spent no time on the skills necessary for entrepreneurship. If anything, Chinese society ranked merchants below peasants, perhaps mindful of the Confucian teaching, "A virtuous man makes his principles his worry, not money." Even wealthy merchants in China failed to train their sons to take over their activities. Their one aim was to retire as a member of the gentry. At the same time, it was recognized that the poor would be concerned with material gain.

Thus, Topley argues that the Hong Kong population is greatly interested in the pursuit of material gain because it is largely a society of peasant refugees who have escaped the restraining bonds of the values and institutions of the traditional Chinese aristocracy and who share the materially oriented values that already existed in Hong Kong before their arrival (cited in Jarvie 1969: 131–32). Gentry influence could not be reestablished because urban residential conditions in Hong Kong do not encourage gentry life and because political leadership rests not on a classical education but on Western-style recruitment into the administration (Jarvie 1969: 187). Status and prestige now come from the acquisition of wealth.

Nicholas Owen also emphasizes Hong Kong's peasant origins, but he attributes the population's entrepreneurial spirit to the fact that immigrants from the mainland were deprived of their rural safety net—that is, they had no village to return to, unlike those who emigrated to the cities in other countries of the developing world (cited in Hopkins 1971: 150). Furthermore, Owen states, the Hong Kong worker leaped from a highly traditional to a highly modern environment. "In other words, the mere act of immigration achieved with great abruptness an economic and social transition which in other underdeveloped countries may take years. The impact is quite distinct from the idea that improved economic performance can be attributed to immigration per se, although the high economic performance of emigrants (for example, Jews, Jamaicans, Indians, Parsees, Scots, and Chinese) provides persuasive evidence that emigration alone may have had a considerable impact" (cited in Hopkins 1971: 152).

Owen, in contrast to Topley, thinks that Chinese peasant society would have had a restraining influence on the entrepreneurial drive of the Hong Kong immigrant. Both authors, however, assume that the Chinese who emigrated to Hong Kong were mostly peasants. There is, however, no empirical evidence to support this idea. According to data from the 1955 Hambro report (see table 2-15), only 14.6 percent of those who emigrated to Hong Kong in the late 1940s and early 1950s were farmers or fishers—in other words, members of China's peasant society. Professionals and intellectuals, whom Topley assumes formed only a small percentage of immigrants, actually accounted for 14.9 percent. Aside from these groups, the largest categories were army and police, business people, and clerks and shop assistants, who together accounted for 47 percent of the immigrant population. Immigrants to Hong Kong were not peasants, nor were they primarily rural gentry. Rather, they were a mixture of members of modern Chinese industrial and urban society. Unfortunately, little research has been done on the structure and values of pre-Communist Chinese industrial society.

Table 2-15. Occupational Structure of Working-Age Immigrant Population, 1955

Occupation	Percentage of total immigrant population
Farmers	14.3
Fishers	0.3
Coolies and domestic servants	1.2
Cottage crafts people	2.1
Industrial laborers	4.0
Independent crafts people	2.8
Hawkers	3.6
Clerks and shop assistants	14.7
Business people	7.9
Professionals and intellectuals	14.9
Army and police	24.4
Others	7.0
Unemployed	3.0
Total	100.2

Note: Total may not add up to 100 because of rounding. The original Hong Kong government estimates are of the working-age population and include a category for "housewives" which gives no indication of the class of those surveyed. It was assumed that the 32.7 percent listed as housewives were evenly distributed across the social backgrounds of the immigrants, and the remaining percentages were scaled against the residual 67.3 percent.

Source: Szczepanik 1958: 155. Szczepanik's data are from the 1955 Hambro Report.

Culturally based explanations of the entrepreneurial behavior of the people of Hong Kong all share a common problem: not everyone in Hong Kong is Chinese. Some of the more successful business people are British, and yet the British today are no one's model of an entrepreneurial and energetic society (Woronoff 1980: 14). Immigrants from India and Pakistan have also done extremely well, again, with no concomitantly spectacular performance at home. What all these groups have in common is that they are immigrants. The Chinese left the mainland either to escape political turmoil or, in the later waves, to gain political and economic freedom. The British went to Hong Kong to seek their fortunes in trade and to penetrate the Chinese market. Even today, immigrants continue to flow to Hong Kong in search of economic success.

The immigrant is the "achievement-oriented individual" whom McClelland describes in his well-known study of entrepreneurship (McClelland 1975). He or she works hard partly out of economic necessity but principally out of achievement-oriented ambition and a belief that individual effort can have an effect on outcomes. The emphasis is on pecuniary gain because money is the most objective measure of individual success. In Hong Kong all these tendencies are intensified. This immigrant society has no traditional forms of status to "tempt" the immigrant away from energetic economic activity. The immigrant works hard in pursuit of pecuniary gain both because of independent internal motivation and because that is precisely the basis of social status. Hong Kong, like the United States in the eighteenth and early nineteenth centuries, is an immigrant society without traditional forms of status, without shared concepts of citizenship, and, admittedly with little culture—but with an overriding focus on hard work and material gain.

If the people of Hong Kong are entrepreneurial because they are immigrants, it follows that many entrepreneurs should be immigrants. As table 2-16 shows, this is definitely the case. Immigrants accounted for 70 to 80 percent of entrepreneurs in the 1970s but for only about 45 percent of the total population.[20] According to the 1966 by-census, 28.0 percent of the economically active population, but only 18.8 percent of those classified as employers or self-employed, were native born (*1966 By-Census*: 38). The argument that the people of Hong Kong are entrepreneurial because they are immigrants appears to be quite strong.

One fact remains unexplained: the rapid decline in average hours of work in the 1970s. On the one hand, this might simply be a result of income effects.[21] On the other hand, one might note that all good (or bad) things come to an end and that people born in Hong Kong after World War II finally came of age in the 1970s. Unlike the immigrant population, the native-born tend to go into the professions rather than business, and they display a much higher political consciousness and tendency toward collective industrial action. Over time they have sparked a gradual social transformation, with more traditional forms of status, such as bureaucratic and professional achievement, gaining some ground over after-tax

Table 2-16. Place of Birth of Entrepreneurs and of the Entire Population,
1971, 1974, and 1978
(percent)

Place of birth	Entrepreneurs			Entire population	
	1971	1974	1978	1971	1976
Hong Kong	34.3	20.0	20.2	56.4	59.0
Mainland China	} 65.7	80.0 {	77.3	42.6	41.0
Other countries			2.4	—	—
Number in sample	210	15	415	—	—

— Not in source.
Source: All data except Hong Kong drawn directly from Sit, Wong, and Kiang 1980: 266. Hong Kong data from Sit 1981b: 12.

income. Hong Kong now boasts "frivolities" such as theater companies and museums. Thus, it is possible that the social transformations engendered by the coming of age of the native-born generation, combined with their probable lower work hours, reduced the average hours of work of the population.[22]

Characteristics of Hong Kong Entrepreneurs

According to a 1978 survey of 400 owners of factories employing between ten and forty-nine workers, Hong Kong entrepreneurs tend to have little work experience before setting up their own firms. Only 21.2 percent of those surveyed had held more than one job, whereas 71.8 percent had held only one job, and 7.0 percent had never been employed (Sit, Wong, and Kiang 1980: 293). Given the 20 percent or more annual turnover rates prevalent in Hong Kong manufacturing (see "The Small-Firm Economy," below), it is unlikely that those who had worked had done so for a long time. Since most entrepreneurs came from reasonably humble origins, this suggests an aggressive and independent orientation.[23] It would seem that the survey respondents worked only long enough to accumulate some capital and technical skills before starting their own firms.

About 60 percent of those who have started their own firms were production operatives in their first job (table 2-17). Considering that most entrepreneurs opened their own firms after holding only one job, this means that the majority of entrepreneurs had production experience but were unlikely to have known much about personnel management, marketing, or finance. This situation is confirmed by Sit's 1975 survey of 159 owners of predominantly small factories in domestic premises, which found that 60.4 percent of entrepreneurs were former manufacturing workers (Sit 1981b: 111).

Table 2-17. Occupations of Entrepreneurs before Establishment of Own Firm
(percent)

Occupation	First job	Second job	Third job
Shareholder	9.0	23.6	57.7
Manager	5.9	2.3	7.7
Administrative staff	24.2	20.2	11.5
Production operative	60.9	53.9	23.1
Number in sample	388.0	89.0	26.0

Source: Sit, Wong, and Kiang 1980: 297.

In addition, most entrepreneurs are unlikely to have had any specialized education to remedy their lack of knowledge of many of the facets
of operating a business (see table 2-18). Close to 72 percent of those
surveyed by Sit in 1978 had no technical or managerial training, and of
the remainder, 23.1 percent had apprenticeship or industrial process
training, both of which are likely to be highly production oriented. Only
5.1 percent had some training in nonproduction areas of business management, namely, accounting and administration. Entrepreneurs were,
however, somewhat better educated than the average production
worker (table 2-19).[24]

Table 2-20 indicates that 51.4 percent of the entrepreneurs surveyed in
1978 set up their firms in the same industry in which they had held their
first job. If second and third jobs are included, the percentage operating
in an industry in which they had previous working experience would
undoubtedly be higher.[25] In a 1975 survey of 159 entrepreneurs, for
example, 63.5 percent were doing "the same type of job" as before, and
9 percent were "in the same line of business" or "had former market
connections" or "training" (Sit 1981b: 111).

Thus the typical Hong Kong entrepreneur can be described as a relatively well-educated immigrant, with a little work experience as a pro-

Table 2-18. Technical and Managerial Training of Entrepreneurs
before Setting up Own Enterprise

Type of training	Number of respondents	Percentage of total
None	298	71.8
Apprenticeship	52	12.5
Industrial process	44	10.6
Accounting	14	3.4
Administration/management	7	1.7
Total	415	100.0

Source: Sit 1978: 288.

Table 2-19. Highest Level of Education of Selected Groups, Late 1970s
(percent)

Level of education	Entrepreneurs, 1978	Economically active population, 1976	Production workers, 1976
No schooling	5.1	13.9	11.8
Primary	36.4	45.4	57.1
Secondary	48.9	34.9	29.6
Tertiary	9.6	5.8	1.4
Number in sample	415.0	—	—

— Not available.
Source: Sit 1978: 289.

duction operative and practically no experience or training in management, who is likely to open a firm in an industry in which he has previously held a job. This last characteristic is what Leibenstein (1968: 73) calls "routine entrepreneurship." Hong Kong appears to be considerably less well-endowed with what he calls N-entrepreneurship (innovating entrepreneurship), although about 35 percent of the entrepreneurs surveyed by Sit did go into industries in which they had no previous experience. It should also be pointed out that although foreign investment has played a central role in identifying new sectors such as electronics, the expansion of these sectors has largely come from firms set up by former production workers in the path-breaking foreign factories.

Table 2-20. Entrepreneurs' First Work Experience and Present Industry, Late 1970s
(number)

Industry of first job	Present industry				
	Wearing apparel	Textiles	Plastics	Electronics	Machinery
Garment/textiles	125[a]	13[a]	6	2	0
Plastics	1	1	49[a]	2	0
Electronics	4	2	5	14[a]	5
Metallic	0	0	5	1	0
Other	67	22	49	3	15
Number in sample	197	38	114	22	20

a. In the same industrial group during first job and as independent entrepreneur: total, 201. Total sample, 391.
Source: Calculated from data in Sit 1978: 295.

Capital Formation

Except in the period before the 1960s, the ratio of gross domestic fixed capital formation (GDFC) to GDP in Hong Kong was considerably higher than in the United Kingdom and the United States but lower than in Japan, a country renowned for its high investment rate (table 2-21).[26]

The Role of Foreign Investment and Other Capital Inflows

The postwar history of foreign capital transfers to Hong Kong begins with the flight of industrial (primarily textile) capital from Shanghai to Hong Kong. The physical capital, monetary wealth, and precious metals that industrialists fleeing from Shanghai and other parts of the mainland brought to Hong Kong must have been immense. Shanghai had been the manufacturing center of China, and that Hong Kong tripled its population in the space of two to three years without suffering a serious economic shock suggests that the colony's capital stock may have doubled or even tripled! Thus the wealth brought in by immigrants was a principal factor behind capital formation immediately after the war.

Indeed, invisible earnings and inflows of capital combined averaged 40 percent of national income between 1947 and 1955, reaching a high of 65 percent during the refugee inflow of 1948–50.[27] It has been estimated that some HK$500 million in overseas Chinese remittances entered and remained in Hong Kong in 1956 and 1957 (Riedel 1974: 112). This would have amounted to 40.4 percent of total investment in the colony (Chou 1966: 72).

Because few data are available on Hong Kong's balance of payments (the IMF does not keep such data on Hong Kong), it is impossible to arrive at accurate estimates of the role of foreign investment in gross domestic capital formation. As Riedel points out, however,

Table 2-21. *Gross Domestic Fixed Capital Formation/GDP, 1953–82*

Year	Hong Kong	Japan	United Kingdom	United States
1953–60	0.15[a]	0.25	0.15	0.18
1961–70	0.24	0.33	0.18	0.18
1971–80	0.23	0.33	0.19	0.18
1981–82	0.30	0.30	0.16	0.17

a. Possibly an underestimate. Using Chou's estimate 1 of GDP yields GDCF/GDP ratios of 0.177 for 1961, 0.201 for 1962, 0.237 for 1963, and 0.256 for 1964. The comparable Hong Kong government figures yield GDCF/GDP ratios of 0.230, 0.270, 0.300, and 0.320.

Source: For Hong Kong: 1953–60, Chou 1966: 72, 81; 1961–65, Hong Kong Government, *Estimates of the Gross Domestic Product 1961–1975,* 23; 1966–79, Hong Kong Government, *Estimates of the Gross Domestic Product 1966–1980,* 12; 1980–81: *Hong Kong Monthly Digest of Statistics,* October 1983: 99; 1982–83: Economist Intelligence Unit 1984: 16–17. Remainder from OECD 1983, 1984.

evidence of a stable foreign exchange rate, an inflating domestic price level and expanding money supply, in the face of a deficit on merchandise trade account indicates that invisible earnings and capital inflow are significant—at least as large as the merchandise trade deficit. Nevertheless, since the trade deficit has been declining as a proportion of GDP while at the same time tourism—the main source of invisible earnings—has been expanding, it can be concluded that the magnitude of foreign capital inflow has been decreasing over time. Thus, whereas it has been argued that "the part played by internal savings was comparatively small (in the 1950s)," this certainly could not have been true in the 1960s. The merchandise trade deficit, of which capital inflow is a part, was equal to only 12 per cent of GDP in 1970, as opposed to 31 per cent in 1955. (1974: 112–13)

Since gross domestic capital formation as a percentage of GDP appears to have increased over time (table 2-21), Riedel's observations suggest that the role of foreign investment in financing domestic capital formation has declined.[28] This in turn suggests that domestic savings as a percentage of GDP have risen substantially over time.

Foreign investment not only improved Hong Kong's flexibility by accelerating the growth of its capital stock, but it also played a vital role in the identification and development of new industries. Fortunately for Hong Kong, the American embargo on trade with China was preceded one or two years earlier by the inflow of textile producers from Shanghai, who were able to provide a new direction for growth.[29] Hong Kong's flexibility was also strengthened by non-Chinese capital. The old British trading "hongs" of Jardine Matheson, Hutchison Whampoa, Swire Pacific, and Wheelock Marden have continued to be part of the key network of trading companies that provides the economy with information on areas of potential growth, although non-Chinese foreign investment did not really begin in earnest until the 1970s.[30] In manufacturing, this investment concentrated in the newly developing electronics and chemical products industries, which held 26.1 percent and 11.9 percent, respectively, of total foreign manufacturing investment in 1978. But foreign investment also assisted in the rapid growth of services in the 1970s. Banks with full or majority foreign interests accounted for 77 percent of all Hong Kong banks in 1976 (Lethbridge 1980: 205). Although the toy and watch industries, among others, developed largely through indigenous entrepreneurship and capital, and although no manufacturing sector has remained dependent on foreign capital, foreign investment has clearly been an important, if not dominant force, in the initial development and subsequent expansion of skill-intensive endeavors, particularly in electronics, chemicals, and banking.[31]

A 1976 survey of fifty-six foreign manufacturing establishments found that the most often cited reasons for investing in Hong Kong were, in descending order, "low corporate taxes," "good economic stability," "lack of exchange controls," "plentiful labor supply," "ideal regional location," and "lack of tariff and quota restrictions" (Lethbridge 1980: 224).

The Role of the Hong Kong Government

Not surprisingly, the Hong Kong government has been described as "minimalist"—its contribution to GDP between 1965 and 1986 barely moved, from 7 percent to only 8 percent.[32] The government is also "thrifty": during 1960–79 more than a third of total government expenditure consisted of capital investment (table 2-22). Its propensity to invest is shown in table 2-23.

Despite its relative unimportance as an economic agent, the government has contributed to the rapid growth of capital, primarily through its laissez-faire policy. This policy, given Hong Kong's excellent geographic location and its abundant, nonmilitant, and industrious labor force, acted as a magnet to Chinese refugees and to foreign capital. Thanks to these inflows, Hong Kong was able to absorb the successive waves of refugees and to continue to grow.

Table 2-22. *Government Capital Formation as a Share of Government Expenditure, 1950–79*
(percent)

Period	Hong Kong	Japan	United Kingdom	United States
1950–54	18[a]	—	—	—
1955–59	27[a]	—	—	—
1960–64	43[b]	—	—	—
1965–69	34	36	21	13
1970–74	34	39	21	11
1975–79	47	37	14	10
1965–79	38	37	19	11

— Not available.

a. Likely to be inaccurate. The denominator is total government expenditures, including transfer payments, which were probably quite small during the 1950s (see Rabushka 1976: 52). This would tend to lead to underestimates. The numerator is Chou's calculation of the government's share in domestic capital formation, which appear to be overestimates. He provides figures of HK$365 million in 1961, HK$468 million in 1962, HK$589 million in 1963, and HK$676 million in 1964. The Hong Kong government's estimates for these years are HK$293 million, HK$382 million, HK$485 million, and HK$510 million (GDP estimates, 1961–75). Thus, Chou's data would tend to lead to an overestimate of the share of investment expenditure.

b. Same as above, except that the problem arose only in the case of the 1960 data. Given four other years of more reliable data, the estimate is likely to be quite accurate.

Source: OECD 1983: detailed tables, pp. 24, 36, 236; 1984: 30–33, 74–75; Chou (966: 72, 8/52; Hong Kong, *Estimates of the Gross Domestic Product 1961–1975*, 23, 29; and *Estimates of the Gross Domestic Product 1966–1980*, 12, 16.

Table 2-23. Government Propensity to Invest, 1950–79
(government share of GDCF/GDP)

Period	Hong Kong	Japan	United Kingdom	United States
1950–54	2.19	—	—	—
1955–59	2.48	—	—	—
1960–64	1.78	—	—	—
1965–69	1.89	1.03	1.10	0.68
1970–74	1.46	1.04	1.03	0.59
1975–79	2.03	1.15	0.75	0.50
1965–79	1.79	1.07	0.96	0.59

— Not available.
Source: Tables 2-21 and 2-22.

The Impact of Spatial Relations

Before World War II, Hong Kong's entrepôt trade and manufacturing were centered on Victoria Harbour, which offered ships 17 square miles of hill-enclosed shelter from typhoons. In 1940 it handled more ships than any other harbor in the world, and 98.7 percent of Hong Kong's registered factories were located in the vicinity of the harbor or in Kowloon (Davis 1977: 118, 204–6). In 1941, 78.7 percent of the colony's population of 1,640,000 was concentrated in 6 square miles on the coast of Hong Kong Island and Kowloon.

Since Hong Kong continued to depend on trade after the war, Victoria Harbour remained the geographic focus of its population and industry, but as the population expanded the city began to spread northward. Thus by 1961 Hong Kong Island and Kowloon together accounted for only 55.3 percent of the total population (table 2-24), although 82.5

Table 2-24. Distribution of Hong Kong's Population, 1961–81
(percent)

Area	1961	1966	1971	1976	1981
Hong Kong Island	32.1	27.8	25.3	23.3	22.7
Kowloon	23.2	18.6	18.2	17.0	15.3
New Kowloon	27.2	36.2	37.6	37.0	31.7
Tsuen Wan	2.4	5.5	6.6	10.3	—
Tuen Mun	0.7	*	0.9	0.8	—
Shatin	0.6	*	0.6	0.8	—
Other towns in New Territories	1.9	9.1	1.9	2.5	—
Rural New Territories	7.6	*	6.9	7.0	—
Marine	4.4	2.8	2.0	1.3	—

* Included in "Other towns in New Territories."
— Not available.
Source: All data except 1981 drawn from Sit 1981b, p. 18.

Table 2-25. Distribution of Manufacturing Employment, 1963–81
(percent)

Area	1963	1967	1973	1977	1981
Hong Kong	22.3	18.3	13.3	14.9	15.3
Kowloon	} 64.0	68.1 {	15.8	17.6	14.8
New Kowloon			49.7	43.8	42.1
New Territories	13.7	13.6			
Tsuen Wan			16.7	18.1	21.3
Rest of New Territories			4.4	5.6	6.5

Note: Categories may not add up to 100 because of rounding. The figures for 1973 refer to establishments with twenty or more persons engaged.

Source: Hong Kong Statistics 1947–67, 63; Hong Kong Monthly Digest of Statistics, July 1975: 58; May 1979: 60; August 1983: 103.

percent of the population and 94.3 percent of registered industrial establishments were still located in the area encompassed by Hong Kong, Kowloon, and New Kowloon (Davis 1977: 63). During the 1960s the movement into New Kowloon stepped up when the government developed the industrial town of Kwun Tong. During the 1970s the population and industrial activity spread into the new towns that the government had developed in the New Territories, particularly Tsuen Wan.[33] Even so, the population and the economic activities of Hong Kong have remained concentrated in an area of 50 square miles. (For the distribution of employment in manufacturing, see table 2-25.)

How do 6 million people live and work in such a small area? Obviously, very closely. In places such as Mong Kok and Sham Shui Po, the population density is greater than 150,000 per square kilometer (400,000 per square mile) and is ranked among the highest in the world (see tables 2-26 and 2-27).

The resulting congestion can be attributed to four interacting factors: (a) rapid and sustained population growth, (b) the topography of the colony, (c) its historical legacy, and (d) government policy. The steep

Table 2-26. Comparative Population Densities, 1967
(population per square kilometer)

Economy or territory	Population density
West Berlin (Federal Republic of Germany)	4,518
Hong Kong	3,486[a]
Singapore	3,367
Netherlands	375
England and Wales	320
Japan	270

a. 1966.
Source: Hopkins 1971: 32.

Table 2-27. Population Densities in Hong Kong Districts, 1961 and 1976
(population per square kilometer)

District	1961	1976
Hong Kong Island	13,303	13,192
Sheung Wan	238,000	—
Wan Chai	209,000	—
Kowloon	84,816	83,104
Mong Kok	—	100,000+[a]
Yau Ma Tei	—	100,000+[a]
Hung Hom	—	100,000+[a]
New Kowloon	27,615	39,729
Overall	2,905	4,138

— Not available.

Note: Overall density figures do not include marine population.

a. Mentioned in Sit 1981b with no date provided. Most recent density data otherwise provided by this source was 1976.

Source: Unless otherwise noted, all data are from Sit 1981b: 14.

topography outside the urban areas (gradient 1 to 3) has made these outlying regions difficult to develop. When the British arrived, they found much of the land in the New Territories leased to local peasants and decided to honor these leases (Chiu and So 1983: 196). Although a large part of the flat land in the New Territories is still under private lease, the government has developed the steeper land in many places, and, despite the cost, it has made a good profit in the process. Since the government is actually the legal owner of all the land, it has legal procedures at its disposal for reacquiring private land, which it used in the development of the new towns in the 1980s (Chiu and So 1983: 196–97).

Clearly, the Hong Kong government, which has always controlled the supply of residential and industrial land, has been the main influence on the location of the population and of economic activity. As a result of historical circumstances, the government focused on minimizing expenditures, maximizing nontax revenue, and operating most services at a substantial profit. Thus, although the government has done a fine job of providing enough housing to put almost half the population in well-balanced estates containing recreation and work areas, as a rule it has financed the capital costs of each program out of recurrent revenue. Consequently, high densities have been set as acceptable standards, with early housing estates providing only 24 square feet per person. The infrastructural development of industrial towns, as explained later, appears to have consistently underestimated the demand for industrial floor space, and this has given rise to tremendous congestion and has encouraged firms to move into residential premises.

A government less concerned with expenditure and a laissez-faire policy would have been willing to buy out leases and engage in deficit-financed development of infrastructure, and conditions could have been considerably better. The development of new towns in the New Territories could have begun in the early 1970s, for example, when the heavy congestion in Hong Kong, Kowloon, and New Kowloon clearly indicated a need for industrial and residential floor space, instead of in the 1980s, by which time further population growth ensured that this new development would not substantially alleviate conditions in the older districts. The Hong Kong government has never viewed extreme congestion as an undesirable condition for which it would be worth sacrificing certain principles of government.[34]

Spatial Concentration, Labor Markets, and Information Flows

With housing in close proximity to industry, and with a good public transport system, workers can easily move from job to job.[35] The spatial compactness has also allowed for the rapid dissemination of information on employment and business opportunities.[36] One survey of large Chinese factories in Kwun Tong found that 52.9 percent used posters as their principal means of recruiting production personnel, whereas only 29.4 percent used newspapers. Factory upon factory is squeezed into multistory buildings, and workers can usually review bulletin boards on the ground floor and find alternative employment in the same building in which they work (Woronoff 1980). In general, information on investment and work opportunities is more easily disseminated when hundreds of thousands of people live within walking and, consequently, conversational distance of each other. This entire process is abetted by the fact that the favorite topic of conversation of Hong Kong's entrepreneurial immigrant population is who is making how much money and the way it is being done.[37]

Hong Kong's labor force has been relatively homogeneous despite the shifts in the economy. An abundant labor supply, brought about by immigration and a natural increase in population, has combined with the relative scarcity of land and capital (despite considerable foreign investment and domestic capital formation) to keep Hong Kong's comparative advantage in manufacturing limited to light manufacturing operations that use mostly unskilled or semiskilled labor, which is quite homogeneous. At most there has been only a short-term decline in productivity in the movement of labor between sectors. In addition, the strongest attribute of the labor force—its discipline and commitment to unremitting hard work—has been of considerable importance in all light industry and has strengthened the homogeneity of the labor force.

Outside of manufacturing, Hong Kong's duty-free and colorful environment has made it a favorite spot for tourists to Asia, leading to strong restaurant, hotel, and retail trades. All of these, again, require little more than hard work and enthusiasm from the labor force. Sooner or later, however, some movement into sectors with substantial amounts of human capital must occur, and at that point labor will become considerably more heterogeneous with respect to shifts between sectors. In Hong Kong this process has begun with the growth of financial services and sophisticated electronics and computer manufacturing industries.

The Capital Market

Hong Kong has a dual financial structure. It is one of the financial capitals of the world, with a tremendous amount of foreign exchange trading and banking activity. At the same time, the domestic stock exchange is small, and the bond market is practically nonexistent.[38] Small and even large firms rely mostly on personal financing. Bank loans make only a small contribution (tables 2-28 and 2-29).[39]

Despite the absence of an integrated market, the financial system appears to be efficient. Hong Kong's congestion and the population's obsession with material gain ensure that information on profitable opportunities is efficiently disseminated. Furthermore, Hong Kong's immigrant population has a cadre of entrepreneurs always ready to exploit such opportunities, and Chinese culture provides institutions from which entrepreneurs can draw start-up and working capital. Interestingly, in a 1978 survey of about 400 entrepreneurs, first-born male children were distinctly overrepresented among entrepreneurs (table 2-30).[40] Just as the pressures to succeed are higher among Chinese first-born male children, so are the financial resources provided for them. Leibenstein (1968) has argued that societies with extended families are frequently sources of entrepreneurs precisely because the resources of the entire group are available to only a few individuals.

The informal banking and loan associations of the Chinese are the *tsou-wuih* (Cantonese phoneticization; literally, "to form an association"), in which friends contribute monthly to a loan fund that each member of the *tsou-wuih* can draw on for a loan through bids. Freedman has described the mechanics of the system:

> Suppose that there were nine members and a promoter, the initial sum collected by the latter being $90. At the first meeting each member paid the promoter $10. At the second meeting tenders were submitted, the highest bid being $2. The successful bidder then collected $10 from the promoter and $10 − 2 = 8 from the other members. Suppose that at the third meeting the successful bidder offered to forgo $2.40; he then received $10 each from the promoter and the previous successful bidder and $10 − 2.40 = 7.60 from each of the remaining seven members. The bids would probably rise at each meeting, but if for the sake of simplicity we assume a flat rate of bidding at $2 throughout, then the very last member (who of course made no bid) came away with

Table 2-28. Sources of Start-up Capital for Manufacturing Establishments, from Various Sources
(percent)

Factories in domestic premises[a]
(number in sample = 136)

Major sources of capital:
  Personal savings: 100.0 percent
  Loans from relatives and friends: 8.1 percent
  Commercial banks: 0.0 percent

Factories with 10–199 employees
(sample size unknown)

Sources of start-up capital:
  Owner's personal capital: 85 percent
  Owner's relatives and friends: 10 percent
  Bank or finance house: 2 percent
  Major customers: 2 percent
  Other sources: 1 percent

Small firms with 20–50 employees
(sample size = 34)

Original capital:
  Owners and family members: 47 percent
  Friends and partners: 20.6 percent
  Relatives: 20.6 percent
  Bank: 3 percent

Firms with up to 200 employees
(sources of initial capital formation; sample size unknown)

		Loans		
Size of firm	Own resources	Private	Bank	Hire-purchase
Fewer than 100 employees	89.0	7.9	1.5	1.6
100–200 employees	88.3	7.6	4.1	—

— Not available.
  a. Average size of thirteen persons engaged; survey appears to have allowed more than one response.
  Source: Lethbridge 1980, Sit 1978, and Mok 1972.

9 x $10 = 90, having paid $74 over a period of nine months and made a profit of $16 at the end.

It was to the advantage of the men who could wait the longest for their money that the periodical bids should be high. People therefore often put in small bids, which they knew would not win, in order to frighten the members who really needed the money into bidding up. . . .

One way of looking at this institution is to see it as a means of procuring relatively cheap credit on a co-operative basis. The promoter paid no interest on what he borrowed, while the members paid

Table 2-29. Sources of Working Capital for Small and Large Firms
(percent)

Firm size (number of employees)	Own capital	Bank loans (part or all)
Fewer than 50	84.1	15.9
50–199	80.6	19.4
200 and more	77.8	22.2

Note: The sample size is unknown. For a sample of 34 small firms (20–50 employees), sources of working capital are as follows: owner and family members, 28.2 percent; friends and relatives, 33.3 percent; banks, 23.1 percent; trade credits and other, 15.4 percent.
Source: Mok 1972.

interest at rates below those demanded by moneylenders and pawn-brokers. (Freedman 1959: 65)

Casual observation indicates that the *tsou-wuih* has been used exten-sively in postwar Hong Kong, Singapore, and Taiwan (China). In Hong Kong—which, like most developing countries and newly industrializing economies, has a comparatively underdeveloped capital market—these associations, along with the concentration of family wealth in the hands of key male members, have made up for the lack of such a market. With the aid of a large band of eager entrepreneurs, this informal market has allowed capital to become concentrated and to respond readily to appro-priate price signals.

The Small-Firm Economy

The average firm in Hong Kong is very small—in contrast to firms in other countries (see table 2-31)—and the size has decreased as the colony has grown richer.[41] Many of these small firms concentrate on wearing apparel. But there are also many in individual sectors in the three- and four-digit categories of the International Standard Industrial Classifica-tion of All Economic Activities (ISIC).[42]

Table 2-30. Birth Order of Entrepreneurs and the Entire Population
(percent)

Birth order	Entrepreneurs	1971 population
First	42.1	28.4
Second	23.2	23.1
Third	16.5	17.4
Fourth	7.5	12.6
Fifth and below	10.7	18.6

Note: Number in sample, 413.
Source: Sit 1978: table 10.12, p. 250.

Table 2-31. Average Size of Manufacturing Establishments in Hong Kong and Selected Economies, 1963, 1972, and 1980

Economy	1963	1972	1980
Hong Kong	37.7	27.9	20.2
Brazil	—	67.2	43.1
Canada	43.5	53.5	52.3
Ecuador	49.9	49.7	46.7
Egypt	—	135.3	—
Germany, Federal Rep. of	135.1	148.5	162.5
Indonesia	32.9	42.7	120.3
Italy	—	128.0	129.3
Japan	17.3	17.9	14.9
Korea, Republic of	22.0	41.0	65.4
Malta	9.4	11.4	18.0
Singapore	47.5	89.1	85.3
Sweden	67.6	69.1	84.1
Switzerland	57.2	74.9	78.5
Thailand	—	49.3	—
United Kingdom	88.4	87.3	60.4
United States	—	59.3	55.0

— Not available.

Note: Unless otherwise specified, all data are persons engaged per manufacturing establishment.

Source: Yearbook of Industrial Statistics, 1972, 1977, and 1981; U.S. 1972 Census of Manufactures, vol. 1, p. 23.

Employment in Hong Kong is heavily concentrated in firms with 20 to 500 workers (table 2-32). It is interesting to compare employment by firm size in Hong Kong and other countries, assuming ten employees to be the dividing line between artisan shops and manufacturing establishments.[43] In Korea, for example, where the average firm size is even smaller than in Hong Kong, proportionately twice as many workers are employed in firms with 500 or more workers. But in Korea establishments with 5 or fewer employees play a relatively greater role than in Hong Kong.

The average size of firms employing ten or more persons in Hong Kong in 1978 was 55.0, whereas in the United States it was 110.9 (1967). Somewhat surprisingly, the average Japanese firm had only fifty-four employees. Small firms play a dominant role in Hong Kong, however, whereas in Japan most of the small firms are satellites of large enterprises (see Anderson 1982: 7, 16–20; Hoselitz 1959: 601, 604; Staley and Morse 1965: 5–8).

Subcontracting

Subcontracting is a primary source of work for both small and large firms in Hong Kong (table 2-33). Most of the subcontracting work of small

Table 2-32. Employment, by Firm Size, Selected Economies
(percentage of total persons engaged in manufacturing)

Size of firm (number engaged)	Hong Kong 1971[a]	1978	Japan, 1967[b]	Republic of Korea, 1978	United States, 1977[a]
1–4	3.7	—[c]	8.4	1.2	
5–9	7.9	11.0	12.1	3.0	1.7
10–19	8.9	9.7	11.0	3.9	3.6
20–49	13.0	15.8	13.6	8.3	8.7
50–99	12.6	15.2	10.4	8.6	10.1
100–199	30.0	14.3	9.3	11.1	18.0[d]
200–499	—[e]	14.7	10.4	16.5	15.6
500–1,000	9.0	10.1	6.6	40.2	13.5
More than 1,000	15.0	9.3	26.7		27.5
Average firm size	25.7	23.7	27.5	20.7	52.8
Average size of firms with 10 or more persons engaged	60.8	55.0	54.2		110.9

Note: Totals do not add to 100 because of rounding.

a. Based on data on number of employees.

b. Figures do not include firms of 1–3 persons engaged; the category 5–9 persons engaged is actually data for firms with 4–9 persons engaged.

c. Included under the category 5–9 persons engaged.

d. Includes firms with 100–249 employees.

e. Included under the category 100–199 persons engaged.

Source: Hong Kong 1971 Census of Manufacturing Establishments, 494; Hong Kong 1978 Survey of Industrial Production, vol. 1, 16; Korea 1967 Census of Manufactures, 582; U.S. 1977 Census of Manufactures, 1–59; and Japan Report on Mining and Manufacturing Census, 1978, 340.

firms is done for local factories and import-export houses (table 2-34), of which there were 14,678 in 1977 handling perhaps half of the colony's trade.[44] The subcontracting work of large firms is principally for overseas customers.[45]

As already mentioned, most Hong Kong entrepreneurs are former production workers with little experience or training in management, marketing, or finance. Subcontracting arrangements simplify the tasks of the small firm manager in a variety of ways.

PRODUCT DESIGN. Small firms do not have to design their own competitive products, but simply produce according to specification. In a 1972 survey of 30 Kwun Tong factories employing twenty to fifty workers, most firms produced according to ordered specifications; two-thirds of the factories had no one specializing in product design and improvement or technical innovation. And in a 1978 five-industry survey of 415 small firms employing ten to forty-nine workers, 68 percent of the firms did not have their own product brand names (Sit 1981a: 171).

Table 2-33. *Work Done for Others as Share of Value Added in 1978*

Size of firm (number engaged)	Percentage of value added
1–9	38.8
10–19	35.5
20–49	29.8
50–99	22.1
100–199	13.4
200–499	12.8
500–999	15.5
1,000 and more	24.5
All firms	22.1

Note: Materials supplied by the subcontractor are netted out.
Source: Hong Kong 1978 Survey of Industrial Production, vol. 2, pt. 5, tables 3.1 and 4.1.

MARKETING. Small firms do not have to market the final product to wholesalers; this task is, logically, also handled by the subcontractor. This arrangement is particularly valuable in the case of export markets, since small firms lack the economies of scale necessary to amortize the information costs associated with overseas trade. Provided that small firms can produce at a competitive price, subcontracting provides a ready market for their output. In 1977 only one out of ten firms employing 10 to 200 workers had a marketing or personnel department (Kwok in Lethbridge 1980: 75). In 1978, 80.7 percent of 415 small firms did not advertise their own products (Sit 1981a: 171).

SOURCING. Subcontractors frequently provide raw materials for small firms to use in producing the subcontracted good. About 30 percent of the value added of small firms is produced under such arrangements (see table 2-30). In 1978, 35.2 percent of small firms relied on other

Table 2-34. *Sources of Orders for Small Manufacturing Establishments (10–49 Employees), Late 1970s*

Source of order	Percent
1. Import-export houses	44.8
2. Local factories	23.9
3. Direct overseas orders	11.1
4. Wholesalers and retailers	4.3
5. Direct sales to consumers	3.4
6. Import-export houses with an element of (2), (3), (4), or (5)	12.0
7. Other combination	0.2
8. Don't know	0.2

Source: Sit 1978: table 14.6, p. 340.

manufacturers and import-export houses as major sources of material supply (Sit 1981a: 173).

SPECIALIZATION. Subcontracting allows small firms to specialize in only one aspect of the production process. In a 1975 survey of 174 small factories in domestic premises, less than 40 percent were involved in the complete process of making finished goods. The majority were linked with other establishments in making, processing, or assembling parts (Sit 1981b: 111). Thus, subcontracting arrangements allow the owners of small Hong Kong firms to concentrate on what they know best: production. Moreover, they are able to concentrate on the particular step in the production process they are most qualified to perform.

Small and medium-size Hong Kong firms also subcontract a significant proportion of their work to other firms in the same size category (table 2-35). In Japan, where subcontracting is also prevalent, most of the work is done by small firms for large ones in a hierarchical structure (table 2-36). In contrast, Hong Kong has a network of mutually interdependent small firms. Each enjoys a high degree of autonomy yet reaps the benefits of economies of scale in design, production, and marketing (Sit, Wong, and Kiang 1980: 343, table 14.10).

If subcontracting arrangements allow small firms to compete with large firms and hence explain the dominance of small firms in Hong Kong, why have these arrangements not been more prevalent in other economies? Such a system could, in principle, be established elsewhere, but it would require import-export houses, with information ties throughout the world, and small firms in need of such services. Hong Kong's prewar history as an entrepôt economy established a base of trading companies that were more than ready to provide the necessary services to the fledgling local manufacturers when the entrepôt trade collapsed in the 1950s.[46] Given the enormous setup costs involved, it is

Table 2-35. Subcontracting in Hong Kong, Late 1970s

Size of firm (number engaged)	Subcontracted work (percentage of value added)
1–9	6.2
10–19	16.5
20–49	16.6
50–99	18.7
100–199	18.8
200–499	13.3
500–999	8.0
1,000 and more	12.7
All firms	14.8

Source: Hong Kong, *1978 Census of Manufacturing Establishments.*

Table 2-36. Utilization of Subcontractors in Japanese Manufacturing,
Late 1970s

Size of firm (number engaged)	Percentage of enterprises using subcontractors	Average number of subcontractors per enterprise
1–3	11.5	3
4–9	33.9	4
10–19	48.4	7
20–29	58.9	9
30–49	64.0	11
50–99	69.3	18
100–199	75.8	23
200–299	77.6	28
300–499	80.3	36
500–999	82.3	84
1,000 and more	83.3	160

Source: Caves and Uekusa 1976: 112.

doubtful whether such a specialized information network could have developed independently.

Labor Costs

Although Hong Kong's labor market is extremely competitive and there are no geographic, legal, institutional, or social barriers to the movement of labor between manufacturing firms, large firms face high unit labor costs (table 2-37).[47] Furthermore, turnover rates appear to increase with firm size (table 2-38).[48] Thus, the higher labor costs of large firms cannot be attributed to firm-specific capital, since the turnover in such firms would decrease with firm size. Instead, large firms are paying higher unit labor costs in an effort to control what might otherwise be unacceptably high turnover rates.[49]

The only way to reconcile the data of tables 2-37 and 2-38 with the lack of formal barriers to the movement of labor between firms is to conclude that Hong Kong's labor force has a preference for working in small firms. This preference could be due to the more rigid organizational structure of large firms, which would inhibit individual self-advancement based on merit (Mok 1972: 52). Or it might be the result of an implicit capital investment by workers in small firms, whereby the worker understands that if the firm expands rapidly, he or she will move up to a managerial position. Hence, the worker in a small firm may gain from the rapid expansion of the firm. In contrast, only a small proportion of production workers in a rapidly expanding large firm would advance to managerial positions. In any case, there seems to be some bias against large firms in Hong Kong's labor market that must be based on preferences, for there are no institutional or legal barriers to the movement of labor.[50]

Table 2-37. *Labor Cost per Employee, by Firm Size and ISIC Sector*
(firm size 10–19 = 1.00)

ISIC sector	Number of employees							
	1–9	10–19	20–49	50–99	100–199	200–499	500–999	1,000 and more
311–12	1.00	—	1.09	1.07	1.24	1.43	—	n.a.
313	n.a.	1.00	—	n.a.	n.a.	—	1.37	n.a.
321	0.90	1.00	1.09	1.20	1.19	1.10	1.10	1.00
322	1.12	1.00	1.06	1.11	1.15	1.13	1.15	1.08
323	1.06	1.00	1.24	1.10	1.05	n.a.	n.a.	n.a.
324	1.73	1.00	1.18	1.34	1.14	1.22	n.a.	n.a.
331	1.11	1.00	1.21	1.25	1.00	n.a.	n.a.	n.a.
332	0.83	1.00	0.91	0.90	1.60	1.08	n.a.	n.a.
341	1.00	—	1.13	1.17	—	—	n.a.	n.a.
342	0.92	1.00	1.16	1.11	1.22	1.47	1.50	n.a.
351–52	0.79	1.00	0.91	1.26	1.10	1.22	n.a.	n.a.
355	1.00	—	—	1.01	—	n.a.	n.a.	n.a.
356	0.99	1.00	1.04	1.07	1.05	0.94	0.94	0.91
361–69	0.79	1.00	0.83	—	—	1.08	n.a.	n.a.
371–72	0.79	1.00	1.05	1.11	1.07	1.28	n.a.	n.a.
380–81	0.93	1.00	0.97	0.95	1.01	0.91	—	—
382	0.85	1.00	1.12	—	1.50	—	n.a.	n.a.
383	1.003	1.00	0.96	0.99	1.05	1.00	1.07	1.09
384	0.92	1.00	1.07	1.07	1.43	—	—	1.18
385	1.00	—	1.20	1.23	1.30	1.34	1.23	—
390	1.02	1.00	0.98	1.02	1.05	—	—	n.a.

n.a. No activity in this size category.

— Not available; because of the small number of firms in this size category, the Hong Kong government does not disclose the data. In cases where data on the 10–19 category were unavailable, the ratios pertain to firms with 1–9 persons engaged. Sectors 314 and 354 are not included in the above comparison because data are lacking on more than one size category.

Source: Hong Kong 1978 Survey of Industrial Production.

The Impact of High-Density Development

In zoning enough land for (crowded) housing, the government may have undersupplied industrial land. According to the 1971 census (Circular 5/72, appendix 1), only 66.9 percent of manufacturing activity took place in industrial buildings, with the remainder divided between residential premises (23 percent), squatter resettlement estates (1.8 percent), and other sites such as commercial office buildings and rooftops (8.3 percent). As table 2-39 shows, the proportion of firms in nonindustrial premises decreased with firm size.

Given the highly segmented construction of residential floor space, large firms are less able to use such premises and are thus driven into the market for industrial premises.[51] Industrial floor space may be in such

Table 2-38. *Turnover Rates of Production Workers, by Factory Size*

Number of production workers	Annual turnover rate (percent)	Number of firms
1–9	17.1	112
10–19	19.9	56
20–49	18.3	63
50–99	19.6	34
100–199	19.1	29
200–499	22.5	15
500 and more	24.7	8

Source: Mok 1972: 42.

short supply, however, that the number of large firms is ultimately restricted.

If industrial congestion is the primary cause of the predominance of small firms in Hong Kong, then as new towns in Hong Kong are established, develop, and mature, large firms should begin to spring up, principally in industrial floor space. But in that case average firm size

Table 2-39. *Manufacturing Establishments, by Type of Premises, 1971*

Size of firm (number of employees)	Domestic premises	Industrial premises	Resettlement estates	Other premises
Number of establishments				
1–4	6,250	128	974	899
5–9	6,483	338	748	571
10–19	3,399	565	273	283
20–49	1,480	1,147	109	118
50–99	256	907	23	42
100–499	89	895	6	17
500–999	5	84	2	0
More than 1,000	0	58	0	0
Total	17,962	4,122	2,135	1,930
Percentage distribution				
1–4	75.7	1.6	11.8	10.9
5–9	79.6	4.2	9.2	7.0
10–19	75.2	12.5	6.0	6.3
20–49	51.9	40.2	3.8	4.1
50–99	20.8	73.9	1.9	3.4
100–499	8.8	88.9	0.6	1.7
500–999	5.5	92.3	2.2	0.0
More than 1,000	0.0	100.0	0.0	0.0
Total	68.7	15.8	8.2	7.4

Note: The sum of the totals does not add up to 100 because of rounding.
Source: Hong Kong 1971 Census of Manufacturing Establishments, 494.

should decline as manufacturing activity continues to grow and, constrained by the limited availability of industrial floor space, is driven into domestic premises in the form of small firms. Furthermore, an economy in which extreme congestion limits average firm size would tend to be characterized by more multiestablishment firms than other economies because proprietors, unable to expand floor space in one location, would simply set up another small establishment at a separate location.

In Kwun Tong—Hong Kong's first planned industrial town, begun in the early 1960s—the average size of factories on reclaimed land declined steadily during the 1960s (table 2-40). Only in 1966, after record construction of 3 million square feet of floor space in 1965 and 2 million square feet in 1966, did the average size of factories rise, presumably as large factories moved into this newly developed floor space. By 1971 the development of Kwun Tong had virtually come to an end; the average size of factories had shrunk to 14.2 employees. Most of the new small factories were located on domestic premises. The Hong Kong government appears to have underestimated the rate at which manufacturing activity in Hong Kong was growing.

Despite the small size of the average firm, the establishment/firm ratio in Hong Kong is usually high—presumably because it is difficult to obtain (and costly to assemble) adequately large contiguous areas of industrial space.[52] The geographic fragmentation reduces the advantages of firm size—another reason why congestion works in favor of small firms.[53]

In sum, small firms are important in Hong Kong, in contrast to other economies with similar technologies and serving similar markets, because of three social and institutional factors peculiar to the colony. First, its prewar entrepôt economy built up a system of trading companies ready to provide specialized sourcing, product design, and marketing services for all firms, thereby eliminating many of the advantages usually enjoyed by large firms in big markets. Second, large firms face higher turnover rates and unit labor costs, which suggests that the labor force prefers to work in small firms. And third, congestion and an inadequate supply of industrial floor space have prevented large firms from becoming established in Hong Kong and have led to the predominance of small and medium-size firms that operate mostly out of domestic and other nonindustrial premises.[54]

These small and medium-size firms are dynamic, however. Although approximately 20 to 30 percent of Hong Kong's small firms close every year, those that do survive frequently expand (see Young forthcoming). In a 1978 survey of 400 owners of factories with ten to forty-nine employees, 27.1 percent had relocated the factory because of expansion, and 56.7 percent reported increased machinery and production capacity, but only 1.7 percent reported decreased capacity.[55] More than 40 percent reported an increase in capacity, number of employees, machinery, total

Table 2-40. The Development of Kwun Tong, 1961–78

Year	Usable nondomestic floor area constructed	Number of factories on reclaimed land	Number of workers in factories on reclaimed land	Average size of factories on reclaimed land	Total number of establishments	Total number of employees	Average establishment size
1961	100+	15,000+	150.0	—	—	—	—
1962	130+	19,700+	151.5	—	—	—	—
1963	626,021	170+	25,000+	147.1	—	—	—
1964	1,069,765	197+	25,336	128.6	—	—	—
1965	3,015,118	343	30,500	88.9	—	—	—
1966	1,931,284	468	49,373	105.5	—	—	—
1967	779,887	503	48,445	96.3	—	—	—
1968	281,922	642	63,000	98.1	879	68,498	77.9
1969	913,601	729	71,200	97.7	1,110	81,898	73.8
1970	2,408,030	808	72,300	89.5	1,315	91,204	69.4
1971	2,260,102	—	—	—	1,619	95,896	59.2
1973	—	—	—	—	—	2,997	16.6
1978	—	—	—	—	—	3,074	14.2

— Not available.
Source: Mok 1972.

sales, and exports (Sit, Wong, and Kiang 1980: 268, 380, 392). Clearly, those small firms that do survive are able to grow.[56]

That the entry of new small firms has contributed to economic expansion and recovery from slumps is illustrated by the recovery from the 1975–76 recession (see table 2-41). Between the fourth quarter of 1973 and the fourth quarter of 1974, manufacturing employment declined rapidly, with small firms of 20 or fewer persons bearing a slightly greater share of the burden. In the fourth quarter of 1975, after a year of stagnation, the economy began a rapid recovery, which raised manufacturing employment to 778,788 persons by the third quarter of 1976, a 24.1 percent increase over that of a year earlier.[57] The recovery began during the fourth quarter of 1975 with an increase in employment of 25,000 persons in establishments with 20–49 workers and was accompanied by increases of 6,000 to 10,000 persons in the medium-size categories. In the meantime, large firms stagnated. In the first quarter of 1976, while the recovery in the rest of the manufacturing sector faltered, firms employing 1–9 and 10–19 persons posted increases of more than 10,000 persons. In the second quarter of 1976 these small firms continued to show gains of 7,000–8,000 persons, while the firms employing 20–499 persons each showed increases of 5,000–7,000 persons. During the same period, large firms finally showed something of a response, with each subcategory registering an increase of 3,000–4,000 persons. By the time the recovery reached its peak in the third quarter of 1976, firms in the 20–49 and 200–499 categories had each posted gains of roughly 10,000 persons. All the other small and medium-size categories showed gains of several thousand, whereas most of the large firms showed slight declines. The increases in employment in the small and medium-size firms were brought about by substantial increases in the number of firms in these categories. Between the third quarter of 1975 and the third quarter of 1976 the number of firms increased from 27,864 to 35,760, or 28 percent in one year! The dynamism of the small-firm economy, operating within a flexible system supported by entrepreneurship and integrated and efficient markets, speaks for itself.

The Political Economy

Although Hong Kong is a colony, it is an independent political entity. Since 1958 it has not been required to submit a budget to the British secretary of state and the influence of the British government has largely been limited to foreign policy (Lin, Lee, and Simones 1979: 150). Until 1974, however, Hong Kong was required to keep its official government reserves, as well as part of the reserves of the banking system, in pounds sterling, the value of which were guaranteed by the British government (Rabushka 1979: 23).[58] At times these reserves have amounted to one-quarter to one-third of Britain's total gold and foreign exchange reserves.

Table 2-41. Role of Small and Medium-Size Firms in the 1975–76 Economic Recovery, Selected Quarters

Size of firm (number engaged)	1973:4	1974:4	1974:4[a]	1975:1	1975:2	1975:3	1975:4	1976:1	1976:2	1976:3
Number of persons engaged										
1–9	75,628	60,932	76,458	83,894	88,192	83,044	81,281	92,189	100,378	105,278
10–19	60,085	48,381	56,123	55,797	64,125	63,104	62,475	73,055	79,650	82,612
20–49	88,124	77,928	87,602	88,062	78,768	79,364	105,754	97,609	103,631	114,335
50–99	86,784	75,147	81,748	80,359	89,346	90,334	103,304	109,787	115,417	119,158
100–199	90,815	80,320	83,987	80,433	92,695	96,266	102,069	104,552	111,632	115,849
200–499	101,525	101,716	101,931	98,538	98,228	100,728	106,038	103,301	108,711	117,472
500–999	62,114	56,682	57,466	55,792	58,930	60,515	59,655	62,397	66,103	61,921
1,000–1,999	41,645	36,228	36,228	31,877	44,382	46,778	51,110	44,219	46,952	48,157
2,000 and more	19,672	18,585	18,585	16,907	9,325	7,498	7,171	11,678	16,372	14,006
All firms	626,393	555,919	600,128	591,659	623,991	627,631	678,857	698,787	748,846	778,788
Number of establishments										
1–9	18,414	15,239	19,558	19,889	19,211	18,432	20,254	20,580	21,460	23,040
10–19	4,450	3,605	4,182	4,163	4,526	4,466	4,639	5,242	5,605	6,022
20–49	2,826	2,555	2,864	2,910	2,475	2,508	3,438	3,071	3,231	3,581
50–99	1,251	1,086	1,180	1,193	1,287	1,301	1,486	1,595	1,676	1,733
100–199	653	586	610	613	667	694	733	761	818	848
200–499	346	343	344	342	333	337	356	353	374	404
500–999	89	82	83	84	87	90	88	92	97	90
1,000–1,999	31	28	28	28	32	33	37	33	36	36
2,000 and more	8	8	8	8	4	3	3	5	7	6
All firms	29,105	25,250	28,857	29,230	28,622	27,864	31,034	31,732	33,304	35,760

(Table continues on the following page.)

Table 2-41 (continued)

Size of firm (number engaged)	1973:4	1974:4	1974:4[a]	1975:1	1975:2	1975:3	1975:4	1976:1	1976:2	1976:3
Proportion of total employment										
1–9	0.121	0.111	0.127	0.142	0.141	0.132	0.120	0.132	0.134	0.135
10–19	0.096	0.087	0.094	0.094	0.103	0.101	0.092	0.105	0.106	0.106
20–49	0.141	0.140	0.146	0.149	0.126	0.126	0.156	0.140	0.138	0.147
50–99	0.139	0.135	0.136	0.136	0.143	0.144	0.152	0.157	0.154	0.153
100–199	0.145	0.144	0.140	0.136	0.149	0.153	0.150	0.150	0.149	0.149
200–499	0.162	0.183	0.170	0.167	0.157	0.160	0.156	0.148	0.145	0.151
500–999	0.099	0.102	0.096	0.094	0.094	0.096	0.088	0.089	0.088	0.080
1,000–1,999	0.066	0.065	0.060	0.054	0.071	0.075	0.075	0.063	0.063	0.062
2,000 and more	0.031	0.033	0.031	0.029	0.015	0.012	0.011	0.017	0.022	0.018
All firms	1.000	1.000	1.000	1.000	1.000	1.000	1.000	1.000	1.000	1.000

a. New series.
Source: *Hong Kong Monthly Digest of Statistics*, May 1975 (p. 5), March 1976 (p. 5), November 1977 (p. 7), June 1977 (p. 7), July 1976 (p. 5), October 1976 (p. 5).

Political Structure

The governor of Hong Kong, who is appointed by the queen of England, presides over the Executive and Legislative councils. The Executive Council meets in camera, consists of six official (government executive) and ten unofficial (private citizen) members, and is charged with advising the governor on all important matters. The Legislative Council meets in public, is composed of twenty-seven official and twenty-seven unofficial members (as of 1982) and, as its name implies, passes all of Hong Kong's legislation. The Legislative Council contains the Finance Committee, which presents the budget to the council every year. The financial secretary, who is without doubt the most powerful person in the Hong Kong government (even more powerful than the governor), sits on the Finance Committee. The unofficial members on the Finance Committee only have the power to reject the financial secretary's budget proposals and cannot directly present their own budgets (Rabushka 1973: 52–53).

The unofficial members of the two councils are appointed by the governor, and their number has increased over the years. Until the early 1970s the unofficial members all came from Hong Kong's economic elite. Since then, the membership has expanded to include trade unionists, teachers, missionaries, and others. Not surprisingly, since they are selected by the government, the unofficial members seldom openly challenge basic government policy. Their principal function is to serve as a conduit of opinion between society and the government, and they periodically ask fairly innocuous questions that are prepared in the Legislative Council. The greatest number ever asked of government officials was ten questions and three supplementaries (in 1966, when K. A. Watson tried to show that the government-run car parks were earning an excessive rate of profit). Nevertheless, on a few occasions the unofficial members have united in opposition to government policy—for example, criminal law legislation in the 1960s—and the government has backed down. In the wake of the growing political activism of the 1980s, however, the unofficial members have begun to play a much more aggressive role in challenging basic government policy.

Aside from the bureaucracy, Hong Kong has several other important government institutions. One is the Office of the Unofficial Members of the Executive and Legislative Councils (UMELCO), which handles complaints against government offices. Established in 1963 to link the unofficial members with the general public, it was reorganized in 1967 but was not significantly strengthened until May 1970, when an administrative officer was provided by the government. Since then, the number of grievances addressed to UMELCO has increased rapidly, and this has allowed unofficial members to play a greater role as a conduit of information between society and the government (see table 2-42). Another important institution is the Urban Council, which runs recreation and social activities in the urban areas. The Urban Council includes elected

Table 2-42. New Cases Submitted to UMELCO, *1969–76*

Year	Number
1966	168
1970–71	834
1971–72	1,208
1972–73	1,689
1973–74	2,812
1974–75	3,115
1975–76	3,304

Source: Lin, Lee, and Simones 1979: 158.

officials, but few people ever bother to vote (in 1973 only 2 percent of the potential electorate did so; see Rabushka 1979: 26). Yet another group of administrators, the City District Officers, work at the local level providing information on government policy, urging participation in community affairs, relaying public opinion and local needs to the central government, and helping individuals with personal problems (Lin, Lee, and Simones 1979: 156). All these institutions appeared, or were significantly strengthened, in the late 1960s after the 1966 Star Ferry riots (discussed below).

Although the labor movement is nominally divided into pro-Communist and pro-Nationalist (Taiwan) factions, neither the Nationalist Kuomintang (KMT) nor the Chinese Communist party (CCP) have much political force in Hong Kong. And although most young people do feel a strong allegiance to mainland China and sympathize to some extent with the CCP's objective of creating a powerful China, during the 1967 riots inspired by the Cultural Revolution CCP members had to resort to bribery to attract demonstrators, and the demonstrations were poorly received by the population. Since then, other interest groups have begun to spring up, reflecting a stronger demand for popular influence in the government, no doubt partially inspired by the 1997 transfer.[59]

Growth of Political Intervention

There were two significant events in the history of Hong Kong's economic and social policy. The first was the development of the public housing program in the early 1950s to deal with the colony's mushrooming population, which by then had increased to about 2 million. At the time, adequate housing was available for only about 750,000 people, with the result that people congregated in huge squatter towns. There they had to contend with rampant disease and crime and crowded conditions (one person to every 12 square feet), and during the typhoon season their dwellings collapsed and were washed downhill. Then, on Christmas Eve 1953, a devastating fire left 50,000 people homeless. In 1954 the government began to build low-cost housing complexes that by the 1980s housed about half the population. Because of the continued waves of immigration and the government's refusal to accelerate the program, however, Hong Kong still has about 200,000 squatters, although the housing program has gradually expanded into new town development, squatter factory resettlement, and even home ownership schemes.

The second event occurred in 1966, when surprisingly widespread and bitter riots broke out in response to a fairly small rise in the Star Ferry fare. (The Star Ferry, which runs between Hong Kong Island and Kowloon, is used by hundreds of thousands of people each day.) The government's own commission of inquiry concluded that the people had reacted in this way because they felt alienated from the government (Hong Kong 1967). There have been only three other serious riots in the history of Hong Kong: (a) a 1956 faction fight between the KMT and the CCP that erupted out of a dispute over the flying of Nationalist flags on the Republic of China's national day; (b) the 1967 CCP-inspired riots, a spillover of the Cultural Revolution in China (Rabushka 1979: 26); and (c) the 1984 taxicab riots. These three riots did not generate any change in government policy.

The 1966 riots, however, totally transformed government policy. Between 1967 and 1976 government expenditure on social services such as welfare, education, and housing increased drastically (see table 2-43), with little direct or specific popular pressure. The following list covers only the highlights of these numerous programs.

- Between 1967 and 1973 thirty-nine provisions of labor legislation were passed, covering issues such as maximum hours of work for women and young people (forty-eight hours), severance pay, maternity leave, rest days per month (four), dangerous work for women and young people under the age of eighteen, and the prohibition of overtime for young people between fourteen and sixteen (Rabushka 1979: 73–74).

Table 2-43. *Government Expenditure on Social Services, 1967–68 and 1976–77*
(millions of Hong Kong dollars)

Service	1967–68	1976–77
Education	289.3	1,376.0
Medical and health	166.9	630.7
Housing	41.5	396.1
Social welfare	20.8	422.1
Labor	4.0	18.7
Total	356.5	2,733.3

Source: Lin, Lee, and Simones 1979: 160.

- An expanded public assistance scheme was begun in 1971 covering, for example, single persons over the age of fifty-five or those unfit for work who had less than HK$70 per month after paying rent (Rabushka 1979: 70).
- Free primary education was instituted in 1971 in all government schools and most government-aided primary schools (Rabushka 1979: 70). A ten-year program was announced in October 1974 with the aim of providing nine years of subsidized education to every child of school age (Lin, Lee, and Simones 1979: 162).
- The City District Officer scheme, begun in February 1968, has given rise to various community-based programs. Mutual aid committees were set up in June 1973, for example, to fight crime in government housing estates, and a campaign to keep Hong Kong clean was initiated in November 1972. (The latter campaign involved more than half the staff of the Department of Home Affairs; see Lin, Lee, and Simones 1979: 165.)
- The UMELCO office was formally established in 1967 and strengthened with an administrative officer in 1970. A system of Green Papers was established in 1972 to invite public views on government policies (Lin, Lee, and Simones 1979: 156, 158, 164).
- The Ordinance for the Prevention of Bribery was passed in 1970 and the Independent Commission against Corruption was set up in 1973 (Lin, Lee, and Simones 1979: 164).
- Approval was given in 1969 to a 1965 proposal on the creation of an urban renewal district (Rabushka 1973: 72).
- An Air Pollution Control Unit was set up in 1970 (Rabushka 1973: 74).

The 1966 riots clearly led the government to play a more prominent role in ensuring a higher quality of life for the people, creating channels of communication between itself and the common people, and establishing institutions to bring people into local government community programs. The 1970s and 1980s saw the continued growth of government intervention in Hong Kong society. In 1977 the government launched a significant new policy with the establishment of the Advisory Committee on Diversification, which was to advise the state on the industrial support facilities and technical backup services needed to help industry diversify. In March 1977, before the committee issued its report, the government established the Industrial Estates Corporation to supervise two high-technology estates in Tai Po and Yuen Long, where land was to be offered at one-seventeenth the market price to suitable applicants willing to introduce new technology or industries (Nyaw and Chan 1982: 462, 463). So far, the estates have been unable to attract many new industries to Hong Kong. Another significant departure from previous policy has been the restraint placed on immigration since 1980, as discussed earlier.

The Hong Kong Government

The character and objectives of the Hong Kong government have been shaped by four basic concepts.

REVENUE MAXIMIZATION AND EXPENDITURE MINIMIZATION. Historically, one of the key directives of the British colonial regulations was that the colonies should be self-supporting, to prevent them from draining the resources of the mother country. As a consequence, the Hong Kong bureaucracy has developed a mentality that concentrates on maximizing revenue and minimizing expenditure. This has led to budget surpluses in almost every year (table 2-44), with the result that total reserves at different times have ranged from 50 to 100 percent of one year's total expenditure. It is not a coincidence that the budget deficit of 1965–66 was followed by an increase in the tax rate on salaries and profits from 12.5 to 15 percent (Rabushka 1979: 24–25, 55). In view of the tremendous contribution that Hong Kong's reserves have made to the defense of the pound sterling, the fiscal conservatism originally prompted by a desire to minimize the drain of the colonies on the home country may have been strengthened by the need to defend the pound sterling, particularly in the early postwar era when Britain still had a substantial influence in the affairs of Hong Kong.

COLONIAL LAISSEZ-FAIRE. It can be argued that Hong Kong's laissez-faire mentality is a result of the government's desire to provide a stable entrepôt port for British trade in the Far East and at the same time to ensure that any possible fiscal demands on the home government would be kept to a minimum. Hong Kong's laissez-faire policy was also greatly affected by the sense of illegitimacy felt by the colonial government. This has had ramifications for social policy, as will be discussed below, and in the economic arena has led the government to focus on revenue from nontax services. In 1970–71, for example, only 25.1 percent of revenue came from profits and salary taxes, while more than one-third came from land sales and other services (table 2-45).

It is commonly said that the Hong Kong government only operates profitable enterprises. The Kowloon-Canton railway, a prime example, has averaged an annual profit of HK$5 million to HK$7 million since 1963. In 1970–71 Kai Tak airport reported HK$81 million in revenues, in comparison with the Civil Aviation Department's total expenditures of HK$13 million (Rabushka 1973: 62, 63). The Hong Kong government runs, and makes a profit on, railways, tunnels, water services, and even car parks—surely not the traditional role of a laissez-faire government. It operates like a business. Rather than imposing taxes to subsidize inefficient services (as most governments do), it provides efficient services so as not to tax. This explains its inordinately high propensity to invest in infrastructure, which is subsequently sold or provided as a

Table 2-44. *Hong Kong Government Finance, 1946–79*
(millions of Hong Kong dollars)

Year	Revenue	Expenditure	Surplus or deficit
1946–47	82.1	85.6	3.5
1947–48	164.3	127.7	36.6
1948–49	194.9	160.1	34.9
1949–50	264.3	182.1	82.2
1950–51	291.7	251.7	40.0
1951–52	308.6	275.9	32.7
1952–53	384.6	311.8	72.8
1953–54	396.9	355.4	41.5
1954–55	434.5	373.3	61.2
1955–56	454.7	402.5	52.2
1956–57	509.7	470.0	40.1
1957–58	584.2	532.7	51.5
1958–59	629.3	590.0	39.3
1959–60	664.6	710.0	−45.4
1960–61	859.2	845.3	13.9
1961–62	1,030.5	953.2	77.3
1962–63	1,253.1	1,113.3	139.8
1963–64	1,393.9	1,295.4	98.5
1964–65	1,518.3	1,440.5	77.8
1965–66	1,631.7	1,769.1	137.4
1966–67	1,817.8	1,806.1	11.7
1967–68	1,900.0	1,766.0	134.0
1968–69	2,081.1	1,873.0	208.1
1969–70	2,480.7	2,032.2	448.5
1970–71	3,070.9	2,452.2	618.7
1971–72	3,541.3	2,901.4	639.9
1972–73	4,936.3	4,300.0	636.3
1973–74	5,240.8	5,169.2	71.6
1974–75	5,875.3	6,255.2	−379.3
1975–76	6,519.5	6,032.2	487.3
1976–77	7,493.5	6,590.9	902.6
1977–78	9,410.2	8,174.1	1,236.1
1978–79	12,374.1	11,162.2	1,211.9

Source: Lethbridge 1980: 49.

service. The average of the excess of government revenue over expenditure in the postwar era has amounted to an annual profit rate of 25 percent on operations (see table 2-45).

SENSITIVITY TO MASS-BASED MOVEMENTS AND CULTURAL ISSUES. All governments must maintain some degree of legitimacy in order to rule, and the Hong Kong government, conscious of its alien nature, has shown itself highly responsive to social unrest such as the Star Ferry riots. Not open to electoral sanctions, the government has tended to resist interest group pressure, although it does attempt to coopt groups and reach a

Table 2-45. Government Revenue, by Source, 1970–71
(millions of Hong Kong dollars)

Source	Revenue	Percent
Duties	414.0	13.9
Rates	333.7	11.2
Internal revenue	1,007.2	33.8
Business profits and salary tax	749.0	25.1
Stamp duties	126.0	4.2
Betting taxes	35.0	1.2
Entertainment	31.0	1.0
Estate duties	23.0	0.8
Licenses and franchises	104.4	3.5
Fines, forfeitures, and penalties	21.0	0.7
Fees of court or office	197.5	6.6
Water revenue	93.4	3.1
Post office	163.3	5.5
Airport and air services	78.7	2.6
Kowloon-Canton Railway	16.4	0.6
Interest, land, and rents	278.2	9.3
Land sales	258.5	8.7
Other	14.3	0.5
Total	2,980.6	100.0

Source: Riedel 1974: 144.

measure of accommodation. It has been particularly receptive to suggestions concerning cultural and social issues, although in certain areas—such as the Chinese demands for capital punishment for murder, rape, robbery, and even wounding—it has adamantly clung to British norms. In the area of economic policy, where it presumably feels more secure, it appears to have hardly ever been influenced by interest group pressure.

SINIFICATION AND BUREAUCRATIC EXPANSION. Over time, the Chinese component in the middle and upper echelons of the Hong Kong government has increased. Most of these people were born in Hong Kong and have a sense of national identity. This characteristic, coupled with the tendency of all bureaucracies to expand their roles, has led to increasing intervention in the society and economy. Thus the housing authority has become involved in activities ranging from providing low-cost housing to a home-ownership scheme. There appears to be a fundamental social need for a minimal standard of housing that warrants a departure from laissez-faire, although it is doubtful whether there is an equally strong social need for home ownership. The 1977 Committee on Diversification is a striking departure from laissez-faire and yet does not appear to have arisen in response to demands from any group. Instead, it reflects the government's impotence and shock over the 1974–75 recession. And yet, Hong Kong's laissez-faire system continued to work during the oil shock. The recession lasted only about nine months, and the 17 percent real GDP growth in the following year was spectacular. The Hong Kong government's locally born technocrats, although strongly indoctrinated in laissez-faire ideology, are, like all technocrats, seeking to apply their skills and expand their area of power and responsibility.

Hong Kong Society

Until the 1980s most people in Hong Kong were politically quiescent. Those born in Hong Kong, however, show a greater interest in influencing government policy than do immigrants. It should also be pointed out that the English-educated people show greater political awareness and activism than the Chinese-educated. The "Chinese" tendency is to view government at worst as a nuisance and at best as something of little concern to the average individual. This view has been reinforced by the political apathy of immigrant groups, who are not likely to have a clear sense of belonging to the society in their new home. With the proportion of native-born and English-educated people on the rise, political activism has been growing.[60]

The fact that manufacturing, commerce, retail activities, and the restaurant trade in Hong Kong are carried out by thousands of predominantly small firms inhibits group organization. If an industry is composed of a few large firms, the firms are much more likely to be able to organize and put pressure on the government when they are faced with economic problems. As the number of firms rises, organizational costs rise exponentially. Collective action becomes almost impossible in an industry with a thousand small firms of fewer than fifty employees. Thus, with the exception of a few wealthy industrialists, capital has limited power. The labor unions do not have that much power either, for they are split into hundreds of friendly societies. Only the white-collar unions constitute a coherent and organized political force.

Some have also argued that Hong Kong's uncertain future as a territory leased from China has been a strong deterrent to active government policy or demands from the populace for government intervention.[61] This suggestion does not hold up, however, when one takes into account the growth of government intervention and widespread political activism in the increasingly uncertain and temporary environment of the 1980s. In particular, during the recent Sino-British negotiations, the people of Hong Kong showed considerable interest in exerting some influence on their political and economic future.

To summarize, Hong Kong's colonial legacy of little intervention, combined with its immigrant Chinese society, weak labor movement, and small-firm economy, fostered noninterventionism throughout the early postwar era. With the growth of an indigenous culture and population, the demand for responsive intervention increased, and the process was abetted by the gradual sinification of the government and the natural tendency for bureaucratic growth.

The Impact of Government Policy on Equity

Despite its small size, the government of Hong Kong has had a considerable impact on income distribution. Some estimates (see tables 2-46, 2-47) suggest the effective tax structure is fairly flat, if not regressive, except in the highest categories of income, where it becomes progressive. The reason is that the government is reluctant to engage in income taxation and consequently relies on excise taxes, as well as the provision of services, for most of its revenue. Government expenditure, however, strongly favors low-income groups (see tables 2-46, 2-47, and 2-48).[62] When Hong Kong's Gini coefficient is adjusted to take into account the distribution of government taxes and benefits, it improves by about 0.03 to 0.04 (table 2-49).[63]

Thus, despite its small share of GDP, the Hong Kong government has clearly had a substantial impact on income distribution, principally through its provision of housing, health, and educational benefits. This disproportionately large impact can be attributed mainly to the efficiency of its bureaucracy (which keeps administrative costs down) and to its lack of defense expenditures. The improvements in income distribution recorded in the 1970s (see table 2-3) could have been the result of

Table 2-46. *Distribution of Taxes and Government Benefits by Income Class, 1971*
(percentage of income)

Monthly income (Hong Kong dollars)	Number of house-holds[a]	Total monthly income	Share of income	Tax payments	Share of benefits
Less than 200	40,587	6,088	0.7	0.5	2.0
200–399	88,650	26,595	3.1	2.0	6.6
400–599	203,738	101,869	11.7	6.7	25.0
600–799	167,883	117,518	13.5	7.5	25.4
800–999	96,241	86,617	9.0	5.9	12.2
1,000–1,199	80,150	88,165	10.1	5.4	10.2
1,200–1,499	61,743	83,353	9.6	6.5	7.0
1,500–1,999	39,878	69,787	8.0	4.5	4.6
2,000–2,499	27,426	61,709	7.1	5.2	3.2
2,500–4,499	26,578	93,023	10.7	14.8	2.7
4,500 and more	13,796	137,160	15.7	40.7	1.2
Total	846,670	871,884	100.0	100.0	100.0

a. Households dwelling on land only.
Source: Hsia and Chau 1978: tables 6.1 and 6.2, pp. 154, 165.

Table 2-47. *Distribution of Taxes and Benefits from Government*
Expenditure, 1971
(percentage of income)

Annual income (Hong Kong dollars)	Taxes	Benefits
0–1,000	6.70	602.78
1,001–5,000	8.97	89.77
5,001–10,000	8.24	36.65
10,001–15,000	7.22	21.42
15,001–20,000	7.44	14.93
20,001–25,000	8.46	14.22
25,001–30,000	8.07	13.41
30,001–40,000	12.45	10.98
40,001–50,000	14.48	10.85
More than 50,000	25.17	8.46
All groups	11.50	21.34

Source: Ho 1979: 115, 130.

the rapid growth of government social services in the era after the Star
Ferry riots. Although the growth of services would not show up in the
census data, they would have enabled the poor to better themselves
economically.

Summary

One of the main factors influencing Hong Kong's economic development was massive immigration, driven by exogenous conditions in
mainland China and encouraged by an open-door government policy.
This, combined with a relatively high natural rate of population growth
(in the early postwar era), rapidly increased Hong Kong's labor force.
Natural growth tended to reduce the age of the labor force until the late
1970s, and immigration has worked to keep the average age of labor at
about thirty-five, but the effect on flexibility has not been great. This
immigrant society is imbued with an entrepreneurial spirit concerned
more with the pursuit of material gain than with labor organization. As
a result, the unions have evolved into friendly societies. Immigration
also brought enormous quantities of capital, primarily from Shanghai.
Foreign investment continued in the 1970s with the arrival of Western
capital drawn by the abundance of labor and the laissez-faire environment. This and the government's propensity to invest have led to the
rapid growth of capital stock.
    Another distinctive feature of Hong Kong's economy is that it is
dominated by small firms. The factors contributing to this situation are
price variation (in general, small firms in the colony face lower labor
costs because the immigrant population finds better possibilities for

Table 2-48. Distribution of Benefits from Government Expenditures, by Income Class, 1981

Monthly income (Hong Kong dollars)	Number of households[a]	Total monthly income (Hong Kong dollars)	Share of income (percent)	Benefits	
				Percentage of income	Percentage of benefits
Less than 600	66,959	33,480	0.6	37.8	2.3
600–999	50,763	40,610	0.8	31.0	2.3
1,000–1,499	112,683	140,854	2.7	23.4	6.1
1,500–1,999	123,231	215,654	4.2	20.9	8.3
2,000–2,499	156,481	352,082	6.8	19.2	12.5
2,500–2,999	119,935	329,821	6.4	17.4	10.6
3,000–3,999	199,242	697,347	13.4	13.7	17.7
4,000–4,999	123,889	557,501	10.7	11.6	11.9
5,000–5,999	84,157	426,864	8.9	10.1	8.7
6,000–7,999	90,992	636,944	12.3	8.3	9.8
8,000–9,999	42,439	381,951	7.4	6.1	4.3
More than 10,000	66,872	1,337,440	25.8	2.2	5.5
Total (monthly)	1,237,643	5,186,548	100.0	10.0	100.0

a. Households dwelling on land only.
Source: Lin 1985: table 6, pp. 408–09.

Table 2-49. Gini Coefficients from Various Studies, Adjusted for the Impact of Government Taxes and Expenditure

Item	Hsia and Chau (1971)	Ho (1974)	Lin (1981)
Before adjustment	0.439	0.4146[a]	0.44
With irregular income and income in kind	0.461	n.a.	n.a.
After government taxes	0.435	0.3930	n.a.
With government benefits	0.411	0.3529	0.41
After all adjustments	0.394	0.3289	n.a.

n.a. Not applicable; no adjustment was made for that factor.
a. Includes adjustment for some sources of irregular income, such as bonuses.
Source: Hsia and Chau 1978; Ho 1974; Lin 1985.

individual advancement in small firms), managerial inputs by trading companies, and the congestion in the colony. The role of the trading companies has its roots in Hong Kong's entrepôt economy, which in turn was shaped by the physical features of the location.

The congestion is the result of rapid population growth, a mountainous terrain, the practice of leasing nonurban land, and the colony's political structure. The last three factors have caused industrial activity to become concentrated within an area of 50 square miles. The congestion (owing to the scarcity of land), as well as the substantial capital and enormous labor inflows, has been responsible for the colony's industrial shifts, until recently restricting the economy to light industries and other low-skill trades. Congestion and the tremendous entrepreneurial drive of the population have served to keep information flows in both the capital and labor markets fairly efficient. The weak labor movement has produced an integrated labor market outside the professions, with no barriers to entry. Although the capital market is grossly underdeveloped, culturally based institutions have provided an informal substitute.

The economy of Hong Kong has also been affected by the political structure of the colonial government, which has emphasized budget surpluses and self-sufficiency (to avoid draining home resources), highly profitable and efficient government services, and nonintervention in the economy. With the growing representation and influence of local Chinese administrators, however, the government has begun playing a greater social and economic role. Responsive intervention has been limited historically by the government's ability to resist all but mass-based pressures, by the diffusion of the political and economic power of both labor and capital, and by the political passivity of the Chinese immigrant population. Nonetheless, the system has worked and thus has obviated the need for either active or responsive intervention.

Hong Kong's economy is truly flexible. Apart from the integrated markets and the age of the labor force, the variables appear extremely favorable and reinforce each other. Entrepreneurship, in the sense of an individual's going out and opening up a firm, for example, is greatly facilitated by the fact that small firms are highly competitive. Without this entrepreneurship and the other elements of the system—the prevalence of small firms, the rapidly growing labor force, and the favorable shifts and spatial relations, not to mention the political structure—there would have been greater pressure for active and responsive intervention, and laissez-faire would have been abandoned.

Instead, the system has been able to sustain itself for forty years, albeit with a few gradual changes instigated by a generation of native-born people in the professions and the governmental structure. For one thing, a lid has been put on immigration, with repercussions for the growth of the labor stock, the age of the labor force, the nature of labor organization, entrepreneurship, capital inflows, and (perhaps) labor costs and the small-firm economy. This does not necessarily mean that the economy will be less flexible in the future, but only that after forty years the system is showing signs of change.

Notes

1. The colony was acquired by the British in three stages. Hong Kong Island itself was occupied by Britain in 1841, during the Opium War, and was ceded "in perpetuity" by China in the Treaty of Nanking of 1842. Kowloon Peninsula was ceded after the Second Opium War under the Convention of Peking of 1860. Following China's defeat by Japan, the New Territories were leased from China for ninety-nine years under the Convention of Peking of 1898. This chapter focuses on Hong Kong's postwar economic development. For prewar history, see Endacott (1964) and Pryor (1983).

2. It is true that the government has run large surpluses during periods of rapid growth and deficits during recessions. These fluctuations, however, seem to be the result of the usual unanticipated movements of tax revenue with the business cycle, combined with the rigidity of preplanned expenditure, rather than any conscious attempt at countercyclical fiscal policy. See Lethbridge (1980: 37–38).

3. Under the silver standard, which lasted until 1935, the Hongkong and Shanghai Bank, Mercantile Bank, and Chartered Bank issued banknotes against silver bullion held in their vaults. Under the sterling standard, which lasted from 1935 until mid-1972, the Hong Kong dollar was pegged to the pound sterling and the banks exchanged pounds sterling with the Hong Kong Government's Exchange Fund for certificates of indebtedness (CIs), against which they could then issue banknotes. Under the quasi–U.S. dollar standard, which lasted from July 1972 until November 1974, the Hong Kong dollar was pegged to the U.S. dollar, but banks could credit their accounts in the Exchange Fund with Hong Kong dollars for the purpose of acquiring CIs. (The expansion of the money supply then occurred by virtue of the 25 percent legal reserve ratio.) Between November 1974 and October 1983 banks continued to be allowed to use Hong Kong dollars to purchase CIs, but the government also allowed the exchange rate to float freely. Hong Kong was thus in the peculiar situation of having a freely determined money supply and exchange rate. The system collapsed in late 1983 when speculation over the outcome of the Sino-British negotiations on the future of

Hong Kong led to a large capital outflow. Since then, Hong Kong has returned to a complete dollar standard, with Hong Kong banks exchanging U.S. dollars for certificates of indebtedness at the fixed exchange rate of HK$7.8 per US$1 (see Greenwood 1984). In January 1978 the government transferred the note-issuing right of the Mercantile Bank to the Hongkong and Shanghai Banking Corporation, which had earlier acquired the Mercantile Bank.

4. The prewar 1941 population was 1,639,337. This, however, included the 750,000 or more immigrants who had entered Hong Kong from the mainland in the four years after the beginning of the Sino-Japanese war in 1937. Thus the arrivals in the mid-1940s were not returning residents but reimmigrants (Davis 1977: 90–92).

5. Naturally, other factors, such as the product and market concentration of exports and the share of agricultural products in total exports, are important determinants of export variability. Although the sample economies differ somewhat with respect to these variables, during the period under study they all exported predominantly light industrial products to the United States. This strong similarity, combined with the magnitude of the difference between Hong Kong's coefficient and those of the other economies, suggests that the conclusion above is warranted.

6. "They [the government] use household income, since a substantial share of income in Hong Kong is earned jointly and pooled by a household. The income figures should be adjusted for household size but data do not permit this. More serious is the fact that [the estimates] . . . derive from different sources, using different definitions for different purposes, different sample designs and frames and, undoubtedly, with different degrees of errors and biases" (Chow and Papanek 1981: 471).

7. The magnitude of the changes shown between 1979–80 and 1981 (a one-to two-year period) is highly questionable and might be something of a statistical artifact. Either income distribution in the 1970s was much worse than indicated by the data in table 2-2, or the 1981 figures grossly overestimate the degree of inequality. Lin (1985), Young's source for most of the 1981 data, cites a 1984 discussion paper by L. Chau, which was unavailable to Young. Cheng's estimates (see table 2-2), presumably derived independently, also show a substantial increase in inequality (in this case between 1976 and 1981).

8. Real GDP per capita increased 9.4 percent in 1961, 5.6 percent in 1962, 7.4 percent in 1978, 3.1 percent in 1979, and 9.7 percent in 1980.

9. Labor's share of national income, which appears to have remained fairly constant at about one-half throughout the late 1940s and early 1960s, rose to 56 percent by 1977. Studies of the manufacturing sector suggest that labor's share declined in the 1960s and early 1970s but then rose from 64.9 percent in 1973 to 69.5 percent in 1976 (Chow and Papanek 1981: 470–71).

10. Another reason is that starting on a new career involves fixed cost. The shorter the workers's remaining participation in the labor force, the less the benefit from a shift.

11. Estimated from more detailed data appearing in Fan (1974), using an arbitrary weight of 77 for those seventy-five or older.

12. From Hong Kong government labor force projections (*Hong Kong Monthly Digest of Statistics*, March 1983, p. 104), Young estimates that the average age of the economically active will be 39.7 in 2001.

13. Table 2-13 shows that the 1980–81 decline apparent in table 2-8 continued in 1982.

14. Woronoff (1980) does not give a date for the figure of 108 unions.

15. In the 1920s, during the period of Nationalist and Communist cooperation on the mainland, the union groups organized extensive strikes.

16. The figures cited include those run by employers' associations (see Hopkins 1971: 245). These apparently accounted for only a small percentage of the above-mentioned services.

17. According to the *1966 By-Census* (vol. 3, table 161), the higher proportion of immigrants in senior government positions is attributable to the predominance of British expatriates in such positions at the time.

18. One would imagine that the predominance of small firms in Hong Kong's manufacturing sector might make the organization of an effective trade union movement more difficult, both because of the organizational costs associated with coordinating so many units and because small firms employ a substantial amount of family labor, which would not organize against the family firm. Young has found, however, that the correlation between average firm size and the degree of unionization in different manufacturing sectors is practically nil. Without adequate data, it was impossible to control for the impact of variables such as skilled male labor and the provision of key services.

19. The figure is somewhat less than the 1968 survey cited earlier, but some allowance must be made for sampling error and the rapid decline in hours of work noted below.

20. Given their average age, immigrants probably accounted for a larger percentage of the economically active, as the data on the 1966 census show. At that time, immigrants made up only 53.8 percent of those born in Hong Kong but 72 percent of the economically active population (*1966 By-Census*: bk. 2: 38). Nevertheless, the differences cited above suggest that immigrants were over-represented among entrepreneurs, particularly because much of the Hong Kong–born population had entered the labor force by the 1970s.

21. Immigrants, arriving almost penniless (not all were wealthy Shanghai-nese entrepreneurs) may work unbelievably hard until they accumulate an asset cushion and then begin to take it somewhat easier.

22. A similar process occurred in the United States in the twentieth century. Both 1976 and 1981 were fairly prosperous years for Hong Kong, with real GDP per capita rising by 15.9 and 7.0 percent, respectively, whereas 1975 and 1982 were recession years. Thus, unless the data discussed above were collected in early 1976 and late 1981, the decline in hours of work cannot be attributed to the effects of the two oil-shock recessions.

23. Only 6.5 percent of entrepreneurs inherited their business. The proportions listing "industrialist/manager," "merchant," "farmer/fisherman," and "skilled/unskilled worker" as their father's occupation were 9.4, 40.1, 21.2, and 17.0 percent, respectively. Others accounted for the remainder. See Sit (1978: 298, 304).

24. Sit, Wong, and Kiang (1980: 290) found a positive correlation between number of employees and proprietor fund and educational levels. It is possible, however, that the correlation was partly due to the fact that entrepreneurs from wealthier backgrounds, who would have started with larger firms, are likely to have been better educated.

25. Unfortunately, Sit, Wong, and Kiang (1980) do not provide this information.

26. Hong Kong appears to have had a rather low rate of capital formation prior to 1960. Our data for those years are based on Chou's estimates, which, when compared with overlapping data for later years provided by the Hong Kong government, appear to underestimate the GDFC/GDP ratio by approximately 6 percentage points (see notes to table 2-21).

27. Szczepanik (1958: 142–43), estimated the precise proportion at two-thirds. His estimates were based on some dubious assumptions, however. Not having data on domestic saving, he assumed that the savings rate was 10 percent. Not having data on capital formation, he assumed a capital/output ratio of 2 and (using the Harrodian growth equation) took the differences in national income between years to derive estimates of total capital formation. After taking into account the proportion financed by the assumed level of domestic saving, he took the residual to be foreign investment. The problem is that the values of practically all the relevant variables were assumed, which makes the results almost meaningless. Szczepanik's general argument, presented in the text, is considerably more convincing.

28. Riedel (1974: 113) claims that foreign investment accounts for only 0.3 percent of total fixed capital formation in manufacturing but provides no source to back up his claim. This figure seems far too low.

29. Substantial manufacturing activity, including textile production, existed in Hong Kong prior to the arrival of the Shanghainese (Davis 1977: 150–60). Nevertheless, there is no doubt that the Shanghainese, with their experience, capital, and managerial staff (which they also brought along) provided a tremendous boost to the development of the textile industry.

30. Of 300 foreign manufacturing establishments in 1976, 182 had been founded after 1970 (Lethbridge 1980: 57).

31. In 1968 U.S. electronics firms—the dominant foreign group in that sector—accounted for 58 percent of the electronics labor force. In 1978 there were 68 foreign electronics firms employing 29,620 people, or 41.2 percent of all the people engaged in the electronics industry (Woronoff 1980: 169). In 1978 there was a total of 768 electronics firms. The following year, the number of electronics firms increased to 1,041, with 20,000 more people engaged in the sector (*Hong Kong Annual Report 1981*: 274). Most of the increase in the number of firms and, consequently, a substantial proportion of the increase in employment must have come from domestic sources, indicating a further decline in the relative importance of foreign firms.

32. The corresponding numbers for Singapore are 10 and 12 percent.

33. The growth in the share of manufacturing employment of Hong Kong Island and Kowloon between 1973 and 1977 is most likely attributable to the fact that the 1973 Census of Industrial Production did not cover establishments with fewer than twenty persons engaged. Hong Kong Island and Kowloon have unusually high densities of small establishments.

34. A number of geographers and urban planners subscribe to this view—that for the sake of fiscal conservatism the Hong Kong government has allowed what most experts consider an unacceptable and avoidable degree of urban congestion.

35. Mok (1972: 45–46) found that 50 percent of the factory employees in Kwun Tong commuted in from other districts and that only 50 percent of Kwun Tong's economically active population was actually employed in the district. The *1966 By-Census* (p. 65, table 104) listed as commuters 9.3 percent of the work force of Hong Kong Island; the figure was 35.2 for Kowloon, 23.0 for New Kowloon, 18.9 for Tsuen Wan (including Tsing Yi and Ma Wan), and 10.2 percent for the rest of the New Territories. Considering that these are large districts, this represents substantial commuting activity. Nevertheless, with the expansion of development (in the late 1980s and 1990s) into the New Territories, where towns are located much farther apart, the fact that 40 percent of the population is tied to low-cost government housing will limit labor mobility.

36. Some studies of Japanese society argue that its geographic compactness was an important factor in the dissemination of technology during its early economic development.

37. Obviously, we are not claiming that money is the sole topic of conversation, only the principal one. Also, conversations among the native-born generation follow less pecuniary lines.

38. With a total capitalization of HK$70 billion and an average daily turnover of HK$30 million in 1977, Hong Kong's four stock exchanges are not particularly large. The market is quite narrow: for example, the ten most active stocks accounted for 60 percent of total turnover in May 1973. The narrowness and the shallowness of the market have led to wild gyrations in response to speculative activity. The stock market is also somewhat unrepresentative of the economy as a whole in that only 16 percent of the 294 equities listed in 1980 were manufacturing concerns, while 41 percent were real estate and construction companies. The bond market is less active than the stock exchange, largely because there is no government deficit financing, and business firms generally do not use it as a source of capital—perhaps partly because, as Jao suggests, the use of leverage is not particularly attractive in a low-tax environment (Lethbridge 1978: 181–84).

39. As tables 2-28 and 2-29 indicate, the results of Sit's survey of small firms with twenty to fifty employees differ considerably in magnitude (but not in kind) from other surveys, including Sit's own survey of small factories in domestic premises. All of these surveys were performed in the 1970s.

40. Of the entrepreneurs surveyed, 94.9 percent were male (Sit, Wong, and Kiang 1980: 244).

41. See Anderson (1982: 6–32); Hoselitz (1959: 601–2); Staley and Morse (1965: 137–40). These researchers do not emphasize the increase in the average size of manufacturing establishments as such, but they do document the decline of firms engaging fewer than ten persons and the increasing importance of large firms, which amounts to the same thing. The rapid decline shown in table 2-31 is principally the result of better statistical coverage of small establishments. Young has estimated that a slight decline in average firm size did indeed occur during the postwar era.

42. In a comparison at the three- and four-digit ISIC level, Hong Kong showed a smaller average firm size than Japan, Korea, Malta, Singapore, the United Kingdom, and the United States in 19 out of 35, 34 out of 35, 13 out of 24, 28 out of 29, 35 out of 35, and 33 out of 35 sectors for which comparable data were available. Young repeated this analysis at the four-digit ISIC level and found that in 20 of the 22 sectors for which comparable data could be found for Hong Kong and Korea, Hong Kong had a considerably smaller average firm size. In the remaining two sectors, Hong Kong firms were only slightly larger than their Korean counterparts.

43. Ten persons engaged is certainly no great technological divide. Nevertheless, a majority of firms engaging fewer than ten persons probably operate in traditional areas serving different markets and using different technologies than the modern sector serviced by the majority of firms with more than ten persons engaged. This is probably more characteristic of developing economies than of industrial economies, where traditional economic activities have for all intents and purposes vanished.

44. In a survey of factories in domestic premises (average size, 13.2 employees) Sit (1981b: 112) found their major marketing channels to be manufacturers (40.9 percent), direct sales (26.4 percent), retailers (11.9 percent), import-export houses (11.3 percent), wholesalers (8.2 percent), and direct export (0.6 percent). A small number (0.6 percent) did not answer the question. The higher and lower

proportions (as compared with the survey in table 2-34) attributed to manufacturers and import-export houses probably reflect the smaller average size of the factories in domestic premises. The high proportion of direct sales to consumers suggests a cottage industry (66.6 percent of the firms surveyed had fewer than ten employees) or the influence of some of the variables discussed by Staley and Morse (1965). Nevertheless, the basic conclusion that import-export houses and other manufacturers were the principal source of orders for small firms, particularly those engaging more than ten persons, remains sound. See also Sit (1981a: 169) and Hopkins (1971: 12, 19–20).

45.   According to the 1978 manufacturing census, export work (as a percentage of total work done for others) by size category of the firm, was as follows: 1–9 persons employed, 0.0 percent; 10–19, 16.1 percent; 20–49, 14.5 percent; 50–99, 23.9 percent; 100–199, 31.3 percent; 200–499, 38.3 percent; 500–999, 25.8 percent; and 1,000 and more, 57.6 percent (see *1978 Survey of Industrial Production*, vol. 2, pt. 5, table 3.1).

46.   Most manufacturing firms in the prewar era were also small. The manufacturing sector as a whole at that time was quite young and one could explain the predominance of small firms as the result of small markets and traditional production. Not much information exists on manufacturing activity at that time.

47.   Admittedly, the relation is not always monotonic. Some of the peculiar fluctuations observed might be the result of aggregation effects—that is, of firms producing substantially different goods, which, however, are all grouped under one ISIC three-digit heading. (Note that at the aggregate manufacturing level labor costs do not rise significantly with firm size.) In general, there seems to be a significant increase in labor costs above the 10–19 employees category. This is not the result of family labor, which is adjusted for by using employees rather than persons engaged. In the 1960s Shanghainese and Western firms, most of which were large, provided considerably greater fringe benefits than Cantonese firms, most of which were small (Hopkins 1971). It is unclear whether the data in table 2-37 capture these additional costs.

48.   The jump in turnover rates occurs after the 100–199 production workers category, while the rise in labor costs occurs after the 10–19 employees category.

49.   Mok (1972: 29) found that 21 percent of the factories he surveyed experienced turnover rates of more than 50 percent. He does not indicate what proportion of these firms were large.

50.   The differences between the labor costs of small and large firms are much greater in other countries, such as Japan. These, however, are usually attributable to institutional or social barriers. The existence of even such a comparatively small variation in Hong Kong is something of a puzzle.

51.   Admittedly, the 1971 census recorded five firms with 500–999 employees and eighty-nine firms with 100–499 employees as operating in domestic premises. This can be seen as a reflection of the desperate attempts by large firms to find any type of floor space rather than as an indication of the suitability of domestic premises for large firms.

52.   In the United States in the mid-1950s the average establishment-to-firm ratio for firms with more than twenty persons engaged was 1.21; it was 1.18 in Japan in 1967. In the 1973 census, the Hong Kong government found an average of 1.38 establishments reported on each return, even though it tried to collect establishment-based data. Thus, at a minimum, Hong Kong has an establishment-to-firm ratio of 1.38 to 1.00, with the actual rate probably being considerably higher.

53. Young (forthcoming) has also found some evidence in favor of a third corollary hypothesis: if the dual assumptions of an undersupply of industrial floor space and an extreme competition for premises are correct, then within mature districts one should rarely observe an increase in the number of large firms. Whenever a large firm ceases operating and its floor space is put up for rent, there is a probability, however small, that this floor space will be split up and rented to several small firms. At that point, that floor space becomes almost irrevocably lost to large firms, as it could only be reoccupied by a large firm if reassembly costs were incurred. Thus, within mature districts there should be a gradual decline in the number of large firms, which is precisely what Young found.

54. Young (forthcoming) examined a number of other possible causes and found the following: (a) casual empirical observation indicates that, given the market instability generated by the sudden imposition of trade barriers and abrupt changes in international prices, entrepreneurs prefer to diversify into different industries rather than expand production within one sector; (b) the existence of ambulatory work groups which perform a number of specialized tasks, such as cutting, ironing, or embroidery in the garment trade, and (possibly) a substantial market for second-hand machinery, are both probably more the result rather than the cause of the economy's being dominated by small firms; and (c) cultural arguments that focus on the "need" of Chinese firms to retain management in family hands, which therefore constrains expansion, are belied by the extensive statistical evidence indicating that Chinese and Western managerial practices in Hong Kong are quite similar (except in the case of extremely small firms). Any differences that do exist can be reasonably ascribed to the fact that Western firms are operating in a foreign culture.

55. This does not contradict Young's (forthcoming) hypothesis on spatial constraints. Small firms engaging 10 to 49 persons should be able to expand and find new premises. Young's hypothesized cutoff point is somewhere between 200 and 500 persons engaged.

56. Owen (1971) argues that a vicious circle of smallness, in which productivity is a rising function of firm size and unproductive small firms are unable to grow, is the reason why Hong Kong is dominated by small firms. Aside from Young's empirical work, which shows productivity and profitability to be a decreasing function of firm size, Young has also shown that the assumptions and methodology that underlie Owen's work are incorrect. Owen did not have the extensive census data available to Young.

57. Although comparisons with periods before 1974 are difficult, the recession, at first glance, would seem to have ultimately benefited Hong Kong's manufacturing sector. The number of persons engaged in registered and recorded establishments in the fourth quarter of 1971, 1972, 1973, and 1974 was 564,370, 578,855, 582,701, and 526,977, respectively (*Hong Kong Monthly Digest of Statistics*, May 1975, p. 5). Although these data do not cover many small firms, it is clear that manufacturing employment grew slowly in the early 1970s. This was probably because of a shortage of labor, as evidenced by the rapid rise in real wages at that time (see table 2-4). After modifying the series twice, the Hong Kong government greatly enhanced its coverage of small firms. A comparison with the data in table 2-41 suggests that the registered and recorded establishments data failed to account for some 75,000 persons engaged. Hence, at most, manufacturing employment in the early 1970s was between 650,000 and 700,000. By the end of the recovery it had risen to almost 800,000. The answer to this puzzle is the entry of 150,000 immigrants in 1973–74, which, combined with the recession, led to a fall in real wages of 9 to 16 percent (depending on the wage series used; see table 2-4) in 1974–75.

58. The one area in which Britain retains special rights is its authority to negotiate landing rights at Kai Tak airport, an important hub airport in the Far East. These rights are usually only granted to foreign carriers if British airlines are given preferential foreign routes (see Rabushka 1979: 23).

59. This refers to the negotiations between China and the United Kingdom over the return of Hong Kong when the lease on the New Territories and Kowloon runs out in 1997. Hong Kong Island was "given" to the United Kingdom in perpetuity, but the British have agreed to return it along with the leased territories in 1997.

60. The proportion of total enrollment in Chinese schools has declined over time.

61. This view is captured in the title of Richard Hughes's (1968) book, *Hong Kong: Borrowed Place—Borrowed Time*.

62. According to the work of the above scholars, government subsidization of university education appears to be the only type of expenditure that favors the wealthy.

63. Hsia and Chau (1978) found government taxation to be fairly neutral, but, somewhat cryptically, when combined with enormously detrimental effects of income in kind, it became quite supportive of income equality, as evidenced by the fact that all adjustments led to a Gini coefficient 0.02 lower than that computed with adjustments for benefits only. Ho's data show that both government taxation and government benefits vastly improve income equality. Although Ho's results seem substantially different from those of Hsia and Chau, they are in fact reasonably similar. Hsia and Chau's adjustments for taxation and benefits lower their Gini coefficient with irregular income from 0.461 to 0.394, for a drop of about 0.067, while Ho's adjustments lower his Gini coefficient from 0.4146 to 0.3289, for a drop of about 0.086. Ho's greater adjustment can be ascribed in part to his imputation of a greater variety of taxes and benefits, such as licenses and other indirect taxes and social welfare and community expenditure than either Hsia and Chau or Lin (see tables 2-46 through 2-48). Adjusting for "excess benefits"—that is, benefits in excess of imputed taxes—by "assuming that extra taxes, sufficient to finance the 'excess' benefits, are collected with no effect on the underlying distribution of total income," Ho found that the Gini coefficient fell from 0.3289 to 0.3040 (see Ho 1979: 139–40).

References

Anderson, Dennis. 1982. *Small Industry in Developing Countries: Some Issues.* World Bank Staff Working Paper 518. Development Economics Department. Washington, D.C.

Caves, Richard E., and Masu Uekusa. 1976. *Industrial Organization in Japan.* Washington, D.C.: Brookings Institution.

Cheng, Tong Yung. 1985. *The Economy of Hong Kong.* Rev. ed. Hong Kong: Far East Publications.

Chiu, T. N., and C. L. So, eds. 1983. *A Geography of Hong Kong.* Hong Kong: Oxford University Press.

Chou, K. R. 1966. *The Hong Kong Economy: A Miracle of Growth.* Hong Kong: Academic Publications.

Chow, Steven C., and Gustav F. Papanek. 1981. "Laissez-faire, Growth and Equity—Hong Kong." *Economic Journal* 91 (June): 466-85.

Commonwealth Foundation. 1975. *Human Ecology and Hong Kong, Report of a Conference Held in Hong Kong in April 1972 by the Commonwealth Human Ecology Council.* Occasional Paper 31. London.

Davis, S. G. 1977. *Hong Kong in Its Geographical Setting.* New York: AMS Press.

Dwyer, D. J., and Chuen-yan Lai. 1967. *The Small Industrial Unit in Hong Kong: Patterns and Policies.* Hull, England: University of Hull.

Economist. 1981. *The World in Figures.* London.

Economist Intelligence Unit. 1982, 1983. *Quarterly Economic Review of Hong Kong, Annual Supplement 1982* and *Annual Supplement 1983.* London.

Endacott, G. B. 1964. *Government and People in Hong Kong 1841–1962: A Constitutional History.* Hong Kong: Hong Kong University Press.

Fan, Shuh-ching. 1974. *The Population of Hong Kong.* Hong Kong: Hong Kong University Press.

Far Eastern Economic Review. 1983. *Asia 1983 Yearbook.* Hong Kong.

Freedman, Maurice. 1959. "The Handling of Money: A Note on the Background to the Economic Sophistication of Overseas Chinese." *Man: A Monthly Record of Anthropological Science* 89 (April): 64–65.

Greenwood, John. 1984. "The Monetary Framework Underlying the Hong Kong Dollar Stabilization Scheme." *China Quarterly* 99 (September): 631–36.

Ho, Henry C. Y. 1974. "Growth of Government Expenditure in Hong Kong." *Hong Kong Economic Papers* 8 (March): 18–38.

———. 1979. *The Fiscal System of Hong Kong.* London: Croom Helm.

Hong Kong. 1967. *Kowloon Disturbances 1966: Report of the Commission of Inquiry.* Hong Kong: Government Printer.

———. 1977. *The 1977–78 Budget: Economic Background.* Hong Kong: Government Printer.

———. 1982. *1981 Economic Background.* Hong Kong: Government Printer.

———. Various years, 1956–66. Annual Reports. Hong Kong: Government Press.

Hong Kong, Census and Statistics Department. 1969. *Hong Kong Statistics 1947–1967.* Hong Kong: Government Printer.

———. 1969. *Hong Kong: Review of Overseas Trade in 1968.* Hong Kong: Government Printer.

———. 1972a. *1971 Census of Manufacturing Establishments.* Hong Kong: Government Printer.

———. 1972b. *Hong Kong Population and Housing Census 1971. Basic Tables and Main Report.* Hong Kong: Government Printer.

———. 1972c. "Type of Premises." Census Circular 5/72. June.

———. 1973. *The Household Expenditure Survey 1973–74 and the Consumer Price Indexes.* Hong Kong: Government Printer.

———. 1976. *1973 Census of Industrial Production.* Hong Kong: Government Printer.

———. 1977a. *Estimates of Gross Domestic Product 1961 to 1975.* Hong Kong: Government Printer.

———. 1977b. *Hong Kong By-Census 1976: Basic Tables.* Hong Kong: Government Printer.

————. 1978a. *Hong Kong Annual Digest of Statistics 1978*. Hong Kong: Government Printer.

————. 1978b. *Hong Kong Population: A 20-Year Projection*. Hong Kong: Government Printer.

————. 1981. *Hong Kong Annual Digest of Statistics 1981*. Hong Kong: Government Printer.

————. 1982a. *Estimates of Gross Domestic Product 1966 to 1977*. Hong Kong: Government Printer.

————. 1982b. *Estimates of Gross Domestic Product 1966 to 1980*. Hong Kong: Government Printer.

————. 1982c. *Hong Kong Annual Digest of Statistics 1982*. Hong Kong: Government Printer.

————. Various issues, 1972–84. *Hong Kong Monthly Digest of Statistics*. Hong Kong: Government Printer.

————. n.d. *Hong Kong Social and Economic Trends 1964/1974*. Hong Kong: Government Printer.

————. n.d. *1978 Survey of Industrial Production*. Hong Kong: Government Printer.

Hong Kong, Commerce and Industry Department. 1965. *The Household Expenditure Survey 1963/64 and the Consumer Price Index*. Hong Kong: Government Printer.

————. 1974. *Annual Statistical Review 1972–1973*. Hong Kong: Government Printer.

————. 1976 Annual Statistical Review. Hong Kong: Government Printer.

Hong Kong, Commissioner for Census Statistics. n.d. *Report on the 1966 By-Census*. Vol. 2. *Tables*. Hong Kong: Government Printer.

Hong Kong, Commissioner of Rating and Valuation. 1962. *Rental Study*. Hong Kong: Government Printer.

Hong Kong, Government Information Services. Various issues, 1979–83. *Hong Kong*. Hong Kong: Government Printer.

Hong Kong, Government Planning Division. 1963. "Tsuen Wan and District Outline Development Plan. Statement to Accompany Plan No. LTW/75."

Hopkins, Keith, ed. 1971. *Hong Kong: The Industrial Colony; A Political, Social and Economic Survey*. Oxford, U.K.: Oxford University Press.

Hoselitz, Bert F. 1959. "Small Industry in Underdeveloped Countries." *Journal of Economic History* 19 (4): 600–20.

Hsia, Ronald, and Laurence Chau. 1978. *Industrialization, Employment and Income Distribution: A Case Study of Hong Kong*. London: Croom Helm.

Hughes, Richard. 1968. *Hong Kong: Borrowed Place—Borrowed Time*. New York: Praeger.

Jarvie, I. C., ed. 1969. *Hong Kong: A Society in Transition*. London: Routledge and Kegan Paul.

King, Ambrose Y. C., and Y. K. Chan. 1972. *A Theoretical and Operational Definition of Community: The Case of Kwun Tong*. Social Research Centre Paper 9. Hong Kong: Chinese University of Hong Kong.

Leibenstein, Harvey. 1968. "Entrepreneurship and Development." *American Economic Review* 58 (May): 72–83.

Lethbridge, David, ed. 1980. *The Business Environment in Hong Kong*. Hong Kong: Oxford University Press 1980.

Lethbridge, Henry. 1978. *Hong Kong: Stability and Change*. Hong Kong: Oxford University Press.

Lin, Tzong-biau. 1985. "Growth, Equity, and Income Distribution Policies in Hong Kong." *The Developing Economies* 23 (4): 391–413.

Lin, Tzong-Biau, Rance P. L. Lee, and Udo-Ernst Simones, eds. 1979. *Hong Kong: Economic, Social and Political Studies in Development*. Hamburg: M. E. Sharpe.

McClelland, David. 1975. *The Achievement Motive*. New York: Irvington.

Miners, Norman. 1981. *The Government and Politics of Hong Kong*. Hong Kong: Oxford University Press.

Mok, Victor. 1972. *The Nature of Kwun Tong as an Industrial Community: An Analysis of Economic Organizations*. Social Research Centre Paper 13. Hong Kong: Chinese University of Hong Kong.

Nyaw, Mee-Kau, and Chan-leong Chan. 1982. "Structure and Development Strategies of the Manufacturing Industries in Singapore and Hong Kong: A Comparative Study." *Asian Survey* 22 (5): 449–69.

OECD (Organization for Economic Cooperation and Development). 1983. *National Accounts*. Vol. 1. *Main Aggregates 1952–1981*. Vol. 2. *Detailed Tables 1964–1981*. Paris.

———. 1984. *National Accounts*. Vol. 1. *Main Aggregates 1953–1982*. Paris.

Owen, Nicholas C. 1971. "Competition and Structural Change in Unconcentrated Industries." *Journal of Industrial Economics* 29 (Oxford): 133–47.

Pryor, E. G. 1983. *Housing in Hong Kong*. Hong Kong: Oxford University Press.

Rabushka, Alvin. 1973. *The Changing Face of Hong Kong: New Departures in Public Policy*. Washington, D.C.: American Enterprise Institute.

———. 1976. *Value for Money: The Hong Kong Budgetary Process*. Stanford, Calif.: Hoover Institution Press.

———. 1979. *Hong Kong: A Study in Economic Freedom*. Chicago, Ill.: University of Chicago Press.

Riedel, James. 1974. *The Industrialization of Hong Kong*. Tubingen, Germany: J. C. B. Mohr (Paul Siebeck).

Sit, Victor Fung-Shuen. 1978. "Hong Kong's Approach to the Development of Small Manufacturing Enterprises." *Small Industry Bulletin for Asia and the Pacific* 15: 89–98.

———. 1981a. "The Nature and Intensity of Subcontracting in Small-Scale Industry." *Small Industry Bulletin for Asia and the Pacific* 17: 169–74.

Sit, Victor Fung-Shuen, ed. 1981b. *Urban Hong Kong*. Hong Kong: Summerson Eastern.

Sit, Victor Fung-Shuen, Siu-lun Wong, and Tsin-sing Kiang. 1980. *Small-Scale Industry in a Laissez-Faire Economy*. Hong Kong: University of Hong Kong.

Staley, Eugene, and Richard Morse. 1965. *Modern Small Industry for Developing Countries*. New York: McGraw-Hill.

Storey, David J., ed. 1983. *The Small Firm*. New York: St. Martin's Press.

Szczepanik, Edward. 1958. *The Economic Growth of Hong Kong*. London: Oxford University Press.

World Bank. 1984. *World Tables*. Baltimore, Md.: Johns Hopkins University Press.

Woronoff, Jon. 1980. *Hong Kong: Capitalist Paradise*. Portsmouth, N.H.: Heinemann Educational Books.

Young, Alwyn. Forthcoming. "Structural Change and Structural Flexibility in National Economies: The Rise and Decline of Industries and Macroeconomic Flexibility." Ph.D. diss. Fletcher School of Law and Diplomacy, Tufts University, Medford, Mass.

Youngson, A. J. 1982. *Hong Kong: Economic Growth and Policy*. Hong Kong: Oxford University Press.

Youngson, A. J., ed. 1983. *China and Hong Kong: The Economic Nexus*. Hong Kong: Oxford University Press.

3 Singapore

Linda Lim
Pang Eng Fong
Ronald Findlay

Singapore is a small island 176 kilometers north of the equator and just south of peninsular Malaysia, to which it is linked by a causeway. Although it covers only 622 square kilometers, it is home to a population of nearly 2.6 million. About 75 percent of its residents are of Chinese descent, 15 percent are Malayan, and 6 percent are Indian. This small, crowded island has no natural resources and depends entirely on the world market, yet it boasts a remarkable economic record: it has developed into a prosperous modern industrial economy and has given its population a standard of living that is the envy of much better endowed nations in the developing world. This chapter explains the reasons for this success.

History and Political Background

Modern Singapore can undoubtedly be credited to the vision of an English colonial administrator, Sir Stamford Raffles, who recognized the island's strategic and commercial value and in 1819 acquired it from its Malay ruler for the British East India Company. Like Malta in the west, Singapore was to be a naval outpost protecting India, the "jewel in the crown" of the British Empire. Singapore, together with Penang and Malacca, became the British Crown Colony known as the Straits Settlements. Its natural hinterland was the peninsula of Malaya, which was composed of federated and unfederated states indirectly ruled by Britain. The island did not begin to realize its potential, however, until the Suez Canal opened in 1869 and steam replaced sail. With the expansion of Malaya's rubber exports, Singapore's entrepôt trade flourished. That trade was conducted by Singapore's British agency houses and smaller Chinese import-export merchants. The port also served as a transit point for migrant labor from India and China bound for Malaya's mines, plantations, and railroads.

In 1942 the British Empire suffered a great blow to its prestige when Singapore fell to Japan, but the British recaptured it in 1945 and the following year made it a separate Crown Colony. At the same time, Penang and Malacca were merged with Malaya. The British had decided to hold on to Singapore as a naval base, recognizing that self-government would eventually be granted to Malaya. Another concern at the end of the 1940s was the bloody guerrilla war that the Chinese Communist party of Malaya (CPM) had begun waging. Things had subsided considerably by the time the Federation of Malaya became independent in 1957. Singapore, meanwhile, was moving slowly toward self-government in all matters except foreign affairs and defense. The crucial question of internal security was eventually handled by a council consisting of three representatives each from Singapore and Britain, with the casting vote held by a representative from the Federation of Malaya. It was with these restrictions that Singapore achieved self-government in 1959.

Even at that time, the population of Singapore was predominantly Chinese, with a good number of Malays and Indians. The Straits Chinese—descendants of the earliest immigrants—had produced an English-educated elite of lawyers and civil servants who dominated the political scene in the early postwar years. Their idea of politics amounted to protecting their interests under an umbrella of British patronage. The rest of the Chinese population was engaged mainly in manual labor and petty trade, was Chinese-educated, and had cultural and political ties with China. This group did not participate in the limited franchise of the early phases of self-government in Singapore before 1959.

The more modern nationalist parties consisted of the Labour Front, founded by the Jewish lawyer David Marshall, and the People's Action party (PAP), formed by a group of students in Britain led by Lee Kuan Yew, also a lawyer. Spurred by their democratic socialist ideologies, both parties pressed for independence. Marshall became the first chief minister of Singapore in 1955, under the Rendel Constitution, which divided power between a British governor and a locally elected chief minister. Marshall resigned a year later in protest against the lack of progress toward self-government and was replaced by Lim Yew Hock. Both of these early leaders were severely tested by Communist-inspired strikes and riots. Although Marshall was a staunch anti-Communist, his liberal sympathies made him shrink from confrontation, whereas Lim did not hesitate to use vigorous measures but was labeled anti-Chinese and a British stooge for doing so.

The PAP soon began gaining support for its radical ideas, particularly from Communist sympathizers in the Chinese community and the labor movement. Lee Kuan Yew had greatly impressed local residents as well as the British authorities with his political skill, which enabled him to remain detached from the often bloody confrontations between the authorities, on the one hand, and the students, on the other. When the political opportunity presented itself in 1959, he carried the PAP to a sweeping victory, winning forty-three out of fifty-one seats in parliament and 53 percent of the total vote of a greatly extended franchise. Lee Kuan Yew became the first prime minister of a Singapore that was self-governing, subject to the limitations on external affairs and internal security.

Once in office, however, Lee sided with the more moderate faction of his party. He soon found himself engaged in a struggle with the radical pro-Communist segments of the PAP and their trade union supporters, who finally left the party in 1961 to form a new left-wing group, the Barisan Sosialis. One of the main points of contention was the political status of Singapore. The PAP leadership felt that the only viable solution for Singapore in the long run was to merge with Malaya, whose conservative Malay-dominated polity had emerged successfully from its conflict with the Communists, thanks to Sir Gerald Templer and his British and Gurkha troops. Perhaps it was the very failure of the armed struggle on the peninsula that led the CPM to intensify its efforts to subvert Singapore through political agitation and infiltration. (It even gained a toehold in the office of the political secretary to the prime minister.) In contrast, the Barisan Sosialis did not want Singapore to join the proposed conservative federation, which included the British North Borneo territories of Sabah and Sarawak, as well as the Federation of Malaya. In a ploy to protect Singapore's interests, it argued for unconditional merger with Malaya (that is, without special clauses), calculating that the populace would back away from such a drastic choice. A referendum in 1962 on the terms of the merger was a triumph for the PAP, for it gave Singapore more autonomy in the new federation than the other constituent units. Several months later, in what was termed Operation Cold Store, the internal security council ordered the detention without trial of many Barisan Sosialis leaders, trade unionists, and student leaders— more than 100 persons in all—and thus quelled any opposition to the merger.

At first, the Malayan leader Tunku Abdul Rahman wanted no part of Singapore or its million or more Chinese, who would, he thought, pose a threat to the Malay majority and to Malay hegemony in the enlarged federation. At the same time, he feared that the political instability of Singapore might give the Communists a chance to turn it into another Cuba, just across the causeway linking the two territories. He felt that Singapore inside the federation would be a lesser evil than Singapore outside. In addition, there were the benefits of Singapore's harbor to consider, not to mention the financial and commercial expertise of its citizens. Singapore, it was thus decided, would become the New York rather than the Cuba of Malaya. In September 1963 the Federation of Malaysia—composed of the former Federation of Malaya, Singapore, Sabah, and Sarawak—came into being.

Five days later, the PAP called a snap election from which it emerged with thirty-seven seats in parliament, against thirteen for the Barisan

Sosialis. Shortly afterward, the government responded to the "direct action" tactics being pursued by the opposition by arresting more Barisan Sosialis leaders, unionists, and students and took steps to break up Barisan-dominated labor unions and other grass-roots organizations. With these measures, it established political peace and enabled the PAP to gain complete control of Singapore politics—which it has held ever since.

Under the terms of the 1963 merger, the federal government was to oversee foreign affairs and defense and the Singapore government labor and education, so as to preserve the cultural autonomy of its own population. Because the financial arrangements were somewhat ambiguous, Singapore was under the impression that it would have fiscal autonomy except for having to make a "contribution" to the central authority; the center, however, expected to collect all revenue directly and to disburse expenditure in Singapore as necessary. The PAP put forward what it called the Malaysian Malaysia program, which provided for equal participation by Malays, Chinese, Indians, and others in a secular democratic state, as opposed to an Islamic Malay-dominated polity in which Chinese and Indians were treated as second-class citizens. The party contested elections on the peninsula in 1964, aiming at urban Chinese constituencies and apparently hoping to displace the Malayan Chinese Association (MCA) as the principal coalition partner of the United Malay National Organization (UMNO) in the ruling alliance.

Not surprisingly, this move prompted the MCA leaders to rally round their long-standing allies in the UMNO, and the PAP won only one seat in the elections. The PAP was also criticized by many Malay leaders for its treatment of the Malay minority in Singapore. On the economic side, any hopes for a Malaysian common market were dashed when the central authorities announced that they did not wish to substitute expensive Singapore industrial products for cheaper foreign imports. The situation grew so tense that rumors of Lee Kuan Yew's impending arrest became rampant, whereupon British Prime Minister Harold Wilson stepped in and issued preemptive warnings to Tunku Abdul Rahman about the possible adverse consequences of such an act. The Tunku responded that separation was the only solution and persuaded all parties to agree. Thus, on August 9, 1965, Singapore became a sovereign nation.

The island was just beginning to recover from the shock of separation when it received a severe economic blow. The British, who had inadvertently succeeded in their plans to make Singapore independent of Malaya, now decided that the price of maintaining the former imperial grandeur of the island was too high and announced that they would be abandoning their naval base there in 1968, well ahead of schedule. British expenditure on the base constituted 20 percent of Singapore's GNP and provided employment for 30,000 civilian workers. Indirect expenditure by British troops and their families provided further sources of employment and income for the local economy. To soften the blow, Britain agreed to hand over its land and facilities gratis and also to provide some economic aid.

In response to these misfortunes, Singapore launched an export-oriented development strategy for which it would eventually become famous and which the other newly industrializing economies (NIEs) of Southeast Asia would adopt. The withdrawal of British aid, like the withdrawal of American aid from Taiwan (China), gave rise to a strategy of the "challenge-response" pattern delineated by Toynbee. In Singapore the strategy generated rapid growth, caused employment to expand, and kept real incomes on the rise for nearly two decades, thereby helping the PAP remain in power. Between 1968 and 1981 the PAP was the only party represented in parliament. It won regular elections with ever-increasing majorities until the general election of December 1984, when it suffered a 12.5 percent decline in its share of all votes cast and two opposition candidates—one of whom had already won a by-election in 1981—won seats in the seventy-nine-member parliament. A few months after the election, the economy plunged into its first severe recession since sovereignty, setting into motion far-reaching economic and political changes.

The Economy

The exponential growth in Singapore's real GDP and in its exports and imports (see figures 3-1 and 3-2) is a clear case of export-led growth, or outward-oriented development. Between 1960 and 1986 the average annual growth rate of per capita GDP was 7.7 percent (table 3-1), and it rose to 8.3 percent between 1960 and 1984, before the recession of 1985–86. This entire period may be divided into five phases, beginning with the years 1960–65.

The period 1960–65 was marked by the growing pains of independence, the stress of the merger with Malaysia, and a confrontation with Indonesia.[1] Nonetheless, per capita income grew at the respectable rate of 5.7 percent a year in this period. In the second period, 1966–73, Singapore was in its "heroic" phase of growth, moving along at the impressive rate of 12.3 percent a year as a result of considerable slack in the economy, combined with institutional changes in the labor market and inducements to direct foreign investment during a worldwide boom during these years. In the third phase, 1973–77, the Organization of Petroleum Exporting Countries (OPEC) oil price shock and the associated world recession pushed growth down to 6.4 percent a year, which was still much higher than growth rates in many other parts of the world. Rapid growth resumed in the fourth phase, 1978–84, reaching 8.7 percent a year. The fifth period, 1985–87, was a time of recession and recovery. Per capita GDP declined by 1.8 percent in 1985 but moved up by 1.9 percent in 1986 and picked up further in 1987. In view of the maturity of the economy, the growth in per capita GDP is expected to be slower (4–6 percent) in the future.

Figure 3-1. GDP at Market Prices, Singapore, 1960–85

Billions of constant 1968 Singapore dollars

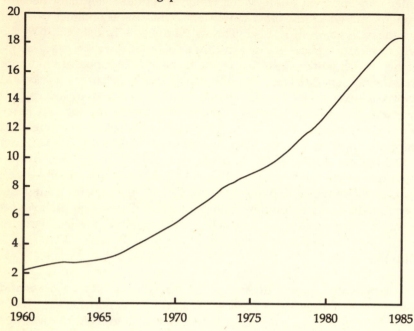

Source: World Bank data.

With rapid growth, unemployment rates fell steadily, from about 9 percent in 1960 to 2.7 percent in 1984 (table 3-1), but after the 1985–86 recession they rose to 4.6 percent.[2] Rapid growth was also accompanied by relatively low inflation, which up to 1973 averaged less than 2 percent a year (table 3-1). In the aftermath of the OPEC oil price shock, inflation rates shot up to 19.6 percent in 1973 and 22.3 percent in 1974. Since then the rates have been low, except in 1980 and 1981, the years of the second oil price shock. These low rates of inflation have been partly the result of government policies restraining domestic demand, especially private consumption, in the face of rapid growth, as explained later in the chapter.

Singapore experienced another important change in the decades after 1960: as table 3-2 shows, there was a massive shift in the proportion of national income devoted to gross domestic capital formation (GDCF). Private consumption fell from nearly 90 percent of GDP in 1960 to 43.9 percent in 1984 before increasing to about 47.5 percent in 1986, a share still far below the level of the late 1970s. Public consumption rose moderately, from 7.5 percent of GDP in 1960 to a peak of 13.3 percent in

Figure 3-2. Commodity Trade, Singapore, 1956–84

Billions of U.S. dollars

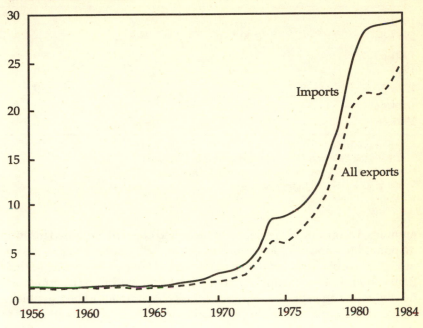

Source: World Bank data.

the recession year of 1985, and since then it has fallen slightly. GDCF rose from 11.3 percent of GDP in 1960 to a peak of 49 percent in 1984, when it exceeded private consumption—mainly because of overbuilding, which had sparked the high growth rate of 1984. Following the recession the share of GDCF in GDP declined to 40 percent in 1986 and is expected to fall even farther because of the construction slump and excess capacity in real estate. Still, over the period as a whole, no other economy in the world has had such a high and sustained rate of investment. At the same time, Singapore reduced its dependence on net imports from 14 percent of GDP in 1960 to less than 3 percent in the boom year of 1984 and down to virtually zero in the recession-and-recovery year of 1986.

The largest structural change associated with this expansion has been the shift from entrepôt trade to the export of manufactures and services (see table 3-3). Reexports from Singapore, which still account for about one-third of total exports, constituted 94 percent of all exports in 1960. The share of domestic exports in GNP rose from about 10 percent in 1960 to 93 percent in 1982 before dropping to 81.8 percent in 1986. This last figure may be misleading, however, since exports are measured in gross

Table 3-1.   Growth, Inflation, and Unemployment, 1960–86
(percent)

Period	Annual growth of per capita GDP	Annual rate of inflation	Unemployment at end of period
1960–86	7.70	3.6	—
1960–84	8.30	3.9	—
1960–65	5.70	1.0	8.9
1966–73	12.30	3.7[a]	4.5
1974–77	6.40	6.6[a]	3.9
1978–84	8.70	4.7	2.7
1985–86	0.05	–0.7	4.6

— Not available.
a. Between 1966 and 1972 the rate dropped to 1.4 percent.
b. Between 1975 and 1977 the rate was 1.3 percent.
Source: Lee 1984: 14; Lim 1986: ix.

amounts, whereas GNP is a net or value added concept. Retained imports amounted to about 143.2 percent of GNP in 1982 but fell to 98.6 percent in 1986. It would be helpful if imports were classified according to their final use for both consumption and investment and their intermediate use for both domestic and export markets. Then it would be possible to arrive at a figure for the import content of exports. One attempt to calculate net domestic exports puts them at 23 percent of GDP in 1982, which seems to be a plausible figure (Sandilands, cited in Tan 1984).

Manufacturing employment grew from 7.5 percent of total employment in 1960 to 19.5 percent in 1982, whereas manufacturing output increased from 12.8 percent of GDP to 21.5 percent over the same period. Productivity in manufacturing thus grew at a lower rate than overall productivity. Since 1982, however, this trend has changed somewhat:

Table 3-2.   Shares of GDP, 1960–86
(percent)

Year	Private consumption	Public consumption	Gross domestic capital formation	Net imports
1960	89.4	7.5	11.3	–14.00
1965	79.2	10.4	21.9	–12.10
1973	62.1	11.0	39.2	–10.20
1977	58.0	10.7	36.2	–2.70
1984	43.9	10.8	49.0	–2.80
1986	47.5	12.1	40.0	–0.07

Source: Singapore Department of Statistics, Economic and Social Statistics Singapore, 1960–1982, table 4.7; and Annual Economic Survey 1986, table A1.4, p. 91.

Table 3-3. Indicators of Structural Change, 1960–86
(percent)

Indicator	1960	1970	1980	1984	1986
Domestic exports as a share of total exports	6.2	38.5	65.6	64.4	65.5
Domestic exports as a share of GNP	10.1	30.5	93.0	81.0	81.8
Retained imports as a share of GNP	57.1	79.4	143.2	105.0	98.6
Manufacturing output as a share of GDP	12.8	20.4	21.5	20.1	20.2
Manufacturing employment as a share of total employment	7.5	19.4	29.5	27.4	—

— Not available.
Source: For 1984–86, *Annual Economic Survey, 1986*, various tables.

manufacturing employment fell to 25.5 percent of total employment in the recession year of 1985, and manufacturing output fell to 19 percent before recovering slightly to 20.2 percent in 1986. The subsequent move toward more capital-intensive and technologically sophisticated goods in the manufacturing sector has probably accelerated since the 1985–86 recession, which forced many labor-intensive industries to close down.

Singapore has also experienced a substantial increase in its incremental capital-output ratio (ICOR), which was about 3 in the period of moderate growth from 1960 to 1965. It fell to 2.5 during the period of expansion from 1966 to 1973, when growth rates were above 12 percent a year, but the investment share almost doubled in this period, from about 20 to 40 percent. From 1973 to 1986 growth slackened, while the investment rate moved past 40 percent. This could indicate capital deepening and long-term investment in infrastructure, but it could also indicate a decline in total productivity, with diminishing returns to capital. Indeed, the rate of return on private capital declined in the 1980s up to the recession, in part because of overinvestment in the construction of new property (Singapore 1986).

Development Strategy

When the PAP was voted into power in 1959, Singapore was an immigrant port city dominated by entrepôt trade and services and operating on laissez-faire principles.[3] Unlike many other developing countries, it did not have an aristocratic class, a landed gentry, or an entrenched military to oppose the PAP. Led by mostly Western-educated intellectuals and professionals, the PAP espoused an anticolonial, social democratic, noncommunalist, and noncommunist ideology and drew its political support from the Chinese-educated working class and the lower middle class. The little opposition it did meet consisted of unorganized complaints from business groups, civil servants, professionals, and the Catholic church (Drysdale 1984: 227). Left-wing opposition from within the PAP's own ranks had been overcome by 1965, and the party's core now consisted of workers, unions affiliated with the National Trades Union Congress (NTUC), community leaders, and the civil service.

The PAP government thus did not have to balance and satisfy the conflicting needs of powerful interest groups to remain in power or to govern effectively. Nor did it have to contend with an entrenched business class that benefited from government regulations or that enjoyed a special relationship with the ruling party, since Singapore had evolved as a laissez-faire economy. Instead, the PAP leadership was able to function more or less autonomously, building and running the government mainly on technocratic principles rooted in its social democratic ideology. It therefore placed continuing emphasis on social policy, particularly mass education, population control, and public housing (see, for example, Lim 1987a).

Initially, the party had no well-defined economic plans. According to Goh Keng Swee, Singapore's first prime minister and a former deputy prime minister, who is considered the chief architect of the economic policies of the 1960s and 1970s, "We produced a formal document called the First Four-Year Plan in 1960, only because the World Bank wanted a plan. We cooked it up during a long weekend. I have very little confidence in economic planning."[4]

Before 1965 the PAP felt that Singapore's economic survival depended entirely on its political viability and hence promoted the merger with Malaysia. Lee Kuan Yew himself admitted that Singapore was never envisioned as a viable economic unit, except as part of its traditional hinterland. Thus the government's development strategy in the first half of the 1960s, before and during the brief union with Malaysia, was to promote import-substituting industries for a Malaysian common market. It did so by offering infant industries tariff protection, which a visiting United Nations industrial survey mission recommended applying selectively in order not to damage the entrepôt trade. In fact, protective import duties were imposed on only two product groups (soap and detergents, and paints) while Singapore was awaiting the formation of a customs union or common market with Malaysia. It was not until separation in August 1965 that tariff and quota protection was substantially increased on a large number of items. But this was not because of pressure from any particular political or interest groups, which would be more likely to oppose such protection in view of the emphasis on entrepôt trade and the lack of domestic manufacturing at the time. Rather, the immediate purpose of protection was to counteract Singapore's persistent unemployment by creating jobs in local industries (Tay 1986).

The government quickly recognized that the domestic market was too small (the population was about 1.5 million in the mid-1960s) for import substitution to be a viable long-term strategy for industrialization. It turned to export promotion instead. Its first step, in the late 1960s, was to reduce tariffs and quotas. Because the import-substituting phase was short and the protective tariff structure relatively low, strong rent-seeking groups did not emerge to resist this change, which in any case was implemented gradually, the last major protective tariffs being removed only in 1980 (Tan and Ow 1983). Because the government avoided direct control measures such as licensing, quotas, and price controls during the import-substituting phase, it kept price distortions and bureaucratic intervention in the economy to a minimum, and the shift in strategy did not generate much opposition.

Pragmatic considerations—rather than ideology, the example of other economies, or interest-group pressure—helped shape the export-oriented industrialization strategy adopted after 1965. The main objective of this strategy was to attract the foreign capital needed to transfer technology, develop new manufacturing activities, and penetrate new markets. Local capital and entrepreneurship were concentrated in their traditional strongholds of entrepôt trade, domestic commerce, and primary production in the Malayan peninsula and were not available to supply the manufacturing technology and market expertise required for world markets. The few industrialists who were present did not think that foreign capital posed a threat to them, since they expected to be producing for noncompeting markets of the world rather than for the regional or local markets. Consequently, a situation of general excess capacity, including high unemployment, prevailed in the mid-to-late 1960s.

From the time that the PAP government assumed power in 1959, it emphasized that Singapore's economic progress would depend in large measure on private enterprise and foreign investment. The conviction that foreign capital was vital to the stability and prosperity of the small nation—indeed to its very survival—grew even stronger after independence. As Prime Minister Lee Kuan Yew (1978) put it: "We never suffered from any inhibitions in borrowing capital, know-how, managers, engineers, and marketing capabilities. Far from limiting the entry of foreign managers, engineers, and bankers, we encouraged them to come." Nor did the PAP, despite its social democratic leanings, frown on profit making:

> Profit is not a dirty word in Singapore. . . . We accept business operations for what they are and do not expect them to perform the functions of philanthropic institutions. Our workers and trade unions hope and expect their employers to make profits, the bigger the better. This is because we understand that it is only when businesses make big profits, that employees can benefit by wage increases, larger bonuses, faster promotion, and improved fringe benefits. (Goh 1973)

To create an attractive investment climate for foreign capital, the government had to ensure social and political stability. In particular it had to change the image of continual labor unrest that had developed during Singapore's political struggles of the late 1950s and early 1960s. As a first step in this direction, authorities introduced legislation in 1968 severely restricting industrial action by workers—a clear swing in favor of the owners of capital that won the PAP the support of both foreign and local employers. At the same time, the government indicated that it would avoid any action that was not in Singapore's national interest or that interfered in domestic politics. Foreign investors who wanted an official guarantee that their Singapore plants would not be unionized were turned away, in part because a significant amount of the PAP's political support came from the moderate majority of the labor movement and was then, as it is now, heavily involved in the NTUC (see Kassalow 1978).

By 1968 the opposition Barisan Sosialis had withdrawn from parliamentary politics, and a boycott by all opposition parties of the 1968 general elections gave the PAP a parliamentary monopoly that it retained until 1981, when it lost a by-election. The party thus faced no political opposition to any of its policies during the young nation's formative years. On the contrary, it has "made the best political use of the uncertainty arising from Singapore's sudden and traumatic separation (from Malaysia), and instilled in the population a sense of siege and a need for national unity" (Pang and Chan 1987).

Singapore's move toward export-oriented industrialization based on foreign capital and technology happened to coincide with favorable trends in world trade. Multinational corporations had begun searching for stable, low-wage offshore manufacturing sites at this time, and hence in late 1967 Singapore had an influx of foreign firms. Its economy was further buoyed by rapid growth and oil exploration in the surrounding regions. The boom hit not only export manufacturing—which included textiles and garments, electrical and electronics products, shipbuilding, and petroleum refining—but also transport and communications and, later, financial services. As foreign firms took over an increasing share of Singapore's manufacturing output, employment, and domestic exports, they created more opportunities for local supporting firms, largely in complementary activities (see Lim and Pang 1982). In the wake of this economic success, foreign investors and local businesses stepped up their support for the government's development policies and programs.

By 1972 the fast-growing, rapidly diversifying economy had not only created jobs for people just entering the work force and for the 40,000 workers laid off when Britain pulled out its military services in 1968 but had also absorbed the backlog of unemployment that had been accumulating since the early 1960s. As Singapore approached full employment, the lower-income groups, in particular, began benefiting from the expansion of the job market and the provision of basic needs (see Pang 1975; Rao and Ramakrishnan 1981).

As a result, the PAP government was able to retain the political support of workers who had sacrificed a great deal when they accepted its wage-restraining policy and pro-employer labor legislation of 1968. But as the labor market tightened and inflationary pressures built up, the government feared that wages would rise sharply and make Singapore less attractive to multinational firms as an offshore location for labor-intensive manufacturing. In 1972 it set up a tripartite National Wages Council (NWC) to recommend "orderly" wage increases.

The government had also given some thought to an alternative strategy—that of shifting away from labor-intensive manufacturing—but it shelved the idea following the 1974–75 recession brought on by the OPEC oil price increase of 1973. Thousands of workers, many of them Malaysian migrant workers, were laid off from export industries such as garments and electronics. When the economy began recovering in 1976, more foreign workers were again employed, but labor shortages also began appearing. In 1979 Goh Chok Tong, now first deputy prime minister and Lee Kuan Yew's immediate heir apparent, announced a second industrial revolution aimed at overcoming this domestic labor problem. Employers were offered incentives to upgrade technology, substitute capital for labor, and shift to less labor-intensive activities. The NWC recommended that wages undergo large (double-digit) corrective increases for three years, from 1979 to 1982, and that employment of foreign labor be restricted. At the same time, Singapore's industrial relations system was restructured to decentralize wage bargaining and perhaps to contain labor's growing bargaining strength in a tight labor market.

This high-wage policy was understandably popular among all workers, but it elicited various responses among foreign investors. Large, long-established firms in labor-intensive export manufacturing (for example, in consumer electronics and electrical household products) were not pleased with the seniority-inflated wage bills they had to pay for their large force of experienced and mostly unionized workers. In contrast, the newer and smaller high-technology firms that employed capital-intensive technology and a relatively small number of young and not-yet-unionized workers were not adversely affected, since labor accounted for only a small proportion of their total costs. Local manufacturers were the hardest hit by the high-wage policy because they were concentrated in the industries with the lowest technology and most labor-intensive exports. Also, they had depended on foreign labor the most and had the least access to large sums of capital and advanced technology (see Lim 1987b).

The high-wage policy, combined with an unfavorable external market environment and the high cost of government-provided services, undermined Singapore's international competitiveness and in 1985–86 pushed the economy into its most severe recession to date.[5] Some multinationals laid off large numbers of workers, and many local firms closed down. As a result, the domestic property sector, which had been massively overbuilt during the construction boom of the early 1980s, plunged further into an already severe slump.

The government appointed a nine-member economic committee to investigate the causes of these new economic problems and to propose solutions. The committee was chaired by Brigadier-General Lee Hsien Loong, the prime minister's thirty-three-year-old son, who subsequently became minister for trade and industry. The members of the committee and of its eight subcommittees were drawn mainly from local and foreign businesses, government ministries, and statutory boards.[6] By including business representatives, the government indicated it was willing to consult private firms (including multinationals) in formulating its economic policy. But no consumers, workers, small businesses, or unions were represented on the main committee, and only one union member served on any of the eight subcommittees. The Economic Committee met for ten months before issuing its report *The Singapore Economy: New Directions* in February 1986. This was essentially a strategic plan for the economy, and one of its goals was to transform Singapore into a "fully developed economy" and "international total business centre" with a better business environment and higher rate of return than in the countries of the Organization for Economic Cooperation and Development (OECD).

Various stages of specific policies designed to bring about economic recovery were implemented before, during, and after the Economic Committee conducted its deliberations. Measures were taken to reduce taxes, fees charged by state agencies and enterprises, and indirect labor costs (especially the compulsory contributions to the Central Provident Fund, which amounted to 50 percent of a worker's wages) and to put a lid on wages for two to three years. The PAP-controlled labor movement and individual unions cooperated, if reluctantly, with the policy. Foreign investors, needless to say, responded enthusiastically and began pouring new investments into Singapore (in part also as a response to the yen-dollar currency realignment of 1986).

Local businesses, however, considered the measures too little, too late, and too short-sighted. They were disappointed that not all their recommendations had been implemented. They were especially upset to hear that they would not be protected against foreign competition (particularly in the service sector) and were being crowded out of the Singapore market (including the domestic labor market) by large multinational and state enterprises. Many local businessmen complained that the government was favoring foreign enterprises and that its support of local industry had become perfunctory and insincere.

Since the 1985–87 recession the government has reduced its emphasis on high-technology industry (which could be said to discriminate against low-technology local enterprises) and has set up a small-enterprises bureau to support promising local ventures—not those in difficulty, but ones likely to be profitable if they had sufficient capital and technical assistance. The government is also looking into ways to stimulate local entrepreneurship and is encouraging Singaporeans to work and do business abroad and to set up their own multinational firms. For the most part, its past and present policies have not intentionally discriminated against local business but have favored large investments and internationally recognized companies, which are overwhelmingly foreign in origin. The current policy of encouraging the multinationalization of Singapore firms again focuses on large units, including state enterprises, because these are the only ones with the capacity to operate internationally.

Local private firms do have the potential to provide an alternative leadership for Singapore: "Politically, the men who control the Chinese Chamber of Commerce and Industry still represent the only homogeneous point of crystallisation for an alternative grouping in Singapore." But their incentive and ability to do so is still limited.

> The old *towkays* (leading merchants) cannot dispute the political changes above and outside their sphere of influence. They cannot dispute the success of the Government's intervention in the economy. But there is resentment that so little thanks comes their way for their entrepreneurial skills, so little recognition of the personal networks into which Singapore plugs in the South Seas and beyond or of the stability that family, clan and company bring to the nation. . . . Resentment has accumulated at being ruled by one who does not have a feel for times past or who does not know in himself what it is to be Chinese. The rest wriggle under the weight of restrictions, the thick layer of bureaucracy and the Government's apparent preference for Western and other foreign businessmen. (Minchin 1986: 225–26)

In sum, Singapore's development strategy has relied heavily on production for the world market. Thus it has given a leading role to foreign investment and multinationals and a secondary role to local capital and labor. Furthermore, the state has directed and intervened in the economy to a considerable extent, as explained in the next section.

State Intervention

As already mentioned, one notable feature of Singapore's development experience is that the state played a prominent role in the economy.[7] Although the PAP did not abandon the colonial administration's commitment to free trade, competition, and free enterprise, it felt that the state should create the physical infrastructure and institutions needed to promote economic growth and should take the lead in establishing new economic activities, especially in industries where the private sector had neither the experience nor the capital to operate successfully. In this the government was initially motivated by practical considerations. When the bureaucratic interests became entrenched, they started carrying direct intervention and economic regulation a little further than was perhaps desirable and set in motion a retreat toward privatization, which is being supported on both pragmatic and ideological grounds.

Besides being the exclusive provider of infrastructure and social services, as are many other governments, the Singapore government engaged in direct production. The main reason for doing so in the 1960s was to build large, high-risk enterprises, such as the National Iron and Steel Mills and Jurong Shipyard. The government also set up state-owned companies to take over some functions from public agencies that had grown too rapidly with a view to safeguarding institutional efficiency and flexibility. In the 1970s it set up many more state-owned enterprises, some in direct competition with private firms. Others were in areas not usually associated with great risk or large capital investments. By the early 1980s the government owned close to 450 companies in a wide range of manufacturing and service industries, including iron and steel, shipbuilding and ship repair, oil refining, petrochemicals, shipping, financial services, air transport, armaments, tourism, and property development. Some are large companies like Singapore Airlines and the Neptune Orient (shipping) Line; others are small ones like Jurong Bird Park and Primary Industries. All these state enterprises operate as profit-making concerns, in keeping with the government's long-standing support of profits and opposition to public subsidies (except for low-income housing, health care, and education).

Shares in these companies are held by one of three government holding firms—Temasek, Shengli, and MND Holding. In addition, forty statutory boards provide a wide range of services, including housing (for four-fifths of the population), telecommunications, utilities, and industrial complexes. Many of these statutory boards—such as the Telecommunications Authority, the Public Utilities Board, and the Urban Redevelopment Authority—are revenue-generating operations. Others—such as the Housing and Development Board (HDB), the Economic Development Board, and the National Productivity Board— are financed by government loans and grants. In 1983 government-owned companies reported a turnover of about 25 percent of Singapore's GDP and profits amounting to close to 10 percent of turnover (Low 1985b). The combined earnings of the seven largest statutory boards that provide public services—the Port of Singapore Authority, the Telecommunications Authority, the Jurong Town Corporation, the Post Office Savings Bank, the Civil Aviation Authority of Singapore, the Public Utilities Board, and the Urban Redevelopment Authority—was in excess of S$1.4 billion in 1984, which was S$300 million more than the profits of the ten most profitable publicly listed companies (*Singapore Straits Times*, 6 April 1985). In 1985 their development reserves, the largest portion of their accumulated surpluses, amounted to S$6.1 billion (Seah 1986: 43).

State involvement extends beyond government-owned enterprises and statutory boards to many other parts of the economy, which the government influences through macroeconomic policies and extensive and selective intervention in various markets. In the land market, for example, the government holds about 75 percent of all land in the country and houses 80 percent of the population. It is also the principal holder of domestic savings channeled through the Central Provident Fund (CPF), the Post Office Savings Bank, and the Development Bank of Singapore; it employs 11 percent of the labor force (and a third of all university graduates); and it intervenes in the labor market, regulating both the supply and the price of labor and controlling its organization.[8] Government revenue accounted for 19.4 percent of GNP in 1984, or 43.5 percent when the current surpluses of state enterprises are included; and public sector gross savings amounted to 64 percent of gross national savings. Government expenditure was 20.8 percent of GNP in 1984, public GDCF was 33.4 percent of total GDCF, and government consumption was 19.9 percent of total consumption. (These particular figures are higher than in Korea but lower than in Taiwan, China.)

With the increase in interventionism and in the power of the public sector, public officials have emerged as a new support group for the government, one with its own interests and sphere of influence. Senior civil servants in particular, many of whom also serve as directors of government-owned companies, wield considerable influence on public activities within the broad policy guidelines laid down by the political leadership. This state capitalism built by civil servants turned entrepreneurs has added a new dimension to the competition between the public and private sector, in that it has alienated local business groups and to some extent the professional classes. The state bureaucracy in Singapore is said to be evolving into a

separate "class" with motivations and interests independent of, and more than simply intermediary between, those of capital and labor. Government members overwhelmingly do not belong to the private property–owning, domestic entrepreneurial class, and some would say that it does not even serve their interests. Their reward comes not from a share of profits—not even the profits of state enterprise—or from corruption, which is nonexistent . . . and only partly from salary and perquisites. . . . Rather it comes from the power of control over the vast assets of the state itself, and indirectly of the private sector as well, and from the reflected glory of the very success the state has created in the economy. (Lim 1983: 761–62)

Private firms have been concerned about the dominance of state enterprises for some time, especially about what they perceive to be unfair advantages given to these firms (see Pillai 1983: 75). The government replies that it is a waste of time to discuss such general complaints and that anyone who is concerned about the widening scope of government enterprises should instead "draw attention to specific cases where mismanagement or privileged treatment and unfair competition has occurred. Where . . . complaints are well-grounded, remedial action will be taken." The spheres of private and public enterprise, the government says, have no clear limits, so why try to define them? "So long as the government substantiates its claims that these enterprises are run on business lines, receive no special privileges and are fully competitive with the private sector, that is sufficient justification for the existence and the expansion of these enterprises" (Goh Keng Swee, quoted in Pillai 1983: 76).

This view held sway until the severe recession of 1985–86, whereupon the state's role in the economy came into serious question, even among government entities such as the Economic Committee, which began calling for the privatization of government-owned companies.

> Now that the companies have succeeded, the government should have no parochial interest in them. Provided they continue to be profitable, well-run companies, it makes no difference to Singapore whether they are owned and managed by the government or by the private sector. To the government, the advantage of selling off these companies, of course for a fair price, will be that civil servants can be freed to concentrate on their primary jobs of administering the country, instead of diverting their energies to running the companies. It will also put an end to complaints from the private sector about special treatment and unfair competition, which will arise no matter how correctly the government companies are dealt with. (Singapore 1986: 16)

Privatization is, however, a complex undertaking (see Low 1985b) that cannot take place overnight. Partial divestment has already begun (with the public sale of a 20 percent share of Singapore Airlines), but it will likely continue gradually for more than ten years. Moreover, the government expects to retain a controlling share of most of the more important companies, but no new businesses will be started up with public funds, except in special circumstances—for example, where it is advisable to spread the risk of a project and obtain financial support outside the private sector. The government will continue to provide an environment conducive to business and create investment opportunities, but the private sector will take on the job of exploiting those opportunities and identifying the best ones to take up. Although the government recognizes that private businesses may make mistakes or miss opportunities, this arrangement is considered a more flexible way of matching up Singapore's resources and opportunities (see Low 1985b: 17).

Again, both pragmatism and ideology appear to be at work here. On the one hand, both the domestic and the international economic environment are making it increasingly difficult for the government to pick winners. Note, too, that many of its past winners (oil refining, shipbuilding, and some newer industries that have not had the chance to become winners, such as petrochemicals) have turned into losers because of changes in the external market—specifically, the onset of worldwide excess capacity. On the other hand, government leaders have been espousing a more laissez-faire ideology since the productivity movement of the early 1980s, which sought to decentralize labor-management relations and make workers less dependent on the state in order to link their fortunes more closely to the performance of the firms employing them. This trend has been particularly evident in the progressive privatization of social services (see, for example, Lim 1987a). Also, Brigadier-General Lee, the minister of trade and industry, appears to have developed a more positive view of market forces than some of his predecessors and has begun calling for more economic flexibility, including institutional flexibility.

Even though the selective divestment of state-owned companies means that the government will no longer be a dominant player in the economy, its role as planner will not change appreciably. State "guidance" (the word now preferred to "intervention") will continue, in part because of the downward inflexibility of prices and wages, on account of institutional rigidities that prevent prices from being always right. Furthermore, because Singapore is small, it is a price taker on world markets that must remain internationally competitive if its export-oriented economy is to survive.

> This, therefore, is the crucial pre-condition for the government to attempt to ensure: That our wages, exchange rates, interest rates, and so on are at levels that make our prices internationally competitive and, at the same time, represent some degree of equilibrium domestically. A balancing act such as this places stringent demands on our institutions and more so on our government planners. It takes sound judgment to decide whether market forces have yielded the right rates that enable Singapore to be competitive internationally. If not, there must be intervention in a timely and careful way to influence key economic variables. (Daniel 1986)

In addition, the government will continue to play the role of regulator but has vowed to reduce the burden of regulation on the private sector. The rate and extent to which both privatization and deregulation proceed will depend on whether bureaucrats try to protect their group interests, which will undoubtedly be undermined if the state plays a smaller part in the economy. (A parallel may be found in Japan, where segments of the bureaucracy have managed to prevent political leaders from removing nontariff barriers consisting of standards and certification procedures and thus from liberalizing the country's trade regime.) As a basic step toward a more flexible economy, Singapore must try to reduce bureaucratic inertia and perhaps even intrabureaucratic rivalry, especially in view of the size and power of the bureaucracy and the degree to which the government relies on it for political support.

Because the state has had such great influence on social and economic affairs, the population has come to depend on it as the provider of basic needs and the creator of wealth and opportunities. The government now fears that such an attitude will be detrimental to work effort and productivity, in that it will sap human dignity and drain public funds, and consequently has begun cutting back on social subsidies (see Richardson 1982: 26).

Politically, such dependence (and the expectations it generates) is a two-edged sword. On the one hand, it means that political support for the government will increase when economic and social development policies are working well, as they did for two decades until the recent recession. On the other hand, it means that support will dwindle when the economy falters or the government tries to reduce this dependence—for example, by cutting social subsidies. Moreover, normal frictions with one's landlord, utility company, transport service, employer, bank, child's school, doctor, and so on, could develop into dissatisfaction with the government itself, which is all these things rolled into one, and more.

Despite the recent moves to reduce its economic role, the government of Singapore retains strong control of the intertwined political and social system that it has shaped. Even before 1965 the PAP government tried to foster attitudes and values favorable to social and economic development and to promote new multiracial grass-roots organizations to supplant social units organized along communal or familial lines (Vasil 1984). Over the years it developed a complex battery of controls and incentives to influence social and economic behavior in many areas, including home ownership, family planning, marriage, childbearing, language use, health habits, moral behavior, community relations, recreation, savings, education and occupational choice, and land transport. By way of example, two current campaigns (backed by incentives and penalties) are aimed at making Singapore the first nation to reverse a declining birthrate and to completely eliminate smoking. This kind of influence, Prime Minister Lee has stated, has been directly responsible for Singapore's economic progress, which would not have occurred "if we had not intervened on very personal matters—who your neighbor is, how you live, the noise you make, how you spit (or where you spit), or what language you use. . . . It was fundamental social and cultural changes that brought us here" (*Economist*, 22 November 1986).

The government has been able to play a strong role in the political, social, cultural, and economic life of Singapore because of the state's highly centralized decisionmaking process. The prime minister and his close colleagues decide on basic policies, although usually after consulting with relevant groups, and these policies are invariably approved by parliamentarians, all but one of whom belong to the ruling PAP. Neither the people of Singapore nor their elected or nominated representatives have had much input into the policies that affect their daily lives. Despite a brief flurry of talk about more participatory democracy after the 1984 general election, when the government lost two parliamentary seats to the opposition for the first time in eighteen years, decisions were still being made from the top down, with the prime minister in firm control.

Today, however, a new generation of political leaders is taking over. Although this new group keeps to the PAP's fundamental political philosophy, it has shown a willingness to yield to the pressure for more consultation, if not more involvement, in policymaking. Some decentralization has even been proposed, through the establishment of town councils with administrative responsibility for particular residential districts. It remains to be seen what if any degree of political liberalization will be permitted after Prime Minister Lee leaves office, or to what extent his successors will be able to pilot Singapore toward a more flexible economy.

Policies and Institutions

The following discussion does not touch on all the developmental policies and institutions with which Singapore has experimented. Rather, it focuses on the most important and distinctive ones.

Industrial Relations

Industrial relations in Singapore have undergone periodic transformations to accommodate or facilitate economic development and to fulfill particular political goals of the ruling party. The 1950s and 1960s were extremely turbulent years for labor because its fortunes were bound up with the anticolonial struggle against the British and the activities of the Malayan Communist party in its own quest for power. Early on, as already mentioned, the PAP government drew part of its support and members from left-wing and militant labor unions, but the split with the Barisan Sosialis and the merger battle with Malaysia took a serious toll on the union leftists, whose leaders were whisked away in a mass arrest in 1962. The left-wing union was later deregistered, and the unions were reorganized under the PAP-led National Trades Union Congress (NTUC), with which 97 percent of all union members (a little more than a quarter of the labor force) are now affiliated.

To ensure the success of its export-oriented development strategy, which hinged on low wages and labor discipline, the government in 1968 passed two labor laws that would contain costs and improve the investment climate in Singapore. The Employment Act standardized the terms and conditions of employment and set limits on negotiable fringe benefits, including holidays, sick leave, overtime, retrenchment and severance terms, and a forty-four-hour workweek. The Industrial Relations (Amendment) Act excluded from collective bargaining such issues as recruitment, retrenchment, promotion, retirement, transfer, dismissal, and work assignments. It also spelled out new procedures for labor negotiation and conflict resolution, including compulsory arbitration.[9]

These political, legal, and administrative actions achieved their aims. They depoliticized the labor movement, established de facto government control over unions, transferred bargaining power from workers to employers, and ushered in an era of labor peace that continues to this day. Since 1968 few man-days have been lost through strikes and other labor actions, and since 1978 there has been no industrial stoppage. (There have been industrial disputes, but all these have been peacefully settled.) Foreign investment has clearly found this labor situation attractive, and the ensuing full employment and rapid growth of real wages have helped keep the peace.[10] The NTUC has therefore become largely a welfare organization for workers. Since 1969 it has concentrated on social, educational, and recreational programs for workers, including childcare and consumer advocacy, and has launched various profitable and professionally managed cooperative enterprises. These have included a number of supermarkets, the largest taxi service on the island, and an insurance company. The NTUC is also represented in tripartite policymaking bodies such as the National Wages Council (NWC) and the National Productivity Council (NPC).

Since the late 1970s the government has, in addition, been instituting some changes to deal with the challenges posed by the increasingly tight labor market and the pressure for economic restructuring. The approach to industrial relations and the methods of wage determination are being decentralized as part of the effort to improve labor-management relations, raise productivity, and make the economy more flexible. Thus, in 1982 the two umbrella industrial unions formed in the late 1960s—the Singapore Industrial Labour Organisation (SILO) and the Pioneer Industries Employees Union (PIEU)—were reconstituted into nine industry-based unions for petroleum workers, electrical and electronics workers, textile and garment workers, and so on. House unions have also been strongly promoted, but not without resistance, and the emerging high-technology industries have been given a boost through amendments to the Trade Unions Act (in 1982) and the Employment Act (in 1984) providing employers with greater flexibility in scheduling labor. For example, employers no longer need to obtain permission from the minister of labor to employ women at night, and twelve-hour shifts (in four-day weeks) are permitted.[11]

These changes have been accompanied by increased government control over the union movement. PAP members of parliament without previous union experience have been appointed to key positions in the NTUC, which has been headed by a cabinet minister since 1978. In effect, the union movement has become "an adjunct of the government," part of the "administrative state" designed to ensure continuing stability (Vasil 1984: 136). In the view of Ong Teng Cheong, a PAP cabinet minister and secretary-general of the NTUC,

> The symbiotic relationship between our party and the NTUC has been the result of the unity of political objectives and the close personal ties of the founders of both the PAP and the NTUC. This relationship must be institutionalised so that continuing rapport between the two organisations can guarantee the well-being of our people. (quoted in Vasil 1984: 136)

In 1985 new PAP members of parliament were thus assigned to work in the trade unions "to gain experience in grass-roots politics" and "acquire a better feel of working class sentiment" (*Singapore Straits Times*, 24 October 1985). Also in 1985, the NTUC launched, with some success, a drive to increase its membership (and, arguably, the segment of the labor force under government control), which had been declining since 1979 (see Lim 1988).

Wages and the Labor Market

In response to the tightening of the labor market in 1972, the government set up the tripartite National Wages Council to formulate annual wage guidelines. These guidelines are not mandatory, but they are fully implemented in public firms and strongly influence wage settlements in private enterprises. The guidelines reduced market fluctuations in wages, narrowed the range of sectoral wage increases, and reduced the differentials across occupations and skills (Pang 1975). Between 1972 and 1978 they sought to promote orderly wage increases and maintain Singapore's international competitiveness in labor-intensive exports. As a result, labor-intensive industries experienced excessive expansion, and growth in productivity declined, especially in manufacturing.[12] Labor shortages thus became worse, and dependence on foreign labor increased, thereby creating a low-wage trap. That is to say, the low wage increases stimulated labor demand but discouraged domestic supply and forced industries to import more foreign workers. In turn, this state of affairs kept wages from increasing. Employers were also discouraged from upgrading their operations, and this delayed the restructuring of the economy.

In 1979 the government responded to the underlying labor shortage by instituting a wage correction, or high-wage policy, to restore wages to market levels, encourage capital-labor substitution and technological upgrading, and reduce dependence on foreign labor. This policy appears to have perceived the relationship between wages and productivity backward. It would be more rational for Singapore to bid labor away from the low-productivity industries if it wants to build a comparative advantage in the capital-intensive sectors. Under the 1979 change, labor costs rose by nearly 20 percent a year for three years, and productivity growth accelerated to 4.6 percent a year between 1979 and 1984. But this was insufficient to reduce dependence on foreign labor, especially in construction, the leader in growth in the early 1980s. A more serious problem was that the high-wage policy sparked a substantial increase in unit labor costs, which reduced Singapore's international competitiveness in relation to that of other Asian NIEs and contributed to the 1985 recession and to the accompanying decline in manufactured exports and employment.

In 1986 the NWC recommended two to three years of severe wage restraint—that is, no increases in wages or fringe benefits—and began stepping up its efforts to increase productivity, hoping thereby to reduce unit labor costs and restore competitiveness. Together with other cost and tax reductions, this policy showed some signs of success, as reflected in the increase in new and expanded foreign investments in 1986 and 1987. Beyond wage restraint, which is a short-run measure, the government is instituting some longer-run changes to make the wage determination system more responsive to the circumstances and performance of individual employers and workers. The move away from across-the-board wage increases actually began in 1981, when the NWC began recommending a range of increases to accord with specific conditions in industries and companies. In 1983 the government reduced its role in the NWC to that of an employer only, and in 1985 it stopped the practice of being the first employer to adopt the council's guidelines. With these moves, the government gradually withdrew from the wage determination process, thus allowing employers or the labor market to get credit for real wage increases. Although the old system may have reaped political benefits, it also made the labor market more inflexible and forced workers to depend on the state.

In 1987 the NWC committee recommended wage reforms that the government subsequently approved and that some of the larger employers proposed to their unions. The most notable reforms are a shift to annual wage negotiations rather than three-year collective agreements, smaller seniority wage increments, and variable bonuses based on company profits and each employee's performance, which are to form a larger component of the wage. Wage bargaining may be based either on profits or on productivity. The NWC will no longer make quantitative recommendations but will become a forum for "reaching a consensus view of the state of the economy" and its outlook every year. In this capacity it will oversee the wage system and foster good industrial relations (Lee 1985a). It is still too early to tell whether these reforms will be widely implemented, although they are being vigorously promoted by Brigadier-General Lee.

The variable admission of foreign labor has been perhaps as important as wage policy in affecting the supply and hence the price of labor. In 1968, the same year that the Employment and Industrial Relations acts were passed, the government relaxed immigration rules to allow employers in Singapore to recruit workers from Malaysia. By 1972 foreign workers accounted for about one in eight workers. Their numbers declined with the 1974–75 recession but picked up again as the labor market tightened in the late 1970s, when workers from nontraditional sources (Indonesia, Thailand, the Philippines, Sri Lanka, and the Indian subcontinent) augmented the traditional supplies from Malaysia. By 1980 up to 11 percent of the labor force consisted of foreign workers (Pang and Lim 1982). In 1981 the government announced that it planned to phase out all foreign labor by 1991 (by 1986 in the manufacturing sector), as part of the desired restructuring out of labor-intensive activities, and special levies were imposed on the wages of foreign workers to discourage their use. Nonetheless, foreign workers, mostly employed in low-skill occupations, accounted for more than half of the growth of the labor force between 1980 and 1984—in large part because of the construction boom during these years.

When the economy—especially construction—went into a slump in 1985–86, tens of thousands of foreign unskilled workers were laid off and returned home. In the face of new concerns about preserving industry and reducing labor costs, and about the unwillingness of Singaporeans to take up many of the unskilled jobs occupied by foreigners, the government decided not to tighten up on foreign labor imports. Rather, it planned to build "a revolving pool of foreign workers on short-term work permits" and to shift from "administrative allocation" to "a more neutral pricing mechanism" to determine the numbers admitted. Labor-short employers in the booming electronics export industry have been not only allowed but encouraged to import foreign labor. Skilled foreign labor has always been liberally admitted, the goal here being "to provide for the retention of skilled workers who can be assimilated as part of our permanent workforce" (Singapore 1986: 105). (In practice these "assimilable" foreign workers have been defined as those of ethnic Chinese origin, from Malaysia, Hong Kong, Macau, and Taiwan, China.)

In its other labor supply policies, the government has moved, since the late 1960s, to promote female participation in the labor force. (For example, it has removed protective restrictions on the employment of female labor and has fostered childcare, part-time work, job sharing, and flexible shifts.) Its goal is to achieve 50 percent female participation by 1995, which is up from the current 46 percent (and the 17 percent at independence). A vigorous pronatalist campaign (including extremely generous tax incentives) is also under way to raise birthrates, which have fallen behind replacement levels, so as to compensate for the rapidly aging population and stave off labor shortages in the future. In addition, the government is promoting the employment of older workers—those over the current retirement age of fifty-five—at lower wages if necessary (Singapore 1986: 105).

Furthermore, the government has invested heavily in Singapore's human resources and continues to do so. In the 1960s it provided primary and secondary education for the growing population, and since the early 1970s educational and training opportunities have been progressively expanded in formal postsecondary and tertiary academic, technical, and vocational institutions. In 1979 it set up the Skills Development Fund (SDF), funded by a 4 percent levy on the wages of low-wage workers, to support the education and training of workers, especially those with few skills, and to help firms invest in new equipment. This move may have distorted resource allocation, artificially cheapening capital in relation to labor and producing the high and rising incremental capital-output ratio noted above. The SDF levy was reduced to 2 percent in 1985 and 1 percent in 1986, and a 2 percent payroll tax was also eliminated, as part of the effort to lower labor costs in the wake of the recession.

The government's economic recovery program includes further plans for preemployment training, postgraduate education, continuing education and training, industry- and employer-based training, professional training, and programs emphasizing "flexible and creative skills" (Singapore 1986: 105). In addition the National Productivity Board (NPB) and other public and private institutions operate a range of programs designed to increase productivity and facilitate the transition from a labor-intensive to a more capital- and skill-intensive industrial structure in which higher value added will, it is hoped, generate higher wages (Tan, Shantakumar, both in You and Lim 1984).

The Central Provident Fund

An institution of great importance in Singapore is the government's Central Provident Fund (CPF), a compulsory savings scheme established in 1955 to provide social security. Initially, the employer and employee each contributed 5 percent of the wage, for a total of 10 percent, which was invested until the worker retired at age fifty-five. In 1968 the contributions were raised to 6.5 percent each. Since then the rates have climbed steadily. They reached 25 percent each, or a total of 50 percent of the wage, in 1984, at which time 77 percent of the labor force was contributing to the CPF. Because labor has consisted, by and large, of young workers and employment has grown rapidly, total CPF funds have swollen to enormous levels (table 3-4). The CPF invests these sums in government bonds, which are used to fund statutory boards and state enterprises or to acquire financial assets abroad.

Table 3-4. Central Provident Fund and Gross Domestic Savings, 1966–85
(thousands of Singapore dollars)

Year	CPF balance	Change in balance	Gross domestic savings	Change as a percentage of savings
1966	416	n.a.	456	n.a.
1967	477	61	515	13
1968	540	63	792	12
1969	632	92	905	12
1970	778	146	1,065	16
1971	988	210	1,260	20
1972	1,316	338	1,976	27
1973	1,771	455	2,959	23
1974	2,414	643	3,548	22
1975	3,235	821	3,820	23
1976	4,066	831	4,644	22
1977	4,945	888	5,200	19
1978	5,981	1,027	5,780	20
1979	7,516	1,535	7,102	27
1980	9,551	2,035	8,723	29
1981	12,150	2,599	10,943	30
1982	15,656	3,506	12,854	32
1983	19,505[a]	3,849	16,282[b]	30
1984	22,670	3,165	18,267	19
1985	26,829	4,159	15,771	23

n.a. Not applicable.
a. CPF Board Annual Report 1985, annex b, p. 32.
b. *Yearbook of Statistics 1985–86*, table 4.2, p. 79.
Sources: CPF Board Annual Report, various years; *Yearbook of Statistics*, various years.

This social security scheme not only costs the government nothing (since workers save for their own retirement), but it also mobilizes domestic savings for the financing of public projects. In the 1960s this enabled the government to build up both its economic and social infrastructure in an inexpensive, noninflationary way, with additional benefits to the workers in the construction of the low-cost public housing units known as Housing Development Board (HDB) apartments. By the late 1970s government surpluses were more than enough to finance public development spending. More and more CPF funds were thus used like foreign reserves, to slow the appreciation of the Singapore dollar and to keep inflation at bay in an era of high wage increases.

Because the fund now serves a multiplicity of goals, its impact on the economy, society, and politics is pervasive and complex, particularly as a result of the changes it has undergone in recent years. After the public outcry against a 1984 proposal to raise the age for the withdrawal of CPF funds from fifty-five to sixty and then to sixty-five, the government agreed to let contributors still withdraw their balances at fifty-five. But it instituted a minimum-balance scheme to ensure that those who use up their withdrawn balances prematurely do not become destitute and thus a burden on the state. To promote filial piety, the government has also introduced a topping-up scheme that allows CPF members to transfer part of their savings or cash to parents over fifty-five years of age as a means of providing support for their old age, thereby further reducing the state's responsibility for social security. For the individual saver, CPF savings are expected to be in excess of postretirement consumption needs, even with retirement and withdrawal remaining at age fifty-five. In other words, the CPF scheme provides more than enough for its members' retirement needs.

Before retirement, contributors may use their CPF balances only to purchase housing or stock in approved public and private companies and to pay hospital bills and some insurance premiums.[13] With the rise in unemployment as a consequence of the 1985–86 recession, the government also considered allowing unemployed citizens to withdraw portions of their CPF balances to meet living expenses during the period of their unemployment. Through the CPF, then, the government ensures that the working population pays for its own social security, health care, housing, and unemployment income, without charge to the government budget (Lim 1987c). The government also uses the fund to control the savings and expenditures of the population, dictating the permissible use and timing of withdrawal of CPF members' funds on the principle, well established in Singapore, that the government knows best—and knows better than the people themselves how they should spend their money.[14]

With the CPF under its control, the government can use these funds to achieve other social or political goals on its agenda, such as its 100 percent home-ownership goal, a cornerstone of the PAP's domestic political strategy. The PAP believes that investing in home ownership will foster social and political stability because it will give ethnically diverse immigrants a clear stake in and commitment to the survival and prosperity of the nation. When the home-ownership scheme started in 1968, the target group was lower-income families in HDB apartments. CPF balances were then used to fund home mortgages for middle-income public housing when the property market became glutted in 1973–74 with units built by the Housing and Urban Development Corporation (HUDC). This service was subsequently extended to private residential properties during the slump of 1977–78. Encouraged by the government not only to purchase housing out of their CPF savings but also to upgrade into bigger and better units, Singaporeans spend a disproportionate amount of their total income on housing, compared with people in other countries. Many are tied down by large mortgages financed from their CPF balances and monthly contributions, which means that they cannot afford to stop working or to malinger. They are thereby indirectly encouraged to fulfill another government goal—promoting hard work and high productivity, as well as high female participation in the labor force (since the savings from two incomes are often needed to afford the high cost of housing).

Another government project supported by the CPF is the COWEC program, which allows employers to deposit part of their contributions to the employees' CPF in a company-held account for company welfare schemes. This was part of the plan to foster company loyalty and improve labor-management relations (with a view to reducing labor turnover and increasing labor productivity) by linking workers' welfare to individual employers instead of to the state (see Lim 1983). Only a few large companies did establish COWEC schemes, which were subsequently cut back in the recession because workers needed their contributions to the schemes to pay their home mortgages after the CPF rates were cut.

Recently the government has begun referring to the CPF as "the nation's nest-egg of last resort," implying that national security depends on it and that therefore a major constitutional change may be in order. The change would be to create an executive president elected independently by the electorate and empowered to veto government expenditure of official reserves (which are bound to contain CPF funds). The proposal, put forth after the PAP lost some voter support in the 1984 general election, represents an attempt by the ruling party to ensure that it will retain some control even if it loses heavily in a subsequent election. Lee Kuan Yew is expected to inaugurate this position when he steps down as prime minister.

In the 1970s the government also started using the CPF as an instrument of macroeconomic policy. Its rates were increased at the same time as NWC wages in order to channel more funds into savings and thereby forestall inflationary surges caused by domestic demand. But the rising CPF rates also added to indirect labor costs and helped erode international competitiveness—problems that culminated in the 1985–86 recession. Despite repeated government protestations to the contrary (even by the prime minister himself), the employers' 25 percent contribution was cut to 10 percent in 1986, leaving the employees' contribution intact, for a total contribution of 35 percent of the wage. This immediately lowered labor costs, as well as workers' savings and income. The government has said that any future increase in the CPF rate will have to be gradual and affordable.

To get a better idea of the impact of the CPF scheme, note first that the outstanding CPF balance—that is, the difference between annual contributions and withdrawals—constitutes a significant fraction of gross national savings (see table 3-4). That ratio rose from 13 percent in 1966 to 32 percent in 1981 but then dropped to 23 percent in 1984. Before the CPF rate cut in 1986, Singapore had both the highest savings ratio (at 42 percent of GDP) and the highest investment ratio in the world. It is thus tempting to conclude that this increased rate of saving helped boost investment and the growth rate. This may be so, but the links are not at all obvious.

In the neoclassical model of a closed economy (where there is no international borrowing and lending and the interest rate is determined purely domestically), savings and investment are directly connected. One can therefore postulate that investment will respond positively to a decline in the rate of interest and that savings will be either inelastic or positively related to the rate of interest. Hence a shift to the right of the savings schedule would lower the rate of interest and increase investment. Full employment would be ensured by flexible wages in the labor market.

Suppose, however, that a Keynesian view is adopted and that output and employment are determined by effective demand, at least in the short run. In such a case the CPF scheme would generate the well-known paradox of thrift. An increase in the propensity to save would shift the investment-savings curve to the left, reducing employment, output, and the rate of interest. As the interest rate fell, investment would increase. To restore full employment, one could either increase government expenditure (or cut taxes) or increase the money supply. An expansionary fiscal policy with the money supply constant would restore full employment but leave investment unchanged, since the rate of interest must remain unchanged. An expansionary monetary policy, however, would lower interest rates and hence raise investment still further. Thus savings would increase once again, in response to the CPF-induced rise in the rate of investment at full employment.

What both of these arguments ignore is that Singapore is highly open to the world capital market and funds are able to move freely in and out of the country at world interest rates. In other words, investment in Singapore, whether by foreign corporations or domestic firms, would be a function of expected profit opportunities in Singapore and the exogenously given world rate of interest. The CPF scheme, by raising labor costs in Singapore and leaving the rate of interest unchanged at its world level, would tend to *reduce*, rather than increase, the level of investment in the country. Since it would also increase saving, there would clearly be a contractionary effect on aggregate demand, which would have to be compensated through a decline in net imports—by a reduction in foreign borrowing or an increase in government expenditure, assuming constant tax rates—for full employment to be restored. If full employment is maintained, except for temporary aberrations, the necessary compensatory government expenditure will likely crowd out *both* private investment and private consumption under the CPF scheme. In short, the scheme expands the role of the government in the economy.

To the extent that the government expenditure consists of social overhead capital or infrastructure payments—for example, for the airports, seaports, and inland transport systems—it can be argued that these public development expenditures help make Singapore an even more attractive manufacturing and financial center and thus encourage greater private investment in the long run. It is only in this somewhat roundabout and tenuous way that the CPF scheme appears to increase private investment in Singapore. Note, too, that with the gradual increase in public sector surpluses, there is less need for CPF funds for public infrastructure, even as the CPF contribution rates have been rising. One troubling aspect of this expenditure is the monumental scale of the public buildings being constructed in the city-state, which add to the extremely high incremental capital-output ratio noted earlier. There is also some question as to whether the investment of publicly managed funds is more productive than private investment, especially in view of Singapore's already well-developed economy. Some might argue, in addition, that when the government encouraged home ownership for social and political reasons, it diverted excessive savings into nonproductive expenditure for consumption (of housing services) and inflated home property values. After these values crashed in 1985–86, the investment was lost and growth declined sharply.

Interestingly, many Singaporeans interviewed in 1984 said they strongly objected to raising the CPF withdrawal age because they wanted to use their retirement balances for productive purposes—most commonly, to start a business and to fund their children's higher education abroad. Such investments in business and human capital should result in higher growth and productivity. Most seemed to think that they could obtain a higher return on their forced savings than the government had. (This may not be true, of course, for if the government offered a lower return on CPF funds, it would also offer lower risk on the investment of those funds.)

The 1986 cut in the CPF rate and the move to put CPF savings to wider use are in line with the government's growing interest in liberalization and privatization and in letting market forces play a greater role in the economy. But the authorities have not ruled out future increases in the CPF rate or suggested that they are considering privatizing CPF management itself, even though they hope to make Singapore a leading center of funds management. The government also continues to emphasize home ownership. More important, it is unlikely to relinquish the social, political, or economic control the CPF bestows. This multipurpose institution and policy instrument, together with its sometimes conflicting goals and functions, is likely to remain intact.

The Government Budget

The government's increasing role in the economy over the years is also reflected in the budget. Between 1966 and the early 1980s revenue from all sources rose from about 17 percent of GDP to 30 percent. During this time current expenditure remained constant (at about 15 percent of GDP), whereas development expenditure doubled its share of GDP (from 6 to 12 percent). Public housing takes the highest proportion of development expenditure (see Asher in You and Lim 1984).

The share of current expenditure in GDP is about the same as in Taiwan (China), and slightly higher than in Korea, but the share of revenue is much higher than in either of the other two economies. Revenue in Singapore exceeds current expenditure by as much as 15 percent of GDP. This is sufficient not only to cover development expenditures but also to accumulate huge cash balances and foreign assets when combined with borrowing against the increments in CPF balances. From 1979 to 1982 the government recorded cumulative surpluses (of revenue over both current and development expenditure) of S$1.3 billion, borrowed S$6.6 billion, presumably from CPF balances, and thus accumulated a total of about S$8 billion in domestic currency and foreign exchange. Even larger surpluses were accumulated between 1982 and 1985.

Singapore is able to accumulate such large surpluses for, basically, two reasons. First, the government's philosophy is that thrift is a virtue and saving is good, whereas spending is not. This might in part reflect the insecurity of a small nation heavily dependent on the world market. This phenomenon has been described as "saving for a rainy day," or having reserves to fall back on in case "the oasis becomes a desert overnight." Confucian traditions may also be involved—note the similarity with Taiwan (China)—or it may simply be the prestige associated with having strong external reserves.

More important, the sterilization of CPF balances as foreign reserves offsets the inflationary effect of large inflows of direct foreign investment, which help create balance of payments surpluses despite persistently large trade deficits. The purpose here is to maintain internal equilibrium, external equilibrium at a stable exchange rate, and high growth rates and employment without inflation. Government over-borrowing via the CPF has a deflationary effect in that it absorbs excess liquidity. The Monetary Authority of Singapore (MAS) intervenes when it supplies Singapore dollars to buy up the foreign currencies brought in as capital inflow. This offsets the drain on public liquidity, increases official reserves of foreign exchange, and retards the appreciation of the exchange rate (Low 1985a). Singapore's external reserves are believed to be worth twice the official estimates; they are invested in foreign assets by the Government of Singapore Investment Corporation (GSIC).

Public Housing and Land Policy

When the PAP government took office in 1959, 8.8 percent of the population was living in the 10,907 public housing units that had been constructed by the colonial government since 1947.[15] The Housing Development Board (HDB) was established in 1960, and by 1965 about 23.2 percent of the population was housed in 54,430 units under its management. In 1985 these figures were far higher, with 84 percent of the population in 551,767 units, 75 percent of them owner-occupied. The term "public housing" is therefore something of a misnomer in Singapore. (Although public housing residents may own equity in the units they inhabit, their ownership rights are restricted in comparison with those of owners of fully private property.) Housing is the largest single item of government development expenditure, accounting for about 40 percent of the total. The share of public residential buildings in total real gross domestic fixed capital formation grew from 6.6 percent in 1965 to a peak of 13.1 percent in 1983 but then dropped to 11.4 percent in 1984.

In recent years the HDB has run current and sometimes overall surpluses. Early on, most public housing was subsidized for low-income groups, but the HDB gradually began providing profit-making housing for middle- and upper-income groups as well. In 1985, for example, housing subsidies for HDB flats (excluding land costs) amounted to S$700 for a three-room unit and S$5,400 for a four-room unit, rising to negative subsidies (profits) of S$10,600 for a five-room improved unit and S$25,200 for an executive apartment. Home ownership for residents at all income levels is financed out of their CPF savings accounts, as explained earlier.

Like the CPF, the public housing program has served a multiplicity of goals beyond the obvious one of meeting a basic social need. In doing so, the government has won a great deal of political support, which may be tempered in the long run by the population's growing dependence on the government and their resentment of controls effected through the HDB. The provision of public housing in the context of large-scale urban resettlement has enabled the government to manipulate the composition of electoral constituencies and thus disperse political opposition. It has also helped to foster ethnic and social integration, and even a national identity, by breaking down traditional patterns of residential segregation and by developing a common HDB life-style. Home ownership has been promoted as a means of achieving political and social stability, and the allocation of public housing has been used as an incentive or disincentive to promote desired kinds of behavior or to discourage undesired ones, particularly with respect to limiting family size and encouraging the three-generation family.

Public housing developments have also become the basis of new forms of social organization and political mobilization. For example, residents' committees led by PAP supporters are now involved in political as well as administrative affairs, and such involvement is likely to increase under the proposed elected town councils that would decentralize responsibility for running these housing developments. If the town councils are taken over by opposition parties, public housing will move to the center of the political arena.[16]

The economic effects of Singapore's public housing program are equally complex. In the early days, public housing subsidized private wages, thereby stimulating employment and probably raising worker productivity, as well as living standards. The construction of public housing itself directly created employment, with further effects on the economy, and it has been used countercyclically. The HDB also built and managed industries in densely populated housing estates, thereby helping to meet the demand for and supply of labor. The impact on private investment and growth was probably positive when housing was largely complementary with private production and consumption, but more recently crowding-out effects may have had a negative effect on private investment.

The effect on income distribution is clearly progressive in that public housing has accounted for a much larger proportion of low-income than of high-income households. Indeed, the Land Acquisition Act empowering the government to acquire land for public purposes without providing full market compensation has been referred to as a "Robin Hood act" by the prime minister himself. It has in effect redistributed land across the board for the benefit of the masses. As mentioned earlier, the government now owns about 75 percent of the land in Singapore.

Public housing is part of the government's broader land-use policy, which includes comprehensive planning and development of land for other public purposes (transport, industrial complexes, educational institutions, recreational and community facilities, and the like). The government also approves and oversees private land use and property development. Because of its large presence in the land and property market, it has been the direct cause of many problems, such as the overbuilding of the early 1980s, the slump in the property market of the mid-to-late 1980s, and the subsequent effect on the rest of the economy, including the labor market.

Direct Foreign Investment

Unlike many other countries in the developing world that have encouraged foreign investment, Singapore has been extremely successful with its strategy of industrialization by invitation.[17] Some believe that Singapore has been able to produce results because its policies were implemented more thoroughly, and with a high standard of integrity.

The main inducements to foreign investment are Singapore's political and financial stability, free trade and capital flows, welcoming government, speedy and efficient processing of investment applications, excellent physical and social infrastructure, strategic geographic location, peaceful labor relations and disciplined labor force, and various tax and other incentives for pioneering projects. These conditions have not changed for the past two decades, although some other factors have. The large, low-cost labor force of the late 1960s has been replaced by more educated, skilled, experienced, and efficient workers, and government investment incentives now put less emphasis on labor-intensive production and more on capital- and skill-intensive activities, including research and development. Singapore also has a budding supplier industry.

Despite its small size, Singapore typically ranks among the top twenty recipients of foreign investment in the world in absolute terms. In the early 1980s it accounted for nearly half of all the foreign investment that went to Asia as a whole (it received about five times more than China in a typical year). More than two-thirds of the U.S. Fortune 100 companies are represented in Singapore, and the well-known multinationals there include Philips of the Netherlands, Siemens of Germany, Ciba-Geigy of Switzerland, General Electric of the United States, and Hitachi of Japan.

Foreign investment became a vital source of the capital, technology, entrepreneurship, and managerial and financial expertise that Singapore required for industrialization. Foreign investment also provided the access to foreign markets Singapore needed to make its export-oriented strategy for industrialization work. Output, employment, and industrial diversification have expanded much more rapidly than would have been the case without foreign investment.

One-third of all firms in Singapore are owned wholly or in large part by foreign establishments, and foreign funds amounted to 40 percent of all investments in the island in 1981. At the end of 1983, more than S$20 billion worth of foreign funds were invested there, 90 percent of which were in the form of direct investment and the remainder in portfolio investment. The rapid influx of foreign investments in the 1970s did not crowd out local investments, which, on the contrary, multiplied nearly tenfold, from S$2.9 billion in 1970 to S$28.9 billion in 1981, in part because of local links created by the foreign enterprises (see, for example, Lim and Pang 1982).

Nearly half of the foreign funds flowed into manufacturing. The amount increased from less than S$100 million in the mid-1960s to well over S$1 billion a year in the 1980s (S$1.8 billion in 1984, S$1.1 billion in the recession year of 1985, S$1.4 billion in 1986, and about S$1.7 billion in 1987). The cumulative total of gross fixed assets is more than S$10 billion. Most of the foreign investments went into the petroleum industry (42 percent of gross fixed assets in manufacturing in 1980), electronics (16 percent), transport equipment and oil rigs (4.5 percent), and precision equipment (4.2 percent). Foreign funds have also flowed into finance and business services and trade.

In 1981 Britain, the United States, Hong Kong, Malaysia, and Japan (in that order) accounted for four-fifths of the foreign equity invested in Singapore. Since then, new investments have come mainly from the United States, followed at a distance by Japan. The average return on foreign capital invested between 1970 and 1981 was 18 percent; it fell in the first half of the 1980s to below OECD levels but has since risen. Large U.S. and British investors whose equity was concentrated in high value added manufacturing reaped returns averaging 19 percent a year, compared with 13 percent for Asian investors, who were interested primarily in small trading firms and in low value added, labor-intensive manufacturing. Between 1970 and 1981 foreign investors earned S$3.2 billion in Singapore and sent out about 60 percent of these earnings—a significant amount, but small in comparison with the S$16.8 billion they brought into the island over this period. Since foreign investments in Singapore are also highly export-oriented, particularly in manufacturing, they have contributed substantially to Singapore's balance of payments surpluses since the late 1960s.[18]

Manufacturing is heavily dominated by foreign capital: in 1984 wholly or majority-owned firms and joint ventures accounted for 71 percent of output, 82 percent of direct exports, and 53 percent of employment and manufacturing. The proportions are higher if minority-owned firms are included. Foreign firms are much more export oriented and have higher value added than local firms. Manufacturing as a whole has become more capital- and skill-intensive, and value added per worker in manufacturing foreign investments has increased, in response to changing local resources and government policy favoring high-technology industries in the 1980s. Singapore is still one of the top world producers of such items as processed petroleum products, oil rigs, semiconductors, computer disk drives, and printed circuit boards, produced mainly in wholly owned foreign subsidiaries.

The share of foreign enterprise in the local economy is reflected in Singapore's "indigenous GDP," or GDP less income earned by foreign firms and individuals. This indigenous share fell from about 90 percent in 1966 to about 75 percent in the early 1980s. Thus, although the strategy of using direct foreign investment as an engine of economic growth has brought benefits in the form of higher levels of employment, productivity, and living standards for the people, it also makes their prosperity increasingly dependent on decisions by foreign firms. Layoffs and reduced investments by multinationals in the 1985 recession, although quickly reversed in 1986, indicate how vulnerable the economy is to a loss of international competitiveness. Dependence on foreign investment also means that the government must control and modify many aspects of social and economic life to ensure a favorable climate for investors.

All the same, the government continues to view foreign investment and exports as crucial to Singapore's economic success. The Economic Committee Report affirms that one of the state's primary goals is to make Singapore an international business center and exporter of both services and manufactures and to create a better business environment and obtain a higher rate of return on capital than in the OECD countries. The experience of the recession has also led to a greater emphasis on nurturing local firms, as well as on attracting and keeping multinationals. The Small Enterprises Bureau set up in the Economic Development Board is expected to help local firms, and the investment promotion agency is trying to attract new foreign investment. Local firms, both state and private, are also being exhorted to invest abroad and become more multinational in their activities (see Pang and Komaran 1985).

Welfare and Income Distribution

Rapid economic growth and expanding employment enabled Singapore to raise the incomes and economic welfare of the population at large.[19] The unemployment rate dropped from 8.9 percent in 1966 to 2.7 percent in 1984 but rose to 4.6 percent in 1986 as a consequence of the 1985–86 recession. By 1984 per capita income had grown by 11 times since 1960 (4.4 times in real terms) and by 5.2 times since 1970 (2.3 times in real terms). The per capita income of US$6,800 and per capita indigenous income of US$6,200 in 1984 caused Singapore to rank in the top quarter of the world's nations by income (twenty-second in 1983), ahead of such European countries as Spain, Portugal, Greece, Italy, and Ireland. Absolute poverty has declined, as indicated by a 1983 survey. Among the poorest 4.8 percent of households (those earning less than S$500 a month, at a time when the poverty level was S$394 a month), 81.1 percent had a television, 55.6 percent had a telephone, 19.3 percent had a washing machine, 13.2 percent had a motorcycle or scooter, 6.2 percent had a videocassette recorder, 1.2 percent had an air conditioner, and 0.8 percent had a piano or organ and a car (Singapore 1982). Two other important factors that contributed to the reduction in poverty were Singapore's smaller families and increased employment.

Various social indicators besides income have shown great improvement since 1960 (see Lim 1987a). The infant mortality rate has fallen by three-quarters and now, at 9.3 deaths per thousand births, is below that of many industrial nations—notably, the United States, Belgium, Austria, Italy, and New Zealand. Life expectancy at birth (seventy years for males, seventy-five for females) is comparable with that of industrial nations, and per capita caloric supply was 115 percent of the average daily requirement in 1983, the same as in Japan and the Scandinavian countries. The principal medical problems among twelve-year-old schoolchildren in 1985 were defective vision (35 percent) and obesity (11 percent of all males), and the main causes of adult death were heart disease and cancer. The literacy rate rose from 72 percent in 1970 to 84 percent in 1980 (more than 90 percent of those under the age of thirty-five), and 60.5 percent of the literate population was literate in two or more official languages. The proportion of the labor force with a secondary education or better also rose, from 28 percent in 1974 to 46 percent in 1980. And 84 percent of the population, and a higher proportion of the lower-income households, live in public housing, a fact that has had a progressive impact on the distribution of housing.

Turning to income distribution, the increase in the shares of government and foreigners in Singapore's GDP has already been mentioned.

Between 1966 and 1984 government revenue rose from 18 to 30 percent of GDP, and the foreign share of GNP rose from 9 percent in 1966 to nearly 20 percent in 1985. The share of wages in GDP rose from 37 percent in 1972 to 46 percent in 1984 (after a slight dip through 1974), whereas the share of profits and rents fell from 54 to 45 percent, after reaching a peak in 1984. In manufacturing, the share of wages in value added fell from about 38 percent in 1965 to about 30 percent in 1980, then rose to 36 percent in 1984 (Singapore 1984: table 1). This rise is apparently the result of the high-wage policy of the early 1980s.

By one estimate, the personal distribution of income, as measured by Gini coefficients, improved from 0.498 in 1966 to 0.448 in 1975 (Rao and Ramakrishnan 1980). By another estimate, they moved from 0.40 in 1972–73 to 0.37 in 1977–78 (Pang 1982: chs. 5 and 6). The magnitude and trend of these figures is similar to those in the other Asian NIEs—Taiwan (China), Korea, and Hong Kong. But the Gini ratio for household income (from the household expenditure survey) decreased from 0.41 in 1972–73 to 0.46 in 1982–83, and the L-index for income distribution by occupation and education (from the labor force survey) worsened in 1982 and 1983 (Islam and Kirkpatrick 1986).

The earlier decline in income inequality was the result of the tremendous increase in low-skill jobs (especially for young and female workers) in labor-intensive, export-manufacturing industries during the rapid growth of the 1960s and 1970s. This made full employment possible. The National Wages Council may also have narrowed wage differentials or prevented them from widening. The apparent worsening of income inequality in the first half of the 1980s probably reflects the particular pattern of economic growth in those years—specifically, the simultaneous rapid expansion of financial and business services employing highly paid, highly educated professionals and of construction employing poorly paid, poorly educated workers, including a large proportion of foreign workers. The government's high-wage policy (which in absolute terms would favor higher-income workers receiving the same percentage wage increase as lower-income workers) and the large upward revision of public sector salaries in 1981–82 may also have affected income inequality.

Factors likely to influence future income distribution include the massive retrenchment and return home of foreign workers in the still-depressed construction sector; the (perhaps temporary) softening of the labor market for certain categories of educated professional workers; the recurring shortages of production workers—especially female workers for booming high-technology export industries; the apparent liberalization of foreign labor supply; and the policy of short-term wage restraints and long-run wage reform in the direction of more flexible and variable wages. On the whole, these factors are likely to create more disparity in incomes, which will be accentuated by recent increases in medical and tuition fees and the likely shift in several years to an item-specific consumption tax. Although because of a progressive system, the posttax distribution of income has heretofore been less unequal than the pretax distribution, recent tax cuts and extremely generous tax rebates to married couples with larger families will probably reduce this progressive effect.[20]

Figures on the ethnic distribution of income indicate that Indians had the highest per capita income in 1966, but the Chinese displaced them in 1974. Malays have always been a rather poor third, although they did have the fastest gain over the 1974–79 period (Pang 1982: chs. 5 and 6). Between 1966 and 1974 Malay mean incomes fell from 84 to 65 percent of Chinese mean incomes, but they had increased to 70 percent of the Chinese mean by 1979. These differences are a function of educational attainment and occupational distribution (which is gradually improving for the Malays), rather than discrimination.

Income distribution by sex has not improved, despite the narrowing of the male-female gap in educational attainment and despite (or because of) the large increase in female labor force participation, from 18 percent in 1957 to 26 percent in 1970 to 46 percent in 1985. Women earn slightly more than half of what men earn, on average. One reason for the differential is that women entered the labor force only recently, and therefore their average age and seniority are lower. Furthermore, sex-segregated, often dead-end, female occupations are overcrowded, and women have a shorter average working life (and more interruptions during it on account of family duties; see Lim 1982, 1988). The current government policies promoting larger families, if successful, are likely to increase income inequality between the sexes since they emphasize motherhood and force employers to discriminate if they are unwilling to bear the costs of frequent childbearing by employees.

Rapid economic growth and greater employment, together with social policies such as public housing, have substantially increased real incomes and the standard of living in Singapore and have virtually eliminated absolute poverty, which, in a full-employment economy, is largely confined to the elderly and disabled. Income distribution improved through 1981 but deteriorated somewhat from 1982 to 1984, in part because of the shift away from labor-intensive export manufacturing. The future pattern of income distribution is as yet unclear, but many signs point to a likely deterioration.

The Political Economy of Affluence

The PAP has completely dominated the politics of independent Singapore. It won *all* the parliamentary seats in general elections in 1968, 1972, 1976, and 1980, lost one seat in a by-election in 1981, and won all but two seats in the seventy-nine-seat legislature in the general elections of 1984.[21] The party won only 64 percent of all votes cast in 1984, however, which was lower than its usual 75 percent or better share of the vote in previous elections. This turn of events has prompted the prime minister to issue periodic statements about the dangers of the one-man, one-vote electoral system which had hitherto served the party well.

It is generally agreed that the PAP retained its mandate in the past because the economy performed so well under its leadership, although some have also pointed to factors such as the apolitical nature of the Chinese and their Confucian attitude toward government, the government's tight political control and people's fears of going against it, and the fragmented and harassed opposition parties that leave voters no choice. Yet PAP popularity declined in 1984, a boom year for the economy. Voters may have been disgruntled by the social policies announced that year (but subsequently, and significantly, withdrawn), which, among other things, proposed raising the CPF withdrawal age and promoted motherhood. But postelection surveys suggested deeper dissatisfaction—especially among younger, more educated voters who now form a larger proportion of the electorate and who seem to want the government to be less intrusive, authoritarian, and arrogant and more responsive, participatory, and liberal. With economic security apparently ensured, voters began calling for more freedom and democracy and for a respite from paternalism and stifling controls.

The recession that followed hard on the heels of the election stirred up further dissatisfaction, particularly with the government's management of the economy. People who had previously allowed the government some credit for the economy's success and their own prosperity were now ready to complain, for they were unaccustomed to the economic distress that befell them. Local businessmen, in particular, blamed their difficulties on excessive regulation, government control over the economy, the competition private firms had to face from public enterprises, the favoring of multinationals, and poor labor, industrial, and property market policies. Some also resented the arrogance and elitism of civil servants; they did not like being dependent on the government for so many aspects of daily life, from housing and transport to education, employment, and television. As the recession deepened, other angry voices rose up—small businessmen who had gone bankrupt, workers who had lost their jobs, school-leavers and university graduates who could not easily find employment to match their expectations and the experience of previous cohorts, and property owners (most of the population!) who found themselves burdened with huge mortgages on properties that were falling in value.

The policies instituted to get Singapore out of the recession, however necessary from an economic point of view, may not have significantly boosted the government's popular support. Although multinationals approved of the cuts in costs and taxes, many local businessmen viewed them as too little, too late, as pointed out earlier. Wage restraint is never popular, especially among labor unions, and the CPF reduced not only workers' real earnings but also the forced savings with which home-buyers financed their mortgages.

Many, however, did seem to approve of deregulation, privatization, and greater support for local private enterprise. But the government is in for some rough sailing here, although it supports these developments in principle and has taken several steps in these directions. Contradictions remain that go beyond mere problems of technical implementation. For one thing, the political leadership is determined to keep the nation's best talents employed in the public sector. As the prime minister is reported to have said (see *Singapore Business Times*, 20 October 1986):

Most of our enterprises have been in the public sector because the public sector had the able men. We have the trained scholars who came back. We staffed these organisations. We built them up. When we say private sector, my next question is: Who in the private sector? Only a few Singaporeans have risen to the top of local offices of [American multinationals]. They can be counted on the fingers of one hand, not even of two hands.[22]

This statement reveals the fundamental assumptions that have weakened the private sector in Singapore. Chief among them is the belief that academic success and an elite education abroad are what produce able men and entrepreneurs and that only Singaporeans who have risen to the top of local offices of American firms are capable private entrepreneurs. As long as this attitude prevails and the government continues to monopolize the island's scarce best talents, it will be difficult to revitalize the economy with vigorous small and large local private enterprises, such as those that are dominant in Taiwan (China), Korea, and Hong Kong. It is probably not coincidental that Singapore has been falling behind these economies in competitiveness.

Another problem for the government is that genuine privatization will mean the loss of economic, political, and social control. Reluctance to surrender this control (or power) will likely retard and limit the privatization process itself and is probably the main reason that two otherwise excellent candidates—public housing and the CPF—are not being considered for privatization, whereas less important ones (such as education, health, and rapid transit) are. In any event, few state enterprises or institutions—certainly none of the important ones—will be completely privatized; even if the government does not retain a majority share, it will most likely still have the largest share and a controlling say in the privatized venture. Thus its control over private capital invested in previously public organizations might actually expand.

In the political arena the government is also faced with the challenge of responding to the presumed desire for greater liberalization without relinquishing control at a time when its continued popularity among voters is uncertain. Searching habitually for bureaucratic solutions and eager to reduce the population's dependence on the state (which, as previously discussed, is a double-edged sword), the PAP recently proposed that elected town councils be established to decentralize the management of public housing constituencies. It also suggested that members of parliament be elected in teams of three, so as to represent adjacent constituencies, rather than individual ones. Within Parliament itself, nine government parliamentary committees, each specializing in a specific area, have been formed to give PAP backbenchers a greater say in the formulation of government policy.

All these measures appear to be aimed at decentralizing power in the Singapore political system, and it remains to be seen how far they will go toward achieving this aim. Already the younger generation of PAP leaders has worked to develop a more consultative style, beginning with the activities of the Economic Committee chaired by Brigadier-General Lee Hsien Loong and with the establishment of a special feedback unit to receive citizens' comments on public policy. In February 1987 the PAP launched a nationwide debate to develop the party's national agenda for its November convention. The agenda was discussed with people throughout Singapore, at small meetings, large dialogue sessions, and public forums, all geared toward "seeking a national consensus on the most important issues facing Singapore and the best ways to deal with them" (*Singapore Straits Times*, 19 February 1987). The issues included race, religion, defense, nation building and the fundamental strategies that have underpinned Singapore's success.

The new generation of PAP leaders—including both Deputy Prime Minister Goh Chok Tong and Brigadier-General Lee—speak frequently of the need to develop a bond with the new electorate of younger, more mature and sophisticated Singaporeans. Many of these individuals have been educated or have traveled or lived abroad and will be demanding more from the government than merely good economic performance. Economic growth itself is bound to slow down in the rapidly maturing economy, so that other factors must develop to bind the political leadership with the people. The PAP leaders know that they must win the trust and the faith of the electorate in order to stay in power. So far they have shown less of a willingness to have trust and faith in the population itself—in its ability to run a successful private economy and a full-fledged political democracy—despite the population's considerably advanced education, experience of the world, and technical and business skills accumulated over the past twenty years.

The paradox of PAP policy is that it is constantly exhorting the population to be resourceful, adaptable, and responsible, while continuing to regard Singapore citizens as politically fickle and economically irrational creatures requiring the constant supervision of technocratic mandarins to prevent them from making the wrong choices. It is up to an increasingly wealthy and sophisticated population to demonstrate to the PAP leadership that its paternalism is becoming an obstacle to the full development of the people's talent and creativity.

Conclusion

Singapore, a nation reluctantly born out of political turmoil, achieved remarkable economic success by relying on a combination of external market forces and government policies, both of which influenced domestic prices and resource allocation and ensured political and social stability. These factors promoted economic development in the 1960s and 1970s. In the 1980s the external markets became more complex and uncertain, and many government policies began to outrun their usefulness. As a result, the state's role in the economy retarded rather than stimulated growth. Together, these factors produced the severe recession of 1985–86, which led the government to pursue recovery through new policy directions.

How Singapore will meet these new challenges will certainly differ from the methods applied in other economies because of the way the government works there: "It formulates policies on purely rational, logical bases. . . . Firstly, there are no pressure groups. . . . Secondly, there are no ideological preconceptions. . . . We cannot afford to be doctrinaire in our approach. Thirdly, where emotions clash with logic and practicality, in Singapore emotions usually give way" (Lee 1985b).

Singapore's leaders recognize that the economy is at a turning point, requiring fundamental shifts in the direction of development policy. With the development of local resources, especially human resources, over the past two decades, the government no longer needs to play a strong role in the economy. Deregulation and privatization are the "rational, logical" policy choices here. Politically, affluence and the increased education and sophistication of the population make the controls favored by the government in the past both unpalatable and unnecessary. Liberalization and democratization are the "rational, logical" policy choices in this area. In other words, Singapore will be unable to go forward smoothly into the 1990s and the twenty-first century unless it dismantles many of the policies and institutions that have served it well in the past. The government recognizes the path that it must follow and has initiated many of the necessary policy shifts. Doubt remains, however, about the extent to which the government will remain committed to carrying out these policies in a more than merely cosmetic way if old habits and emotions, and even pressure groups and ideological preconceptions, should intervene.

Notes

1. In 1963 Indonesia's President Sukarno launched an undeclared war to protest the formation of Malaysia in 1963. The confrontation, which included

bombings in Singapore and a boycott of Singapore's port facilities, ended when Sukarno was deposed by the current president, General Suharto, in 1965.

2. At the trough of the recession in the second quarter of 1986, unemployment rose to 6.5 percent, but recovery in the latter part of the year brought it down to 4.5 percent by the end of the year.

3. This section draws heavily on Pang and Chan (1987) and Lim (1987b).

4. Interview in *This Singapore* (1975: 34).

5. The unfavorable external circumstances included the oil and commodity price slump that hit tourism, shipping, and entrepôt trade, as well as the petroleum and shipbuilding industries; a temporary downturn in the world market for electronics; and intensifying competition in the export of international financial services.

6. The subcommittees were for manufacturing, services, banking and financial services, international trade, local businesses, entrepreneurship development, fiscal and financial policy, and manpower. When further subcommittees that report to these main subcommittees are included, close to 1,000 individuals were involved.

7. This section draws heavily on Pang and Chan (1987) and Lim (1983).

8. Singapore employs a much higher proportion of the labor force than do other countries of the Association of Southeast Asian Nations, the Republic of Korea, Taiwan (China), or Hong Kong.

9. It is widely believed that strikes are illegal in Singapore, but this is so only once the minister of labor determines that a dispute should go before the Industrial Arbitration Court.

10. Because of low or negative inflation, real wages rose by 3 percent in 1985 and 1986, despite nominal wage restraints.

11. For more on the recent changes in the industrial relations system, see Lim and Pang (1984), Smith (1982), Tan (in You and Lim 1984), and Wilkinson and Leggett (1985).

12. Manufacturing productivity rose by more than 9 percent a year in the late 1960s but by only 3 percent a year between 1970 and 1978. Total productivity grew by only 2–3 percent a year in the late 1970s, half the rate in the late 1960s.

13. Hospital bills are paid via the Medisave account, which takes up 6 percent of the wage. Medisave is not an insurance scheme, for it affords protection only in proportion to the individual's actual contribution.

14. The people themselves seem to disagree with this paternalistic assumption, as shown by their objection to the raising of the withdrawal age (see Lim 1987c).

15. This section draws on Lim (1987a).

16. After the general elections of 1984, the government threatened to withdraw state-provided services from public housing constituencies voting for opposition members of parliament, but this did not happen.

17. For some recent studies on foreign investment in Singapore, see Tan (1984), and Chia (1985).

18. Singapore typically runs large merchandise trade deficits, which are more than offset by large surpluses on the service account and the capital account. This allows it to accumulate surpluses in the balance of payments.

19. This section draws heavily on Lim (1988).

20. Since the rebates are based on income tax liabilities, they will benefit those who pay higher taxes more than those who pay lower taxes. A tax rebate of

S$20,000 is being offered for a newborn third child, plus an additional rebate for workers amounting to 15 percent of their earned income.

21. Voting is compulsory in Singapore, but typically many constituencies are not contested by the opposition, and the government wins in a walkover.

22. The "trained scholars" refer to students sent abroad for university education on government scholarships. Quoted in *Singapore Business Times*, 20 October 1986.

References

Chia, Siow Yue. 1985. "The Role of Foreign Trade and Investment in the Development of Singapore." In Walter Galenson, ed., *Foreign Trade and Investment, Economic Growth in the Asian Newly-Industrializing Countries*. Madison: University of Wisconsin Press.

Daniel, Patrick. 1986. "When the Government Is Both Planner and Player." *Singapore Straits Times*, 22 October.

Drysdale, John. 1984. *Singapore: Struggle for Success*. Singapore: Times Books.

Goh, Keng Swee. 1973. "Investment for Development: Lessons and Experience of Singapore, 1959 to 1971." Paper presented at the Third Economic Development Seminar on Investment for Development, Saigon, Viet Nam.

Islam, Iyanatul, and Colin Kirkpatrick. 1986. "Export-Led Development, Labour Market Conditions and the Distribution of Income: The Case of Singapore." *Cambridge Journal of Economics* 10(2):113–28.

Kassalow, E. M. 1978. "Aspects of Labour Relations in Multinational Enterprises: An Overview of Three Asian Countries." *International Labour Review* 3:273–87.

Lee, Hsien Loong. 1985a. "Flexible Wages: A Future Scenario." *Speeches, a Bimonthly Selection of Ministerial Speeches* 9(5). Singapore: Ministry of Communications and Information.

Lee, Kuan Yew. 1978. "Extrapolating from the Singapore Experience." Paper presented at the 26th World Congress of International Chambers of Commerce, Orlando, Fla. Reprinted in Singapore, Ministry of Culture, *Speeches*.

Lee, Soo Ann. 1984. "Patterns of Economic Structure in Singapore." In You Poh Seng and Lim Chong Yah, eds., *Singapore: Twenty-Five Years of Development*. Singapore: Nan Yang Xing Zhou Lianhe Zaobao.

———. 1985b. "Logic and Emotion in Politics." Speech delivered at the 15th anniversary dinner of the Harvard Club of Singapore. Reprinted in *Speeches, A Bi-monthly Selection of Ministerial Speeches* 9(2). Singapore: Ministry of Communications and Information.

Lim, Linda Y. C. 1982. *Women in the Singapore Economy*. Economic Research Centre Occasional Paper Series 5. Singapore: Chopmen.

———. 1983. "Singapore's Success: The Myth of the Free Market Economy. *Asian Survey* 23(6):752–64.

———. 1987a. "An Analysis of Social Welfare in Singapore." In Kernial Singh Sandhu and Paul Wheatley, eds., *Singapore: The Management of Success*. Singapore: Institute of Southeast Asian Studies.

———. 1987b. "Capital, Labor and the State in the Internationalization of High-Tech Industry: The Case of Singapore." Paper prepared for the Conference on

Transnational Capital and Urbanization on the Pacific Rim, Center for Pacific Rim Studies, University of California at Los Angeles.

———. 1987c. "Social Welfare in Singapore." In Kernial Singh Sandhu and Paul Wheatley, eds., *Singapore: The Management of Success*. Singapore: Institute of Southeast Asian Studies.

———. 1988. "Export-Led Industrialisation, Labour Welfare and International Labour Standards." In Lionel Demery and Tony Addison, eds., *Wages and Labour Conditions in the Newly Industrialising Countries of Asia*. London: Overseas Development Institute.

Lim, Linda Y. C., and Pang Eng Fong. 1982. "Vertical Linkages and Multinational Enterprises in Developing Countries." *World Development* 10(7):585–95.

———. 1984. "Labour Strategies for Meeting the High-Tech Challenge: The Case of Singapore." *Euro-Asia Business Review* 3(2):27–31.

Low, Linda. 1985a. "The Financing Process in the Public Sector." *Bulletin for International Fiscal Documentation* 39(4).

———. 1985b. "Privatisation Policies and Issues in Singapore." Staff Seminar Paper 7. National University of Singapore, Department of Economics.

Minchin, James. 1986. *No Man Is an Island: A Study of Singapore's Lee Kuan Yew*. Sydney, Australia: Allen and Unwin.

Pang, Eng Fong. 1975. "Growth, Inequality and Race in Singapore." *International Labour Review* 3:15–28.

———. 1982. *Education, Manpower and Development in Singapore*. Singapore: Singapore University Press.

Pang, Eng Fong, and Heng Chee Chan. 1987. "The Political Economy of Development in Singapore 1959–1986." In Pang Eng Fong and Chan Heng Chee, eds., *The Political Economy of Development in ASEAN*. Singapore: Institute of Southeast Asian Studies.

Pang, Eng Fong, and Rajah V. Komaran. 1985. "Singapore Multinationals." *Columbia Journal of World Business* 20(2):35–44.

Pang, Eng Fong, and Linda Lim. 1982. "Foreign Labour and Economic Development in Singapore." *International Migration Review* 16(4):548–76.

Pillai, Philip Nalliah. 1983. *State Enterprise in Singapore: Legal Importation and Development*. Singapore: Singapore University Press.

Rao, V. V. Bhanoji, and M. K. Ramakrishnan. 1980. *Income Inequality in Singapore: Impact of Economic Growth and Structural Change, 1966–1975*. Singapore: Singapore University Press.

———. 1981. *Income Inequality in Singapore*. Singapore: Singapore University Press.

Richardson, Michael. 1982. "Back to Confucius." *Far Eastern Economic Review* (February 26).

Seah, Richard. 1986. "Tight Grip on a Hoard of Treasure." *Singapore Business* (February).

Singapore, Department of Statistics. 1982. *Report of the Household Expenditure Survey 1982/83*. Singapore.

Singapore, Ministry of Trade and Industry. 1986. *The Singapore Economy: New Directions*. Singapore.

Smith, Patrick. 1982. "The Union Engineers." *Far Eastern Economic Review* (June 25):57–63.

Tan, Augustine. 1984. "Changing Patterns of Singapore's Foreign Trade and Investment since 1960." In You Poh Seng and Lim Chong Yah, eds., *Singapore: Twenty-Five Years of Development*. Singapore: Nan Yang Xing Zhou Lianhe Zaobao.

Tan, Augustine, and Ow Chin Hock. 1983. "Singapore." In Bela Balassa and others, eds., *Development Strategies in Semi-industrial Economies*. Baltimore, Md.: Johns Hopkins University Press.

Tay, Boon Nga. 1986. "The Structure and Causes of Manufacturing Sector Protection in Singapore." In Christopher Findlay and Ross Garnaut, eds. *The Political Economy of Manufacturing Protection: Experiences of ASEAN and Australia*. Sydney, Australia: Allen and Unwin.

This Singapore. 1975. Singapore: Times Publishing.

Vasil, R. K. 1984. *Governing Singapore*. Singapore: Federal Publications.

Wilkinson, Barry, and Chris Leggett. 1985. "Human and Industrial Relations in Singapore: The Management of Compliance." *Euro-Asia Business Review* 4(3):9–15.

You, Poh Seng, and Lim Chong Yah, eds. 1984. *Singapore: Twenty-Five Years of Development*. Singapore: Nan Yang Xing Zhou Lianhe Zaobao.

4 Jamaica

Carl Stone
Stanislaw Wellisz

During the twenty-year period from 1952 to 1972, Jamaica was an exemplar of successful development. Real GDP grew more than 6 percent a year, one of the best growth records in the world. By 1972 the former colony had evolved into a fully independent member of the British Commonwealth with a stable, democratic, two-party parliamentary system. It had become the leading producer of bauxite, tourism was booming, and there was a significant manufacturing industry. Living conditions had improved, and much progress was being made in health and education. True, income distribution was inequitable and there was persistent unemployment, but the People's National party (PNP), led by Michael Manley, had won the 1972 election by a large majority and pledged to bring social reform.

The next fifteen years, however, were filled with economic problems. Between 1973 and 1980 GDP fell every year, for a cumulative decline of 18 percent, and remained virtually at a standstill thereafter. Over the 1965–87 period (which included years of prosperity and years of depression), GNP per capita fell at an annual average rate of 1.5 percent. By the late 1980s Jamaica was among the world's economically least-successful countries.

The changes in Jamaica's fortunes reflect, to some extent, external developments. In the 1950s and 1960s Jamaica benefited from the rising world demand for bauxite and from the growth of U.S. tourism. In the 1970s the demand for bauxite slackened, and oil price increases put Jamaican production at a disadvantage in comparison with that of Australia and other countries. From 1977 on, Jamaica's terms of trade declined precipitously. A large share of the blame falls on economic policy. The PNP government's ambitious program to recast the system along socialist lines proved to be costly and inefficient, while the imposition of a bauxite levy accelerated the decline of the mining sector. The 1980 victory of the Jamaica Labour party (JLP) led by Edward Seaga signaled a reversal of the trend. Initial supply-side measures aimed at reviving the private sector met with limited success, however. The policies of retrenchment with liberalization adopted in 1984 initially depressed the economy; the first definite signs of renewed self-sustained growth did not come until the last two years of JLP rule—too late to save the party from defeat at the hands of the PNP in 1988.

Was the boom of the 1950s and 1960s an isolated episode? Or, was the collapse of the 1970s and the early 1980s a temporary deviation from a long-term upward trend? Jamaica's rich natural resources, educated population, and fortunate geographic location suggest the former. Its sociopolitical structure, which favors direct redistribution and distortionary dirigisme, suggests the latter. Yet both major parties appear to have drawn lessons from past experience, and both now favor a more outward-oriented strategy that promises to lead to self-sustained growth.

Historical Background

Jamaica is the third largest island in the Caribbean, with an area of 4,400 square miles (11,425 square kilometers) and an estimated population (in 1986) of 2.3 million. At the time Columbus discovered the island in 1494, it was inhabited by Arawak Indians. The Spanish took possession in 1509 and enslaved the Arawaks, who soon died out and were replaced by African slaves. When the island fell to the British in 1660, many slaves escaped or were freed by their Spanish masters and settled in the mountainous areas, where they established independent communities and came to be known as Maroons. Despite numerous attempts to suppress the Maroons, they maintained a degree of freedom throughout the slavery period and were joined by later escapees. These communities demonstrated that freedom was possible and their presence, no doubt, fueled the frequent slave revolts.

Popular uprisings persisted after the abolition of slavery. Each successive riot was suppressed, sometimes ruthlessly, but was followed by reform. Thus, in the aftermath of the 1865 Morant Bay Rebellion the planters' self-government was replaced by a Crown Colony government, more attentive to the needs of the common people, and an outbreak of riots in 1938 brought a more permissive attitude toward labor unions and the formation of political parties. The militant tradition of successful mass action persists to this day.

The Economy

The original settlers grew a variety of tropical plants, but under British rule sugar began to play a dominant role; the number of plantations increased from a handful in 1660 to 57 in 1673 and to about 430 by 1739. Large numbers of slaves were brought from Africa to work the sugar plantations. Soon blacks heavily outnumbered the white population; by 1775 there were fewer than 13,000 whites and about 200,000 blacks (see

Black 1983: 122). By the 1820s the whites were also outnumbered by free men of color—that is, descendants of whites and black slave women. Many members of the colored group acquired considerable education and wealth; they went into the professions, took up coffee and pimento farming, and had slaves of their own.[1]

The decline of the sugar plantations started in the early nineteenth century. The labor supply declined after the prohibition of the slave trade in 1807 and even more after the abolition of slavery in 1838, when former slaves left the sugar plantations en masse. In anticipation of this exodus, plantation owners brought indentured laborers from Europe, India, and China but did not succeed in keeping them on the plantations. Virtually none of the Europeans and few of the Indians stayed in Jamaica; the Chinese who settled permanently gravitated toward commerce and, later, industry. Higher labor costs reduced the profitability of production, and between 1830 and 1840 output declined by 50 percent (Eisner 1961: 168).

In the latter half of the nineteenth century Jamaican sugar faced increasingly severe international competition. Originally, sugar imported into Britain from non-British possessions had to pay a customs duty, but in 1846 the British parliament adopted the Sugar Duties Act, eliminating all sugar duties over an eight-year period. This liberalization came at a time of rapid expansion of sugar plantations in Brazil and elsewhere. From 1870 on, there was also increased competition from heavily subsidized sugar beet production. Both the price and volume of production declined, and the value of Jamaican sugar exports fell from J$2.6 million in 1832 to J$418,000 in 1910 (Eisner 1961: 168).

At the turn of the century banana cultivation became the leading economic activity. Banana exports started in 1869 and by 1890 overtook sugar exports. In 1938 bananas accounted for 57 percent of the total value of domestic exports, but in the 1940s plantations were ravaged by the Panama disease. As a result, exports fell from 23 million stems in 1938 to 6.5 million stems in 1949, and recovery since then has been slow (Jefferson 1972: 2–3, 100–104). The slack created by the banana disaster was taken up in the early 1940s by wartime activities. High prices that prevailed in the immediate postwar period and the reintroduction of preferential quotas led Jamaica to revive its sugar industry, which once again became the main source of income.

Before emancipation, slaves were encouraged to grow food on small plots of land allotted to them. Between 1838 and 1850 an estimated 100,000 former slaves left sugar plantations to farm on their own. Some of the small farmers went on to cultivate export crops, but most of them engaged in growing food, which to this day is produced mainly by smallholders.

Since all of the best flat land was occupied by the large plantations, the former slaves settled in the hill country, "either squatting on crown property, or, with the aid of missionaries (notably the Baptists) purchasing small plots of land" (Brown 1979: 61). In many cases their titles to land remained uncertain. As time passed, titles to small property became even more confused, since few of the poor rural inhabitants concluded legal marriages, and heirs' claims were often ill defined. The lack of clear land titles remains a barrier to land improvement and consolidation.

The turn of the century also witnessed mass migration to the cities: the proportion of the population in agriculture declined from 67 percent in 1880 to 54 percent in 1930 (Eisner 1961). Some work opportunities arose in the formal sector—notably in the harbor, in shops and offices, and later, in manufacturing—but most of the migrants from rural areas took informal occupations in services or trade. Petty traders, called "higglers," came to constitute an important socioeconomic stratum. To this day, higglers are specifically exempt from certain taxes and import duties.

Society and Politics

For most of the colonial period the franchise was severely limited by a means test. Two loosely knit parties competed for seats in the local legislative assembly. The Country party was dominated by conservative white farmers, whereas the Town party—to which many colored or brown merchants, planters, and professionals belonged—was in favor of gradual political and social reforms. The property-owning elite expressed little interest in public affairs. Many white planters preferred to raise their families in Britain, where they maintained their main residences, only occasionally visiting the colony. Assembly seats often went uncontested, and election turnout generally amounted to 5 to 10 percent of the eligible voters. At the same time, the planters had close links with British parliamentarians and with British merchant houses having interests in the Caribbean. The planters' lobby (which in 1917 became the Jamaican Imperial Association) sought to secure good markets for staple exports and fought for the reestablishment of preferential treatment.

As the plantations went into eclipse, planters found their power declining and some of their lands being taken over by foreign companies, such as the American Fruit Company and Tate and Lyle. By the 1930s the Jamaica Imperial Association came to be dominated by merchants, professionals, and emerging middle-income and rich peasants. Three new bodies developed out of the Imperial Association: the Sugar Manufacturers Association (dominated by Tate and Lyle and the big sugar family interests), the All Island Cane Farmers Association (controlled by the new rural middle class), and the Employers Federation (dominated by the urban merchants and manufacturing interests). Unlike the traditional planters, the foreign corporations and the urban propertied interests were in favor of democratization. Close ties developed between business leaders and emerging politicians, as for example between Sir Robert Kirkwood, the head of the West Indies Sugar Company (a Tate and Lyle subsidiary), and Norman Manley, the most prominent Jamaican lawyer and a future prime minister.

In 1938 the political situation changed drastically when riots by farm and urban workers erupted in protest against the mistreatment of labor, low wages, and unemployment. The two figures that emerged as the workers' spokesmen, Alexander Bustamante and Norman Manley, were to dominate Jamaica's politics for the next thirty years, and their personalities, as much as ideological differences, determined the country's party structure.

Another important aftermath of the riots was the growth of trade unions. Unions had received recognition under the 1919 Trade Union Act, but until 1938 their activities were severely circumscribed, and their membership was insignificant. Of a total of 262,000 wage earners, 1,080 were union members in 1938 (IBRD 1952: 221). A Royal Commission (the Moyne Commission) appointed to investigate the cause of the strikes recommended that legal obstacles to unionization be removed. Government acceptance of the recommendations permitted Bustamante to build the first strong labor organization, the Bustamante Industrial Trade Union (BITU), which he was to lead until his death in 1977 at the age of ninety-three.

In 1943 Bustamante organized the JLP to give his union a political voice. The same year Manley formed the PNP and sought the support of organized labor. At first Manley wanted to create a British-model trades union council (TUC) that would include Bustamante's union. The latter refused to subordinate itself to the PNP and ultimately (in 1949) the TUC was registered as a union affiliated with the PNP. Thus, two rival workers' parties were born, each with its affiliated unions.

The Economy and the Polity at the Close of World War II

The constitution granted to Jamaica by Great Britain in 1943 introduced a bicameral system, consisting of a House of Representatives elected under universal suffrage and a nominated Legislative Council. Executive power was vested in a council consisting of the governor (who retained the power to override the decisions of the Executive Council on issues of paramount importance), two nominees of the governor, three ex officio members, and five elected representatives.

Political Developments

Both the JLP and the PNP put up candidates at the first general election (1944) held under the new law. At issue were a number of policies, racial factors, and the personalities and ambitions of the two party leaders.

The JLP and the Bustamante Industrial Trade Union (BITU) were led by Alexander Bustamante who emerged as the principal spokesman for the materially and politically militant sector of the urban working class. . . . His political strategies and tactics were essentially that of a populist leader who relied on emotionally charged personal loyalty and charisma. He insisted on keeping his party and union free of any ideological position and maintained an anti-Socialist posture largely because his opponents were professing Socialism. . . .

The opposing PNP and Trade Union Congress party and union were dominated . . . by divergent factions of middle class professionals among whom was a group of Socialists. . . . Its militant leaders articulated fierce sounding Socialist rhetoric that frightened the economic elites. (Stone 1973: 35)

In the 1944 election Norman Manley and the PNP championed independence. Bustamante, in contrast, advocated maintaining ties with Great Britain and warned that independence would replace the rule of a white elite with that of a local brown elite, to the detriment of the black common man.

Manley, for all his radical backing, held moderate opinions, akin to those of the middle-of-the-road leaders of the British Labour party. An Oxford-educated barrister, he was, in many ways, more acceptable to the middle and upper classes than Bustamante. Indeed, in the 1938 events Bustamante was thought to be the rabble-rouser and Manley the moderate. Bustamante, the leader of the black working class, was himself light-skinned and the cousin of Manley.

While both parties have always been multiclass and multiracial alliances, drawing their support from all strata of Jamaican society, their ideological perspectives and political appeal reflect consistent differences. The PNP has always been somewhat left of center and has consistently advocated sweeping changes in the economy and society. The JLP has always been more conservative, pragmatic, and oriented toward stability rather than change. The principal differences in outlook are summarized in table 4-1.

Despite these differences, both parties have many features in common. They share a belief that the state should provide aid and welfare to the poorer classes through social policies and public spending programs, that the state should provide economic policy leadership for the private sector and assume a central role in promoting economic development through state-funded projects, that some state regulation of the economy is necessary in the national interest, that the state must provide social services for the citizens and economic services and infrastructure for those engaged in production, and that the state has a responsibility to engineer changes through social reforms and legislation. Most important, the PNP and the JLP are both committed to the intensive use of political patronage; that is to say, the scarce benefits that flow from government policies and expenditure in the form of jobs, housing, contracts, and so on should be allocated to party supporters. In a sense,

Table 4-1. Differences in the Fundamental Perspectives of the JLP
and the PNP

PNP *(party of change)*	JLP *(party of stability)*
Socialist, supporting state ownership and cooperatives as a policy priority	Capitalist, defending free enterprise
Advocacy of radical economic and social changes (redistribution of land, worker ownership, and worker management)	Incrementalist approach to policy changes
Advocacy of big government and state control of the economy	Supportive of an active but limited role for the state in the economy, with a greater reliance on market forces
Advocacy of a more activist role in international and regional affairs and a high-profile role in multilateral bodies (Group of 77, United Nations, nonaligned movement)	Advocacy of bilateralism, close ties with strong allies, and a low-profile role in world affairs
Promotion of closer links with the developing world in foreign policy	Emphasis on closer links with Western countries
Strong presence of leftists in party circles	Distrust toward intellectuals and leftists

Source: Authors' compilation.

it is possible to view the two-party system in Jamaica as a continuing struggle between rival patronage machines.

In the 1944 election, twenty-three of the thirty-two contested seats were won by the JLP. The PNP, lacking a strong grass-roots organization, won only four seats, and five seats went to independents. In the five years that followed, the unions opposed to the BITU gained in membership and gave increased support to the PNP. In the second general election (1949) the PNP won a plurality of votes (43.5 percent to 42.7 percent for the JLP) but only thirteen seats, while the JLP obtained seventeen seats, and independents two seats. The two-party system was firmly established.

The 1944 election marked the defeat of an attempt to organize a party favoring business interests: the Jamaica Democratic party, which stood for laissez-faire and was backed by the "oligarchs," won no seats. Yet despite their defeat at the polls, the influence of business interests remained powerful: the colonial authorities gave all the nominated seats on the Legislative and Executive councils to businessmen and property owners. Business, however, increasingly relied on lobbying to foster its interests (Phillips 1977), particularly after 1953, when a constitutional reform abolished the nominated seats and gave the elected representatives control over the administration through a ministerial system.

The diversification of owners' interests led to the decline, and eventual demise, of the Jamaica Imperial Association.[2] In its stead, two business lobbying organizations were formed in the late 1940s and early 1950s. The Jamaica Manufacturers Association, founded in 1947, became a strong advocate of protectionism and fiscal concessions in favor of local manufacturing industry. A revitalized Chamber of Commerce, incorporated under the Companies Law of 1950, specialized in representing merchant interests. These two organizations were influential in fostering a policy of dirigisme espoused in the late 1940s and early 1950s by the colonial authorities.

Economic Conditions

Agriculture was the mainstay of the economy in the immediate postwar period. According to the 1943 census, 45 percent of the gainfully employed population was in agriculture and only 12 percent in manufacturing (table 4-2). A strikingly high percentage of the labor force was employed in personal services, a category that consists mainly of household servants (mostly female) but also includes hotel personnel. Wage and salary earners accounted for about 57 percent of the economically active population.[3] In agriculture laborers were slightly outnumbered by farmers and cultivators. In manufacturing there were 16,000 wage and salaried workers and 43,000 artisans and unpaid family laborers. The commercial sector was dominated by higglers.

Table 4-2. Labor Force by Industry Group, 1943

Sector	Gainfully employed		Wage and salary earners	
	Thousands	*Percent*	*Thousands*	*Percent*
Agriculture	228.0	45.1	105	36.5
Mining and quarrying	0.6	0.1	1[a]	0.3
Manufacturing	59.2	11.7	16	5.6
Construction	34.1	6.8	13	4.5
Public utilities	1.3	0.3	—	—
Commerce	39.5	7.8	7	2.4
Transport and communications	11.4	2.3	10	3.5
Personal services	81.3	16.1	59	20.5
Other services	21.1	4.2	11	3.8
Other and unspecified	28.5	5.6	66[b]	22.9
Total	505.0	100.0	288	100.0

— Included in manufacturing.

a. Includes fishing and hunting.

b. Includes 9,000 clerical workers and 57,000 miscellaneous laborers (doing odd jobs).

Sources: For gainfully employed, census data from Jefferson 1972: 30. For wage and salary earners, Jamaica, Department of Statistics, *National Income of Jamaica,* 1943 and 1946.

At that time Jamaica had 66,000 farms (a farm being defined as having at least 1 acre or a 1942 product valued at £15 or more) and 146,500 small plots. More than half of the farms (57 percent) consisted of holdings of 6 acres or less. Such farms occupied only 6 percent of the farmland. At the other extreme, the 500 largest farms (0.75 percent of the total), with 500 acres of land or more, occupied 60 percent of all farmland. Most of the land of small farms was under cultivation, whereas much of the land on large farms was in pasture or lying fallow.

Large estates, located in the alluvial plains, were devoted mainly to the production of export crops (notably, sugarcane, bananas, and coconuts) and some livestock for the domestic market. The output of small farms, located mostly in the hills, appears to have been fairly evenly divided between export crops and foodstuffs for the home market.[4]

The estates were quite efficient, with sugarcane yields 60 to 75 percent higher than those of the small farmers who delivered their cane to the estates for milling.[5] Small farms were unproductive because of poor soil conditions, undercapitalization, and backward technology. A third of the cultivated land was leased, much of it on a year-to-year basis, and many farmers lacked clear title to the land they owned. As a consequence many farmers were unable to borrow against their land and obtain financing for modernization. The Ministry of Agriculture and numerous private organizations extended technical aid to farmers, but their activities lacked coordination and were somewhat ineffectual (IBRD 1952). Many small farmers supplemented their income by providing services to other farmers and by taking odd jobs, thus creating a pool of part-time wage labor (Smith 1956: 16–17, 66–68).

Manufacturing consisted mainly of processing local agricultural products. In 1951 sugar mills accounted for 29 percent of total factory employment, while food-processing enterprises in general employed 69 percent of all factory workers and generated 60 percent of the gross value added by manufacturing. Fewer than 10 percent of workers were employed in import-substituting industries that relied on imported raw materials, such as shoe and garment manufacturing, furniture, and woodworking (Smith 1956: 68).

In 1950 and 1951, the earliest years for which such data are available, gross value added by agriculture, including fisheries, amounted to 30.6 percent (1950) and 26.7 percent (1951) of GDP, at factor cost. In both years, manufacturing generated only slightly more than 11 percent of GDP, with sugar, rum, and other food-processing activities accounting for more than half of the gross value added by manufacturing (table 4-3).

Agricultural and processed agricultural products played an even greater role in export trade. In 1950 sugar and confectionery products accounted for 42 percent of total exports and the food, beverages, and tobacco category as a whole for 94 percent.[6] Imports consisted mostly of consumer goods and fuel, with a low volume of raw materials and capital goods.

Table 4-3. *Percentage Distribution of* GDP *at Factor Cost, 1950–51*

Sector	1950	1951
Agriculture	30.6	26.7
Mining	0.2	0.3
Manufacturing	11.3	11.2
Sugar, rum, and molasses	3.1	3.0
Other food processing	3.1	3.0
Construction	7.6	10.9
Public utilities	1.1	1.0
Distribution	15.2	15.9
Transport and communications	7.1	6.6
Ownership of dwellings	5.9	5.3
Government	6.1	6.8
Miscellaneous services	15.0	15.2

Note: Totals do not add up to 100.0 because of rounding.
Source: Jamaica, Department of Statistics, *National Income of Jamaica,* 1956.

THE GROWTH RECORD. Jamaica's economy apparently passed from a period of stagnation just before World War II into a wartime boom that lasted until 1946, but it lapsed into a decline in the succeeding four or five years. Since the country's GNP estimates are in current terms and no GNP deflator is available to convert them into constant prices, inferences must be based on the cost of living index (see table 4-4). Much the same pattern emerges from the data on employment and output. Real wages rose rapidly between 1943 and 1946 and then declined. The real wage level in 1950 appears to have exceed the 1943 level by only 8 percent (table 4-5).

Table 4-4. *National Income Estimates, Selected Years, 1938–50*
(Jamaican pounds)

Year	National income at current factor prices[a]		Indices of estimated national income at constant prices	
	Total (thousands)	Per capita	Total	Per capita
1938	20,319	17.8	93[b]	100[b]
1942	33,300	27.1	100	100
1943	40,500	32.5	118	116
1946	63,800	43.2	176	167
1947	70,000	52.7	165	153
1950	85,000	60.6	151	133

a. 1942 = 100.

b. The cost of living index begins with August 1939. Since between mid-1938 and mid-1939 there was reasonable price stability, our calculations are made on the heroic assumption that between 1938 and 1939 prices did not change.

Sources: For 1943–47, Jamaica, Central Bureau of Statistics, 1947; for 1950, IBRD (1952: 4, n. 3). For cost of living index, used as a deflator, Jamaica, Central Bureau of Statistics, *Abstract of Statistics,* various issues.

Table 4-5. Wages and Prices, 1942–52

Year	Index of nominal wages in the Kingston area (1943 = 100)	Cost of living index (1939 = 100)	Kingston area real wage index[a] (1943 = 100)
1942	—	152	—
1943	100	157	100
1944	109	159	108
1945	119	159	118
1946	127	165	121
1947	142	194	115
1948	150	235	100
1949	168	245	108
1950	177	257	108
1951	202	295	108
1952	—	325	—

— Not available.
a. Estimated by deflating the nominal wage index by the cost of living index.
Sources: Jamaica, Central Bureau of Statistics, Abstract of Statistics, various issues.

The wage pattern reflects fluctuations in the demand for labor: indices of employment in the Kingston area, where most industry was (and still is) concentrated, show a rapid rise in manufacturing employment between 1943 and 1946–47 and stagnation thereafter (table 4-6). Employment in public utilities continued to grow in the late 1940s but declined in the services and distribution trades. Output figures show a similar pattern: although the production of sugar rose rapidly between 1943 and 1951, the production of most other commodities appears to have stagnated, particularly in the late 1940s.

THE UNEMPLOYMENT PROBLEM. The main economic problem of the early postwar era, as perceived at the time, was unemployment. High unemployment and underemployment dated back to the 1930s, if not earlier, and were among the major causes of the 1938 riots.[7] Although unemployment declined during the war, 60 percent of the island's 284,000

Table 4-6. Indices of Employment in the Kingston Area, 1943–51

Sector	1943	1944	1945	1946	1947	1948	1949	1950	1951
Manufacturing	100	113	131	155	159.0	145.5	146.5	150.5	158.5
Public utilities	100	98	101	122	121.8	115.8	134.8	152.5	157.9
Wholesale and retail trade	100	101	112	109	112.0	110.7	113.3	109.0	104.3
Services	100	101	112	109	112.0	110.7	113.3	109.0	104.3

Source: Jamaica, Central Bureau of Statistics, Digest of Statistics, various issues.

wage earners worked less than forty weeks in 1942 (table 4-7), and 54,000 adults (22,000 men and 32,000 women) under the age of twenty-five who had never had a gainful occupation were looking for work (Jamaica 1945: 13–14).[8] In 1946 the unemployment rate in the Kingston area was 15.5 percent among the population over the age of fourteen (Standing 1981: 49), and in the 1950s and 1960s it averaged about 18 percent (Jamaica, Department of Statistics, various years).

One explanation given for the endemic unemployment in the Kingston area was labor market segmentation. Disequilibrium arose, some said, because job-seekers "queued up" for high-paying jobs in "protected" sectors and, while doing so, were able to survive by taking advantage of the prevailing sharing ethic (a good man was expected to help his less fortunate friends and kinsmen) or by engaging in illicit activities (Maunder 1960: 4–36; Tidrick 1975: 306–42). Other economists were not convinced that unions had raised wages significantly above the labor opportunity costs but failed to give a cogent alternative explanation of the unemployment phenomenon.[9]

What proportion of the Jamaican unemployment was truly involuntary? A 1945 report by the government-appointed Economic Policy Committee headed by F. C. Benham acknowledged that, as the 1942 census figures showed, "only a third of the wage earners were fully employed" but that "the situation is much less serious than the figures suggest," for "most people do not want to work for long hours in a hot climate.[10] They prefer to have a lower standard of living and more leisure; they are not educated to appreciate a higher standard of living, and would rather take life easily than add to their material comforts" (Jamaica 1945: 14). In view of these considerations, the committee concluded that there was no need to take extraordinary measures to increase employment.

Table 4-7. *Average Number of Weeks Worked by Wage Earners, 1942*

Weeks worked	Number of wage earners
0	8,431
1–9	16,802
10–19	41,106
20–29	61,204
30–39	39,139
40–49	27,898
50–52	83,740
Not specified	5,790
Total	284,110
Never gainfully employed[a]	54,156

a. Among work-seeking adults under the age of 25.
Source: Census of 1942 (see Jamaica 1945).

Even those who take strong exception to the Benham committee findings agree that the way unemployment is measured in Jamaica yields higher figures than the standard method used in other countries:

[In Jamaica] the unemployed comprises those persons "looking for work" together with persons "wanting work, available for work." This latter category includes persons . . . actually engaged in home or other duties not classified as part of Economic Activity, but who were willing and able to accept work. (Jamaica, Department of Statistics, 1971)

During the 1970s only about 40 to 45 percent of the unemployed were actually seeking work when surveyed (Standing 1981: 58), as was the case in the semiannual labor force surveys conducted by the Statistical Institute of Jamaica in October 1983, April 1984, and October 1984. Only 44 percent of the unemployed were currently seeking work, while 25 percent of the unemployed had never held a job and were not looking for work (Standing 1981: 58). These figures are, however, subject to a large margin of error. Ten percent of the individuals who said that they received on-the-job training also claimed that they had never held a job! Nonetheless, it is safe to conclude that under the usual definition of unemployment—meaning nonworking individuals who are actively looking for work—Jamaican unemployment estimates would be reduced by more than 50 percent, although the problem would still be of considerable magnitude.

In any case, in the 1940s and 1950s political leaders believed that job creation was of primary importance.[11] They were concerned about the number of jobless, the rapid growth of "unproductive" jobs, and the decreasing participation in the labor force by women (Lewis 1950: 3–5). Job creation was also emphasized by the World Bank, which in 1952 warned that "the percentage of unemployed must be reduced if Jamaica is to develop a stable economic and political system" and stated that employment needed to be increased by 45 percent in the decade 1952–62.

POVERTY AND EQUITY. In the 1940s income was distributed very unevenly. Average annual wages and salaries in manufacturing were more than three times as high as those in agriculture (table 4-8). The self-employed apparently fared worse than urban workers, and subsistence farmers constituted the poorest group.

Despite slow economic growth and the uneven income distribution, the standard of living in the immediate postwar period was improving. The country was being rapidly electrified: domestic electricity sales rose from 3 million kilowatt hours in 1943 to 12 million in 1951. As standards of hygiene improved, the infant mortality rate fell from 9.3 to 8.1 percent of live births, while life expectancy, estimated at 51.25 years in 1945–47, rose to 55.73 years by 1950–52.[12]

Table 4-8. *Average Annual Earnings, Wages, and Salaries, by Economic Sector, 1943*
(Jamaican pounds)

Sector	Number	Average annual earnings[a]
Agriculture and forestry (including stockraising)	105,000	13.3
Quarrying, mining, fishing, and hunting	1,000	50.0
Manufacturing	16,000	46.9
Construction	13,000	38.5
Transport and communications	10,000	50.0
Trade and commerce	7,000	107.1
Services	70,000	33.6[b]
Recreational	300	66.7
Professional	5,900	144.1
Public	4,800	141.7
Personal	59,000	12.7
Clerical	9,000	166.7
Miscellaneous, laborers (doing odd jobs)	57,000	12.3
All occupations	288,000	29.5

a. Excluding income in kind.
b. Income figures for services subgroups, as given by the source, do not add up to the total for services.
Source: Computed from Jamaica, Central Bureau of Statistics, *National Income of Jamaica,* 1943, 1946.

ECONOMIC POLICY. The British government had traditionally favored conservative finance, laissez-faire, and free trade within the empire, and tariffs (if any) were imposed for revenue only. During the period of political transition, the Jamaican government continued this policy of financial conservatism and between 1942 and 1952 ran frequent surpluses and developed substantial accumulated balances.[13]

At times, however, the government had departed from laissez-faire, even before World War II. In 1935 the colonial government enacted the Safeguarding of Local Industries Law, under which the Privy Council awarded monopoly rights to the Jamaica Match Industry, Ltd. The company was granted high tariff protection and guaranteed an 8 percent (later increased to 10 percent) after-tax profit; the subsidies it received under this proviso between 1943 and 1953 totaled J$780,000. Similar privileges were given to companies producing processed milk and other products.

With the wartime disruption of normal trade, industries were given natural protection, but as soon as the war ended, the government resumed its selective granting of privileges. The Hotel Aid Law of 1944, for example, gave duty-free import privileges and accelerated depreciation to approved hotel ventures; textile ventures received protection in

1947; and a 1948 law gave protection and granted a monopoly franchise to a cement manufacturer. Other laws in this period protected the motion picture industry and button manufacturing.

Agricultural policy also deviated from the free-market ideal. To cope with the shipping shortage during World War II, the government took control of the export of all major crops.[14] After a transition period following the end of the war, control of the export of major commodities was entrusted to statutory boards composed of representatives of producers and of the government.[15] The boards had an export monopoly; they negotiated terms with foreign buyers, set prices for growers, and provided other services, such as the distribution of fertilizers at subsidized prices (Jamaica, Ministry of Trade and Industry, 1954).

Toward the end of World War II there was a shift in Westminster's policy. In 1944 the Colonial Office issued a paper asserting that the colonial governments should help private interests diversify and industrialize the local economies. The paper argued that if private initiative was lacking, the local colonial governments should assume entrepreneurial functions (Widdicomb 1972: 80–81). This policy recommendation coincided with the program of the PNP, which, as early as 1939, demanded "the institution of Statutory Industries Boards supported by adequate legislative power for the protection and safeguarding of local industries" (see Widdicomb 1972: 78). By the 1949 election the PNP was pushing for a comprehensive plan of industrialization that called for the use of protection and tax incentives and for the establishment of a National Industrial Development Corporation to assist private investors and develop new industries on its own account (Widdicomb 1972: 79).

Not surprisingly, the policy of government-sponsored industrialization was opposed by Jamaican landed interests and importers. Opposition also came from the JLP. Although labor had no objection to protective measures or fiscal laws that would help industry (indeed, the 1949 Pioneer Industry Act was adopted under a JLP administration), it was against direct government investment on the grounds that it led to socialism.

Expert opinion was divided. In its 1945 report, the Economic Policy Committee concluded that Jamaica's economic future lay in modernized and diversified agriculture, to be fostered by price supports, subsidies, and government-sponsored extension work. Industry could, at best, absorb only a small fraction of the growth of the labor force. As a consequence, the social cost of government-sponsored industrialization would be unreasonably high in relation to the social benefit. Even so, the committee endorsed aid to industry through tariff exemptions on capital goods and income tax holidays for new enterprises, as well as publicly financed industrial research and vocational training.

In contrast, W. Arthur Lewis argued that "land [in Jamaica and in the other West Indian islands had] reached the limit of its capacity some thirty or forty years ago," that agriculture was on the decline, and that mechanization had pushed people off the farms. Industrialization was therefore essential for the creation of productive jobs. The government should foster industry because under laissez-faire new enterprises would take advantage of economies of agglomeration and gravitate toward areas that had already been industrialized. To attract foreign funds and to nurture domestic capital and entrepreneurs, the government should provide infrastructure, build and lease factory space at reasonable rents, and grant fiscal concessions and tariff protection. In some cases it might be necessary to grant monopoly rights, but these should be accompanied by price controls. In matters of national interest, the government might also be called on to start and operate industries that were privately unprofitable. Its industrial development policy would be entrusted to an agency patterned after the Industrial Development Company of Puerto Rico, "the most intelligent model of what is required. . . . The great advantage of having a special agency . . . is that it can treat each case on its merits" (Lewis 1950: 51–52). In sum, this could be described as dirigisme and the discretionary use of incentives.

The Ten-Year Plan of Development for Jamaica, adopted in 1946, reflected the views of the Economic Policy Committee. Public expenditure was to be devoted to economic and social overhead and agriculture.[16] Industry was to receive fiscal concessions, but only a negligible sum was allocated to industrial and trade development (table 4-9).

Before long, however, greater emphasis was being placed on industrialization and a larger role for the government.[17] Under the 1949 Pioneer Industry (Encouragement) Act, firms introducing new products or techniques to Jamaica could qualify for a postponement of their corporate profit tax and for the duty-free importation of all capital goods. In 1951 import duties on steel, iron, nonferrous metals, crude rubber, and leather were lowered to help industries making use of these inputs, and other tariffs were revised to safeguard against regressivity in the degree of

Table 4-9. *Sectoral Allocation of Funds, Ten-Year Plan of Development for Jamaica, 1946–56*
(thousands of Jamaican pounds)

Sector	Original provision	Revised plan
Agriculture	6,030	6,616
Education	3,302	2,093
Public health	5,564	6,117
Communications	1,742	1,611
Industrial and trade development	400	400
Social welfare	1,774	1,011
Miscellaneous	724	338
Total	19,536	18,187

Source: Jamaica 1951.

fabrication.[18] The 1951 revision of the Ten-Year Plan allocated more funds to development (principally of agriculture), at the expense of social expenditures (table 4-9).

In keeping with the revised plan, the government launched two public development corporations in 1951: the Agricultural Development Corporation (ADC), which was to do research on various crops, particularly on rice; and the Jamaica Industrial Development Corporation (JIDC), which was to "stimulate, facilitate and undertake the development of industry."[19] The JIDC was to give financial and technical assistance to new industries, to industries whose development would cause either a reduction in imports or an increase in exports, and to industries that employed a high proportion of labor in relation to capital. The JIDC was also to develop industrial sites and lease out factory space at moderate rental rates. During its first year the JIDC received J$470,000 in government grants in support of its program; between 1952 and 1971 it received more than J$16 million of government funds (Widdicomb 1972: 167).

To sum up, between 1944 and 1952 Jamaica continued to be an agricultural country with no major structural transformation yet in sight. Following a short wartime boom, national income appears to have stagnated. From an institutional point of view, this was a period in which Jamaica moved from laissez-faire to economic leadership by the government, which put in place mechanisms of control that were to become the basic economic institutions of independent Jamaica.

The 1952–72 Boom

During the two decades between 1952 and 1972 Jamaica enjoyed unprecedented prosperity and growth, fueled by the rapid development of the bauxite and alumina industry and of tourism. Stimulated by the inflow of foreign exchange, GDP grew at an average annual rate of 6.3 percent, which at the time was hailed as an "economic miracle."[20]

Politics and Society

Between 1952 and 1962 Jamaica passed from limited self-rule to complete independence. In 1953 it set up a Westminster-model parliamentary system, with the colonial authorities retaining residual control. In 1959 it gained full internal autonomy, and in 1962 complete independence within the Commonwealth.

THE POLITICAL PARTIES. During this transition the country's two parties alternated in power: the JLP held office until 1955, when the PNP won the general election. The PNP won again in 1959, but in 1962 the government passed to the JLP, which remained in power for the next ten years.

These changes had little impact on policy, for the PNP of the 1950s and 1960s was much more moderate than the party that had contested the

1949 election. In 1952, after a sharp split, the Socialist faction was expelled from the party leadership, and Norman Manley assumed complete party control. This change made the PNP more acceptable to the wealthy, who until then had supported the JLP as the lesser of two evils. In the same year a new PNP-affiliated union was formed. Known as the National Workers Union (NWU), it sought recruits among rural workers, who had previously backed Bustamante.

As a result of these changes the PNP and JLP became strikingly similar, right down to their development strategies. Both tried to attract foreign investment to activities requiring large blocks of capital and technical expertise, while giving government guidance and protection to domestic investment.

SOCIAL TRANSFORMATION. The economic prosperity of the 1952–72 period transformed the structure of Jamaican society. The middle strata of professionals and white-collar workers grew from 13 percent of the labor force in 1943 to 22 percent in 1970, production workers grew from 13 percent of the labor force to 24 percent, the number of peasants declined, and society became more urbanized.

There emerged a new class of merchant-manufacturing families who came to dominate the private sector in modern Jamaica. They did not develop out of the planter class, but mainly from the more enterprising merchants who had expanded from small beginnings early in the twentieth century.

Members of these business families rarely entered into politics formally, but in the 1950s and early 1960s many of them served the government in a technical or advisory capacity. Most of the politicians elected in the early postwar years had little formal education—except for a few trained in law and in medicine—or administrative experience. Consequently, they tended to rely on outside advice when dealing with complex policy issues and naturally turned to business leaders, with whom many of them had personal ties. Since the state had begun expanding its role in economic affairs, businessmen had a personal stake in policy formation. Indeed, powerful private family interests competed among themselves for inside influence over policymaking by cultivating politicians and top bureaucrats as strategic allies. Foreign corporations also became influential as new foreign capital entered the economy in such important areas as bauxite mining, tourism, manufacturing, finance, and banking.

Between 1938 and the early 1950s party organizations were relatively undeveloped, and both the JLP and the PNP relied heavily on trade unions to mobilize grass-roots political support. In the 1950s and 1960s trade union membership expanded rapidly, but, paradoxically, their political influence declined. The leaders of the two parties became involved in affairs of state and lost much of their populist intensity, for they had come to regard organized labor as just one of several competing interests.

As their membership expanded, the unions became increasingly involved in collective bargaining, to the detriment of their political activities.[21] No longer political reference points for party loyalty, the unions became less capable of delivering votes, and the parties began seeing them as little more than a source of recruits and a place for an aspiring politician to build a populist image. The unions became a voice of the labor aristocracy, whereas the political parties turned into strong community-based organizations that concentrated on mobilizing the bottom 40 percent of the population—including the unemployed and the poor, who looked to the parties for patronage benefits and handouts.

Labor relations remained tense as employers continued their bitter fight against the unions, even after the advent of political democracy. They viewed trade unionism in their family-owned enterprises as a sign of worker disloyalty and resented union attempts to restrict their freedom to hire and fire, set work norms, dictate pay and working conditions, and mete out rewards and punishments. The master-servant ideology that had created a rigid color-class hierarchy divided between the privileged white and light-skinned employers, on the one hand, and the poor black working class, on the other, did not make for easy recognition of workers' rights.

The workers, on their side, resented the unwillingness of owners and managers to accept the rights that unions had already won in Europe. Past experience had led union leaders to believe that extreme militancy was the only way to bring management to the bargaining table. Neither side was willing to compromise. Jamaica became one of the most strike-prone countries in the world; violence and lockouts were frequent occurrences.

Historically, Jamaican society has tended to associate strong leadership with action-oriented or charismatic personalities, rather than with persons distinguished by intellect or depth of thought and ideas. Intellectuals, therefore, did not enter directly into politics. Instead, many of them served as advisers, mostly to PNP politicians. From their main base at the University of the West Indies, the left-wing intellectuals exerted significant influence on public opinion throughout the 1950s and 1960s. They consistently advocated a nationalist, statist, and socialist economic policy. They criticized the capitalist character of the economy, its ownership by foreigners and by a domestic racial minority, the ideological conservatism of the traditional political leaders, U.S. influence on the country, human rights violations and police brutality, income inequality, and the manipulation of the interests of the poor by power-seeking party machines. These charges helped set the stage for the ideological shifts of the 1970s.

The social changes that had accompanied the economic boom of the 1950s and the 1960s were reflected in the composition of Parliament. During the early 1940s about 70 percent of the parliamentary representatives and candidates had lower-middle-class occupations (clerks, teachers, small businessmen, ministers of religion, druggists, trade unionists, and the like). Only 10 percent were medium and big farmers, merchants, and manufacturers. The remaining 20 percent came from the high-income and high-status professions (lawyers, doctors, engineers, and so on).

As the economy grew and diversified, the high-status professions came to include a growing number of managers, technicians, and administrators. The proportion of parliamentarians drawn from this group increased to 50 percent, whereas the share of the lower-middle-class occupations dropped to 30 percent and that of the business sector totaled about 12 percent. Trade union representation was now only about 5 percent, against 11 percent in the 1940s. Cabinet posts were monopolized by the high-status professions and persons from business and trade union backgrounds.

THE STATE AS AN INTEREST GROUP. During the 1960s a new generation of highly trained professionals and technocrats emerged in key positions in the public sector and within the ranks of the political parties. This change was facilitated by the opening of the University of the West Indies on the island and the return of Jamaicans educated in the United Kingdom, Canada, and the United States. Many graduates entered the public sector, where their training was in greater demand than in the private sector. The rapid upgrading of educational levels within the upper ranks of the Jamaican civil service over the postwar years can be seen in table 4-10.

The new policy-shaping institutions such as the Central Bank, the Development Bank, and the Planning Agency began to rely less on advice from the private sector and more on the highly educated party and bureaucratic leadership. The new power relationship is reflected in the country's first five-year development plan, for 1963–68, prepared by

Table 4-10. *Educational Levels of Civil Servants, 1955 and 1981*
(percent)

Year and characteristic	Postsecondary	Secondary or less
1955		
Managerial	8	92
Professional	28	72
1981		
Managerial		
Under 35	82	18
35 and over	42	58
Professional		
Under 35	68	32
35 and over	49	51

Sources: Administrative Staff College reports, and research by Carl Stone.

the JLP government under the policy leadership of the then minister of development and welfare, Edward Seaga. Under the plan, the government was to have a larger role in the economy. By providing employment and boosting consumer demand for construction projects, the government would stimulate activity in the private sector. At the same time, it would balance economic development against social needs to see that the benefits of development had a wider distribution. Although the intention was to encourage private effort and enterprise, such enterprises would operate to the advantage of the community:

> Government will participate as much as necessary in the productive sector in order to ensure that necessary production is not neglected or abandoned by unresponsive private efforts. . . . But real economic power represented by ownership or control of land and other assets has remained in the hands of a very limited group in the community. It is essential that the basis of such ownership should be widened. (Jamaica, *Five-Year Independence Plan*)

This development plan, masterminded by the JLP leader who was to become prime minister in 1980, was clearly designed to establish a new role for the government—as an intervener on behalf of the poorer classes, a regulator of the private sector, and the prime mover in stimulating growth. The foundation was being laid for what might be called the "political management" of the economy. Indeed, the plan redefined the power relationship between the public and private sectors and made the private sector the junior partner in directing policy.

As policymaking organs distanced themselves from business, powerful families made an effort to safeguard their interests by maintaining close personal ties with top politicians. But the interests of businessmen as a group came to be represented by organizations such as the Jamaica Chamber of Commerce, the Jamaica Manufacturers Association, the Jamaica Hotel and Tourist Association, and the Sugar Manufacturers Association. Most of the active membership and leadership of these associations came from the smaller and less influential businesses that needed to work through a lobby to influence policymaking.

By the early 1970s these private sector organizations and the state were in sharp conflict over JLP and PNP price control measures; JLP policies seeking to increase the tax take from the private sector; JLP and PNP policies seeking to expand government ownership and control of public utilities; the backing of trade union politicians for unions engaged in disputes with business interests; the unwillingness of elected political leaders to deal harshly with trade union violence; violations of the law and breaches of no-strike rules governing essential services; JLP policies seeking to nationalize insurance and financial institutions; and PNP proposals for land reform and land tax revisions. Private businesses complained that these policies were not only adverse to business interests but were often adopted without even consulting those directly concerned, who did not have an opportunity to respond until the policies were about to be implemented.

Despite these conflicts, the leaders of the business lobbies tried to be supportive of the government. They feared the government's power and the possible reprisals from political leaders who might view their criticisms as political attacks. The government was only criticized in public in extreme situations, when vital business interests were being threatened, and only after other channels of response had been exhausted. When the government seemed opposed to business interests on ideological grounds, however, as happened under the PNP in the 1970s, businessmen, in self-defense, openly joined with political opposition forces.

ECONOMIC DEVELOPMENT. The 1950s and the 1960s were a period of prosperity for Jamaica (table 4-11). Growth was fueled by the bauxite-alumina industry and by tourism, but other sectors expanded rapidly as well. There was some slowing down in 1958 and 1961–62 because of the uncertainty that accompanied the transition to independence. Once business confidence was restored, however, growth resumed, albeit at a somewhat slower pace than in the 1950s.

The bauxite industry, which grew from an insignificant beginning in 1952 to a leading world position in 1962, was the main engine of growth. Bauxite expansion slowed in the 1960s, but in the latter part of the decade the rapid expansion of alumina production capacity gave new impetus to the economy (table 4-12).

Table 4-11. GDP *at Constant Market Prices, 1950 and 1955–72*
(millions of 1974 Jamaican dollars)

Year	GDP	Growth rate (percent)
1950	585.8	n.a.
1955	913.4	9.3
1960	1,276.2	6.9
1961	1,291.9	1.2
1962	1,294.1	0.2
1963	1,332.1	2.9
1964	1,432.3	7.5
1965	1,541.9	7.7
1966	1,593.5	3.3
1967	1,614.3	1.3
1968	1,696.4	5.1
1969	1,773.5	4.5
1970	1,980.8	11.7
1971	2,042.9	3.1
1972	2,231.8	9.2

n.a. Not applicable.
Source: World Bank data.

Table 4-12. Jamaican Bauxite and Alumina Production, 1952, 1962, and 1972

	Bauxite		Alumina	
Year	Thousands of metric tons	Percentage of world production	Thousands of metric tons	Percentage of world production
1952	420	2.7	0	0.0
1962	7,615	24.4	665	6.3
1972	12,989	18.8	2,087	8.7

Note: Data in parentheses indicate percentage of world production.
Sources: Bauxite 1952 and alumina 1962 from Jefferson 1972: table 6.3. Percentages from World Bank estimates and American Bureau of Metal Statistics 1965–75.

Tourism also played an important, although less crucial, role. The number of tourist arrivals rose rapidly during the early and middle 1950s but fell off toward the end of the decade in the face of political uncertainty and the increased competition from other Caribbean countries. In the late 1960s rapid growth resumed (table 4-13). By 1972 the number of tourist arrivals was more than four times that recorded in 1955, and tourist expenditures amounted to 36.8 percent of the value of exports.

The expansion of hotel facilities in the 1950s acted as a stimulus to the construction industry. Manufacturing continued to thrive in the 1950s and 1960s, as did the financial institutions and several other major sectors of the economy (table 4-14).

This trend was sustained by a high rate of investment. The ratio of total investment to GDP rose from 10.2 percent in 1950 to 23.9 percent in 1959. In the early 1960s the ratio declined, to a trough of 17.9 percent in 1963, but then turned back up to reach a peak of 32.1 percent in 1971.

Domestic savings also rose steadily, from about 13 percent of GDP in the early 1950s to an average of about 22 percent in the second half of the

Table 4-13. Jamaican Tourism, Selected Years, 1955–72

	Total expenditures (millions)		Expenditures per visitor			
Year	Number of tourists (thousands)	U.S. dollars	1974 Jamaican dollars	U.S. dollars	1974 Jamaican dollars	Expenditures as percentage of GDPa
1955	122	15.1	63.9	123.8	523.8	7.0
1960	227	40.3	73.1	177.5	322.0	5.7
1965	317	64.7	102.7	204.1	324.0	6.7
1970	415	95.5	134.9	230.1	325.0	6.8
1972	494	134.7	167.7	272.7	339.4	7.5

a. At constant 1974 prices. This ratio is not intended to reflect the contribution to GDP but simply to provide a rough indication of the relative importance of tourism in the national economy.
Sources: World Bank data: Jefferson 1972.

Table 4-14. Growth of Value Added at Constant Factor Cost, 1952–72
(percent a year)

Sector of activity	1952–59[a]	1959–72[b]
Agriculture, forestry, and fishing	2.2	2.2
Mining, quarrying, and refining	20.5	8.0
Manufacturing	8.6	5.4
Construction and installation	16.1	3.2
Electricity, gas, and water	10.7	9.9
Transport, storage, and communications	7.8	7.5
Distributive trades	8.8	2.1
Financial institutions	8.6	6.0
Ownership of dwellings	0.4	1.9
Public administration	7.8	8.7
Miscellaneous services	9.8	5.1
GDP at constant factor cost	8.3	5.0

a. At 1965 factor prices.
b. At 1960 factor prices.
Sources: Jamaica, Department of Statistics, and IBRD estimates.

1960s. Housing and other construction, agriculture, and industries producing for the home market were entirely financed from domestic sources.

Foreign investment, consisting mainly of private flows, financed about 30 percent of domestic capital formation over the period as a whole. About half of the foreign inflow went to the mining industry, which was entirely foreign-financed, and the rest into hotels, banking, and export-oriented manufacturing.

During 1960–65 the inflows of private foreign finance averaged only J$9 million a year. By 1966 the economy had overcome the initial uncertainty connected with the transition to independence, and, with the expansion of alumina capacity and the growth of tourism, foreign investment rose to a peak of 64 percent of total fixed private investment in 1971. In 1972, however, foreign financing dropped to 41 percent on the completion of a program for expanding alumina capacity (table 4-15). Thus far, foreign finance had had both a strengthening and a destabilizing effect; the latter took on important proportions in the 1972–80 period.

MONETARY AND FISCAL POLICIES. In 1961 the Bank of Jamaica was established, and the country went off the sterling standard, but its currency remained pegged to the pound sterling for the next ten years. The economic expansion of this period was supported by a basically conservative macroeconomic policy.

The government's budget on current account showed a surplus throughout the period. On average, government savings accounted for close to 30 percent of total domestic savings. The overall deficit, which

*Table 4-15. Total Private Fixed Investment and Net Private Capital Inflows,
1960–72*
(millions of Jamaican dollars)

Year	Fixed investments	Inflows	Inflows as percentage of fixed investments
1960–65	92[a]	9[a]	10
1966	123	38	31
1967	143	47	33
1968	185	92	50
1969	211	84	40
1970	273	137	50
1971	243	155	64
1972	246	91	41

a. Annual average.
Sources: Bank of Jamaica and World Bank estimates.

stood at 1.1 percent of GNP in 1960, increased slowly, reaching 4.4 percent
of GNP in 1971—still a moderate figure by most standards. Public debt
denominated in local currency amounted to 7.4 percent of GNP in 1960
and to 10.2 percent in 1972, while the ratio of foreign debt to GNP equaled
8 percent in 1960 and 9 percent in 1972.[22]

In 1960 total government expenditures amounted to less than 17
percent of GNP. Toward the end of the decade there was a sharp increase
in government expenditures, and by 1971–72 the ratio was close to 24
percent. To meet the country's financial needs the government imposed
a land improvement tax in 1968 and travel, hotel, and additional consumption taxes in 1969. In the same year it also increased the progressiv-
ity of income taxes, and it imposed a company profit tax in 1970.

Jamaica's current account balance was in deficit from the mid-1950s
until the end of the period under consideration, but since capital inflows
exceeded the current deficit in almost every year, the overall balance was
generally in surplus. The 1972 currency crisis was the one untoward
incident that marred the otherwise positive picture. After the collapse of
the Bretton Woods agreement, Jamaica decided, in late 1971, to maintain
its link with the British pound, and early in 1972 the Jamaican dollar was
revalued from US$1.20 to US$1.30 per Jamaican dollar, while the trade-
weighted average of the Jamaican real exchange rate appreciated by
some 10 percent (see Gavin 1989).

At the same time, the island experienced a consumption boom, related
to the expansionary monetary policies undertaken by the government
in an election year. The stimulus given to imports was magnified by
speculative purchasing: it was generally (and rightly) believed that the
new exchange rate could not be sustained, and there were short-term
capital outflows. Although the volume of exports rose, their value did

not change, because of a slight decline in the price of bauxite. To make matters worse, the current account crisis coincided with a deterioration in the capital account. With the program for expanding the alumina industry nearing completion, investment in mining declined from J$107 million in 1971 to J$50 million in 1972, and, as noted earlier, total private foreign investment declined from J$155 million to J$91 million.[23]

By the end of 1972 reserves had fallen sharply. The Jamaican dollar was permitted to drift downward, quantitative import restrictions were imposed, and the government drew on its credit from the IMF. Although the crisis revealed some mistakes in macroeconomic policy, few in the government suspected the extent of the difficulties that would plague the country in the next decade.

THE BAUXITE-ALUMINA INDUSTRY AND THE STRUCTURAL TRANSFORMATION OF THE ECONOMY. The boom years saw a profound structural transformation of the economy. Within twenty years agriculture's contribution to GNP and foreign exchange earnings declined precipitously, while manufacturing, mining, and services gained sharply in relative importance. Although farm products continued to be exported, bauxite-alumina and tourism emerged as the prime earners of foreign exchange.

The importance of Jamaica's bauxite deposits was not fully recognized until the 1940s, but even then they could not be commercially exploited until the standard processing method (the Bayer process) was adapted to the characteristics of the ore. In 1950, after negotiations with potential developers, the government of Jamaica offered conditions no less (and perhaps more) favorable than those of Suriname and Guyana, the region's other sources of the mineral.[24] Since the original agreement linked fiscal payments to the volume, not the value, of exports, Jamaica derived no benefits from the rapid rise in the world price of aluminum that occurred in the early 1950s. The agreement was renegotiated in 1957 to take the product price into account, raising the royalty-cum-tax payments from 2s8d (shillings and pence) per ton to 13s–16s, depending on the price of aluminum and the dollar-sterling exchange rate.

The three American producers—Alcoa, Reynolds, and Kaiser—developed mines to supply their U.S.-based processing facilities, and Alcan, a Canadian company, built an alumina-processing plant on the island. Jamaica exported all of its bauxite and 25 percent of its alumina to the United States, supplying 40 and 10 percent of U.S. bauxite and alumina requirements, respectively (Hughes 1984: 42). Thus, the fate of the Jamaican industry hinged on conditions in the U.S. market.

The U.S. government had strongly encouraged the aluminum industry to expand by allowing it to qualify for accelerated depreciation (a five-year writeoff) under the 1950 Defense Production Act. Aluminum ingots produced within five years of the start of an operation could be sold to the U.S. government strategic stockpile if there were no willing commercial purchasers, so that the risk of overexpansion of processing capacity was virtually eliminated. Reynolds and Alcan received U.S. government loans, repayable in aluminum ingots for the stockpile, to help finance the investment in their Jamaican operations.

The strategic stockpiling policy also generated direct demand for Jamaican bauxite. The original goal, 2.6 million tons, was reached by 1958. Under pressure from the Jamaican government the purchases continued, and the stockpile reached 8.9 million tons by the end of 1965. Large purchases were made again in the 1980s to bolster the Jamaican economy under the Seaga regime.

The first commercial shipments of bauxite were made in 1952; local processing of bauxite into alumina began in 1953. Over the next five years production increased at a phenomenal rate, rising from 420,000 tons in 1952 to 4.7 million tons in 1957, when Jamaica became the world's leading producer, and to 13.0 million tons in 1972 (see table 4-12). Exports of alumina began in 1953 with 29,000 tons and reached 2.1 million tons in 1972. By then, bauxite production capacity was rated at 14 million tons, about half of which could be domestically refined to produce 2.7 million tons of alumina.

The growth of the bauxite-alumina industry led to the formation of an enclave operating under a separate fiscal regime and having weak links to the rest of the economy. The industry is capital-intensive: in 1962 employment stood at 4,000, and in 1972 it reached a peak of 7,000. Although the industry pays high wages in comparison with the rest of the economy, wages account for less than 20 percent of gross value added.[25] The ratio of intermediate inputs to gross value of output does not even reach 25 percent (Girvan 1971: 44), and a substantial proportion of inputs, notably fuel, is imported. The most important link to the local economy is the demand for transport and construction services—the latter arising mainly in periods when capacity is being expanded.

Despite these weak links, Jamaica's economy became increasingly dependent on the bauxite-alumina industry, which by 1972 accounted for more than 12 percent of the island's GDP (table 4-16). What is more important, during the 1952–62 period the share of bauxite and alumina in total exports increased from 2.3 to 48.4 percent, whereas that of agricultural products (mainly sugar, rum, molasses, and bananas) fell from 79.3 to 40.8 percent. By 1972 bauxite and alumina accounted for two-thirds of export earnings (table 4-17). Bauxite and alumina also became one of the leading sources of government finance: by fiscal 1961–62 the industry was supplying about 16 percent of government revenues and paying more in taxes than the rest of the corporate sector (Girvan 1971: 61).

The bauxite-alumina boom had a dampening effect on the production of other tradables, notably agricultural output, while stimulating the demand for nontradables (see Corden 1984: 355–80). Agriculture's share of GDP fell from 27.7 percent in 1952 to 11.9 percent in 1962 and 9.1 percent

Table 4-16. GDP by Industrial Origin, 1952, 1962, and 1972
(percent)

Sector	1952	1962	1972
Agriculture, forestry, and fishing	27.7	11.9	9.1
Mining	0.0	9.6	12.2
Manufacturing	12.5	13.7	14.3
Construction	11.0	10.8	11.3
Electricity, water, and gas	1.0	1.2	1.6
Transport, storage, and communications	6.0	8.0	7.3
Wholesale and retail trade	16.7	16.0	13.9
Banking and insurance	1.8	4.5	6.6
Ownership of dwellings	4.9	3.3	2.7
Central and local government	5.3	7.3	9.4
Miscellaneous services	13.1	13.8	11.6

Note: Data in this table do not agree with World Bank data. The World Bank figures indicate a decline in the share of mining in GDP between 1965 and 1970, during which time bauxite and alumina production increased by more than 50 percent, while total output increased by only a third.

Sources: Jamaica, Department of Statistics, *National Income and Product Accounts*; 1952 estimates adjusted by Jefferson 1972: 42.

in 1972. Between 1954 and 1972 the ratio of value added by nonbooming tradables to GDP fell at a rate of 1.1 percent a year, and the ratio of nonbooming exports to GDP fell an average 3 percent a year.[26]

ROLE OF THE GOVERNMENT. During the 1950s and the 1960s the government took an increasingly active role in promoting and regulating economic development. In the early 1950s government investment amounted to less than 20 percent of gross national savings (see Jefferson 1972: tables 3.1, 9.1, and 10.1). By the early 1960s this ratio had jumped to 30 percent and by 1972 to more than 60 percent (table 4-18). In 1962–63 economic services were allocated 40 percent of the capital budget; social services (including education, health, housing, and welfare), 24 percent; and community services (roads, sanitation, fire protection), 22 percent.[27]

Table 4-17. Composition of Domestic Exports, 1953, 1962, and 1972
(percentage of f.o.b. value at current prices)

Export	1953	1962	1972
Bauxite and alumina	11.4	48.5	62.7
Sugar and bananas	60.0	30.2	15.2
All others	28.6	21.2	22.1[a]

a. Includes reexports.
Sources: Bank of Jamaica and IMF.

Table 4-18. Gross National Savings and General Capital Expenditure, 1962–72
(millions of Jamaican dollars)

Year	Gross national savings	Capital expenditure	Capital expenditure as percentage of savings
1962	85	25	29
1963	107	25	23
1964	89	30	34
1965	106	36	34
1966	120	38	32
1967	127	40	32
1968	144	51	35
1969	156	55	35
1970	197	73	37
1971	169	90	53
1972	176	110	63

Note: Government capital expenditure refers to fiscal years ending March 31.

Sources: Jamaica, Department of Statistics, *National Income and Product* 1972; Ministry of Finance and World Bank estimates.

As part of its economic program the government created a number of new parastatals, among them the Jamaica Industrial Development Corporation (JIDC) and the Agricultural Development Corporation (ADC), launched in 1952, as discussed earlier; the Small Business Loans Board, set up in 1956, which extended to small enterprises loans of less than J$2,000; and the Agricultural Credit Fund and the Development Finance Corporation (DFC), established in 1959. (In 1969 the DFC became the Jamaica Development Bank.) The DFC was empowered to extend medium- and long-term loans to industry and to low- and middle-income housing schemes, as well as to tourism, which the JIDC was not entitled to do. In 1969 the Jamaica National Export Corporation was created to take over the JIDC's export-promotion functions. These various corporations answered to different ministries—the JIDC to the Ministry of Trade and Industry, the DFC to the Ministry of Finance, and the ADC to the Ministry of Agriculture. Thus, quasi-governmental bodies proliferated with little or no functional coordination.

Between 1952 and 1970–71 the major development agencies received a total of J$70 million in government funds, but their investments had only modest results. A detailed analysis of JIDC activities found that the agency spent 45.6 percent of its J$16.2 million grant on administrative and promotional activities, and it devoted J$1.7 million to constructing industrial estates and factory buildings and J$2.3 million to portfolio investment. Subsequently, J$2.3 million of the portfolio investment had to be written off (Widdicomb 1972: 166–70).

The most important indirect measures adopted by the government consisted of incentives granted to industry. The Industrial Incentives

Law of 1956 (IIL), which remains in force, extended and made more generous the provisions of the Pioneer Industry Act of 1949. Under the IIL manufacturers of approved products can qualify for income tax exemptions of up to ten years, commencing up to three years from the time the company starts production. In designated development areas the tax holiday can be extended to fifteen years and can even be extended to income tax on dividends distributed during the holiday period. Manufacturers of approved products can also import raw materials and capital goods duty-free.[28]

Applications for concessions under the IIL are reviewed individually by the Industrial Development Corporation, which makes its recommendations to the minister of commerce. Approval may be given under either the "new product" or the "other" category. A new product is designated as such if less than 20 percent of domestic demand is satisfied by approved domestic manufacturers. The "other" category includes enterprises that use domestic raw materials, are labor-intensive, or produce an input of importance to domestic industry.

The Export Industry Encouragement Law (EIEL), also adopted in 1956, provides the same concessions as the IIL. In addition, enterprises manufacturing exclusively for export may import duty-free all raw materials and capital goods without time limit. To qualify, production must be performed in-bond, and the only domestic sales permitted are those to another export manufacturer.

Although the incentive legislation of the mid-1950s granted industries the same privileges in selling on the internal or external markets, the trade regime became increasingly biased in favor of import substitution. Import duties were gradually raised and made more progressive in line with the stage of fabrication, but they remained moderate, not surpassing 35 percent ad valorem (except on a few luxury items). At the same time, the government made extensive use of quantitative restrictions to protect designated domestic manufacturers and, in many cases, granted them virtual monopoly power. Starting with a quota on shoe imports in 1952, the restricted list contained about 50 items by the time of independence, and by 1968 the number had grown to 158. Some of the quotas were narrowly defined; others—for example, "clothing, all categories"—were so broadly defined that they offered protection to an entire branch of industry.

Under the incentive system, the size of the quota is negotiated at the time a new firm gains approval and is calculated as a function of the firm's capacity to satisfy the domestic market. Normally, only one firm is approved as a manufacturer of a given product—ostensibly to achieve economies of scale. Theoretically speaking, nothing prevents firms that do not benefit from the incentive privileges from eroding the monopolies that are thus created. In practice, however, it is often more profitable to find an unexplored opportunity of import substitution and obtain monopoly privileges, instead of competing with established firms.

Table 4-19. Number of Firms Approved under the Industrial Incentives Law (IIL) and the Export Industry Encouragement Law (EIEL), 1956–85

Year of approval	IIL	EIEL
1956–60	27	22
1961–65	148	48
1966–70	79	53
1971–75	52	47
1976–80	39	27
1981–85	14	57

Source: Planning Institute of Jamaica.

The industrial incentive laws created a bias against the production of exportables. Between 1956 and 1980, 345 firms applied for fiscal privileges under the Pioneer Industry Encouragement Law (PIEL) and the Industrial Incentive Law (IIL), compared with the 197 applicants under the Export Industry legislation (table 4-19). In 1972 EIEL firms paid J$3.1 million in wages, while firms benefiting from domestic privileges paid J$18.6 million.[29] According to the Jamaica Industrial Development Corporation, total sales amounted to more than J$127 million for the former and less than J$13 million for the latter. In 1972, 68 percent of the firms benefiting from IIL privileges were either 100 percent Jamaican-owned or had majority Jamaican ownership, whereas 63 percent of EIEL firms were either fully foreign-owned or had majority foreign ownership. The average investment per worker amounted to J$10,900 in IIL firms but only J$778 in EIEL firms (1972 figures). It is easy to see why Jamaican manufacturers favored a protectionist policy and why foreign-owned firms were footloose and ready to liquidate their Jamaican operations should the business climate turn unfavorable.

The economic growth of the 1950s and 1960s enabled party leaders to fulfill some of their promises to the newly enfranchised masses, beginning with help for the poorer classes, which included expanded education and health services, the construction of low-income housing, schemes of support for small farmers, and national insurance for retired workers. The rise in social welfare expenditures as a percentage of GDP is shown in table 4-20.

Between 1950 and 1970 primary school enrollment grew from 64 to 85 percent of children of school age, and secondary school enrollment expanded from 6 to 58 percent (table 4-21). This is in sharp contrast to the marginal increases before the advent of universal adult suffrage (1944). The massive rise in secondary school enrollment was facilitated by the increase in the number of government tuition scholarships in the early 1950s and the large increase in the number of secondary school buildings.

Improved environmental hygiene (better water supply, nutrition, and health services) led to a dramatic decline in infant mortality and a rise in

Table 4-20. Government Social Expenditure (Health, Education, Housing, and Welfare), Selected Years

Year	Social expenditure as percentage of GDP
1938	2.8
1960	5.6
1970	6.4
1975	12.1

Source: Planning Institute of Jamaica, *Economic and Social Survey*, various issues.

life expectancy. Jamaica now ranks far above other developing countries in health indicators and is close to the standards of the highly industrialized nations (table 4-22).

The JLP constructed new public housing at a rate of 1,500 units a year during its two terms of office between 1962 and 1972.[30] The PNP, during its two terms in office from 1972 to 1980, built an average of 2,500 units a year, with the rate of construction accelerating as the country approached the 1980 elections. In total, approximately 50,000 housing units were constructed by successive PNP and JLP governments between independence in 1962 and 1985; this figure represents 75 percent of the new housing built over this period.

Public housing not only has social and economic value but also provides opportunities for political patronage and for establishing political strongholds through the careful selection of tenants. Typically, the JLP and PNP governments pack their housing schemes with persons who are strong party supporters and in this way create tightly knit, politically partisan communities.

Consistent with their commitment to social reform, successive JLP and PNP governments initiated extensive social legislation. The National Insurance Act (1965) replaced the traditional poor-relief institutions with old age pensions, disability benefits, and various benefits for the dependents of all workers contributing to the scheme.

Table 4-21. Growth in Educational Opportunities, Selected Years, 1920–70
(percent)

Year	Primary school enrollment (ages 5–14)	Secondary school enrollment (ages 15–19)
1920	51	3
1944	58	4
1950	64	6
1960	65	15
1970	85	58

Source: Jamaica, *Statistical Yearbook*, 1926–72 issues.

Table 4-22. Health Indicators in Selected Countries

Country	1937	1950	1960	1970	1980
Infant mortality per 1,000 live births					
Jamaica	118	81	63	36	22
Mexico	140	90	74	71	65
Sri Lanka	158	71	63	51	47
United States	57	29	26	20	15
Venezuela	135	67	72	51	42
Malaysia	170	81	69	41	32
Life expectancy at birth					
Jamaica	—	61	64	68	70
Mexico	—	56	58	62	65
Sri Lanka	—	60	62	67	69
United States	—	69	70	71	73
Venezuela	—	57	59	66	66
Malaysia	—	52	57	64	67

— Not available.

Sources: West Indian Royal Commission Report 1938; World Bank 1980; Overseas Development Council 1978.

The government also tried to help poor farmers. During the colonial period agricultural extension services were available only to big farmers producing traditional export crops, such as sugarcane and bananas. In the 1950s and the 1960s these facilities were extended to small farmers and geared to their needs. To cope with these expanding tasks, the government increased the technical staff in its agricultural departments from 45 in 1930 to 676 in 1970. As a further help to small farmers, the government developed credit and marketing facilities and instituted land-distribution schemes that increased the number of farmers owning their own land from 60 percent in 1943 to 80 percent in 1962. And when the government was criticized for failing to provide sufficient jobs, it launched a public employment scheme (1968). The budget of this program grew from J$5.2 million in fiscal 1968–69 to J$8.2 million in fiscal 1971–72, thus contributing to the growing budgetary burden of social expenditures.

INCOME INEQUALITY AND UNEMPLOYMENT. Despite Jamaica's prosperity and the government's efforts to help the poor, inequality and unemployment persisted in the 1950s and 1960s. In 1958, for example, the lowest two deciles of households in the country had a 2.2 percent share of total income, whereas the wealthiest 5 percent of households had a 30.2 percent share (table 4-23). Moreover, one-fifth of all households earned less than J$50 a year. The Gini coefficient, 0.61, is among the highest in the world.[31]

Table 4-23. *Income Share of Jamaican Households, 1958*
(percent)

Decile of household	Income share
1–2	2.2
3	2.5
4	3.5
5	4.7
6	6.1
7	8.3
8	11.2
9	18.0
10 (first 5 percent)	13.3
10 (second 5 percent)	30.2

Source: Ahiram 1958: 337.

On average, urban income was 2.4 times greater than rural income. The poorest fifth of the urban households was 3.5 times as wealthy as the poorest fifth of the rural households—a statistic that points to the severity of the rural poverty problem.

Labor income was highly dispersed (table 4-24), in large part because of differences in skill. In 1965 the average weekly wage of skilled workers in large establishments was two and a half times as high as that of unskilled workers; in some occupations (for example, public utilities), the differential was even higher (table 4-25). The wages of skilled workers reflect the ease with which these workers migrated to the United States and Canada, and manufacturers have perennially complained of a skill shortage.

Wages for workers at the same skill level in different industries also varied greatly. In 1965 the average weekly wage for all unskilled workers was J$9.20, whereas unskilled bauxite mine workers earned J$27.00 (Jefferson 1972: 38). Unskilled agricultural workers (other than those on

Table 4-24. *Distribution of Labor Income, 1968, 1972, and 1974*
(percent)

Percentage of households	1968	1972	1974
0–60	25.0	20.0	16.0
0–80	47.2	39.3	32.0
0–90	63.3	57.0	48.3
0–95	75.0	65.0	60.0
0–100	100.0	100.0	100.0
Gini coefficient	0.53	0.60	0.67

Source: World Bank estimates.

Table 4-25. *Wage Rates by Sector, 1965*
(average weekly earnings, Jamaican dollars)

Sector	All workers	Skilled workers	Unskilled workers
Agriculture (excluding sugar)	6.6	19.2	5.8
Agriculture (sugarcane)	9.0	24.2	7.8
Mining	42.4	49.4	27.0
Sugar (factory)	16.2	21.8	11.0
Other manufacturing	14.8	18.0	10.0
Construction (private)	20.8	28.8	13.8
Construction (government)	7.6	19.4	6.8
Public utilities (electricity)	35.2	37.4	10.6
Public utilities (water and sanitation)	8.2	17.6	7.0
Commerce	24.0	28.6	11.4
Transport, storage, and communications	19.6	27.8	14.0
Miscellaneous services	13.8	20.8	11.2
Weighted average	14.4	24.6	9.2

Source: Jefferson 1972: 38.

the sugar plantations) earned the lowest wage, although many supplemented this income with earnings from their own small farms.[32]

Unemployment, as measured by the Statistical Institute, declined in the early boom years. In 1953 it stood at 17.5 percent (it was 25.1 percent in 1943), and by 1960 it was down to 13.5 percent, a low figure by Jamaican standards (table 4-26). By 1972, however, it was up to 22.8 percent. Over the 1953–72 period as a whole, employment rose by 19 percent and the labor force grew by 27 percent. Had it not been for emigration, which siphoned off an estimated 50 percent of the increase in the working-age population, the situation would have been much worse.

Table 4-26. *Employment and Unemployment, Selected Years,
October 1943–October 1972*

Year	Labor force	Employed	Unemployed	Unemployment rate (percent)
1943	555,600	416,100	139,500	25.1
1953	634,900	523,900	111,000	17.5
1957	658,100	545,500	112,600	17.1
1960	654,600	566,100	88,500	13.5
1968	727,000	592,300	134,600	18.5
1969	753,900	624,300	129,500	17.2
1972	808,900	624,400	184,600	22.8

Sources: Jamaica, Department of Statistics, *The Labour Force: 1973*; for 1943–60, Jefferson 1972: 28.

Why unemployment was high and ever-growing in Jamaica's rapidly growing economy can be explained by a number of factors. As already mentioned, the booming bauxite-alumina industry did not create a significant number of direct jobs. Furthermore, it handicapped Jamaica's export-oriented agriculture and thus slowed job creation there. In manufacturing, the policy of protecting import-substituting industries favored relatively capital-intensive enterprises, and the unions concentrated their actions on protected sectors. In the face of mounting unemployment, real wages in unionized industry rose by more than 1 percent a year between 1967 and 1972. The labor market became increasingly segmented as a growing proportion of the population engaged in marginal occupations or remained unemployed.

Summary

The boom years of 1952–72 brought rapid economic and social progress to Jamaica. At the beginning of the period it was an agricultural country emerging from colonialism and largely dependent on expatriate managers and administrators. Within less than a generation the economy became diversified and the administration self-reliant. The transition was achieved with a remarkable lack of disruption.

There were, to be sure, some signs of weakness. The bauxite-alumina boom depressed the production of tradables, and the economy became more dependent on foreign exchange earnings from the bauxite-alumina industry—a trend encouraged by the government's policy of promoting import substitution. This was also a period of rapid growth for government enterprises, which were, for the most part, inefficiently run. Indeed, public administration expanded faster than GDP. Although monetary and financial stability continued throughout most of the period, the 1971 balance of payments crisis showed that the economy was vulnerable to errors in macroeconomic policy.

The Manley Government, 1972–80

Despite the unprecedented prosperity of the late 1960s, the JLP government found the electorate growing more and more dissatisfied. People complained that income disparities and unemployment were as serious as ever, that the government was corrupt, and that the favoritism it practiced verged on the persecution of its political opponents.

Political Developments

By 1970 the PNP, which promised to bring good government and social reform, was clearly gaining popularity. The decisive factor in the 1972 election was not any substantive issue, however, but the personality of the PNP's leader, Michael Manley, the son of Norman Manley: "Manley's awesome popularity in 1972 was based on a charisma that drew on Rastafarian imagery, a watered-down black power appeal, and an intelligent and persuasive oratory adaptable to the streets or a boardroom. Manley pledged 'Better Must Come,' that 'It's time for a government of love' to be achieved through 'Power for the People'" (Kaufman 1985: 71).

The oratory apparently had broad appeal: Manley's main support came from the middle class, the better-to-do workers, and the wealthy (table 4-27). In the general election held in February 1972, the PNP received 56.4 percent of the vote, which at the time was the largest majority ever obtained by either party under universal suffrage, and it won thirty-six of the fifty-two seats in the legislature.

During its first two years in power, the PNP introduced a number of moderate social reforms, but starting in 1974 it moved in the direction of "democratic socialism." The government tightened controls over the private sector, acquired a number of enterprises, and undertook some new industrial and commercial initiatives. These measures, and the increasingly radical oratory of the PNP leaders, polarized society. The mass media became more partisan in debating controversial policy and ideological issues. The public agenda broadened to encompass many issues that had never been publicly debated before, such as race and class, and people grew more vocal about national policy issues. They began supporting or criticizing government policies on phone-in radio programs and in letters to the editor in the island's two daily newspapers, and the number of strikes, many of which were politically motivated, rose sharply (table 4-28). There were also frequent cases of land seizure and of violent battles between youth gangs associated with the two parties.

By 1976 the PNP had lost the support of the middle and, especially, the upper classes, while its popularity among workers, the unemployed, and intellectuals increased. Thus it regained the profile it had before the 1952

Table 4-27. Political Support, by Class of Worker, 1972–86
(percent)

Class	1972		1976		1980		1986	
	PNP	*JLP*	*PNP*	*JLP*	*PNP*	*JLP*	*PNP*	*JLP*
Unemployed and unskilled workers	52	48	60	40	40	60	65	35
Skilled and semiskilled wage workers	61	39	72	28	48	52	63	37
White-collar workers	75	25	57	43	37	63	56	44
Business management and high-income professionals	60	40	20	80	14	86	31	69
Small farmers	47	53	45	55	35	65	57	43

Source: National polls by Carl Stone.

Table 4-28. Average Number of Strikes and Man-Days Lost Per Year, 1964–83

Period	Number of strikes	Man-days lost
1964–67	64	178
1968–71	79	178
1972–75	142	346
1976–79	175	—
1980–83	94	—

— Not available.

Note: According to Stephens and Stephens (1986: table 2.10), in the years 1976, 1977, and 1979 there were, on average, 163 strikes per year, with an average of 101,000 man-days lost.

Sources: For number of strikes, Jamaica, *Statistical Yearbook*, 1949–79; for days lost, Stephens and Stephens 1986: table 2.10.

"purge" and scored a triumph in the 1976 election, winning forty-seven of the sixty electoral seats.[33]

The new PNP programs proved to be costly, however, and the government resorted to massive internal and external borrowing to keep them going. These difficulties were compounded by a decline in the demand for Jamaican bauxite and alumina (severely aggravated by a government-imposed levy), a slump in tourism, and a flight of capital and entrepreneurs. Soon after the 1976 election the government had to abandon most of its social projects and, despite protestations to the contrary, follow an IMF-type austerity program. These measures, in turn, alienated the left and brought about a drastic decline in PNP support among the unemployed and workers. The JLP emerged from the violence of the 1980 general election with 58.8 percent of the vote. The PNP, with only nine of the sixty members in the legislature, now found itself on the opposition benches.

THE PNP'S SHIFT TO THE LEFT. A number of factors caused the PNP to move toward the left during the 1970s. A new wave of populist radicalism had emerged outside the two major parties in the 1960s and had fomented violent protests. This movement articulated race and class issues and challenged the political system for selling out to conservative interests. Its activist support came from a small group of militant black intelligentsia who spoke out against racial and class oppression and the absence of social justice in Jamaica. A number of bright militants within this movement emerged as leaders within the PNP, among them D. K. Duncan and Arnold Bertram.

Both the leaders and activists in this movement rallied behind the new PNP head, Michael Manley, who had succeeded his father, Norman Manley, in 1969. The younger Manley had limited his activities to trade unionism before he took over the PNP's leadership. A newcomer to the political scene, he seemed to be unblemished by corrupting connections with the established politicians and power structure. The new radicals embraced Manley, and he in turn felt his political mission was to radicalize Jamaican politics in order to incorporate the alienated elements into the mainstream of the country's political system.

Manley was influenced by the radical thinking of the local university intelligentsia, who were highly critical of Jamaica's so-called neocolonial economic policies and dependence on foreign capital in the 1950s and 1960s and who favored socialist solutions and nationalist strategies of economic ownership and control. Manley was also driven by a desire to establish himself as a leader of the developing world. This required close collaboration with the existing radical leftist leaders of the nonaligned developing countries, such as Fidel Castro, Julius Nyerere, Muammar Qaddafi, and Houari Boumedienne, all of whom were ostensibly committed to socialism as a strategy for development. The influence of radical allies in the developing world, the radical activists within the PNP, a personal commitment by Manley to find a path toward a more self-reliant and nationalist economic policy, and Manley's trade union background (which increased the importance of workers in his eyes) all converged to push the party further to the left and eventually to break down the two-party consensus that had marked Jamaican politics up to that time.

Manley's succession to leadership coincided with the emergence of a new technocratic leader of the JLP, Edward Seaga, whose managerial style sharply contrasted with Manley's radical populism. These differences widened the ideological differences between the two parties, which increased even further during the economic crisis of the mid-1970s.

Despite these differences, most of the measures adopted by the PNP in the 1970s were some variation of steps taken by the JLP between 1962 and 1972 (table 4-29). There was no sharp shift from free enterprise to socialist planning; rather, the preexisting dirigiste trend was accelerated and radicalized.

CHANGES IN POWER RELATIONS. During the 1970s the political influence of the private sector declined considerably. The PNP deliberately set out to reduce capitalist influence over national policy in order to project itself as a party of the poor and to increase the role of party activists and mass organizations. In accordance with socialist doctrine, the PNP wanted an enlarged public sector that would assume many of the functions previously carried out by private enterprise.

Although a few prominent businessmen remained close to the PNP leadership and some companies made considerable profits during this period, the majority of the capitalist class felt threatened by PNP policies and withdrew their support from the government. For the first time since independence, business as a group created a unified lobby, the Private Sector Organization of Jamaica (PSOJ). Unlike the existing associations

Table 4-29. Continuities in Party Policies

Major JLP policies, 1962–72	PNP reaction, 1972–80
Initiated local ownership of financial institutions	Continued
Established machinery for price controls	Continued
Initiated state ownership of utilities	Extended
Initiated state acquisition of idle lands for allocation to small farmers	Extended
Established state agency to run sugar industry	Extended
Continued lease of government lands to small farmers	Extended
Established Agricultural Marketing Corporation	Continued
Developed large low-income housing projects	Continued
Initiated national insurance	Criticized, but continued
Continued rent controls	Extended
Expanded scholarships to high schools and increased secondary education	Continued
Developed National Cultural Festival promoting local music and folk culture	Continued

Source: Authors' compilation.

representing various sectors of the business community, this was an umbrella organization, and it had the full and active support of the most influential business interests. The PSOJ reviewed government policies and attempted to influence public opinion by making the private sector's views on economic issues known.

Government-business relations steadily deteriorated in the face of growing trade with the Soviet bloc countries and a strong Cuban presence (diplomats, doctors, construction workers, and political activists). Private businesses began to fear that the country was heading toward communism and interpreted the increasing incidents of crime against businessmen as politically motivated attacks mounted to force private entrepreneurs out of the country. Panic within the private sector weakened the economy, inciting PNP hostility toward the business class and feeding claims that business was in collusion with the U.S. Central Intelligence Agency to destabilize the government. There was a considerable flight of capital. Enterprises were closed, tax payments evaded, and investments shelved. A climate of antigovernment hysteria paralyzed economic activity in the private sector, and the collaborative relationship it had maintained with the public sector in the previous two decades gave way to confrontation.

CHANGES IN THE DECISIONMAKING PROCESS. Public decisionmaking took on some important new structural features during the 1970s.

- The prime minister began dominating the policy agenda and coordinating policy implementation. His office became like the U.S.

White House in that it exercised leadership over the principal areas of government policy.

- The governing PNP exercised even tighter control over the policy agenda than the JLP had in the 1960s. New cadres of handpicked policy advisers with party connections were brought into government ministries and the prime minister's office. These advisers supported policy leaders and strategists in the governing party by operating as their resource persons.

- With policymakers relying more on new party advisers and outside consultants, the policy role of senior professional civil servants dwindled. This trend was reinforced by the practice of giving senior appointments to people who supported the governing party's ideology.

- Policies were debated and decided on in mass meetings of the governing party's rank and file. As a consequence, the general interest in policy matters deepened, and cabinet members began feeling greater pressure from below. These open debates also widened the ideological divisions within the party and sharpened competition among politicians.

Thus, administrative and political power shifted from the bureaucracy to the hands of the PNP.

Socioeconomic Goals and Policies

The economic and social policies of the Manley government rapidly evolved from moderate reformism to full-fledged democratic socialism. In the 1972 election manifestos, Manley and other PNP activists had railed against Jamaica's excessive dependence on foreign investment and had called for industrial development based on domestic raw materials and for increased food output. They also called for greater social justice through more progressive taxation, subsidies on essential commodities, and educational and youth employment programs (Stephens and Stephens 1986: 67–68). They made no mention, however, of the form of ownership or the means of production. By contrast, in its 1974 Declaration of Principles the PNP stated that the aim of domestic policy should be "ultimate control by and in the name of the people of the major means of production, distribution, and exchange." The private sector was to be an integral part of the mixed economy, but private activities were to be controlled in the service of society (Stephens and Stephens 1986: 106–8).

Economic reforms were in step with the new ideology. Foreign-owned public utilities, electricity, urban transport, telephones, and several major banks were bought out by the government. The government acquired majority ownership of the cement, gypsum, and steel industries and initiated several ambitious projects, but some of them (for example, the construction of a refinery) had to be abandoned for lack of funds. The Jamaican Bauxite Mining Co., Ltd., a government holding company formed in 1975, took a 51 percent equity position in the bauxite mining operations of the multinationals operating in Jamaica (Kaiser and Reynolds) and a minority position in the other two firms there (Alcoa and Alcan).

In addition to capturing the "commanding heights" of the economy, the government acquired a number of faltering businesses, including several hotels. Many of these purchases were made under pressure from the owners, who, alarmed by the deterioration of the economy and the trend toward socialism, were anxious to sell out. At the same time, private enterprise continued to be granted incentives under the Industrial Incentives (Regional Harmonization) Law, which was passed to bring Jamaican legislation in line with that of the other countries of the Caribbean Economic Community (CARICOM).

In agriculture, the government used the marketing board mechanism to extract a rent from export crops (sugar, bananas, citrus, coffee, cocoa, coconuts, tobacco, and pimento and other spices) but kept production for the home market relatively free of price controls. The resulting bias is reflected in growth figures. Between 1972 and 1980 the production of export crops declined at an annual rate of 6.1 percent, whereas the production of domestic crops rose 0.8 percent a year.[34] To relieve rural poverty, the government launched a land-lease program that provided public land to landless peasants at low cost. In another major experiment, it formed sixteen workers' cooperatives on 26,800 acres of sugar estates it had bought from foreign companies.[35]

In the first five years of its tenure, the Manley government improved public health services, raised the level of pension and poor relief payments, and launched an adult literacy program. A public works program, IMPACT, was started in April of the same year with the aim of giving employment to a full-time equivalent of 20,000 workers. During fiscal 1974–75 this program alone cost J$38.4 million, or 7.7 percent of government current expenditure.

To improve low-income housing, the government launched a J$20 million scheme in January 1974 that was to provide housing for families with incomes of less than J$1,200 per year. This was followed in 1975 by a National Housing Trust scheme, to be financed by contributions from employers and employees.[36] A worker could withdraw his contribution after seven years, a salaried employee after twenty-five years. Between 1974–75 and 1980–81, total contributions to the trust amounted to J$102.6 million. The trust sponsored its own housing schemes and became a source of mortgage financing for public and private housing (Davies 1984b).

A national minimum wage of J$20 for a forty-hour week that took effect in November 1975 led to pay increases for about 25 percent of all workers. At the same time, the government issued guidelines on salary increases, with the aim of reducing the wage spread.[37] It put out new wage and salary guidelines in 1976 and in subsequent years and made the income tax more progressive so as to level income disparities and provide financial support for its increasingly burdensome welfare policies.

Most of the government's new schemes proved to be expensive, ill-conceived, and mismanaged. The nationalized enterprises could, in principle, provide the government with much-needed current revenue, but in practice, most of them incurred losses. The farmers' cooperatives ran up enormous debts and had to be liquidated by the successor government. The high-wage policy left Jamaica's producers unable to compete in their markets, and the burden of the state's welfare schemes grew heavier.

In aggregate, the Manley program pushed government current expenditures up from about 14 percent of GDP in 1972 to more than 30 percent in the closing years of the decade. These expenditures far outpaced the revenues from increased taxes and the bauxite levy, and consequently the current account, which had a surplus in 1974–75 and 1975–76, slid into a deficit in 1976–77 that amounted to 19.5 percent of GDP. In the following year the deficit declined, but only because the government was forced to trim its program.

The Bauxite Levy

One of the most important and controversial moves of the Manley government was to impose a levy on bauxite production (Young 1987). In the short run, the levy relaxed the foreign currency constraint on the economy; in the longer run, however, it contributed to the decline of alumina and bauxite production in Jamaica.

In the late 1960s Jamaica began to lose its primacy as a bauxite producer to newer fields, notably in Australia. In 1968 Australia produced only half as much as Jamaica, but by 1971 it had caught up, and by 1974 it was producing a third more than Jamaica. Guinean production did not come on stream until the 1970s, but it, too, grew very rapidly in the subsequent years. Between 1970 and 1974 Jamaica's output of bauxite grew by 18 percent compared with 42 percent for the world as a whole.

In the 1950s and 1960s world consumption of aluminum grew at 9 percent a year. Between 1960 and 1984 the annual rate slowed to 2.7 percent, mainly because of the worldwide recession triggered by the 1973 and 1979 oil price shocks and because of the increasing use of plastics. Moreover the oil price increases put Jamaica at a disadvantage with respect to coal-using producers such as Australia. According to World Bank estimates, an increase of US$10 per barrel of oil raises the cost of alumina production in Jamaica by US$15 to US$29, depending on the plant. Even more important, aluminum reduction is a fuel-intensive process, and the increases in the price of fuel forced U.S. aluminum plants (the main buyers of Jamaican alumina) to relocate to energy-rich countries.

A production levy imposed by the Manley government struck another blow to Jamaica's bauxite and alumina industry. Manley's original intention was to organize an international cartel of bauxite producers patterned on OPEC. The producing countries, however, failed to agree on a general scheme for limiting output or to impose a uniform royalty rate, and on April 15, 1975, Jamaica, acting alone, imposed a levy on bauxite production equal to 7.5 percent of the average realized price of aluminum ingot.[38] The levy brought about a sixfold increase in taxes, raised alumina production costs by some US$30 per ton, and made Jamaica, which had been among the world's lowest-cost producers, one of its highest.

In the years that followed the imposition of the bauxite levy, the bauxite and alumina industry went into decline. In 1974 Jamaica produced 15.3 million tons of bauxite and 2.9 million tons of alumina, but the corresponding figures for 1975 were 11.6 million tons of bauxite and 2.3 million tons of alumina (table 4-30). By 1983 the output of bauxite had declined by a half and that of alumina by more than a third. In 1974 Jamaica's main customer, the United States, purchased 52 percent of its bauxite import requirements from Jamaica; within ten years that proportion declined to 40 percent, and the proportion of alumina that the United States imported from Jamaica fell from 25 to 13 percent.

The immediate effect of the Jamaican levy was to raise the government's revenues from bauxite and alumina production from US$27 million in 1973 to US$180 million in 1974 (table 4-31). During the first ten years of the levy the industry paid the government a total of US$1,691 million on 111 million tons of bauxite. In the ten years before the levy, the industry had produced 114 million tons of bauxite, for which it paid the government only US$270 million in taxes and royalties (data from Jamaica Bauxite Institute quoted in Davies 1984c).

Table 4-30. Jamaican Bauxite and Alumina Production, 1972–80

Year	Bauxite		Alumina	
	Thousands of metric tons	*Percentage of world production*	*Thousands of metric tons*	*Percentage of world production*
1972	12,989	18.8	2,087	8.7
1973	13,600	18.1	2,506	9.2
1974	15,328	18.2	2,874	9.8
1975	11,570	15.0	2,259	8.5
1976	10,296	12.8	1,639	5.9
1977	11,434	13.5	2,047	6.7
1978	11,736	13.8	2,141	6.9
1979	11,505	12.9	2,074	6.4
1980	12,064	13.0	2,395	6.9

Source: American Bureau of Metal Statistics 1965–75 and 1973–83 and most recent data.

Table 4-31. Government Earnings from the Bauxite Industry, 1964–73
(millions of U.S. dollars)

Year	Taxes and royalties	Year	Levy earnings[a]
1964	20.52	1974	179.99
1965	22.09	1975	150.43
1966	27.53	1976	139.40
1967	24.29	1977	180.99
1968	24.33	1978	194.25
1969	29.49	1979	190.28
1970	35.95	1980	205.71
1971	30.21	1981	192.99
1972	28.42	1982	135.51
1973	26.95	1983	121.34
Total	269.78		1,690.89

a. Does not include royalty payments.
Source: Davies 1984a: 4.

An idea of the importance of the levy can be obtained by comparing the foreign exchange earnings with the rise in the cost of oil imports associated with the 1973 and 1979 oil price shocks. Between 1974 and 1978 the proceeds from the levy more than covered the rising cost of oil. Following the second shock, the cost of oil imports continued to climb, but the proceeds from the levy fell, leaving a progressively widening gap (table 4-32). It is clear, nevertheless, that the levy greatly eased the country's balance of payments problem.

Even from a long-run point of view the imposition of the levy does not seem to have been a serious mistake—a proposition that can be backed by an admittedly crude calculation of the present value of revenues accruing to Jamaica from bauxite and alumina. Suppose that in the absence of the levy, the industry's output and total annual payments had remained at the levels of the early 1970s.[39] At the beginning of 1974 the present value of the corresponding income stream, reckoned at a 10 percent discount, would have equaled J$772 million at 1973 prices. The present value of actual 1974–83 receipts discounted to the beginning of 1974 equals J$796 million (1973 prices).[40] It is possible, of course, that output would have continued to grow, had it not been for the levy; however, the industry was not wiped out by the levy, so the two biases work in opposite directions. On balance, the imposition of the levy does not look like a fatal mistake, although it was poorly timed and in all likelihood was excessively high.

It is obvious, however, that the proceeds of the levy were used injudiciously.[41] The PNP government intended to invest most of the proceeds to create an alternative source of income, in anticipation of the exhaus-

Table 4-32. Levy Earnings in Relation to Nonbauxite Oil Imports, 1974–83
(millions of U.S. dollars)

Year	Levy earnings	Nonbauxite-related oil imports	Levy – imports
1974	180	139	+41
1975	150	146	+4
1976	139	147	–8
1977	181	154	+27
1978	194	141	+53
1979	190	201	–11
1980	206	261	–55
1981	193	268	–75
1982	136	281	–145
1983	121	278	–157

Note: Davies's levy data do not agree with those of Davis. Davies's paper having been published at a later date, his figures are assumed to represent the revised and corrected data. Similarly, Davis's 1981 oil import figure is not used, since the 1983 economic survey presents a revised figure.

Sources: For 1974–80 oil import data, Davis 1982; for 1974–82 levy data, Davies 1984c; for 1981–83 data, Planning Institute of Jamaica, *Economic and Social Survey*, 1983.

tion of the island's bauxite deposits (see Hughes 1984: 47). In fact, the lion's share of the levy proceeds were used to cover the government's mounting budgetary deficits.

Between 1974 and 1982 the Capital Development Fund (CDF), created to receive and dispose of the levy proceeds, received US$1,495.1 million (see table 4-33). To meet the government's fiscal demands, US$1,074.8 million was transferred to the budget, leaving US$420.3 million for investment.[42] A large proportion of the investment fund was held in reserve or employed by the central bank, and US$19.1 million was placed in government debentures. In total, only US$157.7 million went for productive investment; most of that amount was used to acquire private businesses, to finance the government's bauxite enterprises, and to construct housing. Despite their merit, these endeavors did not contribute appreciably to the goal of creating alternative sources of income to the bauxite-alumina industry.

Fiscal, Monetary, and Trade Policies

To overcome the balance of payments crisis it inherited from the previous regime, the Manley government placed quantitative restrictions on imports of consumer goods and on foreign travel. From mid-1972 the Jamaican dollar (along with the pound sterling, to which it was linked) was allowed to float downward in relation to the U.S. dollar. In January 1973 Jamaica delinked its currency from the pound sterling and deval-

Table 4-33. *Levy Inflows into the* CDF *and Transfers to the Consolidated Fund, 1974–83*
(millions of U.S. dollars)

Year	CDF inflows[a]	Transfer to consolidated fund	Transfer as percentage of inflows
1974	117.2	60.4	51.6
1975	167.0	120.9	72.4
1976	113.5	93.4	82.3
1977	224.8	164.9	73.3
1978	115.7	102.6	88.6
1979	194.3	165.3	85.0
1980	234.8	90.9[b]	38.7
1981	199.7	196.8	98.5
1982	128.1	79.6	62.1
1983	195.8[c]	202.2	103.2
Total	1,690.9	1,277.0	75.5

a. Includes inflows of arrears for previous years and therefore may not coincide with actual earnings for a particular year.

b. A larger sum was slated to be transferred, but the elections of 1980 delayed the parliamentary action necessary.

c. Includes an amount that represents a prepayment against future production.

Source: Hughes 1984.

ued it a further 5.6 percent against the U.S. dollar, for a total devaluation of 18 percent; subsequently it established a new parity of J$1.00 for each US$1.10.

These measures restored confidence temporarily, but the rising budgetary deficits caused reserves to fall once again. Toward the end of 1973 the government drew on IMF credit. At the same time, it subjected all imports to licensing and set quotas to prevent the value of imports from exceeding J$645 million, or about J$40 million (7 percent) above the 1973 level. Additional duties were imposed on imported spirits. The sales tax on durable consumer goods was raised, and the retail price of gasoline was nearly doubled. Jamaican citizens were given six months to repatriate their foreign investments. The government put tight controls on credit expansion and made plans to reduce its fiscal expenditure (see Brown 1981: 1–51).

Following the imposition of the bauxite levy (June 1974), import and credit controls were relaxed. There was also a marked relaxation of fiscal discipline. The first two PNP budgets, for 1972–73 and 1973–74, saw government expenditure increase by 21.4 percent and 23.2 percent, respectively. During the same period the nominal budgetary deficit rose by more than 150 percent, although in 1973–74 it still amounted to only 5.6 percent of GDP. For fiscal 1974–75 the government budgeted a 63 percent increase in total expenditures and a 117 percent increase in capital expenditures.

Despite a transfer of J$85 million from the CDF to the budget, the fiscal deficit increased to 9.6 percent of GDP, and in fiscal 1976–77 it reached 23.9 percent of GDP. By then, the government could not even cover its current expenses out of levy-transfer revenue. Between 1973 and 1976 the volume of money in circulation doubled, and, despite price controls, the consumer price index rose from 71.5 to 117.1 (January 1975 = 100).

To stem the price-wage spiral, the government not only put ceilings on salary increases (as mentioned above) but also limited pretax dividends to 7 percent of a company's net worth and froze all rents, rolling some of them back to 1971 levels. In 1976 the Price Commission was charged with determining the price of about 100 commodities (mostly important foodstuffs). All other prices were regulated, broadly speaking, to keep price rises from outrunning increases in costs. To keep down the cost of living, the government granted subsidies to imports of basic commodities. In 1976 the subsidies cost J$43.9 million. By 1977 the cost had risen to J$157.0 million, that is, to 19 percent of the government's current expenditures (Brown 1981: 32).

Steps were also taken to reduce effective demand. In 1976 the government put a sales tax on beer and cigarettes and raised property, company, and income taxes for the J$10,000-plus bracket. In 1977 it raised the income tax on earnings in excess of J$20,000 from 60 to 70 percent and that on earnings in excess of J$30,000 to 80 percent. In addition, it imposed taxes on gasoline, telephone calls, and various other items.

These measures proved largely ineffective. With the Jamaican dollar pegged to the U.S. dollar, the real exchange rate rose, and the balance of payments deteriorated. The foreign reserves of the Bank of Jamaica dwindled from J$138.6 million at the end of June 1975 to J$58.5 million at the end of December. By March 1976 they were negative.

In October 1975 the government took steps to reduce the balance of payments deficits through strict licensing of capital goods imports.[43] Imports from CARICOM countries, heretofore freely admitted, were also put under license.[44] In 1976 a number of luxury imports were banned, and capital goods quotas were tightened. In 1977 another 128 items were added to the banned list, including, among others, motorcars, bicycles, air conditioners, and toilet preparations. Restrictions on current industrial inputs were progressively tightened, and it is claimed that by 1977 they were hampering production in several branches of industry, including garments, footwear, and metal fabrication.

These measures were still unable to remedy the budgetary and foreign balance situation. The government was forced to seek IMF help and in July 1977 signed an agreement under which US$79.6 million was to be made available to Jamaica over a two-year period (ending June 1979). Under the agreement Jamaica was required to take effective steps to restore the central bank's foreign reserves, restrict domestic credit expansion, and limit foreign medium- and long-term borrowing. It did not have to curtail social programs, however, or remove price controls and subsidies. It was also permitted to maintain a dual exchange rate (put into effect the previous year), as well as quantitative restrictions on imports. Thus, the distortions were there to stay, while credit was to be tightened.

Attempts to implement this program of austerity without liberalization put a further dampener on an already depressed economy. Jamaica failed to pass the December 1977 IMF performance test, and the agreement was abrogated. But there was no alternative source of funding, and in May 1978 the government signed a US$240 million three-year extended fund facility (EFF) agreement with the IMF. This time the IMF insisted on comprehensive reforms. A single exchange rate was to be reestablished and the Jamaican dollar devalued. Price controls and subsidies were to be phased out, but during the transition period wage increases were to be subject to a ceiling, in order to reduce real wages by 25 to 30 percent. Taxes were to be raised and budgetary expenditures curtailed, and domestic credit was to be tightened.

To conform to the new agreement, the PNP government had to abandon its projects and policies, thus alienating its left-wing supporters. But the government did not succeed in meeting all the IMF conditions, and in September 1979 payments were suspended. Negotiations with the IMF were resumed but were finally broken off by the government in March 1980. By the time of the 1980 election, the PNP had abandoned or suspended its efforts to reform the economy and society; and it had also failed to obtain the foreign aid needed to restore economic stability.

Economic Performance

Although 1971 and 1973 were reasonably prosperous years, real GDP declined every year between 1973 and 1980, for a total fall of more than 15 percent (see table 4-34). The principal causes of the decline were the collapse of the bauxite-alumina and tourist industries, the flight of capital and entrepreneurship, and shortages of industrial inputs (see table 4-35). Mining, manufacturing, and construction had suffered severe declines. Government services constituted the only major sector to register vigorous growth. The pattern of expenditure on GDP had shifted drastically: there was a virtual collapse of capital formation. Private consumption declined, and public consumption rose sharply (table 4-36). Both exports and imports declined, the latter more sharply; the narrowing of the trade balance reflects the drying up of direct foreign investment.

Despite the economic collapse, total employment kept rising, albeit at a slow rate, and labor productivity plummeted. Employment in the public sector increased by a spectacular 57.6 percent between 1972 and 1976, growing from 10.8 percent of the total in 1972 to 15.7 percent in

Table 4-34. GDP *at Market Prices, 1970–80*
(millions of constant 1974 Jamaican dollars)

Year	GDP
1970	1,967
1971	2,027
1972	2,213
1973	2,241
1974	2,153
1975	2,144
1976	2,010
1977	1,966
1978	1,976
1979	1,941
1980	1,830

Source: Statistical Institute of Jamaica.

1976. A deceleration of employment formation in the closing years of the decade, combined with the rapidly growing labor force, led to a spectacular rise in the unemployment rate, which reached a high of 31.1 percent in 1979 (table 4-37).

The rising real wages, mounting labor strife, and anticapitalist PNP oratory sparked capital flight and an exodus of businessmen and managers. Jamaican statistics do not indicate the occupational characteristics of emigrants, but since about half of these Jamaicans went to the United

Table 4-35. GDP *by Sector of Origin, 1973 and 1980*
(millions of Jamaican dollars at constant 1974 prices)

Sector	1973	1980	Percentage change
Agriculture	146.9	143.8	–2.1
Mining and quarrying	181.6	117.0	–43.2
Manufacturing	401.1	304.9	–24.0
Electricity and water	22.2	24.6	+10.8
Construction and installation	225.7	114.7	–49.2
Wholesale and retail trade	481.9	311.2	–35.4
Transport, storage, and communications	124.3	126.9	+2.0
Financial and insurance services	91.6	115.5	–26.0
Real estate and business services	208.9	229.5	+9.9
Government services	250.9	368.3	+76.3
Miscellaneous services	125.9	99.5	–21.0
Nonprofit organizations	39.9	19.8	–50.4
Imported service charges (–)	60.3	76.9	–27.5
GDP at market prices	2,240.5	1,899.1	–15.2

Source: Jamaica, Central Statistical Office.

Table 4-36. Expenditure and GDP, 1973 and 1980
(millions of Jamaican dollars at constant 1974 prices)

Item	1973 Expenditure	1973 Percentage of total	1980 Expenditure	1980 Percentage of total	Percentage change
Consumption	1,730.9	88.0	1,646.9	90.0	–6.1
Private	1,359.0	69.1	1,202.2	65.7	–11.6
Public	371.0	18.9	444.7	24.2	+19.9
Investment	673.0	34.2	229.0	12.5	–66.0
Gross fixed capital formation	664.8	33.8	206.9	11.3	–68.9
Change in stocks	8.2	0.4	22.1	1.2	–85.4
Exports	680.2	34.6	648.8	35.5	–4.6
Imports	974.8	49.6	695.2	38.0	–28.7
GDP	1,966.7	100.0	1,829.5	100.0	–7.0

Source: Jamaica, Central Statistical Office.

States during the 1970s, data from the United States can provide some indication of the magnitude of the managerial exodus.[45] Before 1976 administrators and managers did not exceed 1.6 percent of Jamaican immigrants to the United States. In the late 1970s this proportion rose more than 5 percent, reaching 7.2 percent in 1977. Between 1977 and 1979, 2,888 managers and administrators emigrated to the United States; only 1,816 were recorded in the preceding eleven years.

Table 4-37. Employment and Unemployment, October 1972–October 1984

Year	Labor force	Employed	Unemployed	Unemployment rate (percent)
1972	808,900	624,400	184,600	22.8
1973	801,200	621,600	179,600	22.4
1974	820,100	650,600	169,500	20.7
1975	865,600	684,300	181,300	20.9
1976	895,500	679,100	216,400	24.2
1977	917,900	699,200	218,700	23.8
1978	949,200	702,100	247,100	26.0
1979	962,500	663,400	299,100	31.1
1980	1,006,900	737,300	269,600	26.8
1981	1,022,900	761,400	261,500	25.6
1982	1,048,600	756,300	292,300	27.9
1983	985,400	722,700	262,700	26.7
1984	971,400	724,700	246,700	25.4

Sources: Jamaica, Department of Statistics, *Statistical Abstract*, selected volumes; Jamaica Department of Statistics, *The Labour Force 1973*; for 1983, Planning Institute of Jamaica, *Economic and Social Survey*, 1984.

The riots and political violence of the Manley era also made Jamaica a much less attractive vacation spot. Tourism declined rapidly, particularly during the rather violent 1976 elections. By 1977 tourist expenditures in constant Jamaican dollars had fallen almost a third below the 1972 level (table 4-38). With the gradual return of social and political stability in the late 1970s, the industry slowly recovered. Since the rest of the economy remained shaky, the economic importance of tourism increased, as shown by the rising ratio of tourist expenditures to GDP.

The position of labor improved in the early years of the Manley regime. Unemployment fell by 2 percentage points, to 20.9 percent in October 1975. Wages improved: in the two and a half year period from April 1974 to October 1976, real wages of men and women rose by 10.0 and 25.7 percent, respectively.

With the continued decline of the economy and the introduction of austerity measures in the late 1970s, however, labor lost all of the gains of the early 1970s, and more. By 1980 the shares of labor and capital had reverted back to those of the early 1970s. The unemployment rate stood at 26.8 percent in 1980, having peaked at 31.1 percent in the preceding year. Between October 1976 and November 1980 the real wages of men fell by 32.8 percent and those of women by 41.9 percent (Kaufman 1985). From April 1974 to November 1980 the real wages of men and women fell 26.1 and 27.0 percent, respectively. During that six-year period GDP per capita fell by 21.7 percent. When the rising unemployment rate is

Table 4-38. *Jamaican Tourism, 1972–80*

Year	Number of tourists (thousands)	Total expenditures (millions)		Expenditures per visitor		Expenditures as percentage of GDPa
		U.S. dollars	1974 Jamaican dollars	U.S. dollars	1974 Jamaican dollars	
1972	494	134.7	167.7	272.7	339.4	7.5
1973	517	127.3	150.7	246.2	291.5	6.7
1974	531	133.3	121.2	251.0	228.2	5.6
1975	553	128.5	96.5	232.4	174.6	4.5
1976	471	105.8	71.8	224.6	152.4	3.6
1977	387	105.5	63.7	272.6	164.7	3.2
1978	533	146.9	112.4	275.6	210.9	5.7
1979	594	195.4	156.5	329.0	263.4	8.1
1980	529	240.7	165.8	455.0	313.4	9.1

a. At constant 1974 prices. This ratio is not intended to reflect the contribution to GDP but simply to provide a rough indication of the relative importance of tourism in the national economy.

Sources: For 1972–79, World Bank estimates; for 1980, Economist Intelligence Unit 1986, 1987.

taken into account, it is apparent that labor bore its full share of the economic decline.

By 1980, after a 26 percent decline in the preceding seven years, GDP per capita stood at approximately the same level as that recorded in 1964. The economy was distorted by quantitative restrictions. The Bank of Jamaica's net reserves stood at minus US$500 million and external public debt at US$1.5 billion.[46]

The Seaga Regime, 1980–88

In the October 1980 election the JLP won an overwhelming victory, securing fifty-one parliamentary seats to the PNP's nine. The PNP was further weakened by a split between the right wing led by Michael Manley, who was reelected party president, and a left-leaning faction led by D. K. Duncan, the general secretary. This conflict contributed to the JLP's landslide victory in the local elections held in March 1981.

Political Developments

The slow pace of economic recovery under JLP rule and the scandals connected with the conduct of government enterprises helped the PNP recover some of its support and prestige, despite continuous squabbling within the party.[47] But the 1983 Grenada expedition, in which Jamaica played an active part, created an outburst of enthusiasm for the JLP. Taking advantage of this opportunity (and fearing that the new austerity measures on the government's agenda would erode JLP support), Seaga called an election for December 15, 1983, although the next regularly scheduled election was not due until October 1985. The PNP accused Seaga of violating a pledge to compile a new voters' register (the existing register effectively disenfranchised 200,000 potentially eligible young voters who, according to public opinion polls, would have secured a PNP victory) and boycotted the election. The boycott allowed the JLP to govern for the next four years without parliamentary opposition, but all the while the PNP resorted to a variety of pressure tactics and its popularity increased. Polls taken at the time of the 1986 local elections indicate that more than 50 percent of each social group, except for business and high-income professionals, favored the PNP (see table 4-27). Even among businessmen and high-income professionals, a substantial 31 percent supported the PNP.

The JLP victory marked the end of populist politics. Technocratic control over policy was reasserted, while party and mass influence dwindled. The responsibility for formulating and overseeing policy became concentrated in the office of the prime minister, who retained the finance and defense and communications portfolios, while his brother-in-law controlled the key tourism and mining ministries.

The return to power of the JLP strengthened capitalist influence. Some business leaders obtained government jobs; others were nominated members of the Senate or were made chairmen of statutory boards; still others served as unofficial advisers. Access to power was limited to the big business families, however, especially to those that had helped finance the JLP campaign, and to foreign business interests.

Although policies had begun moving to the right somewhat, there remained a degree of distrust between government and business. The communication gap became even more difficult to close when the prime minister continued exercising policy control, showed no interest in toning down centralization or personal rule, and made no effort to heed private sector advice on many issues. In response, the business lobbies once again appealed to public opinion in an effort to influence policy direction. They also sought the backing of the staffs of aid agencies, especially the U.S. Agency for International Development (USAID), and tried to find allies among U.S.-based pressure groups (such as the Heritage Foundation) that shared the private sector's ideological outlook.

The trade unions, too, were having their problems. They had lost much of their influence after a good number of their leaders—notably Michael Manley, Pearnell Charles, Clifton Stone, Carlyle Dunckley, and Errol Anderson—had moved into party positions. Without personalities of national stature at the helm, the unions proved to be no match for the tough, no-nonsense leadership of Prime Minister Seaga. Labor lost its clout once the public sector gained ascendancy, as was all too clear when 1,200 government and public enterprise workers lost their jobs as a result of a futile effort at a general strike in 1985. The unions could no longer protect workers or deliver benefits in this increasingly hostile climate. The average number of strikes per year fell to the levels of the early 1960s.

The PNP government of the 1970s and the JLP government of the 1980s differed most sharply in their foreign policy: whereas Michael Manley had sought an alliance with Cuba, Edward Seaga cooperated closely with the United States. In the domestic field, Seaga's government reversed the trend toward the nationalization or communalization of the means of production. The legal measures the PNP used to manage the economy remained virtually unchanged, however, although the controls were generally relaxed. The pendulum had swung too far left in the 1970s and there followed, in the 1980s, a corrective movement, but not a counterrevolution.

As the 1989 election approached, both parties moved toward the center. Seaga drew away from the most unpopular liberalization measures, and, in an effort to broaden his political appeal, included a labor union leader in his cabinet. Manley, on his part, repudiated the socialist experiment. His government would favor the working class (he pledged to restore union rights curtailed by the Seaga government and to institute a massive public works program), but it would also create conditions favorable to private enterprise, especially to small and medium-size business. There would be no resumption of nationalization; Manley even agreed to the privatization of broadcasting facilities, although he objected to the method proposed by Seaga. Good relations with the United States would be maintained, and the Cubans would be asked to keep a low profile. The two parties thus resumed their traditional stance, one slightly "right" and one slightly "left" of center, both wooing the same constituency, and both pursuing basically the same economic strategy.

The Economy

When the JLP took over in 1980, they found that they had inherited a tightly controlled, virtually insolvent economy. The number of tourist arrivals was 10.9 percent lower than in the previous year; manufacturing output, hampered by shortages of imported inputs, was down 11.6 percent; sugar and banana production were at record lows; and GDP was declining, as it had every year since 1974 (with the exception of 1978). The 1980 budget deficit amounted to J$986 million (or 20 percent of GDP), and the foreign current account deficit was J$296 million (according to IMF statistics). The only good news was that bauxite production had risen from 11.5 million tons in 1979 to 12.1 million tons in 1980.

The poor state of the economy was by far the most important reason for the JLP victory. Public opinion polls showed that the majority of the electorate blamed the government for the unemployment and the shortages and regarded economic recovery as the foremost election issue (Stone 1982: 70, 74).

In its electoral campaign the JLP promised to restore business confidence and to bring more efficient management, but it stopped short of formulating an overall program for recovery. Once in office, Seaga was urged by the IMF and by other international lenders and donors to adopt measures of retrenchment and liberalization. Within Jamaica there was support for change, but specific reform measures met with strong opposition from powerful interest groups. Consumers—especially those in the lower-income groups—did not want to see price controls lifted, subsidies eliminated, or the currency devalued, and they strongly objected to increases in the price of government-provided goods and services. The powerful lobby of manufacturers of import-substituting goods favored an overvalued currency (for the sake of cheap input imports) and quantitative import restrictions (to protect them from foreign competition). Entrenched business enterprises that had benefited from credit rationing feared the removal of interest rate ceilings. Workers fought against the closing of inefficient public enterprises, against job retrenchment, and against real wage cuts. The JLP leadership itself took an ambivalent attitude: on the one hand, it favored change; on the other, it was reluctant to give up the discretionary powers that gave it command over the economy and generated political support.

In 1980 the JLP government opted for liberalization without austerity. The government hoped that the relaxation of controls (and the pledge of no further nationalization) would give a powerful stimulus to the private sector. Output would catch up with pent-up demand, and equilibrium would be restored without recourse to politically unpopular retrenchment measures. To prevent food and fuel prices from increasing, the Jamaican dollar was not to be devalued. To avoid heightening the unemployment problem, public employment was not to be reduced through dismissal.

Foreign borrowing would also be necessary over the short term to bridge the time gap between the import response to liberalization and the production response. Medium- and long-term credit was to be used to finance the infrastructural improvements required to foster the growth of industry, agriculture, and tourism. Within three to four years, however, the economy would be showing a 4.5 percent self-sustaining growth rate, whereupon the trade gap would narrow and long-run stability would be restored.

In 1981 the IMF granted Jamaica a $560 million EFF, thus implicitly agreeing with the recovery strategy.[48] The first tranche of loans was given unconditionally. The release of further tranches, spaced out over three years, was made contingent on the satisfaction of quarterly macroeconomic "performance criteria," which were, however, more lenient than those imposed on the Manley regime.[49]

The supply-side measures paid off. The improved availability of inputs stimulated production. Despite a fall in bauxite prices, the value of exports in current terms grew by 2.2 percent; GDP rose, in real terms, by an estimated 2.6 percent, or about twice as fast as originally foreseen in the recovery plan; and the IMF targets were readily satisfied.[50]

In 1982, however, export earnings from bauxite-alumina and sugar declined, and Jamaica failed to pass the IMF external balance of payments test. After another failure, in March 1983, the IMF withdrew its support.

In 1983 the fiscal and external balance deteriorated further. Because of its no-dismissal pledge, the government was unable to make sharp cuts in current expenditures, and the modest economies it did achieve were roughly offset by the increase in interest payments caused by the rise in public debt. In fiscal 1983–84 the overall deficit climbed to 15.8 percent of GDP, from 12.4 percent in 1979–80. With a faster inflation rate than that of its trading partners and a fixed exchange rate, Jamaica saw its competitiveness decline: by the end of 1983 the real exchange rate had risen to the level reached on the eve of the 1978 Manley devaluation (see Gavin 1989). The policy was clearly untenable; pressure mounted to replenish the stocks of production inputs and consumer durables. Exports stagnated while imports boomed. The balance of payments situation was further aggravated by a capital outflow approaching US$300 million. Jamaica had lost US$326 million in reserves and was US$91 million in arrears on accumulated payments.

The agreement reached late in 1983 after renewed negotiations with the IMF and with the World Bank marks a policy watershed: for the next several years the Jamaican government took a series of measures to reduce aggregate demand and eliminate government waste. It introduced new taxes in 1984–85 and put a cap on wage increases in the public sector. In addition, it reduced subsidies on essential items, which led to a 20 percent increase in the price of gasoline, a 40 percent increase in transport fares, a 60 percent increase in air fares, and higher prices for drugs and soap. It also announced that 5,000 civil servants would be dismissed.

IMF pressure and economic circumstances forced the government to renege on its no-devaluation pledge. In January 1983 a dual exchange system was introduced to induce the expenditure of "black" foreign exchange on legitimate imports. The central bank continued to sell U.S. dollars at J$1.78 per US$1.00 for imports of basic foods, drugs, and educational supplies and for the servicing of foreign debt. Currency for all other imports was to be purchased from commercial banks at a free rate, expected to range from J$2.50 to J$3.00 per US$1.00.[51] Exporters received half the proceeds at the free rate and half at the official rate.

In the course of the 1983 negotiations, the IMF insisted on setting the value of the Jamaican currency at a uniform, realistic level. The exchange rate was unified, the Jamaican dollar was devalued, and in 1984 a currency auction system was put into effect. The value of the Jamaican dollar declined—at first gradually, reaching J$5.77 per US$1.0 on September 5, 1985, but then precipitously, to J$6.40 on October 24. Fearing adverse public reaction, the government intervened at that point. By mid-November the rate rose back to J$5.50. Although the auction system was formally retained, the government thereafter resorted to a combination of market operation and pressure on bidders to maintain a fixed parity.

The austerity measures met with strong opposition. In April 1983, 100,000 civil servants and other government employees held a three-day strike to protest the ceilings on wage increases. A year later widespread riots erupted in response to rising food prices. The protests reached a climax in June 1985, when six trade unions, including the pro-JLP Bustamante Industrial Trade Union, organized the first postindependence general strike to demand that the government curb the inflation rate, increase public sector wages, and put an end to dismissals aimed at reducing public sector employment.[52]

The government resisted the protesters' demands, but it took steps to soften the impact of the reforms, beginning with a number of direct measures to keep the cost of living down. It restored subsidies on basic commodities in 1983, and in 1984—with the help of U.S. PL 480, the European Economic Community (EEC) Food Program, and the Italian government—it launched a food stamp program that was to benefit close to 1 million people.[53] In 1987, as part of the agreement with the IMF to keep down the inflation rate, Jamaica reimposed price controls on basic foods, medicines, and textbooks and also on animal feed, fertilizers, pesticides, and herbicides. The government also improved public sector wage offers and delayed reductions in the number of private sector jobs.

On the whole, the reforms were put into effect with great vigor. Largely as a consequence of public employment cuts and wage restraint, current fiscal expenditure declined from 31.6 percent of GDP in 1983–84 to 26 percent in 1985–86. In 1986 the government introduced a reform of personal and corporate taxes. A highly complicated and steeply progressive tax system was replaced by one with a broad base, a high initial threshold, and a flat 33⅓ percent rate above the threshold. Government revenues rose sharply (table 4-39). By fiscal 1986–87 the current deficit had turned into a current surplus. Sharp cuts in new capital spending led to a curtailment of the overall deficit from 15.3 percent of GDP in 1983–84 to 2.5 percent in 1986–87.

The last two budgets of the Seaga regime showed some relaxation of fiscal discipline. Public opinion polls indicated widespread dissatisfaction with the lack of government attention to social services; the last preelection budget (1988–89) scheduled a 67 percent increase in the capital expenditure of the Ministry of Education and a 123 percent increase in that of the Ministry of Health.[54]

SECTORAL POLICIES. Improved export performance was essential to the success of Seaga's renewal strategy. To promote the growth of exports in the short run, it would be necessary to revitalize the bauxite-alumina industry, the traditional export crops (sugar, bananas, citrus, coffee), and tourism. In the longer run, there was the possibility of exporting nontraditional agricultural products.

The key export policy issue facing the Seaga regime was what to do about the bauxite levy. A reduction in the levy could mean a short-run decline in fiscal revenues, which the government could ill afford, and there was some uncertainty about the long-run fiscal benefits. Moreover, the 1980 production figures seemed to indicate that the 1979 reduction had been sufficient to restore Jamaica's competitive position and stimulate a return to full capacity utilization.[55]

Initially, the government decided to make no changes in the levy arrangements; instead, it opted for a production-boosting strategy patterned on that of the previous regime. The government offered to enter into joint ventures with foreign business enterprises or governments to modernize existing facilities or start new ones.[56] BATCO, a public marketing company set up by the Manley government, sought to find markets outside those dominated by the integrated multinational producers.[57] In

Table 4-39. Central Government Operations, 1980–81 to 1988–89
(millions of Jamaican dollars)

Item	1980–91	1981–82	1982–83	1983–84	1984–85	1985–86	1986–87	1987–88	Preliminary 1988–89
Current account revenue	1,118	1,503	1,650	1,791	2,678	3,143	4,361	4,862	5,466
Current expenditure	1,550	1,715	1,861	2,394	2,818	3,253	3,755	4,189	4,991
Current account surplus	-369	-213	-212	-603	-140	-110	606	672	475
Capital revenue	11	6	—	4	8	8	—	168	59
Capital expenditure	472	643	657	508	447	591	922	1,163	1,433
Pass-through[a]	—	—	—	89	70	90	43	157	202
Overall surplus	-830	-849	-869	-1,196	-649	-783	-350	-479	-1,101

— Not available.

a. Guaranteed loans to the private sector.

Source: Jamaica, Ministry of Finance and Planning.

1985 the government set up a second marketing organization, the Jamaican Overseas Marketing Company, with headquarters in Switzerland.

The government estimated that, with the help of such measures, production would soon surpass the level of 15 million tons reached in 1974 and would rise as high as 18 million tons by 1983–84. Although demand was buoyed by the U.S. decision to replenish its strategic stockpile, production remained stagnant in 1983 and 1984 (table 4-40). The levy was reduced to 6 percent (with incentives to modernize and to produce at more than 70 percent of plant capacity), but in 1985 output declined further.[58] A strong world demand buoyed output to 7.9 million tons in 1987, only to be followed by another decline in 1988. In the eighth year of its tenure the government negotiated new agreements with Alcoa and Alcan under which the levy was cut to 3 percent of the average realized ingot price and a 33⅓ percent tax was imposed on realized (net of levy) gross profits.

Agricultural policies, too, underwent an evolution. In the first phase the government attempted to improve productivity while keeping (with some exceptions) the institutions inherited from the previous regime. Disappointment with the results led to institutional reform.

As of 1980 sugar was still the most important commercial crop and, next to bauxite and alumina, the main source of foreign exchange (table 4-41). Sugarcane was grown on 26 percent of the cultivated land, or 112,000 acres, down from 168,000 acres in 1970. Plant disease (rust and smut), labor unrest, and factory breakdowns caused by antiquated machinery, lack of replacement parts, and poor management led to a steady decline in yields. Production in 1980 amounted to 270,000 tons and in 1981 it declined to 202,000 tons—not enough to satisfy domestic demand and fill Jamaica's highly profitable quota on the EEC market.

When Seaga assumed office, about half the sugar was produced on publicly owned estates. At the end of the 1980–84 campaign the National Sugar Company, which ran eight state sugar mills, had an accumulated

Table 4-40. Jamaican Bauxite and Alumina Production, 1980–85

	Bauxite		Alumina	
Year	Thousands of metric tons	Percentage of world production	Thousands of metric tons	Percentage of world production
1980	12,064	13.0	2,395	6.9
1981	11,606	13.2	2,556	7.5
1982	8,158	10.4	1,761	5.9
1983	7,682	9.8	1,907	6.1
1984	8,733	9.4	1,713	4.9
1985	6,217	6.9	1,512	4.4

Source: American Bureau of Metal Statistics 1973–83 and 1985.

Table 4-41. Volume of Major Export Crop Production, 1980–84

Product	Unit (thousands)	1980	1981	1982	1983	1984
Sugarcane	Tons	270	202	198	205	197
Bananas	Tons	33	31	21	23	11
Citrus[a]	Boxes	1,117	883	933	676	570
Coffee[b]	Kilo	854	837	1,067	1,066	1,326
Cocoa	Kilo	1,326	1,564	1,260	1,964	1,910

a. Deliveries to paving and processing plant.
b. Total exports of unroasted coffee.
Source: Planning Institute of Jamaica, Economic and Social Survey, various issues.

deficit of J$89 million, (US$50 million at the then-ruling exchange rate), while the debt of the sugar cooperatives was J$39.1 million, or US$21 million (Economic Intelligence Unit 1981). The Seaga government dissolved the cooperatives and placed the land they cultivated (as well as some other government-owned land) under the management of Tate and Lyle. With the help of World Bank and Canadian loans, the government-owned estates were replanted with improved cane, and modern machinery was purchased. Ultimately, some of the inefficient factories were closed, and some were privatized.

Despite the reforms, growers did not reach the 330,000-ton target set for 1983. Output in the 1980s fluctuated between 185,000 and 205,000 tons. In most years Jamaica had to import sugar to satisfy its EEC and U.S. sugar quotas, as well as its domestic demand. But because of a decline in free market prices and successive cuts in the U.S. import quotas, less and less urgency was attached to rehabilitating the industry.

Efforts to revitalize banana exports were more successful. In 1979, 64,000 acres were devoted to growing bananas, and 62 percent of the cultivated land was in smallholdings of 5 acres or less. The average yield was only 3 tons per acre, although large estates averaged 13 tons per acre. Except for some local consumption, the bananas were exported through a state monopoly, the Banana Marketing Company, which set prices at a low, uniform level that gave no incentive to produce a high-quality fruit. As a result, Jamaican bananas commanded low prices on the international market. In the United Kingdom, however, Jamaica had a 25 percent share of the protected-price import quota, which, typically, it was unable to fulfill.

The JLP government attempted to increase banana output and improve the quality by sponsoring modern, privately managed, joint-venture plantations and by abandoning marginal farms. The original goal of increasing exports from 33,000 tons in 1980 to 120,000 tons by 1983–84 proved to be quite unrealistic.[59] Instead of rising, output declined 11,000 tons in 1984, and Jamaica's share of the U.K. market fell from 11 percent in 1980 to 4 percent.

More radical measures followed. In 1985 the government liquidated the state-owned Jamaican Banana Company, selling or leasing about 100,000 acres of land and discharging 2,300 workers. In the same year the grower-controlled Banana Export Company (formed to replace the Banana Marketing Company) raised producer prices on high-quality fruit by 50 percent. By 1987 quality had improved and exports had surpassed 34,000 tons. There was a similar evolution in the strategy to revitalize the other traditional export crops (tobacco, citrus fruits, coconuts, cocoa, and coffee).

The government also granted subsidies to promote nontraditional agriculture. Several farms established with government backing to grow winter vegetables for export to the United States encountered production, transport, and marketing difficulties, and by the late 1980s most of them had closed down. In contrast, the cultivation of mangoes and cut flowers and the efforts at pisciculture met with great success.

Some of the agricultural initiatives were dictated primarily by social considerations. The Agro 21 program launched in 1983, for example, was designed to help small farmers. In the course of the next four years the government leased 30,000 acres and sold 40,000 acres to smallholders. Under another program, initiated in 1987, formal property titles were given to 36,000 small farmers who did not have a clear legal right to the land they cultivated.

In another important shift, Seaga's regime moved away from the long-established policy of import-substituting industrialization toward an emphasis on exports. The first move in this direction was taken in 1982, when 64 out of 380 products were removed from the quantitative restriction list and licensing procedures were simplified. Import licensing was abolished in April 1984 for most raw materials and capital goods and in April 1985 for most consumer goods. All price controls (except for basic food items) were also gradually phased out. In 1986 the government undertook a tariff reform program aimed at simplifying tariffs and reducing disparities. By April 1988 the maximum tariff (including the stamp duty) was reduced to 60 percent. The ultimate goal (to be achieved by 1991–92) was to have a nominal tariff ranging from 5 to 30 percent.[60]

The industries oriented toward the home market, which were depressed as a consequence of the measures taken to reduce effective demand, were further hurt by increasing foreign competition. Protection in the form of quantitative import restrictions was no longer granted under the Industrial Incentives Act, and the number of firms seeking and gaining approval under the act fell by half. At the same time, devaluation and greater freedom of trade favored export orientation. The number of approvals under the Export Industry Encouragement Act doubled (see table 4-19), and activity in free-trade zones grew rapidly. These zones were established primarily to exploit the ease of access into the U.S. market under the Caribbean Basin Initiative. Textile and clothing manufacturers benefiting from a U.S. quota became the principal employer, and their workers numbered close to 20,000 by late 1987. Industry, in the aggregate, remained virtually stagnant between 1980 and 1984. Since then, however, it has experienced some growth, spearheaded by the export-oriented textile and clothing sector.

Tourism in Jamaica was hard hit by the recession associated with the oil price shocks of the 1980s and then suffered a further blow from the bad press given to PNP socialism, which fueled the fear of disorder. In the 1980s the situation improved on all counts. Tourist arrivals and expenditures as a percentage of GDP rose rapidly. In 1987, for the first time, the number of tourists exceeded 1 million (table 4-42).

PRIVATIZATION AND RETREAT FROM DIRIGISME. One of the first acts of the Seaga regime was to provide assurance that nationalization had come to a halt. In subsequent years the government privatized a number of enterprises in order to obtain much-needed finance and achieve greater managerial efficiency. Enterprises that were entirely or partly privatized included the National Commercial Bank, the Caribbean Cement Company, and a number of hotels. In 1982, however, the government purchased a local refinery from the Exxon Corporation rather than agree to a price increase demanded by the company.

Although the government had loosened controls over the private sector, it retained the principal instruments for guiding the economy. It continued to grant preferential treatment to selected enterprises under the Industrial Incentives acts, and the 1982 amendment to the 1971 Agriculture Incentive Act gave it more power to influence agricultural investments.[61] The November 1982 launching of the National Develop-

Table 4-42. Jamaican Tourism, 1978–87

Year	Number of tourists (thousands)[a]	Total receipts (millions of U.S. dollars)
1978	530	156
1979	586	199
1980	529	242
1981	546	284
1982	662	338
1983	776	399
1984	834	407
1985	833	407
1986	942	516
1987	1,031	598

a. Total of stopover visitors and cruiseship passengers.
Sources: Jamaican Tourist Board and Bank of Jamaica.

ment Bank of Jamaica (to replace the Jamaica Development Bank, which had gone bankrupt) enabled the government to use commercial and financial institutions and credit unions to maintain and extend its financial influence over medium-term financing of industry, tourism, and mining. The scope of the State Trading Corporation (renamed the Jamaica Commodity Trading Company Ltd.) was expanded to include motor vehicle imports.

ECONOMIC PERFORMANCE. During the first three years of the Seaga government, GDP grew at a slow pace (see table 4-43). With retrenchment came two years of GDP decline. Thus, between 1981 and 1986 GDP at constant prices fell by 1.1 percent and GDP per capita by 9.0 percent. In 1987 the economy, buoyed by a rise in demand for bauxite, grew more than 5 percent for the first time since the 1970s. In 1988 the improvement continued, although it was interrupted in September by Hurricane Gilbert, the worst such storm in a century.

From 1980 to 1987 the economy underwent a major transformation. The share of GDP (at current prices) generated by bauxite declined from 14 to 7 percent and that of agriculture from 8 to 6 percent, whereas the contribution of manufacturing rose from 16 to 22 percent. The service sector grew rapidly, but the share of GDP generated by the government shrank from 14 to 9 percent.

Despite the fluctuations in income, aggregate employment rose throughout the period, reflecting a structural transformation that favored labor-intensive sectors such as tourism and export-oriented manufacturing. Since 1985 there has also been a marked decrease in the unemployment rate (table 4-44).

The trade figures reflect this transformation of the economy. The value of traditional exports (bauxite-alumina, sugar, and the other traditional export crops) fell from US$826 million in 1980 to US$460 million in 1987, but nontraditional exports (manufactured goods and some agricultural

Table 4-43. GDP, 1980–87
(millions of constant Jamaican dollars)

Year	GDP	Percentage increase from previous year
1980	1,830	–5.7
1981	1,877	2.6
1982	1,899	1.2
1983	1,942	2.3
1984	1,926	–0.9
1985	1,836	–4.6
1986	1,870	1.8
1987	1,968	5.2

Source: Statistical Institute of Jamaica.

Table 4-44. Labor Force and Employment, 1980 and 1988
(thousands)

	1980		1988		
Item	Number (thousands)	Percentage of total employed	Number (thousands)	Percentage of total employed	Percentage change 1980–88
Labor force	960.3		1,077.4		21.9
Total employed	698.7	100.0	874.3	100.0	25.2
Agriculture	26.1	37.4	257.9	29.4	–1.2
Mining	8.2	1.2	6.0	0.7	–17.1
Manufacturing	73.0	10.6	136.0	15.6	86.3
Construction	25.0	3.6	45.7	5.2	82.8
Transport, communications, and utilities	34.7	5.0	42.6	4.9	22.8
Commerce	87.6	12.5	137.2	15.7	56.6
Public administration	104.1	14.9	76.4	8.7	35.3
Other services	105.0	15.0	172.5	19.7	64.3
Total unemployed	261.8	27.3	203.4	–22.3	
Unemployed job seekers	107.1	11.1	87.3	–9.8	

Note: Labor force, employment, and unemployment figures for 1980 are averages of April and October survey data; for 1988, they are averages of April and November survey data.

Source: Statistical Institute of Jamaica.

products such as flowers and winter vegetables) rose from US$115 million in 1980 to US$232 million in 1987. Of the nontraditional exports, clothing grew at the fastest rate, from US$6.5 million in 1980 to US$102 million in 1987, with most of the increase occurring after 1985. Thus, in a period of a few years Jamaica was transformed from an economy almost entirely dependent on bauxite-alumina and sugar exports to one with a diversified export mix (table 4-45).

The merchandise balance shows no clear trend. As table 4-46 indicates, imports rose during the years of the supply-side policy and later declined under the impact of the austerity measures, while exports fluctuated from year to year. Nevertheless, thanks to the increasing income from tourism, the external current account balance improved radically, especially after 1985.

In one respect, however, Jamaica's international position experienced some deterioration: during the first five years of the decade external debt almost doubled, while the ratio of debt-service payments to the value of exports of goods and of nonfactor services rose from 20 to 43 percent (table 4-47). By 1987 nearly half of export earnings was being channeled into the payment of interest and amortization.

Table 4-45. *Composition of Commodity Trade, 1980–87*
(percent)

Commodity	1980	1981	1982	1983	1984	1985	1986	1987
Bauxite and alumina	78	79	69	63	64	54	52	49
Other traditional	10	9	12	14	15	16	18	18
Nontraditional	12	13	19	23	21	30	30	33
Clothing	—	—	2	2	5	7	9	15

— Not available.
Source: Jamaica, Central Statistical Office.

Summary of the Seaga Years

The Seaga regime removed most of the direct controls over the economy and restored internal and external balance. It thus managed to arrest Jamaica's economic deterioration. But the recovery was far from spectacular. To what extent was that attributable to exogenous factors?

Jamaica entered the 1980s facing declining terms of trade (table 4-48), and high world interest rates also posed an obstacle to recovery. In other respects, however, external circumstances were highly favorable, particularly the recovery of the U.S. economy, which led to a rapid revival of tourism. Politically, Seaga had a powerful ally in the Reagan administration. Jamaican goods received special treatment in the United States under the Caribbean Basin Initiative, and there was a substantial rise in U.S. aid. The IMF also adopted a more flexible attitude than it had shown toward the Manley administration.

Internally, the government enjoyed a high degree of autonomy. Between 1980 and 1983 Seaga had a solid parliamentary majority. From 1983 on, there was no parliamentary opposition. This does not mean that the government exercised absolute power—far from it. Reforms met with strong opposition from organized pressure groups, and the regime had to perform a delicate balancing act. If it moved too slowly, it risked

Table 4-46. *Merchandise Trade and Current Account Balance, 1981–86*
(millions of current U.S. dollars)

Year	Exports	Imports	Commodity balance	Current account balance
1981	974	1,296	−323	−337
1982	767	1,209	−442	−409
1983	686	1,124	−439	−359
1984	702	1,037	−335	−335
1985	569	1,004	−436	−304
1986	598	844	−246	−108

Source: IMF, *International Financial Statistics*.

Table 4-47. External Medium- and Long-Term Public Debt and Debt Service, 1977–88
(U.S. dollars)

Year	Debt		Debt service	
	Millions	Percentage of GDP	Millions	Percentage of exports
1977	1,045.5	33.3	159.1	16.4
1978	1,203.9	55.8	158.6	14.7
1979	1,451.1	60.5	273.8	23.5
1980	1,867.6	70.0	263.3	19.3
1981	2,293.1	77.2	438.8	31.3
1982	2,694.3	81.8	408.4	32.8
1983	2,988.5	82.6	381.4	30.7
1984	3,222.9	135.8	394.8	31.5
1985	3,616.9	180.3	503.0	43.4
1986	3,650.5	150.2	616.0	47.8
1987	4,013.4	140.4	774.5	49.4
1988[a]	4,008.8	—	771.8	—

— Not available.
a. Preliminary figures.
Sources: Bank of Jamaica and World Bank Debt Reporting System.

Table 4-48. Terms of Trade, 1974–87
(millions of U.S. dollars)

Year	Unit value of exports[a]	Unit value of imports	Terms of trade
1974	25.9	26.8	96.6
1975	39.1	31.0	126.1
1976	38.7	33.3	116.2
1977	41.7	41.8	99.8
1978	68.3	59.5	114.8
1979	85.7	75.7	113.2
1980	101.5	97.8	103.8
1981	102.7	108.2	94.9
1982	100.0	100.0	100.0
1983	103.2	128.8	80.1
1984	207.0	229.1	90.4
1985	239.0	326.9	73.4
1986	245.1	291.7	84.4
1987[b]	288.2	316.2	91.1

a. Excludes reexports.
b. Preliminary figures.
Source: Statistical Institute of Jamaica.

losing international financial support, but rapid reform could cost it domestic support.

Objection may be taken, however, to the timing of the reforms. The supply-side strategy pursued before 1983 neglected the fact that direct controls under the Manley regime had kept in check the pent-up domestic purchasing power generated by an expansionary fiscal and monetary policy. In the absence of measures to reduce aggregate demand, the relaxation of imports had an adverse effect on the balance of payments. External debt mounted rapidly, imposing a heavy burden on the future. Moreover, recovery was hampered by the lack of policy credibility. Retrenchment, coming in 1984 and in 1985, depressed the economy, and recovery did not come until the close of the decade.

The timing was also poor politically. An early call for sacrifices could have been justified as being necessary to undo the errors of the previous regime. No such justification could be found for measures taken in midstream. Although growth followed the adjustment, it came too late to save the regime.

Politics gives, in fact, a clue to the timing of the reforms. In the late 1960s Seaga was a leading architect of Jamaican dirigisme and a forceful spokesman for economic planning. On coming into power in 1980 he sought to correct the errors of judgment of his predecessor, but not to dismantle the system that Manley had helped to build. In the end, pragmatism (and the pressure of donor and lending agencies) won over idealism, and the economy was liberalized. The same pragmatic reasons underlie Manley's shift away from democratic socialism and the acceptance by his new administration of free-market principles.

Conclusions

The most striking feature of the Jamaican experience is the important role history has played in the development of the island's economy and polity since World War II. The heritage of slavery and colonialism created a society highly stratified along both ethnic and class lines, with a strong tradition of militancy among the urban working class as well as the rural poor. The British administrative and business leaders at the top of the colonial pyramid were removed after independence, and their place was taken by an new elite consisting largely of lawyers and intellectuals in the PNP and labor and business leaders in the JLP. The problem for this emerging elite was to satisfy the aspirations of their less fortunate fellow citizens for jobs and higher living standards, in the context of a highly open economy with a British-type political system.

Jamaica departed from the common pattern of other newly independent British colonies in that it had a genuine two-party system from the outset rather than a single coalition, as in the case of the Congress party in India, the Anti-Fascist People's Freedom League (AFPFL) in Burma, or the PAP in Singapore (which quickly suppressed its rivals). The fact that elections have been held regularly and that incumbents have often been soundly defeated at the polls is a record of which Jamaica can be proud, even though the violence that has frequently been associated with the electoral process is deplorable.

The state in Jamaica is the coveted prize in a continuing two-party contest, a Hotelling-type duopoly. As this chapter has explained, the parties have engaged in the competitive provision of housing, public employment, and other benefits. The result has been a vast increase in the government's share of GDP, which tripled from 6.0 percent in 1965 to 19.4 percent in 1983. Although much of the expansion came during the Manley regime of 1972–80, the earlier JLP governments of 1962–72 also engaged in this process. Under the Seaga administration, which had to contend with a great deal of external pressure, the share of the government shrank to 9 percent of GDP, but once again there was heavy domestic pressure for better social services.

In the 1950s and 1960s the bauxite bonanza financed not only social expenditure but also the diversification of the economy. To a large extent, however, investment went into highly inefficient import substitution industries that drained, instead of adding to, the pool of scarce foreign exchange resources available to the country. The import-substituting strategy had the backing of the domestic business sector, which found it easier to obtain privileges from the government in licenses and contracts than to produce for the world market. The government, too, gained; the discretionary granting of protection from foreign competition and of other privileges gave the administration a powerful tool with which to control industry and hence secure the political support of the business sector.

In the 1950s and 1960s the system worked fairly well. Revenues from bauxite and alumina and from tourism began rising, and the government's current account was in surplus. The Manley government's attempt to introduce democratic socialism disrupted growth, and fiscal expenditures soared. The bauxite levy provided the government with additional revenue in the short run, but soon, in combination with unfavorable external developments, it led to a sharp decline in production. The currency was maintained at an artificially high level to preserve the standard of living of workers whose consumption basket was heavily weighted with imported foodstuffs. Overvaluation heightened the balance of payments problem, whereupon the government introduced direct controls that only made the situation worse. Most serious of all, capital fled the country and skilled workers emigrated to the United States and Canada.

The JLP government, in power from 1980 until 1989, undertook the task of restoring the economy. At first it attempted to do so within the traditional dirigiste framework. Disappointing results and pressure from lenders and donors gradually forced the government to adopt a more free-market stance. The PNP won the 1989 election but, in view of the government's recent experience, decided to rely heavily on private enterprise and on free markets, a decision that marked a considerable departure from the policies followed since independence.

Thus, once again, the two rivals appeared to be moving toward the center. The lost decades of the 1970s and 1980s have perhaps taught both parties some bitter lessons about how a small open economy can survive in a highly uncertain world.

Notes

The authors wish to thank Alwyn Young for his numerous valuable contributions to this chapter.

1. It is claimed that 50,000 slaves had colored masters in 1826; at the time of emancipation in 1838 there were, in total, 311,000 slaves in Jamaica (see Black 1983: 123).

2. In 1960 the Imperial Association changed its name to the Farquaharson Institute of Public Affairs and became a small, insignificant group defending private enterprise interests.

3. It must be noted that the census figures in table 4-2 are not strictly comparable with the figures given in the National Income Statistics.

4. In 1961, according to the census, more than 40 percent of farms under 5 acres were growing crops mainly for local consumption, while 52 percent of the farms in this size group grew mainly export crops. See *Five-Year Independence Plan* (Jamaica 1963–68: 17).

5. The World Bank reported, however, that large livestock properties were characterized by low yields. See IBRD (1952: 13). The World Bank's estimates were based on figures supplied by the Sugar Manufacturers Association.

6. The 1951 figures are 48 and 92 percent, respectively (Jamaica, Central Bureau of Statistics, *Digest of Statistics, 1952*, no. 12).

7. For a discussion of the unemployment problem during the Great Depression, see Orde-Brown (1939). Urban unemployment in Jamaica was noticed as early as 1861, at which time, however, the sugar planters had difficulty in securing adequate labor. See Sewell (cited in Standing 1981: 48–49) and the West Indian Royal Commission Report (the Moyne Commission), quoted in Jefferson 1972: 4.

8. In the computation of percentages, the "not-specified" category was netted out.

9. In 1943 only 12 percent of wage laborers were unionized (by 1950, however, membership rose to 25 percent), and only a fraction of workers was covered by the minimum wage law enacted in the wake of the 1938 riots. It is conceivable, of course, that employers, facing an undisciplined and militant labor force voluntarily pay a wage exceeding the labor opportunity cost, thus creating a pool of involuntary unemployment. For a theoretical exploration of this concept, see Calvo (1979: 102–7).

10. The committee was appointed in 1944 by the governor-general to conduct a systematic economic survey and to recommend policies designed to ensure full employment without detriment to the general standard of living.

11. As we shall see, the importance of the unemployment problem as a political issue persists to this day.

12. Jamaica, Central Bureau of Statistics, *Digest of Statistics* (various issues); life tables for British Caribbean countries 1959–61 as given in Jamaica, Department of Statistics, *Annual Abstract of Statistics* (1967).

13. In many years, however, the surplus was smaller than the grants obtained under colonial development and welfare schemes.

14. To safeguard the banana plantations, the British government purchased the entire crop suitable for export at guaranteed prices. Since no shipping facilities were available, the bananas were then sold in Jamaica at (lower) free-market prices.

15. Legislation establishing the boards including the Coffee Industry Regulation Law (Law 43 of 1948), the Citrus Marketing Plan (under the Agricultural Marketing Law 1949), the Cocoa Marketing Law (Law 40 of 1951), and the Banana Board Law (Law 24 of 1953). Until 1952, the British Ministry of Food purchased the entire sugar surplus; subsequently, sugar exports were subject to international agreements.

16. Under the Citrus Expansion Program, which started in 1947, the government gave growers low-interest loans for fertilizer and provided insect and disease control. This was the most ambitious agricultural project undertaken under the plan.

17. For an account of the discussions that preceded the policy shift, see Widdicomb (1972: 77–93).

18. These modifications followed the recommendations of the *Report of the Committee on the Revision of the Customs Tariff* (Jamaica 1950).

19. *Report on the Revision of the Ten-Year Plan of Development for Jamaica*, as approved by the House of Representatives on November 28, 1951 (Jamaica 1952: 3, 16).

20. The figure is for the average annual growth rate of GDP at constant market prices between 1950 and 1972, as calculated from the World Bank data bank. Other data sources yield somewhat higher estimates.

21. Trade union membership grew from 67,000 in 1950 to 78,000 in 1960 and 150,000 in 1970. In the last year, unions included 35 percent of all wage earners.

22. Based on figures from IMF, *International Financial Statistics*, which do not necessarily agree with the figures of Jamaica, Ministry of Finance, or with those of the World Bank.

23. The drop in foreign investment reflects, in part, the revaluation of the Jamaican dollar in relation to the U.S. dollar.

24. A royalty of 1 shilling per long ton was imposed on exported ore and a royalty of 10 pence per ton was imposed on ore used locally to produce alumina. In addition, the bauxite-exporting companies were to pay a 40 percent tax on a notional profit of US$0.60 per ton and processing companies a 40 percent tax on actual profits. Royalty payments were to be lower for output exceeding 1 million tons. This contract is difficult to compare with the contracts concluded with Suriname and Guyana because of differences in the cost of mining and transport and in the chemical composition of the ore (see Girvan 1971).

25. Girvan (1971: 46) estimates that between 1959 and 1966 wages accounted for 14.8 percent of the value added in the production of dry bauxite, taxes for 31.2 percent, depreciation for 11.1 percent, and net profit for 41.6 percent. When the ore is also considered, wages account for 17.8 percent of the gross value added.

26. Nonbooming tradables are defined here as being equal to the sum of all agricultural products, all manufacturing products, quarrying, and oil refining. The decline in the relative importance of nonbooming tradables (NBTs) was more

accentuated during the initial period of bauxite-alumina growth. During 1954–72 as a whole the NBT/GDP ratio fell at an annual rate of 13 percent. Nonbooming exports are defined as all exports except alumina and bauxite.

27. General services (administration, defense, justice, police) amounted to 3 percent, the balance consisting of "other N.E.C." (2 percent) and of statistical discrepancies (8 percent).

28. The granting of the various privileges is not automatic; each case is considered on its merits, and the fiscal concessions and trade protection are negotiable.

29. The wage bill of manufacturing firms receiving no privileges (most of which produced mainly for the home market) amounted to J$81.3 million.

30. According to World Bank estimates, family formation between 1950 and 1960 averaged about 3,000 families a year. Net additions to the housing stock are said to be approximately equal to the growth in the number of families. There are, however, no estimates of the number of housing units going out of use or of total housing stock.

31. Total income is defined as "annual money income of wage earners, non-wage earners, and other income recipients before any deductions," excluding "income in kind, gifts, payments to pension funds and similar institutions on behalf of workers [and] receipts from capital transactions" (Ahiram 1958: 335).

32. Some of the differentials—for example, between nonunionized rural and urban wages—are equilibrating; others reflect relative union strength, as well as the magnitude of the monopolistic profit that can be shared between the owners and workers. The matter is highly complex and has never been thoroughly investigated, but see Brewster (1968).

33. The improvement in the PNP's electoral performance between 1972 and 1976 might be partly attributable to the fact that in the 1972 election, because the rolls had not been revised since 1969, no one under the age of twenty-three could vote, while in the 1976 election those eighteen and older were able to vote.

34. It should be noted, however, that output rose sharply in the mid-1970s, while in the closing years of the decade there was a moderate decline.

35. In 1970 Tate and Lyle, the major sugarcane estate and factory owner, announced its intention to give up farming in Jamaica. The following year the government purchased from Tate and Lyle 60,000 acres of sugar land and put them back under WISCo (a Tate and Lyle subsidiary) for management. Other private lands were also acquired and managed directly by the government. The transfer of management of some of the lands to workers' cooperatives, which occurred under the Manley regime, largely resulted from pressure by a workers' self-management movement (see Feuer 1984).

36. Employees were to contribute 2 percent of their pay to the trust and employers 3 percent of the wage bill, or 1.5 percent of operating cost, whichever was greater.

37. Under the original order, applicable for a period of six months, salaries of up to J$7,000 per year could be raised, on expiration of current contracts, to the real level prevailing at the end of the last contract expiration period to June 1973. Salaries between J$7,000 and J$12,000 could be raised by up to the amount of raises allowed for those earning less than J$7,000 a year, those between J$12,000 and J$16,000 were to be given half that increase, and salaries in excess of J$16,000 were totally frozen.

38. The levy was to be raised to 8 percent on April 1, 1975, and to 8.5 percent on April 1, 1976. In fact, however, the levy was not raised to 8 percent until 1976. In 1977 it was lowered to 7.5 percent. Under a 1979 agreement a 7.5 percent levy

was to apply to output below 85 percent of capacity of each company and a 7 percent levy was to apply to output above 85 percent of capacity. A proviso was also made that the levy would be lower if ingot prices exceeded a stated limit. The average levy paid in 1965 was 6.5 percent.

39. A somewhat optimistic assumption, given the stagnation of world demand for bauxite and alumina during the late 1970s and early 1980s and the appearance of more efficient producers such as Australia and Guinea.

40. The average annual value of taxes and royalties collected by the Jamaican government between 1970 and 1973 was J$30.3 million (Davies 1984c: 4; all figures use 1973 Jamaican dollars). The average annual value of wages and salaries paid by the bauxite-alumina industries between 1970 and 1972 was J$32.5 million. Similarly, the average value of materials and services purchased was J$26.8 million, which contributed perhaps J$13.4 million to value added. Given Jamaica's high unemployment rates, we may assume that these payments went to otherwise unemployed factors. Bauxite-alumina indirect taxes between 1968 and 1970 amounted to J$0.86 million. We assume a figure of J$1 million for average indirect taxes between 1970 and 1973. From these estimates, one arrives at annual earnings from the bauxite-alumina industry of J$77.2 million.

41. This section is based on Hughes (1984: 40–77) and Davies (1984c: 167–94).

42. The successor JLP government followed the same policy as the PNP government. In fact, the proportion of proceeds transferred to the budget rose after 1980.

43. Capital goods import licenses were restricted to continuing construction projects and essential capital projects. The value of capital goods imported in the remaining months of 1975 was to be deducted from the 1976 license quota, and payments had to be delayed until 1976.

44. The Caribbean Free Trade Association (CARIFTA) treaty of 1968 established free trade among Commonwealth countries of the Caribbean. The free-trade provisos of CARIFTA were preserved under the Caribbean Economic Community (CARICOM), which superseded CARIFTA in 1973.

45. Until the late 1960s the United Kingdom was the principal destination of Jamaican emigrants; 158,630 Jamaicans entered Britain between 1955 and 1962. After the imposition of additional immigration restrictions in 1962, this number fell, with only 32,700 Jamaicans entering Britain between 1962 and December 1968. According to the *Caribbean Yearbook* (1979/80: 319), in the 1970s the mainstream of Jamaican immigration was distributed as follows:

Country	1972	1973	1974	1975	1976
United States	13,427	9,963	12,408	11,076	9,026
Canada	3,092	9,363	11,286	8,211	7,282
United Kingdom	1,620	1,872	1,397	1,394	1,198
Total	18,139	21,198	25,091	20,681	17,506

46. The relative importance of external and internal factors in the 1974–80 decline is the subject of a heated debate, briefly summarized in Bullock (1986: 127–76).

47. The most notorious event was the acquisition of the Terra Nova Hotel by the National Commercial Bank for J$6.5 million. The property was valued at no more than J$4.1 million. When the fact became known, Mr. Seaga asked the bank's board to resign.

48. In addition, to make up for a (temporary) shortfall in traditional exports, the IMF granted Jamaica US$48 million in 1981 and US$24 million in 1982 in compensatory finance facility. IMF support paved the way for other international financing. During the first year in office, the government obtained US$450 million from the Caribbean Group for Economic Development and US$50 million from the U.S. government. Total public and private loans amounted to about US$1 billion. Foreign finance and aid were forthcoming throughout the government's term of tenure. USAID grants and loans alone amounted to US$750 million during the 1981–86 period. (U.S. assistance was, however, drastically cut in 1987–88.)

49. The conditions that accompanied the 1981 EFF included a schedule of reduction of the budget deficit and of the balance of payments deficit. Ceilings were placed on domestic bank credit to the public sector and on new public sector or government-guaranteed foreign borrowing. The government was to refrain from introducing a multiple exchange rate system, and it was not to resort to new trade restrictions for balance of payments purposes.

50. The accuracy of this often-quoted figure for GDP growth is open to doubt. Between 1980 and 1981 the number of tourists rose from 528,800, to 546,100 but all the other major productive sectors stagnated. Bauxite production declined from 13,064,000 tons in 1980 to 11,606,000 tons in 1981, and levy earnings decreased from US$206 million to US$193 million. The Planning Institute of Jamaica estimates that value added by manufacturing rose by 0.2 percent, but the physical indices show a decline in output of virtually all major commodities except rum. The volume of production of main agricultural commodities declined, and the value of agricultural exports fell by 13 percent, from US$169 million to US$149 million. The United States is virtually the sole buyer of Jamaican bauxite. Sales of Jamaican alumina are geographically more dispersed. In 1974 34 percent of alumina exports were destined for the United States, while Norway and the United Kingdom accounted for 22 and 16 percent, respectively. By 1983 sales to the United States ranked third, behind Canada and the United Kingdom.

51. To placate Jamaica's CARICOM partners, who objected to the dual system, an intermediate tier, applicable to CARICOM imports, was introduced in August 1983.

52. In contrast to the rapid expansion of public sector employment under Manley, public sector employment under Seaga fell from 110,500 in 1980 to 92,600 in 1984.

53. In 1983 the government imposed a hotel industry tax to capture windfall profits (estimated at $200 million) resulting from devaluation. One-half the proceeds of the tax was used to subsidize basic food items.

54. The 1988–89 fiscal expenditures were to be further swollen by measures taken in the wake of Hurricane Gilbert.

55. Under a two-part levy system instituted in 1979 a lower rate applied to production in excess of 85 percent of plant capacity.

56. Despite some promising openings, these efforts proved largely fruitless.

57. Contracts with several countries, including the U.S.S.R. and Yugoslavia were successfully negotiated, and over the years BATCO's activities became increasingly important. In 1984 bauxite exports amounted to 4.54 million tons, of which BATCO handled 1.68 million tons.

58. To replenish its strategic stockpile, the U.S. government purchased 1.6 million tons of Jamaican bauxite in 1982, with payment in cash and agricultural products. In 1983, 1 million tons of bauxite were purchased for cash, and 1 million tons were swapped for dairy products.

59. The 1980 figure reflects hurricane damage. During the 1970s exports fluctuated between 68,000 tons and 80,000 tons a year.

60. A number of reforms, including tariff rationalization, had to be undertaken as a condition of World Bank structural adjustment loans.

61. Under the 1982 amendment agricultural undertakings could quality for tax concessions (five-to-nine-year income tax holidays, exemption from payment of consumption and sales taxes on inputs, and tax deductions on interest paid on long-term loans), for concessionary loans (at interest no higher than 3 points above the Bank of Jamaica's minimum discount rate), and for relief from import duties.

Bibliography

Ahiram, E. 1958. "Income Distribution in Jamaica, 1958." *Social and Economic Studies* 13(33):333–69.

Ambursley, Fitzroy, and Robin Cohen. 1983. *Crisis in the Caribbean*. London: Heineman.

American Bureau of Metal Statistics. Various issues. *Non-Ferrous Metal Data*. Washington, D.C.

Ayub, Mahmood Ali. 1981. *Made in Jamaica: The Development of the Manufacturing Sector*. Baltimore, Md.: Johns Hopkins University Press.

Barnett, Lloyd G. 1977. *The Constitutional Law of Jamaica*. Oxford, U.K.: Oxford University Press.

Barry, Tom, Beth Wood, and Deb Preusch. 1984. *The Other Side of Paradise: Foreign Control in the Caribbean*. New York: Grove.

Beckford, George. 1972. *Persistent Poverty: Underdevelopment in the Plantation Economies of the Third World*. New York: Oxford University Press.

Black, Clinton V. 1983. *History of Jamaica*. London: Collins.

Blake, J. 1961. *Family Structure in Jamaica: The Social Context of Reproduction*. New York: Free Press.

Blume, Helmut. 1968. *The Caribbean Islands*. London: Longman.

Bonnick, Gladstone G. 1984. "Jamaica: Liberalization to Centralization and Back?" In Arnold C. Harberger, ed., *World Economic Growth*. San Francisco: ICS.

Brewster, Havelock. 1968. "Wage, Price and Productivity Relations in Jamaica, 1957–62." *Social and Economic Studies* 17(2).

Brown, Adlith. 1981. "Economic Policy and the IMF in Jamaica." *Social and Economic Studies* 30(4):1–51.

Brown, Aggrey. 1979. *Color, Class and Politics in Jamaica*. New Brunswick, N.J.: Transaction Books.

Bullock, Colin. 1986. "IMF Conditionality and Jamaica's Economic Policy in the 1980's." *Social and Economic Studies* 35(4):127–76.

Calvo, Guillermo A. 1979. "Quasi-Walrasian Theories of Unemployment." *American Economic Review* 69(May):102–07.

Carnegie, James. 1973. *Some Aspects of Jamaica's Politics, 1918–1938*. Kingston: Institute of Jamaica.

Chernick, Sidney. 1978. *The Commonwealth Caribbean*. Baltimore, Md.: Johns Hopkins University Press.

Colonial Office. 1944. "The Planning of Social and Economic Development in the Colonial Empire." Paper on Colonial Affairs 3. His Majesty's Stationery Office, London.

Corden, W. M. 1984. "Booming Sector and Dutch Disease Economics: Survey and Consolidation." *Oxford Economic Papers* 35:355–80.

Cumper, Gloria. 1972. *Survey of Social Legislation in Jamaica.* Kingston: University of the West Indies, Institute of Social and Economic Research.

Davies, Omar. 1984a. *An Analysis of Jamaica's Fiscal Budget.* Occasional Papers Series. University of the West Indies, Department of Economics, Mona, Jamaica.

———. 1984b. *Housing, The Basis for a National Policy in Jamaica.* Occasional Paper Series. University of the West Indies, Department of Economics, Mona, Jamaica.

———. 1984c. "Jamaica's Fiscal and Foreign Exchange Budgets and the Impact of the Bauxite Levy, 1974–1983." *Jamaica Bauxite Institute Journal* 3(1): 167–94.

———. 1986. *The State in Caribbean Society.* Kingston: University of the West Indies.

Davis, Carlton E. 1982. "Energy and the Jamaican Bauxite Alumina Industry." *Jamaican Bauxite Institute Journal* 2(1).

Drake, Paul, and Eduardo Silva. 1986. *Elections and Democratization in Latin America, 1980–85.* Berkeley: University of California Press.

Eaton, George. 1975. *Alexander Bustamante and Modern Jamaica.* Kingston: Kingston Publishers.

Economist Intelligence Unit. Various issues. *Quarterly Economic Review.*

Eisner, Gisela. 1961. *Jamaica 1830–1930: A Study of Economic Growth.* Manchester, U.K.: University of Manchester Press.

Feuer, Carl Henry. 1984. *Jamaica and the Sugar Workers' Cooperatives: The Politics of Reform.* Boulder, Colo.: Westview.

Gavin, Michael. 1989. "Macroeconomic Policy in Jamaica 1972–1980." Columbia University, Department of Economics, New York.

Girvan, Norman. 1971. *Foreign Capital and Economic Under-development in Jamaica.* Kingston: Institute of Economic and Social Research.

Graham, Norman, and Keith Edwards. 1984. *The Caribbean Basin to the Year 2,000.* Boulder, Colo.: Westview.

Greenfield, S. M. 1961. "Socio-Economic Factors and Family Form." *Social and Economic Studies* 10(1):72–85.

Henriques, Fernando. 1953. *Family and Color in Jamaica.* London: Granada.

Henry, Paget, and Carl Stone, eds. 1983. *The Newer Caribbean: Decolonization, Democracy and Development.* Philadelphia, Pa: ISHI.

Henry, Zin. 1970. *Labour Relations and Industrial Conflict in Commonwealth Caribbean Countries.* Port of Spain: Columbus.

Hicks, John R., and Ursula K. Hicks. 1955. *Report on Finance and Taxation in Jamaica.* Kingston: Government Printer.

Hughes, Wesley. 1984. "Mineral Taxation and Economic Development: The Use of Jamaica's Production Levy Earnings, 1974–83." *Jamaica Bauxite Journal* 3(1):42.

Institute of Economic and Social Research. 1981. *Public Sector Issues in the Commonwealth*. Special issue of the institute's journal. Kingston.

IBRD (International Bank for Reconstruction and Development). 1952. *The Economic Development of Jamaica*. Baltimore, Md.: Johns Hopkins University Press.

Jacobs, H. P. 1973. *Sixty Years of Change 1806-1866 - Progress and Reaction in Kingston and the Countryside*. Kingston: Institute of Jamaica.

Jamaica. 1945. *Report of the Economic Policy Committee*. Kingston: Government Printer.

Jamaica. 1950. *Report of the Committee on the Revision of the Customs Tariff*. Kingston: Government Printer.

———. 1951. *Report on the Revision of the Ten-Year Plan of Development for Jamaica*. Kingston: Government Printer.

Jamaica. Various issues. *Statistical Yearbook*.

———. n.d. *Five-Year Independence Plan 1963–1968*. Kingston.

Jamaica, Central Bureau of Statistics. 1947. *Quarterly Digest of Statistics* 6 (January–March).

———. Various issues. *Abstract of Statistics*.

———. Various issues. *Digest of Statistics*.

Jamaica, Department of Statistics. 1958. "The National Income of Jamaica, 1956." Kingston.

———. 1971. *The Labor Force: 1968*. Kingston.

Jamaica, Department of Statistics. 1981. *National Income and Product*. Kingston.

———. Various issues. *Continuous Social and Demographic Survey*. Kingston.

Jamaica, Ministry of Trade and Industry. 1954. *Review of the Developments in Trade and Industry in Jamaica during the Period 1944–1954*. Kingston: Government Printer.

Jefferson, Owen. 1972. *The Postwar Economic Development of Jamaica*. Kingston: Institute of Social and Economic Research.

Jones, Edwin, Derek Gordon, and Phyllis Green. 1983. *Employee Morale in the Jamaican Civil Service*. Kingston: Administrative Staff College.

Kaufman, Michael. 1985. *Jamaica under Manley, Dilemmas of Socialism and Democracy*. Westport, Conn.: Zed Books.

Kuper, Adam. 1976. *Changing Jamaica*. Kingston: Kingston Publishers.

Lacy, Terry. 1977. *Violence and Politics in Jamaica 1960–70*. Manchester: Manchester University Press.

Lewis, Gordon. 1968. *The Growth of the Modern West Indies*. New York: Monthly Review.

Lewis, W. Arthur. 1950. "The Industrialization of The British West Indies." *Caribbean Development Review* 2(1).

Looney, Robert. 1987. *The Jamaican Economy in the 1980's: Economic Decline and Structural Adjustment*. Boulder, Colo.: Westview.

Manley, Michael. 1974. *The Politics of Change: A Jamaican Testament*. London: Andre Deutsch.

———. 1975. *A Voice at the Workplace: Reflections on Colonialism and the Jamaican Worker*. London: Andre Deutsch.

———. 1976. *The Search for Solutions*. Ontario: Maple House.

———. 1982. *Jamaica—Struggle in the Periphery*. London: Writers and Publishers Co-op.

Mau, James. 1968. *Social Change and Images of the Future*. Cambridge, Mass.: Schenkman.

Maunder, F. W. 1960. *Employment in an Underdeveloped Area: A Sample Survey of Kingston, Jamaica*. New Haven, Conn.: Yale University Press.

Metallgesellschaft. Various issues. *Metal Statistics*.

Mills, G. E. 1974. "Public Policy and Private Enterprise in the Commonwealth Caribbean." *Social and Economic Studies* 23(2).

Mintz, Sidney, and Sally Price, eds. 1985. *Caribbean Contours*. Baltimore, Md.: Johns Hopkins University Press.

Munroe, Trevor. 1972. *The Politics of Constitutional Decolonization: Jamaica 1944–1962*. Kingston: Institute of Social and Economic Research.

Nettleford, Rex. 1970. *Mirror Mirror-Identity, Race and Protest in Jamaica*. Kingston: Collins and Sangster.

Norris, Katrin. 1962. *Jamaica: The Search for an Identity*. Oxford, U.K.: Oxford University Press.

Orde-Brown, G. St. J. 1939. *Labour Conditions in the West Indies*. Cmd. 6070. His Majesty's Stationery Office, London.

Overseas Development Council. 1978. *Disparity Reduction Rates in Social Indicators*. London.

Payne, Anthony, and Paul Sutton, eds. 1984. *Dependency under Challenge: The Political Economy of the Commonwealth Caribbean*. Manchester, U.K.: Manchester University Press.

Phillip, George. 1987. *A–Z of Industrial Relations Practices at the Workplace*. Kingston: Kingston Publishers.

Phillips, Peter. 1977. "Jamaican Elites: 1938 to Present." In Carl Stone and Aggrey Brown, eds., *Essays on Power and Change in Jamaica*. Kingston: Jamaica Publishing House.

Planning Institute of Jamaica. 1984. *Economic and Social Survey*. Kingston.

———. *Quarterly Economic Report*.

Pollard, Stephen K., and Douglas H. Graham. 1985. "The Performance of the Food-Producing Sector in Jamaica 1962–1979." *Economic Development and Cultural Change* 33(4):731–54.

Post, Ken. 1978. *Arise Ye Starvelings: The Jamaican Labor Rebellion of 1938 and Its Aftermath*. The Hague: Nijhoff.

———. 1981. *Strike the Iron: A Colony at War: Jamaica 1939–1945*. Atlantic Highlands, N.J.: Humanities.

Ramsaran, Ramesh. 1985. *U.S. Investment in Latin America and the Caribbean*. London: Hodder and Stoughton.

Schultz, Donald, and Douglas Graham. 1984. *Revolution and Counterrevolution in Central America and the Caribbean*. Boulder, Colo.: Westview.

Sherlock, Philip. 1980. *Norman Manley: A Biography*. London: Macmillan.

Smith, M. G. 1956. *A Report on Labor Supply in Rural Jamaica*. Kingston: Government Printer.

Standing, Guy. 1981. *Unemployment and Female Labour, A Study of Labour Supply in Kingston, Jamaica.* New York: St. Martin's.

Statistical Institute of Jamaica. 1986. *The Jamaican Economy: 1985.* Kingston.

—————. *Bank of Jamaica, External Trade of Jamaica.* Kingston.

Stephens, Evelyn H., and J. D. Stephens. 1986. *Democratic Socialism in Jamaica.* London: Macmillan.

Stone, Carl. 1973. *Class, Race and Political Behavior in Urban Jamaica.* Kingston: Institute of Social and Economic Research.

—————. 1974. *Electoral Behavior and Public Opinion in Jamaica.* Kingston: Institute of Social and Economic Research.

—————. 1980. *Democracy and Clientelism in Jamaica.* New Brunswick, N.J.: Transaction Books.

—————. 1982. *Work Attitudes Survey.* A report to the Jamaican government. Kingston: Earl.

—————. 1986a. *Class, State and Democracy in Jamaica.* New York: Praeger.

—————. 1986b. *Power in the Caribbean Basin: A Comparative Study of Political Economy.* Philadelphia, Pa: ISHI.

Stone, Carl, and Aggrey Brown, eds. 1977. *Essays on Power and Change in Jamaica.* Kingston: Jamaica Publishing House.

—————, eds. 1981. *Perspectives on Jamaica in the Seventies.* Kingston: Jamaica Publishing House.

Tidrick, Gene M. 1975. "Wage Spillover and Unemployment in A Wage-Gap Economy: The Jamaican Case." *Economic Development and Cultural Change* 23(2):306–42.

United States, Department of Labor. 1967. *Labor, Law and Practice in Jamaica.* Washington, D.C.

Wedderburn, Judith, ed. 1986. *A Caribbean Reader on Development.* Kingston: Friedrich Ebert Stiftung.

West Indian Royal Commission Report (Moyne Commission). 1938. Cmd. 6607. London.

Widdicomb, Stacey H., Jr. 1972. *The Performance of Industrial Development Corporations: The Case of Jamaica.* New York: Praeger.

World Bank. 1980. *World Tables.* Baltimore, Md.: Johns Hopkins University Press.

Young, Alwyn. 1987. "Decline of the Jamaican Bauxite Industry." The Political Economy of Poverty, Equity, and Growth Project. Working Paper. Columbia University, New York.

5 Mauritius

Stanislaw Wellisz
Philippe Lam Shin Saw

Mauritius is a small volcanic island 61 kilometers long and 47 kilometers wide located in the Indian Ocean 800 kilometers east of Madagascar. The population of the island is about 1 million, and about half of its 1,865 square kilometers is arable. Mauritius has several island dependencies, the largest being Rodrigues, which lies 560 kilometers farther east. Rodrigues has an area of 104 square kilometers and a population of slightly more than 35,000.

Mauritius has rich volcanic soil that can support a variety of agriculture. The subtropical climate is also favorable, and, owing to the mountainous terrain, there is a diversity of subclimates. Rainfall is ample, especially in the upland areas. The only serious impediments to agriculture are cyclones, which occur almost every year during the summer months and reach destructive force every five to six years, and occasional droughts. The island has no other natural resources except for its beautiful landscape and good beaches, which make it attractive to tourists. There is a good natural harbor at Port Louis, but Mauritius lies far from present-day sea-lanes.

Historical Background

When the island was discovered by the Portuguese in 1510, it was uninhabited.[1] Neither the Portuguese nor the Dutch, who gained control of the island in 1658, established permanent settlements there (although the latter attempted to do so on two occasions). These visitors caused a great deal of harm to the local flora and fauna, exterminating the dodo and destroying the hardwood forests covering the land.

The first permanent settlement was established in 1722 under the aegis of the French East India Company. In 1766 Mauritius became a French colony. In 1810 it came under British rule, but the settlers were guaranteed their cultural rights, and the French legal system was preserved. After World War II it enjoyed an increasing degree of autonomy and in 1968 became a fully independent member of the Commonwealth.

The French settlers established sugar plantations and brought slaves from Madagascar and East Africa to work the land; by the end of the eighteenth century the whites were outnumbered by a margin of four to one. The slave trade was outlawed in 1807, and in 1839, following a four-year transition period, slavery itself was abolished.

In the eighteenth century entrepôt trade was as important to the island's economy as the plantations, but it declined under British rule. Subsequently, the plantations flourished, and the area under sugarcane increased fivefold between 1820 and 1840.

When the slaves were freed, many of them left the plantations, and indentured workers were brought in from India to satisfy the growing demand for labor. Initially, these workers were repatriated at the end of their five-year contracts, but later many settled permanently. The first arrivals came the year slavery was abolished, and by 1850 net immigration was up to 55,700. By 1860 it had reached 101,000. Thereafter the influx of Indians tapered off rapidly and came to a halt after 1880, by which time Indians were in the absolute majority.

The Chinese constitute the most recent ethnic group to have arrived, beginning with a few in 1830 and with greater numbers in the mid-nineteenth century. Originally this group consisted almost exclusively of men, but women began arriving after World War I.[2]

Of the several languages spoken on Mauritius, the predominant one is Créole, a French-based dialect spoken by the mixed-blood (Créole) population.[3] The small, influential group of Franco-Mauritians speak French, as do educated individuals of all ethnic backgrounds. The island's several newspapers and most radio and television broadcasts use French. English is the official language, and intermediate and advanced education is mainly in English, with French as a foreign language. At the elementary level, however, there are also French, Hindi, Tamil, and Chinese schools. Despite this apparent confusion, many people believe that their mastery of both English and French gives them an important advantage in trade relations.

The Economy

In the early years of British rule, from the early 1830s to the late 1860s, Mauritius had a booming economy. In 1826 Great Britain granted Mauritian sugar a privileged import duty status that only the British West Indies had enjoyed up to then. Producer prices in Mauritius climbed from 26 shillings per 100 pounds in 1823 to 58 shillings in 1826. The area under sugarcane expanded from 26,000 acres in 1820–30 to 40,000 in the following decade, 59,000 in the 1840s, and 110,000 in the 1850s (Varma 1980: 86, 82–83). Sugar production rose from an average of 23,000 metric tons in the latter half of the 1820s to 55,000 tons in 1850 and 130,000 tons in 1860.[4]

In the subsequent decades growth decelerated, and the area under cultivation increased marginally, reaching 124,000 acres in 1861–1900 and 127,000 in 1901–08. Technical improvements raised sugar output by 45 percent between 1860 and the turn of the century, but the crop became less profitable.

The economic slowdown of the late 1800s was largely due to exogenous factors. For one thing, Great Britain ended its preferential system in 1846, leaving producers in Mauritius (and in the West Indies) exposed to free competition for the first time. To make matters worse, Great Britain imposed a duty on all sugar imports in 1854; this tariff was lifted in 1874 but was reimposed in 1901. At the same time, other European countries were busy protecting their burgeoning sugar beet industry. As a result, Mauritius turned to India for an assured sugar market, which, however, proved less lucrative than the British market in the colonial preference period.

Another problem was the slowdown in the shipping trade, after the great boom of the 1850s and 1860s. In 1850 alone, Port Louis had been visited by 470 ships, with a total displacement of 136,000 tons. After the repeal of the Navigation Laws in the following year lifted restrictions on the trade activities of non-British ships, the harbor saw even more trade, particularly after the discovery of gold in Australia, which opened up a vast market for transshipped goods. In 1858 the number of ship arrivals jumped to 825 and their total displacement to 308,000 tons (Toussaint 1974: 95). But the opening in 1869 of the Suez Canal, which made the route from Europe to India and Australia vastly shorter, and the arrival of the steamship, which the harbor facilities of Port Louis could not handle, brought the era of unbounded growth to an end.

Mauritius also fell victim to natural disasters in the second half of the century. A cholera epidemic in 1854 left 17,000 dead, and malaria, brought in from India, killed about 50,000 people between 1866 and 1868 (Toussaint 1974: 99). In 1892 a particularly violent cyclone destroyed a great deal of property and claimed 1,200 victims. Port Louis, already abandoned by much of the population because of malaria, was virtually wiped out by a fire in 1893. Cattle and draft animals were repeatedly struck by disease, and in 1902 a surra epidemic killed virtually all the horses and mules on the island, with a devastating effect on sugar harvesting and transport in two consecutive years (Varma 1980: 95).

Mauritius enjoyed a brief resurgence in the years following World War I, thanks to the Imperial Preference System, created in 1919, which once again provided the sugar market with some protection. Prices climbed, and sugar output in 1920 surpassed 259,000 tons. But by the late 1920s and especially the 1930s, the island became weighed down by unprecedented difficulties, and the economy remained in a depressed state until the eve of World War II.

The Constitutional Regime

Mauritius was unusual among British colonies in that the socially and economically dominant local group was European in origin. Before the British takeover, the French settlers enjoyed a high degree of self-government. The British were at first unwilling to grant autonomy to a largely hostile group, yet they were careful not to alienate the island's elite.[5] At the same time, colonial officials felt bound to protect the interests of other social groups, particularly the colored (mixed-blood and African) and Indian population.

It is, perhaps, because of this inherently difficult situation that the governor retained absolute power for so long, although by 1825 a governing council, consisting of the governor assisted by four ex officio members, had been set up. This body was replaced in 1832 by a council consisting of the governor, seven ex officio members, and seven Mauritians appointed by the governor.

True representative government began only in 1885, with the adoption of a constitution and the establishment of a new council, consisting of—in addition to the governor, eight ex officio members, and nine nominated members—ten elected members. A means test severely restricted the franchise to the white and the richer mixed-blood population, although the governor did appoint an Indian to the council as early as 1886. Even so, it was not until 1926 that Indians won elective seats (Mannick 1979: 49–53). This constitution remained in force until after World War II.

Social Stratification

The island's economic structure generated a deep conflict of interest between the propertied classes and the laborers. In the nineteenth century it took little skill to cultivate and process sugarcane, and most of the output was exported. As a result, the landowners were clearly interested in pursuing a low-wage policy and thus turned to India, which could provide them with a virtually unlimited flow of cheap labor.

The indenture system that replaced slavery not only put the landlords in a particularly strong position but also lent itself to easy abuse. In response to numerous appeals to the Crown on behalf of the workers, successive commissions were appointed to investigate working conditions, and several laws were passed to protect the Indian workers (see Varma 1980: 66–77). In 1907, on the recommendation of a royal commission, further Indian immigration was formally prohibited, and this move strengthened the position of Mauritian workers.[6] A labor law of 1922 abolished long-term contracts tying workers to estates and regulated terms of employment. Government regulation was not always effective (in fact, an 1867 law designed to protect the workers was interpreted in a way that would keep the workers under control), but the paternalistic approach allayed the anger of the workers and at times (notably in 1871) prevented the eruption of violence.

The conflict between the rich landowners and the poor laborers was defused somewhat by the gradual rise of two middle-income groups. The first consisted of Créoles, some of whom had acquired property and education even before the abolition of slavery and had taken on commercial, administrative, or professional jobs. The second group, consisting of small and medium-size (and a few large) sugar planters, originated with Indian field bosses, known as *sirdars*, who enriched themselves by providing workers to plantations, supervising them, and lending them money. In the latter part of the nineteenth century, the *sirdars* began seeking land of their own, obtaining it from plantation owners who, faced with falling sugar prices and increasing labor costs, were willing to convert some of their less productive land to sharecropping or to parcel it outright (North-Coombes in Toussaint 1972: 262; see also Allen in Bissoondoyal 1984). By the turn of the century almost 32 percent of cultivated land devoted to sugar had been sold or leased by the estates.

Politics

Following the introduction of the 1885 Constitution, the voting population split into two rival groups: the Oligarchs (who in 1905 founded le Parti de l'Ordre), and the Progressives. In 1907 the latter group, supported by colored voters and the more liberal whites, organized into a formal party, the Action Libérale. Mass participation in politics did not begin, however, until 1936 with the establishment of the Mauritian Labour party (le Parti Travailliste), which was organized on the model of the British Labour party by Dr. Maurice Curé, a Créole leader, with Rama Sahadeo, an Indo-Mauritian, as secretary general.

The Labour party soon came to play a central role in Mauritian politics. Amid the widespread strikes and workers' riots of 1937, the party emerged as the workers' spokesman. In 1940 Dr. (later Sir) Seewoosagur Ramgoolam, a prominent member of the party, was nominated to the council, where he distinguished himself as a champion of worker's rights and an advocate of independence (Varma 1975).

In the aftermath of the 1937 riots the government appointed a commission of inquiry (the Hooper Commission) to appraise the economic situation of the plantation workers and small farmers. In accordance with the commission's recommendations, the government in 1938 adopted an industrial association ordinance legalizing trade unions, although it restricted the scope of their activities. Industrial disputes were to be brought before a conciliation board appointed by the governor, and strikes were to be permitted only if a dispute had not been resolved within thirty days. When labor troubles flared up again in 1943, the government finally relaxed the restraints on workers' organizations.

The first trade unions were local in character, and most of them were confined to skilled workers until 1943, when agricultural workers banded together to form the Amalgamated Labourers Association.[7] Thereafter, trade unions came to play an important role in public life, although they did not form a single, politically united bloc.

World War II to 1962

The period between World War II and 1962 marked the end of the ancien régime. These were the years in which the island made rapid progress toward self-rule and then independence. It still had a sugar plantation economy, but its problems were increasing, and a radical reorientation in economic policy was obviously needed.

The Economy

In contrast to World War I, which had little effect on the economy, World War II virtually cut the island off from its main customers and sources of supply. As a result, the government ordered estates and large planters to plant food crops. Since food was still in short supply right after the war, the authorities introduced a system of subsidies and guaranteed prices that was removed when imported food became freely available once again. Subsequently, food production declined rapidly.

Sugar production, deprived of markets, fell during World War II. In 1945 output amounted to only 138,000 tons (Toussaint 1974: 121)—barely 8,000 tons more than in 1860. After the end of hostilities the industry recovered rapidly with the aid of a British government loan of 2.5 million pounds sterling and high world prices. A further stimulus to growth came in 1951 when the Commonwealth Sugar Agreement granted Mauritius a sugar quota at preferential prices.[8] Sugar output reached 457,000 tons in 1950 and exceeded 530,000 tons in 1953.

The recovery restored the primacy of the sugar industry. In 1958 sugarcane generated 35 percent of GNP (table 5-1) and employed 55,000 persons, or about 35 percent of the economically active population. Other agriculture accounted for less than 10 percent of GNP. Some marginally profitable tea, tobacco, and copra plantations had survived, largely through government backing, but nonsugar agriculture consisted largely of small subsistence farms that sold some of their produce on the local markets. Manufacturing industries were the source of 6 to 7 percent of GNP and employed fewer than 10,000 workers.[9] Beverages, wood products, and clothing—all for domestic use—were among the industrial products. The tourist industry boasted a single mediocre hotel located in Port Louis, far from any beach.

In this highly open economy, exports contributed 47.5 percent of GNP in 1957–58, and imports 40.4 percent of gross domestic expenditure. Sugar and molasses accounted for 98 percent of exports, tea and copra

Table 5-1. *Structure of GNP at Factor Cost, 1958*

Economic sector	Millions of rupees	Percent
Agriculture, forestry, and fishing	206	31.3
Sugar	147	22.3
All other	59	9.0
Mining and quarrying	1	0.2
Manufacturing	121	18.4
Sugar	78	11.9
All other	43	6.5
Construction	30	4.6
Electricity and water	11	1.7
Transport, storage, and communications	76	11.6
Wholesale and retail trade	67	10.2
Banking, insurance, and real estate	12	1.8
Ownership of dwellings	45	6.8
Public administration and defense	24	3.7
Other services	61	9.3
GDP	654	99.4
Plus factor income from rest of world	4	0.6
GNP	658	100.0

Source: Meade and others 1961: 44.

being the only other significant export commodities. Food, drink, and tobacco accounted for about 30 percent of total imports, which is not surprising since the country was heavily dependent on imported staples. Another 30 percent of imports consisted of other consumer goods, and most of the balance was made up of fuel, transport equipment, agricultural machinery, and fertilizer.

Foreign investment in Mauritius was virtually nonexistent, but Mauritians invested abroad, mainly in sugar plantations in continental Africa and South America. Mauritian planters, finding limited investment opportunities at home, established foreign subsidiaries, as it were, in their field of expertise.

During the 1950s the country was relatively prosperous. Per capita GNP in 1957 was estimated at MR1,097 (about 82 pounds sterling).[10] Employee compensation ranged from a low of 51 percent of national income (in 1956 and 1957) to a high of 55.5 percent in 1954. Despite the presence of a wage-fixing mechanism and the existence of labor unions, wages responded to market forces. Because of the nature of the sugar industry, there was considerable seasonal unemployment, but in the peak season there seemed to be no shortage of jobs. Although the area devoted to sugarcane cultivation increased by about 3 percent a year in the 1950s and GNP rose (albeit at a slower pace), income failed to keep pace with population growth, increasing the danger of a long-run decline in incomes and of rising unemployment.

Society and Politics

In 1962 the island of Mauritius had a population of 345,000 Hindus, 110,000 Muslims (of Indian origin), and 23,000 Sino-Mauritians; 204,000 inhabitants were classified as "general population." This last category included Créoles, people of pure African and Malagasy origin, and about 12,000 Franco-Mauritians.

The Franco-Mauritians, as already mentioned, constituted a land-owning and professional elite. The twenty-five large millers' estates that occupied about 51 percent of sugarcane land belonged to Franco-Mauritian families (Toussaint 1974: 75). The Franco-Mauritians also invested in local trading companies and abroad. Most of the Hindus still worked as rural labor, although many had made considerable economic and social progress. In the late 1950s the island had 2,700 planters' estates ranging in size from less than 10 arpents to more than 200 arpents (1 arpent = 1.043 acres). Some were cultivated by tenant farmers, but the majority were freeholds, mostly Hindu-owned (Nababsing and Virahaswami in Virahaswami 1977). Other Hindus became white-collar workers or joined the professions, and they came to occupy most of the public administration positions.[11] The Sino-Mauritians were predominantly in trade; the Muslims provided the bulk of urban labor. Many of the Créoles were sugar estate foremen and supervisors, skilled workers, and white-collar workers. People of pure African origin constituted the least advantaged group: most of them were in subsistence farming and in low-skill jobs.[12] These ethnic divisions were not ironclad, and members of all communities could be found in all occupations.

Following World War II, the British Labour government took steps to give the island greater autonomy and to democratize the regime. Consultations on reform, organized in 1947 by the then governor-general, McKenzie Kennedy, brought to light the conflict between representatives of the (mostly) Hindu laborers and the (mostly) Franco-Mauritian and Créole propertied classes. The former overwhelmingly supported the Labour party program, which called for universal suffrage, single-seat constituencies, self-government, and, ultimately, full independence. The latter, fearing Hindu domination and socialism, opposed universal suffrage and demanded to have their rights protected. If suffrage was to be instituted, they favored separate ethnic rolls or, at the very least, proportional representation.

An order-in-council issued on December 19, 1947, represented a compromise between the two groups. It created a Legislative Council consisting of forty members—nineteen elected, twelve nominated, and eight ex officio. The governor, as head of the council, had the tie-breaking vote. The means test was abolished, and all adult males literate in one of nine languages—English, French, Créole, Gujarati, Hindustani, Tamil, Telegu, Urdu, or Chinese—were given the vote. (In 1945 only 12,000 people were entitled to vote, in contrast to the 72,000 allowed to vote in the 1948 election.)

Once the franchise was extended, the lines of ethnic and political division were redefined. The historic enmity between the Franco-Mauritian oligarchs on one side and the Créoles and progressive French on the other was now forgotten, and the two groups made common cause against the workers, mostly of Indian origin.

In the 1948 election, the first to be held under the new rules, communal considerations played a dominant role. Hindu candidates captured eleven of the nineteen elective seats; eight went to colored Créole candidates and one to a white candidate. Following the election, Dr. Ramgoolam reorganized the Labour party (which had declined in importance during the war years) to give it a broader ethnic base and a more clearly socialist outlook. Eighteen of the nineteen elected members of the council supported the Labour party, whose supremacy was diluted only through the appointment of conservatives to the council (Mannick 1979: 128–29). In the next general election, held in 1952, the Labour party won thirteen seats, a white-dominated conservative grouping (the Ralliément Mauricien) two, and independents four. At the time it seemed that the island's politics would soon be dominated by a single party.

In the governmental structure introduced in 1947, a sharp line was drawn between the (mostly elected) Legislative Council and the Executive, which remained in the hands of the governor and of appointed officials. Moreover, a large proportion of the adult population remained disenfranchised. Starting in 1955, successive conferences were held in London to promote further reform. These meetings gradually led, by 1965, to a full parliamentary system and, ultimately, to independence in 1968.[13]

The first general election under universal suffrage took place in 1959. There were 277,500 registered voters. Four parties presented candidates: the Labour party, the Comité d'Action Musulman (CAM), the Independent Forward Bloc, (IFB), and the Parti Mauricien Social Démocrate, (PMSD). The CAM was organized in 1958 with the express purpose of defending the rights of the Muslim population; in other respects its program coincided with that of labor, and the two parties formed an election alliance. The IFB, also organized in 1958, concentrated on specific socioeconomic issues; its main drawing card was the personality of its founder, S. Bissoondoyal, and its support came primarily from the Hindu community.[14] All the parties except the PMSD favored independence. The PMSD, which represented Créole and Franco-Mauritian interests, was constituted in 1955 to replace the exclusively white Ralliément Mauricien, whose head became the PMSD's first leader. In 1966 Gaëtan Duval, a charismatic Créole lawyer and politician, became party leader. Duval steered his party toward multiethnicity, but it remained mainly Créole in character.

In the election, Labour won twenty-six seats, the CAM five, the IFB six, and the PMSD three.[15] The three pro-independence parties formed a coalition government, with the PMSD remaining in opposition. The results confirmed the strength of the Labour party, but they also marked the emergence of a multiparty system in which ethnicity and individual leadership played as great a role as ideology or class interests and in which coalitions succeeded each other in office.

Rules adopted by the Labour party in 1957 forged, in theory, a strong link between trade unions and the party. Under these rules trade unions, cooperative societies, and other collective bodies received the right to become affiliated members. In practice, however, unions as such did not play a dominant role in the 1959 and 1963 elections. Not all of them chose to become party affiliates, and even those that did were mostly concerned with issues of immediate interest to the workers rather than with national politics.

Economic and Social Policies

When the Labour government took office in Great Britain, the colonial government of Mauritius assumed an activist economic policy and embraced the concept of planning. In March 1945 Mauritius established the Central Development and Welfare Committee, which immediately prepared the ten-year welfare and development plan for the period from 1946–47 to 1956–57. In 1955 it launched a capital expenditure program for major infrastructure projects, including modernization of the harbor and airport.

In implementing the plan, the government relied mainly on the private sector and interfered only sporadically with the market mechanism. For example, it took some measures to encourage agricultural diversification. Between 1947 and 1949 the government used price supports to promote the growing of food crops; in 1955 it turned over some Crown lands to tea planting to encourage the tea industry, which also received government-financed technical aid; and it granted tobacco growers protection from foreign competition and subjected them to planting quotas. But the sugar industry was also encouraged; it received a loan from Great Britain and assistance from the newly created Mauritius Sugar Industry Research Institute. A modest step to encourage manufacturing was the 1954 Customs Tariff Ordinance, which gave the governor-in-council the right to change the duty schedule if a particular product had to be imported for an object or an enterprise beneficial to the colony.

In an effort to promote social welfare, the government established a social security scheme for plantation workers to which both employers and employees contributed and a wage tribunal empowered to fix plantation workers' minimum wages. The government took charge of importing rice and flour, selling these products at cost and at times subsidizing them to lower the cost of basic wage goods. Steeply progressive income taxes were imposed on the wealthy.

From 1947 to 1949 the government conducted a spraying campaign to eradicate malaria, which had plagued the island since the mid-nineteenth century. This action virtually eliminated the disease, greatly improving the population's well-being and making the workers more productive. At the same time, it created a new problem: a rapid increase in population growth.

The Population Explosion

The island's population had received an earlier infusion with the inflow of indentured workers during the sugar boom of the first half of the nineteenth century. When the boom subsided, no more workers were brought in, and disease—mainly malaria—checked the growth of the resident population. Thus, before World War II the population grew at only 0.5 percent a year. By 1958, with malaria eradicated and general sanitary conditions greatly improved, the rate jumped to 3 percent a year.

In mid-1957 Mauritius had 594,000 inhabitants, of whom 317,000 were of working age. At the time, that figure was expected to reach 490,000 by 1972.[16] Given the limited possibilities for emigration, more than 90,000 new jobs would have had to be created between 1960 and 1972 to handle the projected increase (Meade and others 1961: 60). The long term looked even more alarming; according to United Nations estimates, constant fertility and declining mortality would bring the population up to 2,869,000 by 2002 (Titmuss 1961: 42–66, 251–91).

There appeared to be no simple solution to the problems posed by population growth. Sugar plantations were unlikely to provide more job opportunities, since the land under cane could not be expanded, and technological improvements were, if anything, likely to reduce the demand for labor. Moreover, there was little scope for generating more sugar income. The large millers' estates were, in general, run efficiently, and, short of a major technical breakthrough, yields could not be expected to increase rapidly. The productivity of the planters' estates was much lower, but there seemed to be no way to improve output other than through socially unacceptable consolidation. In addition, demand was becoming more limited. The island's sugar quotas amounted to 518,000 tons, and the domestic market could absorb only another 23,000 tons. Any excess would have to be sold on the free international market at uncertain, variable prices, which would be insufficient in some years to cover production costs.

Prospects for other industries did not seem much better. Geographically isolated and without natural resources or industrial experience, the island seemed to have little opportunity for producing for the world market, despite its low wage rates and high literacy rate (85 percent of the total population). The only hope seemed to lie in agricultural import substitution through crop diversification. Some products for home use could also be manufactured reasonably efficiently on a small scale, but the domestic market was too small to support inward-oriented industrialization.

The Meade Report

In 1959 the government of Mauritius appointed a committee headed by James Meade "to make recommendations concerning the action to be taken in order to make the country capable of improving the standard of living of its people, having regard to the current and foreseeable demographic trends" (Meade 1961: xv). The commission's report, presented in 1961, came to play a major role in policy formulation in the last years of the colonial period and in the early years of independence.

The Meade Commission found that the existing marketing arrangements gave planters an incentive to overexpand sugar production. The Sugar Syndicate, the sole exporter, paid the producers the average price realized on all sales. Since the quota price exceeded the free-market level, the price paid to the producer was higher than that realized on the syndicate's marginal sales. To correct the distortion, the existing sugar export duty of 10 to 30 cents a ton would have to be replaced by a 5 percent export tax, the future level of the tax to be adjusted depending on the need to regulate output. The proceeds of the tax could be used to finance diversification and restrain sugar production. The commission examined the prospects for various other crops and concluded that substantial benefits could be achieved through compulsory changes in land use, the institution of price supports, government-sponsored research, and improved storage facilities. It also recommended the formation of marketing boards.

Import-substituting industrialization was also to be promoted. The customs tariff system was to be revised and all anomalous cases eliminated where the duty on raw materials exceeded that on the finished good. Tariffs were to be progressive in accordance with the degree of fabrication, but to avoid the creation of "tariff babies," the progression would have to be moderate. Certain industries likely to be efficient at low output volume, such as the manufacture of household utensils, were to be given special protection. The government was to set up an industrial development board that, among other things, would be responsible for the development of industrial estates and would advise the government on the granting of tax holidays for selected new enterprises. In short, the report urged the government to encourage diversification and industrialization through the use of fiscal incentives and disincentives.

The report recommended wage restraint. Wages had to remain low if the growing mass of workers were to find employment. Low wages were also the only hope for the rise of export-oriented manufacturing.

Import Substitution Strategy, 1963–72

When Mauritius finally achieved independence in 1968, it found itself facing communal riots, a left-wing challenge, serious economic difficulties caused by deteriorating terms of trade, and a rapidly growing population and labor force. Despite the magnitude of its difficulties, the government held a steady policy course, adhering to the general strategy adopted by the colonial regime. It also introduced measures to diversify the economy, as recommended by the Meade Report, although, for political reasons, it did not pursue a low labor costs policy, as was also recommended.

Political Developments

In 1963 the Labour party of Sir Seewoosagur Ramgoolam won 40 percent of the popular vote. The PMSD, the sole party to oppose independence, won 20 percent. Thus, the move toward independence pressed forward, culminating in a constitutional convention in London in 1965 at which delegates proposed a Westminster-type constitution. A modified version acceptable to the opposition was introduced in 1966. It established a voting system, ensured ethnic balance, and created a seventy-member Legislative Assembly with sixty-two elected members, of whom sixty would come from three-member constituencies and two from a single two-member constituency in Rodrigues. The remaining eight seats were allocated to "best losers" to ensure that each of the four recognized ethnic groups would be represented approximately in proportion to their relative numerical strength. The allocation of seats was not supposed to change the party balance of the elected members.

A general election, amounting to a referendum on independence, was held on August 7, 1967. The Labour party and its allies, the IFB and the CAM, won 56 percent of the votes and forty-seven assembly seats, while the opposition PMSD won twenty-seven seats (table 5-2). After six months of full self-government, the country became independent on March 12, 1968.

That year serious riots broke out between the Créoles and the Muslims. To preserve national unity, the Labour party formed a coalition government together with the CAM and the PMSD. But then another challenge emerged in the form of a new party, the Mouvement Militant Mauricien (MMM), supported mainly by younger leftists and by radical trade unions in the General Workers' Federation.

This radicalization of Mauritian politics perhaps reflected the frustration of citizens who saw their country become independent yet found economic power still in the hands of the Franco-Mauritian oligarchy and most of the nonwhite population as poor as before. To make matters worse, the postwar baby-boom generation was reaching maturity, and unemployment was rising. Nonetheless the government pursued much the same policies as it had in colonial times.

Table 5-2. Results of Elections to the Legislative Assembly, 1967–83

Political group	1967	1976	1982	1983
Independent Forward Block	12			
Comité d'Action Musulman	5			
Labour party	26	28	2	14
PMSD	27	8	2	5
Parti Socialiste Mauricien			18	
Mouvement Socialiste Mauricien				27
MMM		34	42	22
Organisation du Peuple Rodriguais			2	2
Total	70	70	66	70

Note: In 1982 only four "best losers" were assigned.

In protest, the Marxist MMM and the radical unions—which had been organized largely through the efforts of Paul Bérenger, a leftist Franco-Mauritian—pressed for direct action to deal with these problems. In 1971 the MMM organized strikes and riots, to which the government responded by calling off the general election scheduled for 1972, declaring a state of emergency, banning public meetings, and imprisoning the radical leaders. Stability was preserved, at the cost of the temporary suspension of the democratic system. The ruling coalition remained in power until 1976 and, after that year's election, was reconstituted for another five years.

The Economy

In the 1960s and the early 1970s the economic fortunes of Mauritius were still inextricably tied to those of the sugar industry. After two severe cyclones in 1960 damaged the sugar crop and caused GNP to drop some 12 percent from its 1959 level, a bumper crop in 1963 and relatively good prices raised GNP 31 percent over the previous year. Nonetheless, during the 1960s as a whole real GNP showed little or no growth, while the population rose 2.8 percent a year; hence GNP (and GDP) per capita declined (table 5-3).

In line with the Meade Commission recommendations, the government adopted various measures to diversify production, beginning in 1961 with a 5 percent levy on sugar exports, which was raised to 6 percent in 1971. In 1964 it established the Development Bank to provide long-term financing for industry. Most important was the introduction of the industrial development scheme.

The development scheme offered the holders of development certificates (DCs) a holiday from corporate taxes and from taxes on dividends. A DC company could apply for protection from foreign competition, either in the form of higher tariffs or (since 1969) a quota. Unless the industry was already heavily protected, the request was likely to be

Table 5-3. GDP at Constant 1976 Market Prices, 1960–72

Year	GDP (millions of rupees)	Growth rate (percent)	GDP per capita (rupees)	Growth rate (percent)
1960	2,274	–1.3	3,445	–1.3
1961	2,794	22.9	4,139	20.1
1962	2,816	0.8	4,075	–1.5
1963	3,207	13.9	4,537	11.3
1964	2,986	–6.9	4,130	–9.0
1965	3,082	3.2	4,165	0.8
1966	2,972	–3.6	3,925	–5.7
1967	3,102	4.4	4,008	2.1
1968	2,888	–6.9	3,647	–9.0
1969	3,031	4.9	3,742	2.6
1970	3,019	–0.4	3,642	–2.7
1971	3,148	4.3	3,743	2.8

Source: World Bank data.

granted. Under the initial scheme, capital goods could be imported duty-free for a period of three years, and certificate holders could apply for an exemption from duties on raw materials. There was also a provision—little used in practice—for refunds on the import duty content of exports. A complex procedure was introduced to ensure that certificates were granted only to industries "of importance to the island's economy," but the criteria were vague and arbitrary. The question of measuring the economic costs and benefits of import substitution was not raised until almost twenty years later.

Yet import substitution appeared to give the only promise of industrialization. Mauritian entrepreneurs lacked production or marketing experience and seemed unlikely to go into export-directed manufacturing. It seemed just as unlikely that foreign capital would flow into this small, remote country that was showing increasing signs of political instability. Nevertheless, it did have a ready market for import substitutes, which, although small, was highly protected. There also was a ready source of capital, generated by sugar profits. As mentioned earlier, before independence these tended to be invested in sugar plantations abroad; with the imposition and gradual tightening of capital export controls, they became available for domestic investment.

During the 1960s about 100 development certificates were granted to a variety of industries, including food processing, furniture making, and the production of plastic products, dry cells, and paint. Although statistical information is lacking, DC companies appeared to rely on relatively capital-intensive methods, which is not surprising in view of the possibility of importing capital goods duty-free and the government's high-wage policy. In total, DC firms employed fewer than 5,000 workers.

In its wage policy the government struck a compromise between economic and political considerations. From the political standpoint, the

Labour party recognized that its main support came from the Hindu community, a large part of which was employed in the sugar industry. But sugar workers were demanding higher wages and legal protection, for they were still being treated like indentured laborers, hired and dismissed at will. To retain labor support, the government instituted a wages council in 1963 and empowered it to set minimum wages in the sugar sector. In 1966 it issued the Security of Employment (Sugar Industry) Ordinance, giving job security to permanent sugar workers, that is, those who worked more than a certain minimum number of days per year (see Chesworth 1967: 252–79).

The first wage order, issued in the 1963 bumper crop year, set the minimum wage 25 percent above the previous year's average level. In subsequent years the minimum was either raised or held constant, depending on the profitability of the sugar crop and on the cost of living. As a consequence, the system introduced a downward rigidity in the money wage.

Initially, the minimum wages applied to the sugar sector only, but because of the sugar industry's important position in the island's economy, they served as guides for labor negotiations in other sectors. Eventually, wages councils were set up in other industries, in effect removing wage bargaining from the individual firm to the industry level.

Between 1958 and 1968 the cost of labor rose by 50 percent, whereas the cost of living increased by only 12 percent. This rise in real wages occurred at a time when labor demand was constant because of overall stagnation, while the population in the economically active age bracket (fifteen to sixty-five) was growing at an annual rate of 2 percent.

There is no doubt that the high-wage policy was at variance with the need to create employment, but there is some question as to how much more employment would have been generated in the short run if wages had been more flexible. In sugar production the ratio of labor to output is virtually fixed in the short run, with volume determined by the preferential quota. The import-substituting industry is relatively insensitive to costs, since the degree of protection it receives under the development certificate scheme is a function of the cost differential between production and imports. To be sure, the high-wage policy encouraged the use of relatively capital-intensive methods in manufacturing, but given the size of the sugar industry, the overall effect must have been quite small. High wages, however, reduced rents and profits, and therefore investment. The policy undoubtedly had adverse effects on job creation in the long run, but in the short run high wages bought social peace at relatively little immediate economic cost.

According to official figures, unemployment in Mauritius rose from 2 percent of the labor force in 1962 to 13 percent in 1972. These figures are unreliable, however, since the unemployment register does not include the names of all those who seek work and does not automatically drop the names of those who have found work. In any case, the problem was serious enough for the government to launch an emergency public works program, which at its peak (during the third quarter of 1967) employed 30,000 workers, or 18 percent of all wage earners. This program and other welfare measures put a severe strain on the government budget. Up until fiscal 1964–65 the government had a current account surplus that it could use for public investment. In the next two years it incurred a deficit of about Rs 20 million and was forced to scale down the program.

The greatest success was achieved in the area of population control, through two private family planning schemes introduced in 1963. There was, of course, no immediate effect on the rate of growth of the labor force, but within the next seven years the crude birth rate dropped from 40 per thousand to 27 per thousand (Deveaux and others 1983). In 1972 the population reached 826,000, but that was 3,000 lower than the lowest projection made twelve years earlier. In 1982 the population stood at 963,000—almost exactly at the lowest projection.[17] According to current estimates, Mauritius is likely to have between 1.2 million and 1.4 million inhabitants by the turn of the century and will thus escape "the truly terrifying prospect" of a population almost triple that size, as contemplated by Meade.

The Sugar Boom and Its Aftermath, 1972–79

The 1970s, in contrast to the faltering 1960s, was a period of unprecedented economic growth, triggered by a sugar boom that improved the country's terms of trade.[18] The rapid growth of export-oriented manufacturing and an expansionary budgetary policy also contributed to prosperity (see table 5-4 and figures 5-1 and 5-2).

World sugar prices began to rise in 1971, and between 1972 and 1975 producer prices on Mauritius more than tripled. In 1973 and 1974 Mauritius had exceptionally good crops. In 1975 close to 30 percent of the crop was destroyed by a cyclone, but high prices on the world market sus-

Table 5-4. GDP *at Constant 1976 Market Prices, 1972–79*

Year	GDP (millions of rupees)	Growth rate (percent)
1972	3,410	8.3
1973	3,819	12.0
1974	4,156	8.8
1975	4,193	0.9
1976	4,707	12.2
1977	5,075	7.9
1978	5,368	5.8
1979	5,674	5.7

Source: World Bank data.

Figure 5-1. GDP *at Market Prices, Mauritius, 1958–86*

Billions of constant 1976 Mauritian rupees

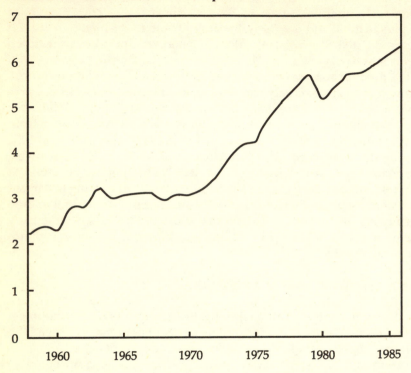

Source: World Bank data.

tained the economy. The boom reached its peak in 1975–76; after that prices fell rapidly.[19] Extensive foreign borrowing by the government delayed the effects of the collapse until the end of the decade, by which time the mounting foreign debt had brought the country to the verge of bankruptcy.

Politics of the Boom Years

Although the government suppressed the left-wing revolt and called off the 1972 election, it was clearly conscious of the pressure from the left. The policies of the boom period indicate that the Labour party and its allies tried to steal the MMM's thunder by introducing a series of measures aimed at improving social services, education, and conditions of work. But it was by and large foreign policy issues that broke up the ruling coalition and forced a general election in 1976.[20] The Labour party, buoyed by the prosperity of the preceding years and by its populist

Figure 5-2. Commodity Trade, Mauritius, 1950–84

Millions of U.S. dollars

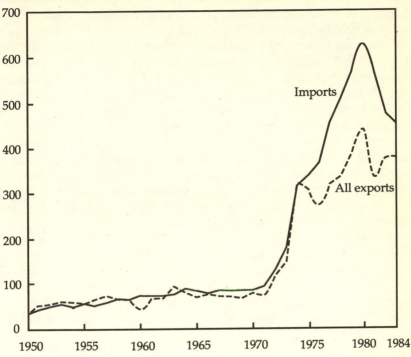

Source: World Bank data.

policies, won enough seats to form another coalition government, but the MMM emerged as the single largest party and firmly established itself as a major force.

Social Policies

In 1973 the Industrial Relations Act replaced the wages councils with a single National Remuneration Board (NRB) composed of representatives of the government and of employers' and employees' organizations. The NRB was empowered to set minimum wages for the private sector by industry and by occupational category, and in practice actual wages closely conformed to its levels (see Mauritius Employers' Federation 1984). Thus, the NRB has in effect eliminated bilateral wage bargaining, thereby reducing the influence of unions and making the government the arbiter of labor disputes.

One obvious disadvantage of such a system is that administered wages are unlikely to balance labor supply and demand. On the plus side, the willingness of management and labor to adhere to the NRB rulings helps defuse industrial conflicts, and the harmonious atmosphere will undoubtedly act as a magnet to foreign investment and facilitate industrial growth.

During the first phase of the boom the wage councils, and later the NRB, pursued a policy of moderation: real wages in the sugar industry rose only slightly, while money wages in other industries failed to keep pace with the rise in the cost of living. In 1973, however, the salaries commissioner, appointed to review the conditions of work for civil servants, recommended that salaries be increased on average by 30 percent and that they be indexed. The recommendations were accepted. The terms of the award were subsequently extended to all public corporation employees, and the cost of living adjustments were legislated for all workers in both private and public employment. Until 1979, cost of living increases were granted twice a year to all workers; since then, the adjustments have been made yearly.

The NRB awards made in 1974–76 led to real wage increases in all parts of the economy and brought day wages (for unskilled workers) and weekly wages (for skilled workers) closer together. Over the 1971–76 period as a whole, real wages of workers paid by the day rose by 46 percent in the sugar industry and by 18 percent in manufacturing industries, whereas real wages of workers paid by the week rose by only 10 percent.[21]

Another innovation in this period was employment compensation for termination, instituted under the Labour Act of 1975. All workers with more than a year's service were entitled to receive severance pay proportional to the length of service. Employers planning to dismiss ten or more workers had to notify the Termination of Contracts of Service Board in advance. A 1982 amendment provided further job protection by introducing a 120-day waiting period between notification and dismissal.

The government invested heavily in health and educational facilities, water and sewerage, and low-income housing. The share of the current budget devoted to social services also grew, from 40 percent in 1970–71 to 52 percent by 1973–74. This increase, however, is entirely accounted for by a rise in rice and wheat flour subsidies, granted to keep down the increase in the cost of living and to help the poor.[22] In 1973–74 (the first year such payments were made) subsidies amounted to Rs 107 million (or 20 percent of the recurrent budget), and they were even higher in the following years.

In short, in the boom period the government sought to favor labor by raising real wages and extending social services. These policies proved difficult to reverse. Indeed, after the boom subsided, social expenditure, both on capital and on current account, continued to rise. Transfers to private schools rose from a negligible amount in 1972–73 to Rs 23 million by fiscal 1977–78. A decision to make all secondary education free pushed the transfers up to Rs 104 million in fiscal 1978–79. By that time social expenditures accounted for 10 percent of GDP, putting an unbearable strain on the nation's resources and necessitating a sharp and painful readjustment.

Fiscal and Budgetary Policy

The higher revenues of the boom period were still outpaced by expenditures, and the government moved to increase the sugar levies. In 1973 the 6 percent sugar export tax was replaced by a graduated tax. Planters exporting less than 20 tons were exempt from the tax, while estates that exported 5,000 tons or more were subject to the highest tax, initially set at 9 percent.

The graduated tax was highly popular, for it affected mainly the wealthy Franco-Mauritians. While the boom lasted, the tax did little economic harm, for it merely forced the large estates to share their rents with the state. But with the end of the boom, the government's need for revenue increased, and the tax, instead of being removed, was made more steeply progressive (table 5-5). Thus the most efficient area of the sugar industry was heavily penalized; large estates suffered losses and became progressively decapitalized. The sugar tax quickly became a leading sociopolitical issue that was not resolved until the end of the 1980s.

The tax increase notwithstanding, the government ran a deficit in the boom years. In 1970–71, the last fiscal year before the boom, Mauritius had a Rs 9 million surplus on its current account and an overall deficit of Rs 61 million. By 1973–74 there was a current account deficit of Rs 19 million and an overall deficit of Rs 259 million. Reckoned at constant prices, government revenues increased by 40 percent within three years, but deficits grew by a factor of 6.[23]

Table 5-5. Sugar Export Taxes, by Crop Year, 1973, 1977, and 1979
(percent)

Export volume (metric tons)	1973	1977	1979
Less than 20	0	0.0	0.0
20 or more, but less than 75	6	6.0	10.5
75 or more, but less than 1,000	7	7.0	12.25
1,000 or more, but less than 3,000	8	9.0	15.75
3,000 or more	9	13.5	23.625

Note: The 1979 rate includes a 75 percent surcharge designed to capture the revenue increase resulting from rupee devaluation. In 1983 the surcharge was reduced to 50 percent; in 1983 the 75 percent surcharge was reinstated, but exporters of up to 75 tons were exempted from duties.

Source: Mauritius Chamber of Agriculture.

To finance the deficit the government resorted heavily to domestic (mostly central and commercial bank) borrowing. Public debt rose from Rs 381 million in July 1971 to Rs 1,021 million in July, 1975 (table 5-6).

As the boom subsided, the gap between revenues and the steadily growing expenditures widened. Between fiscal 1975–76 and fiscal 1978–79 fiscal revenues rose by 33.2 percent and expenditures by 80.5 percent, while the consumer price index (based on the 1960 purchase basket) rose 35.7 percent. By 1979 the fiscal deficit amounted to 13 percent and public debt to 48 percent of GDP.

To mitigate inflation and to preserve the trade balance in the face of budgetary deficits, the government resorted to ever more stringent controls. Price controls were imposed on all important products. Bank credit to the trade sector was frozen at the 1976 level. Commercial banks were required to increase the proportion of their assets in the form of cash or government bonds, and in 1979 the Bank of Mauritius suspended its rediscount facilities. These restrictions impeded the formation of private credit without limiting the expansion of government credit; between 1976 and 1979 the share of net claims on the government in domestic credit increased from one-third to more than one-half. Quantitative restrictions were gradually extended to all imports. Nevertheless, there was a drain on foreign reserves, which by the summer of 1979 were barely sufficient to cover one week's imports.

Export-Oriented Industrialization

With the sharp rise in sugar profits during the boom years, gross savings rose from an average of 12.8 percent of GDP in 1964–66 to 15.2 percent in

Table 5-6. *Central Government Budget, Fiscal 1970–71 through Fiscal 1975–76*
(millions of rupees)

Item	1970–71	1971–72	1972–73	1973–74	1974–75	1975–76
Current revenue[a]	260	294	377	515	745	1,077
Current expenditure	251	268	311	535	734	991
Current balance	9	26	65	–19	–11	85
Capital revenue[b]	14	1	1	5	46	18
Capital expenditure	84	101	127	245	259	423
Capital balance	–70	–99	–126	–240	–213	–405
Overall balance[c]	–61	–74	–61	–259	–203	–320
External borrowing	12	9	18	39	58	37
Internal borrowing	60	104	109	84	306	207

a. Excludes transfers to capital budget.
b. Excludes transfers from current budget.
c. Overall deficit equals external plus internal borrowings plus changes in reserves.
Source: Mauritius, Central Statistical Office.

1970–72 and to a peak of 34.2 percent of GDP in 1974–75. Traditional investment opportunities were limited, however. The domestic sugar industry was adequately capitalized, while investment in foreign plantations was impeded by capital export controls. Easy import substitution possibilities had been almost exhausted.

New investment opportunities were opened up by the Export Processing Zone (EPZ) law adopted in 1970. This law exempted from all import duties enterprises producing solely for export, regardless of their location. Foreign stockholders were permitted to repatriate profits from EPZ enterprises and the original capital investment. EPZ enterprises also received a ten-year corporate tax exemption. A similar law was adopted for the hotel industry.

It is estimated that during the 1971–76 period sugar profits financed 50 percent of capital formation in the rapidly expanding EPZ sector. The balance of the investment came from abroad. The advantage of Mauritius for foreign-financed "footloose industries" is that under the Lomé and Yaoundé conventions, its manufactured products have free access to the EEC, subject to content provisions.[24] The same privilege is enjoyed by other developing countries, but Mauritius enjoys greater political and social stability than most of them and has a superior infrastructure. Mauritius also benefits from the restrictions imposed by the EEC and the United States on exports from Hong Kong, as well as from the uncertainty concerning that colony's future.

In 1971 the EPZ sector consisted of nine enterprises employing 644 people and accounted for 1 percent of total export earnings. Five years later, Mauritius had eighty-five EPZ enterprises, mostly in the clothing sector, with 17,171 employees. The EPZ export share had increased to 13 percent. Few of the tasks in EPZ factories were physically demanding, and since the minimum wages for men were markedly higher than those for women in the early years, the EPZ factories employed women almost exclusively (table 5-7).

After 1976 the rate of growth of EPZ industries declined drastically. Sugar profits dried up, there was a worldwide recession, and, because of its economic difficulties, Mauritius no longer appeared to be a good place to invest.

Aftermath of the Boom

In September 1971 employment in large establishments stood at 142,000, including 17,000 relief workers.[25] In December of the same year there were 30,600 registered unemployed. Four years later employment rose to 173,000, the number of relief workers fell to 6,000, and registered unemployment dropped to less than 20,000. When the boom subsided, job creation slowed down. Nevertheless, by September 1979 total employment surpassed 199,000, while the number of registered unemployed at year's end stood at 23,000.

Table 5-7. Employment in EPZ Industries, 1971–86

Year	Male labor	Female labor	Total labor
1971	214	430	644
1972	384	2,204	2,588
1973	770	5,030	5,800
1974	1,088	7,881	8,469
1975	1,670	8,591	10,261
1976	3,478	13,693	17,171
1977	3,087	14,385	17,474
1978	3,186	15,137	18,323
1979	3,381	17,361	20,742
1980	3,854	17,490	21,344
1981	4,473	19,128	23,600
1982	4,393	19,083	23,476
1983	4,807	20,719	25,526
1984	7,913	29,609	37,522
1985	14,883	39,068	49,813
1986	24,202	49,813	74,018

Source: Mauritius, Central Statistical Office.

The sugar industry, which was still the dominant activity, did not directly generate new jobs. (Between September 1971 and September 1975 the number of sugar workers rose from 54,800 to 57,800; it then leveled off for a year, and by September 1979 it had declined to 52,700.) Rather, jobs were created mainly in manufacturing. Employment there rose from 9,800 in September 1971 to 22,500 in September 1975, to 35,600 in September 1979. Export-oriented industries operating under the 1970 EPZ legislation were responsible for most of this increase.

The efficiency of this growth in resource allocation continued to be hampered by the division of the economy into a highly protected inward-looking sector and an outward-looking free-market sector. A completely outward reorientation was politically unfeasible in the 1970s, however, since protection was the key to the prosperity of the import-substituting industry and DC certificate holders constituted a powerful lobby. But the DC certificate holders were not disturbed by the formation of an export-oriented enclave: on the contrary, they welcomed it as another potential source of profits. Mauritian labor also favored economic segmentation: the high-wage sector—sugar and import-substituting industries—constituted a male enclave. The EPZ industries employed women, whose earnings supplemented family incomes and who did not compete with the men. For the export-oriented industries, too, the enclave solution had obvious advantages in that the quasi-extraterritorial status provided a degree of protection against the government's dirigiste tendencies.

Other policies of the boom period left a more problematic legacy. The economic segmentation was a typical Mauritian compromise: a socially acceptable and economically satisfactory, although not an optimal, solution. The overvaluation of the currency made Mauritius less attractive to foreign investors. Steeply progressive taxes hurt the sugar industry. Overspending needlessly stimulated the economy. And the attempt to cushion the subsequent recession saddled the country with a debt-making readjustment.

Retrenchment and Recovery, 1979–88

The policy of fiscal expansion and direct controls in place following the end of the sugar boom proved untenable, and in 1979 the government turned to the IMF and the World Bank for aid. The two institutions were willing to extend credit, but they insisted that Mauritius curtail costly social programs, return to fiscal conservatism, and remove controls.

Retrenchment eroded the government's popularity, and the MMM scored an overwhelming victory in the 1982 general election. Recognizing the economic constraints, the MMM pursued much the same policies as the previous government. After a political split and a general election, another coalition was formed, with the MMM once again in the opposition.

Despite the political turmoil, the successive governments pursued remarkably consistent economic policies. Without abandoning their populist stance and their dirigiste tendency, they cut public expenditure and liberalized the economy. After a brief hiatus the economy responded, opening a new period of export-led growth (see table 5-8).

Political Developments

In the course of the campaign preceding the 1976 general election, the ruling coalition pledged to take further steps to foster equality, raise real wages, and improve health and educational facilities. Measures taken in

Table 5-8. *Annual GDP Growth Rate at Constant Prices, 1976–86*
(percent)

Year	Growth rate
1976	16.7
1977	7.0
1978	4.0
1979	3.6
1980	−10.0
1981	6.4
1982	5.8
1983	0.4
1984	4.7
1985	6.8
1986	8.9

Source: Mauritius, Central Statistical Office.

the years 1976–79 to redeem these pledges overstrained the available resources. Retrenchment policies, undertaken after 1979 under pressure from the IMF and the World Bank, gave the opposition MMM the opportunity to accuse the government of selling out to the international institutions.

The Labour party then began losing support, and the MMM seemed to provide an attractive alternative. Since its inception, the MMM had steadily moved away from doctrinaire socialism toward moderation, and from direct action toward a parliamentary system. The party manifesto, issued in 1970, and further elaborated in 1976 (see Mouvement Militant Mauricien 1970, 1976), called for widespread nationalization and for worker self-government. But as the economic crisis of the late 1970s intensified, Paul Bérenger, the party's leader, put increasing emphasis on a "new social consensus" and played down the party's Marxian doctrine (see Obeegadoo 1984).

This move allowed the MMM to form an electoral alliance with the Parti Socialiste Mauricien (PSM), a moderate, predominantly rural Hindu group that had broken away from the Labour party in September 1979. The joint MMM-PSM electoral campaign presented the proposed cabinet as a highly responsible group, ready to replace Labour's "tired old men" who had ruled since preindependence days. The electoral manifesto promised to increase employment, raise minimum wages, and provide more welfare. The socialist features of the program were limited to a wealth tax that would affect only a small group of the very rich, the nationalization of two money-losing sugar mills, and the acquisition of a 50 percent share in the hotel industry. At the same time, the MMM pledged to promote free enterprise and to attract private foreign investment.

In the 1982 election the MMM and the PSM won all the parliamentary seats. Once in power, the new government concentrated on improving macroeconomic management and relegated nationalization to a more propitious time. This strategy of moderation won the MMM support from a wide spectrum of Mauritian opinion (and gained the government foreign support), but it alienated the party's more radical wing. Measures such as a proposed reduction in rice and flour subsidies and a contemplated reduction in sugar export taxes caused widespread dissatisfaction. Personality conflicts and ethnic friction made the situation all the more difficult. After nine months of MMM rule, Paul Bérenger resigned from his post of minister of finance and took most of the MMM deputies into the opposition. The MMM prime minister, Aneerood Jugnauth, amalgamated his (mostly Hindu) MMM followers and the PSM to form a new party, the Mouvement Socialiste Mauricien (MSM).

In 1983 Jugnauth, unable to command a parliamentary majority, called a general election, in which the MSM was allied with the Labour party and with the PMSD. The core of the MMM now consisted of urban, predominantly Muslim, workers, but the party enjoyed widespread support among the poorer and the more radical members of the island's ethnic groups and intellectuals. The MMM obtained 46 percent of the popular vote, but it received only twenty-two parliamentary seats to forty-eight for the MSM and its allies.

Members of the alliance shared a dislike for the MMM but otherwise had little in common. The ruling coalition represented a wide spectrum of political opinion that was plagued by personal animosities and in later years by scandals. Yet, despite defections, it held together. The government's popularity owed much to the increasing prosperity. In 1987 the alliance again won a general election, although, as in 1983, the MMM won more votes than any other party.

Economic Retrenchment

In 1979 the country found itself on the verge of insolvency. Between the end of 1972 and the end of 1979 the foreign debt outstanding and disbursed rose from US$32.6 million to US$226 million, and the annual debt service from US$2.2 million to US$18.9 million. Grants and concessionary loans were increasingly difficult to obtain, and commercial bank terms hardened. The average interest rate on loans rose from 2.9 percent in 1973 to 10.3 percent in 1979, while their average maturity contracted from thirty-five years to ten years. Foreign exchange reserves (defined as net assets of the banking system) fell from Rs 406 million at the end of 1972 to minus Rs 206 million at the end of 1979.

In October 1979 the government signed a stand-by agreement with the IMF enabling Mauritius to draw a total of SDR 73 million over a two-year period.[26] In accordance with the agreement, the Mauritian rupee was devalued on October 23, 1979, by about 22.9 percent. The agreement specified a schedule for reducing the fiscal deficit, imposed limits on government short- and medium-term borrowing, and called for a higher discount rate and private credit ceilings.[27]

Toward the end of 1979 and early in 1980 Mauritius was hit by cyclones and floods that destroyed a third of the crop and caused extensive damage to housing. Emergency relief measures prevented the government from adhering to IMF conditions, but because of the circumstances it was able to obtain a waiver, and the stand-by arrangements were not interrupted. A new agreement signed in September 1980 provided, in addition to the SDR 40 million already drawn, SDR 35 million for one year to help with the balance of payments. A third standby agreement, signed in December 1981, provided a further SDR 30 million, and a fourth balance of payments support agreement for SDR 49.5 million was reached in 1983. These agreements contained detailed fiscal and monetary policy clauses and called for wage restraint.

The cumulative effect of the austerity measures undertaken in the early 1980s was quite dramatic. The fiscal deficit declined, at current

Table 5-9. Fiscal Deficit, Fiscal 1981–82 to Fiscal 1986–87
(millions of rupees)

Item	1981–82	1982–83	1983–84	1984–85	1985–86	1986–87[a]
Total revenue	2,288	2,825	3,122	3,562	4,131	5,036
Total expenditure	3,673	3,985	3,980	4,386	4,770	5,456
Deficit	1,384	1,160	858	824	639	420
Deficit as percent- age of GDP	12.6	9.5	6.4	5.4	3.7	2.1

a. Includes grants.
Source: Bank of Mauritius, *Annual Report*, various issues.

prices, from Rs 1,384 million (12.5 percent of GDP) in 1981–82 to Rs 424 million (2.2 percent of GDP) in 1986–87 (table 5-9). The balance of payments also improved; in 1985, for the first time in a decade, there was an overall surplus on the external account (table 5-10).

After a further devaluation, the rupee was delinked from the SDR and linked to a trade-weighted currency basket in February 1983.[28] Its value declined against the dollar for the next two years but rose in 1985–87 (table 5-11).

Liberalization and Structural Reform

In 1982–83 the MMM and its successor government reached an understanding with the IMF and the World Bank on a structural adjustment program to run through fiscal 1985–86 (see Mauritius 1983). The agreement called for a close monitoring of public sector investments, liberalization of the economy, and structural reform.[29]

Table 5-10. Balance of Payments, 1975–79
(millions of rupees)

Year	Surplus or deficit
1975	351
1976	–514
1977	–328
1978	–330
1979	–634
1980	–161
1981	–922
1982	–484
1983	–513
1984	–253
1985	258
1986	1,718

Source: Mauritius, Central Statistical Office.

Table 5-11.   Average Exchange Rate, 1978–87
(Mauritian rupees per U.S. dollar)

Year	Exchange rate
1978	6.16
1979	6.31
1980	7.68
1981	8.94
1982	10.87
1983	11.71
1984	13.80
1985	15.44
1986	13.74
1987	12.88

Source: IMF statistics.

The restructuring proceeded apace. In December 1983 import quotas were lifted from 22 commodities; a further 193 were freed in April 1984 and 60 more in August (see Mauritius 1985). Finally, in February 1985 the quotas were eliminated altogether, although some tariff duties were raised to give additional protection to domestic import-substituting industries. Most of the domestic price controls were also removed, and after the broad liberalization that occurred in 1985 only rice, flour, bread, potatoes, sugar, frozen fish, cement, and petroleum products remained under controls.

There was also a partial relaxation of quantitative credit restraints, although a complex formula was retained to decide how much credit each bank would be permitted to extend. The formula gave preference to export-oriented industry and it discriminated against commercial credit, thus acting as a restraint on imports.

To reduce dependence on import duties, the government introduced a 5 percent sales tax in 1983 and in 1984–86 overhauled the entire tax system with the help of IMF experts. In order to encourage corporate profit retention, the tax on undistributed profits, levied at a rate of 66 percent on private and 55 percent on public companies, was replaced by a uniform 35 percent tax on total profits under the Finance Act of July 26, 1984. The number of personal income tax brackets was reduced from eight to four, and the marginal rate applying to the top bracket was lowered from 70 to 35 percent. Tax revenue declined at first; but thanks to improvements in the tax collection system, the initial dip was largely made up within two years.

The Sugar Export Tax

In December 1982, in accordance with the World Bank agreement, the government appointed a three-person commission to propose changes in policy toward the sugar industry. In June 1984 the commission published two separate reports. One, signed by its chairman, Dragoslav Avramovic, a senior adviser to the United Nations Conference on Trade and Development (UNCTAD), found that the sugar export tax penalized large efficient units and recommended that export taxes be replaced by a profit tax (see Commission of Inquiry on the Sugar Industry 1984b). The other report, signed by the two Mauritian members, stated that the export tax should not be changed (see Commission of Inquiry on the Sugar Industry 1984a).[30] Both reports called for the establishment of a sugar authority. This recommendation was immediately accepted.

In February 1985 the Sugar Authority published an action plan (see Mauritius Sugar Authority 1985) designed to increase efficiency by concentrating cane milling in larger units. This move had been advocated by the owners but opposed by workers, who, however, now agreed to it on being guaranteed reemployment. Measures were also proposed to facilitate the transfer of land and to foster research and development.

On the export tax issue, the government moved gradually in the direction dictated by considerations of efficiency. The Sugar Sector Package Deal Act eliminated the export duty on the first 1,000 metric tons. The rate was set at 15.75 percent for the next 2,000 tons and at 23.625 percent for the remainder. The 1988 Sugar Industry Efficiency Act raised the exemption to 3,000 tons and lowered the average duty paid by the corporate sector (defined as the nineteen sugar mills and twenty-one sugar plantations) from 20 to 13.5 percent. Once again, a feasible compromise was found between economic efficiency and political desirability.

Export-Oriented Industrialization

The policy of fiscal balance, devaluation, and wage restraint improved the competitive position of export-oriented manufacturing industries. As of 1985 the minimum wage rate for male workers ceased to apply to EPZ enterprises, making the hiring of men more profitable.[31] The proportion of male employees rose from 21 percent in December 1984 to 33 percent in December 1986 (see table 5-7). Henceforth, EPZ enterprises ceased to be an almost exclusive enclave of women workers.

In 1985 the tax regime was changed to encourage the establishment of more permanent enterprises. In contrast, the 1970 scheme, which provided a ten-year tax holiday followed by taxation at ordinary rates, favored short-term projects that would cease operation at the end of the exemption period. The new scheme eliminated the tax holiday but limited the profit tax to 15 percent. To encourage the reorientation of import-substituting enterprises toward foreign markets, enterprises that sold both at home and abroad were allowed to reduce corporate taxes in line with the volume of their export business.

World economic recovery improved export prospects. Somewhat paradoxically, the growing protectionism in the United States and the EEC also worked in favor of Mauritius. Export constraints, voluntary or otherwise, imposed on major exporters (notably, Hong Kong) worked in favor of countries whose exports did not as yet threaten the industrial countries. To be sure, as the Mauritian textile and clothing industry expanded, it too became subject to U.S. constraints, but it retained free access to the EEC. Foreign capital was readily available, particularly from Hong Kong investors who feared the consequences of the forthcoming transfer of sovereignty over the colony and were attracted to Mauritius by the presence of a Chinese community there.

The new export-led boom that followed boosted EPZ employment 190 percent between 1983 and 1986. By mid-1988 the value added by export-oriented enterprises was about 12 percent of GDP—double the share of five years before. Tourism also developed rapidly. Between 1981 and 1987 the number of arrivals rose from 119,000 to 208,000, and gross earnings increased from Rs 450 million to Rs 1,786 million. Thus the structural transformation of Mauritius from a monoculture to an outward-oriented diversified economy that began during the sugar boom gathered new force after the hiatus of the late 1970s.

Social Policies

The main political parties in Mauritius are progressive in the sense of striving to foster the interests of labor and of the poorer strata of society. As a consequence, when the IMF and the World Bank insisted that Mauritius curb real wages and reduce social expenditures, the government found itself on the horns of a dilemma. To its credit, the government succeeded in adhering to the loan guidelines and in maintaining industrial peace without losing popular support.

It succeeded in this respect in part by mitigating redistribution toward the rich. Thus, at the time of the 1979 devaluation it imposed a 75 percent surcharge on the export tax to capture any windfall profits that devaluation might create. In November 1979 it raised wages by 13 percent, of which 4 percent was partial compensation for the 8 percent increase in the consumer price index of the previous year and 9 percent was to offset the anticipated cost of living effect of the devaluation. The wage increase wiped out half the adjustment effect of the devaluation. It should be noted, however, that for the first time since 1973 wages were not adjusted to reflect in full the increase in the cost of living. In subsequent years wage restraint was exercised, with real wages remaining virtually stable until 1987 (table 5-12).

In another important but unpopular retrenchment measure, the government reduced rice and flour subsidies. In 1981–82 the subsidies were equal to about 46 percent of the c.i.f. value of the two commodities, and the Rs 230 million in subsidy expenditure accounted for 20 percent of the

Table 5-12. Index of Real Average Monthly Earnings of Daily Paid Laborers in Large Establishments, September 1980–September 1988

Year	Index
1980	100.0
1981	103.2
1982	99.8
1983	105.9
1984	98.4
1985	97.9
1986	102.6
1987	122.1
1988	114.4

Note: For a definition of large establishments, see note 25.
Source: Mauritius, Central Statistical Office, *Biannual Surveys of Employment and Earnings.*

budgetary deficit. By fiscal 1985–86 the subsidies had declined to Rs 72 million, or to less than 15 percent of the c.i.f. value.

The wage restraint (and subsidy curtailment) notwithstanding, real per capita GDP increased by 28 percent between 1983 and 1987, and the real income of the median household rose by about 18 percent. This improvement in well-being reflects the rising ratio of employment to population. In the course of the four years, employment rose by 124,000, of which 40 percent represented total increased employment of women, 6 percent that of men, and 38 percent unemployment reduction, while the growth of the working-age population accounted for only 16 percent. Thus, with more jobs per family unit, the policy of wage restraint proved to be socially acceptable. But in 1987, in the face of continuing job creation and the near exhaustion of labor reserves, real wages rose rapidly.

A Look into the Future

The economic achievements of Mauritius are a tribute to the enterprising spirit of the population and the moderation and wisdom of the political leadership. To an uncomfortable degree, however, progress is a result of the preferential trade policies pursued by the large powers.

Sugar still accounts for more than 12 percent of GDP, and it is the largest net earner of foreign currency. Sugar cultivation is profitable because quota prices in the EEC (which buys close to 75 percent of the sugar output) and the United States (which accounts for another 2 percent) exceed the world price by a factor of 3. Should the support level be lowered, or should the share of the quota granted to Mauritius be reduced, the industry could be in deep trouble.[32]

Trade preferences also sustain export-oriented industry to a large extent. About 87 percent of all workers in EPZ factories are employed by the garment industry; nearly 70 percent of EPZ exports go to the Common Market, mainly France and Germany. This industry could be seriously hurt if other low-wage countries in a better geographic location (for instance in eastern and central Europe) were to develop a garment industry and obtain the same EEC privileges as Mauritius.

There are no easy solutions to the island's problems. Diversification into industries requiring higher skills would run up against stiff competition from the newly industrializing economies with their more highly skilled labor. The island's tourist capacity is limited. And although it might be possible to convert land under sugarcane to the cultivation of other tropical export crops, for the time being the government is pursuing a policy of agricultural import substitution with little, if any, attention to comparative advantage.[33] There are signs, too, of a return to dirigiste policies, which have done little harm as yet but may stem further growth if they are intensified.[34]

Concluding Remarks

In the past twenty-five years Mauritius has enjoyed considerable prosperity. It has evolved into a semi-industrialized, export-oriented economy with remarkable speed, in view of its history as a monoculture and its remoteness from sources of raw material and from the markets needed to support diversification. The campaign to create new jobs and control population growth removed the specter of an island brimming with people with nothing to do. The country, not so long ago classified among the poorest, now ranks comfortably in the middle-income group. And despite ethnic diversity and class differentiation, Mauritius has preserved a democratic multiparty system.

These accomplishments are all the more remarkable in view of the lack of congruence not only between ethnic groups but also between the island's linguistic, religious, and occupational groups. Because intergroup relations are dynamic and constantly undergoing change, one may well ask whether Mauritians can ever be expected to form a strong interlocking society (Benedict 1961: 51).

This diversity, it seems, has been a decided advantage. In their effort to coexist, the various groups have admittedly sought second-best solutions, which are neither fully efficient in the economic sense nor fully satisfactory in political or social respects. Yet, by ensuring that no one group will pursue selfish interests, they have also safeguarded the progress of society as a whole. Although the ruling coalitions have in many cases been unstable, they all represent a consensus and have managed to maintain a steady and consistent policy course. Through compromise solutions, Mauritians have devised what may be an imperfect system, but one that has worked.

Notes

1. For the history of Mauritius and of the nearby islands, see Toussaint (1972, 1974).

2. Some 300 workers were brought from China in that year, but they refused to work in the sugar fields. The majority were repatriated, while the rest took urban jobs.

3. In France the term Créole is applied to the French born in the colonies; in the United States it is used to denote people of mixed European and non-European origin. Here the term is applied to the broad spectrum of Mauritian population who have some French ancestors but are not considered to belong to the Franco-Mauritian group. According to the 1952 census 95 percent of the population spoke Créole, 20 percent French, and 2.7 percent English (Benedict 1961: table VI).

4. As Varma (1980: 95–96) notes, however, the progress was far from uniform. The industry had to withstand periodic cyclones and droughts, not to mention infestations of pests and parasites. In 1840 otaheite, a variety of cane that grew particularly well in Mauritius, was affected by the *maladie blanche*, which caused sugar output to drop from a peak of 41,000 tons in 1840 to 27,500 tons in 1843, the lowest level since 1828. The 1840 level was not surpassed until 1845.

5. For a colorful description of the pro-French policies of early British governors, see Roy (1960: 70–113).

6. At the request of the estate owners who faced a labor shortage during the 1919–23 sugar boom, 1,500 Indian immigrants were brought in to work in the cane fields. On landing, the immigrants found work conditions so difficult that more than half requested repatriation (see Varma 1980: 79).

7. Among the early unions were the Mechanical and Technical Workers Trade Association, the Plaines Wilhelms and Black River S.E. Artisans I.A., and the Pamplemousses Mechanical and Technical Workers I.A. (see Algoo 1985: 34–56, 61–72).

8. Under the agreement, signed in December 1951, Commonwealth exporting territories agreed to limit their individual exports to the United Kingdom to specified quotas, the prices to be fixed annually at a level reasonably remunerative to efficient producers. A single price applied to all exporting territories. Under the 1958 International Sugar Agreement, Commonwealth countries received a quota, to be allocated in proportion to the Commonwealth Sugar Agreement quotas. Production exceeding the quotas set under the two agreements could be sold (subject to certain restrictions stipulated in the agreements) on the free market, usually at much lower prices.

9. According to the 1964 Census of Industrial Production, private manufacturing enterprises with three or more employees accounted for 19,000 of the persons employed; about half of that number were in sugar factories.

10. The Mauritian rupee was pegged at Rs 40 = 3 pounds sterling.

11. In 1952 Indians (Hindus and Muslims) constituted 67 percent of the population; they occupied 53 percent of the civil service jobs and 27 percent of the professional positions (Benedict 1961: 27).

12. A poignant description of the condition of the Mauritians of African origin is given by Mourba (n.d.).

13. The various stages of negotiation are succinctly outlined in Fovoreu (1970: 25–29). For a more detailed analysis, written from the point of view of the Labour party, see Varma (1976). In 1957 four elected members of the

Legislative Council were appointed observers to the Executive. The 1958 Mauritius (Constitution) Order-in-Council established an Executive Council of twelve ministers, three of them ex officio members and nine nominated by the governor from among the elected members of the Legislative Council. In 1961 the leader of the majority assumed the title of chief minister; henceforth the government was required to consult him on the appointment of ministers and on the dissolution of the Legislative Council. In 1961 the chief minister became a prime minister, and the Legislative Council became the Legislative Assembly. The assembly, in addition to the forty elected members, had fifteen nominated members, and the Cabinet had to include members of all political parties that won assembly seats. A full parliamentary system was adopted in 1965, and independence within the Commonwealth was proclaimed in 1967 (see Fovoreu 1970: 26–29).

14. The IFB advocated the social security system and was particularly concerned with the problem of unemployment. It also favored the formation of cooperatives.

15. The next general election (in 1963) brought no substantive changes in the distribution of seats.

16. The lowest projection showed a working age population of 488,000; the highest, 496,000.

17. The figure is merely an estimate, since 1982 was not a census year.

18. The terms of trade, reckoned on a 1970 basis, declined from 105 in 1964 to 100 in 1970; they rose to 133 in 1974 and reached 168 in 1975.

19. As a result of forward contracts signed with British importers, the price obtained by Mauritius lagged behind the world price. In 1974, when the world price stood at Rs 3,700 per ton, Mauritius obtained only Rs 2,300 per ton, but in 1975, when the world price dropped to Rs 2,702 per ton, Mauritius was paid Rs 3,115 per ton. In 1976 the size of the crop compensated in part for the further drop in prices, and the full impact of the slump in sugar prices was not felt until 1977.

20. Sir Gaëtan Duval and his PMSD favored a pro-Western policy and a rapprochement with South Africa; the Labour party leaned toward neutralism and favored close ties with India.

21. Relative wage movements cannot be explained in market terms. Throughout the period there was substantial unemployment among daily workers, but it was much lower among the more highly skilled workers paid by the week. Employment in the sugar industry rose by less than in other areas of the economy (both in percentage and in absolute terms).

22. In the face of the rising inflation of the 1970s, the government also attempted to control the price of necessities by imposing price controls on thirty-five basic commodities, mostly foodstuffs. Net of subsidies, the share of the recurrent expenditures devoted to social service remained invariant.

23. For the purposes of this calculation the current price figures were deflated by the consumer price index. The results are not appreciably changed if the implicit GNP deflator is used instead.

24. These provisions specify the percentage of the content that has to originate in the EEC or in one of the ACP (Africa, Caribbean, and Pacific) countries that were signatories of the convention.

25. Large establishments are defined as (a) sugar plantations with 25 arpents or more of land, (b) tea plantations with 5 arpents or more, (c) all flue-cured tobacco establishments, (d) all other private establishments employing ten or more workers on the day of the survey, and (e) all central or local government

departments. The data are obtained through a biannual survey. Estimates of small business and self-employment are highly unreliable.

26. SDR 19 million was made available immediately under the upper credit tranche, and SDR 54 million was granted under the supplementary financing facility.

27. Fiscal austerity called for a reduction in rice and flour subsidies.

28. On September 27, 1981, the rupee was devalued from Rs 10 to Rs 12 per SDR.

29. Low-priority items were to be shelved. No project in excess of Rs 100 million was to be undertaken without prior consultation with the World Bank.

30. The two Mauritian members were Jagadish Manrakhan, vice-chancellor of the University of Mauritius, and R. S. Pillay, director of audit. On July 5, 1983, in place of Mr. Pillay, who resigned, the governor appointed R. Sithanen, a transport economist.

31. In 1984 the minimum wage for male and female workers in EPZ enterprises was Rs 29.38 and Rs 17.46 per day, respectively. The lowest minimum wage for a male worker outside the EPZ was Rs 34.37. The minimum wage for a woman in EPZ employment was set in 1985 at Rs 19.99 per day and in 1986 at Rs 20.99 per day (none for men). Outside the EPZ the lowest wage for men was set at Rs 37.41 in 1985 and at Rs 39.29 in 1986.

32. Since World War II the highly protected U.S. and European sugar beet industries have grown rapidly; hence there is a danger that imports will be drastically reduced or that support prices will be lowered.

33. Import substitution is promoted through price supports and through incentives for interline planting of crops, such as potatoes, in the cane fields.

34. In 1987 and 1988 the government pursued a policy of rapid rises in real wages; in the latter year a number of price controls were reimposed to stem the accelerating inflation.

References

Algoo, Rajpalsingh. 1985. *Le mouvement syndical à l'Ile Maurice*. Port Louis: Artisans and General Workers' Union.

Bank of Mauritius. *Annual Report*. Various issues.

Benedict, Burton. 1961. *Indians in a Plural Society: A Report on Mauritius*. Colonial Research Studies 34. London: Colonial Office.

Bissoondoyal, U. 1984. *Indians Overseas: The Mauritian Experience*. Moka, Mauritius: Mahatma Gandhi Institute.

Chesworth, D. P. 1967. "Statutory Wage Fixing in the Sugar Industry in Mauritius." *International Labour Review* 96:252–79.

Commission of Inquiry on the Sugar Industry. 1984a. *Report*. Port Louis: Government Printer.

———. 1984b. *The Human Factor, The Sugar Industry and Mauritius: A Vision for the Future*. Port Louis: Government Printer.

Devaux, Michel J. C., and others. 1983. *Mauritius: Recent Developments and Prospects*. Washington, D.C.: World Bank.

Fovoreu, Louis. 1970. *L'Ile Maurice*. Paris: Berger Levrault.

Mannick, A. R. 1979. *Mauritius: Development of a Plural Society*. Nottingham, U.K.: Spokesman.

Mauritius Employers' Federation. 1984. *Trends in Wages and Salaries, 1970-1983: A Compilation of Guidance Notes*. Port Louis.

Mauritius, Ministry of Agriculture, Fisheries, and Natural Resources. 1985. *A Re-structuration Programme for the Sugar Industry*. Port Louis: Government Printer.

Mauritius, Ministry of Finance, 1983. "Letters to The Managing Director, International Monetary Fund, and to The President, World Bank." Port Louis.

Mauritius, Sugar Authority. 1985. *Action Plan for the Sugar Industry 1985–90*. Port Louis.

Meade, James E., and others. 1961. *The Economic and Social Structure of Mauritius*. London: Methuen.

Mourba, Suresh. n.d. *Misère noire (Ou Réno sur l'histoire de l'Ile Maurice)*. Port Louis: Swan Printing.

Movement Militant Mauricien. 1970. *Pour une ile Maurice possible*. Port Louis.

————. 1976. *Pour Une Ile Maurice Libre et Socialiste*. Port Louis.

Obeegadoo, Stiv. 1984. *From Revolution to Reformism: The Political Dynamics of Mauritian Society and the Evolution of the Mauritian Militant Movement*. Port Louis: S. Obeegadoo.

Roy, J. N. 1960. *Mauritius in Transition*. Allahabad, India: Samelan Mudranacaya.

Titmuss, Richard M. 1961. *Social Policies and Population Growth in Mauritius*. London: Methuen.

Toussaint, Auguste. 1972. *Histoire des Iles Mascareignes*. Paris: Berger-Levrault.

————. 1974. *Histoire de l'Ile Maurice*. Paris: Presses Universitaires de France.

Varma, Moonindra Nath. 1975. *The Struggle of Dr. Ramgoolam*. Quatre Bornes: N. M. Varma.

————. 1976. *Road to Independence*. Quatre Bornes: N. M. Varma.

————. 1980. *The Making of Mauritius*. Rev. ed. Quatre Bornes: N. M. Varma.

Virahaswami, Raj. 1977. *The Characteristics of Island Economies*. University of Mauritius.

6 Malta

Ronald Findlay
Stanislaw Wellisz

Malta, the largest island of the Maltese archipelago, lies 93 kilometers south of Sicily and 290 kilometers east of Tunisia. It has an area of 246 square kilometers. Fresh water is in short supply on the island, and the soil is poor, although the stone found there is highly suitable for buildings. Aside from its people, the only inherent assets of Malta are its strategic location and excellent natural harbor.

Economic and Political Background

In 1530 the Holy Roman Emperor Charles V invited the Knights of St. John, who had lost Rhodes to the Ottoman Turks, to settle in Malta. Because of its strategic location, the island provided the knights with a new base from which to continue their defense of the western Mediterranean against the Turks. In the Great Siege of 1565 the knights withstood the forces of Suleiman the Magnificent and remained in possession of Malta until dislodged by Napoleon in 1798. The Maltese population revolted against the French and, with the help of a British naval blockade, forced the invaders to surrender. In 1802, not wanting to see the knights return, they voluntarily assented to the sovereignty of the king of England. The knights left Malta a rich legacy in the Cathedral of St. John and the many public buildings in which the present government conducts most of its business.

Under the Treaty of Paris of 1814 Britain formally came into possession of Malta and in 1827 made it the headquarters of the British Mediterranean fleet. During the Crimean War (1854–56) Malta was a supply and ship-refitting station for the British forces. After the opening of the Suez Canal in 1869 the island became a key point on the Mediterranean route to India and was the site of a large naval dockyard. During World War I it was used as a base for the British expedition to the Dardanelles, and in World War II it played a crucial role in the allied defense of the Mediterranean against the Axis powers. The people of Malta were awarded the George Cross for their gallant defense of the island against German aerial bombardment. In the Cold War years following World War II, Malta became a base for the North Atlantic Treaty Organization (NATO).[1]

Thanks to the island's strategic location, revenues from outside sources have bolstered its economy for centuries. The Knights of Malta, for example, drew revenues from the whole of western Christendom (see Balogh and Seers 1955: vii). In fact, during the period of the knights' rule and throughout the nineteenth century, Malta had a dual economy. In rural areas the principal occupations were subsistence farming, fishing, and cotton weaving. The more advanced part of the economy was concentrated around harbor areas, where the main activities were related to servicing the military establishment. The Maltese constructed buildings and fortifications for the military, worked in shipyards, and supplied the stores. After the opening of the Suez Canal, entrepôt trade became an important activity.

Economic Situation in the 1950s

Malta continued to depend on the military through the mid-1950s. Of a total of 82,580 persons gainfully employed in 1954, 3,600 were in the armed forces, 18,900 were civilian employees of the defense department (navy shipyard workers alone numbered 12,000), and 8,860 were employed by the public administration. By contrast, only 8,130 were gainfully employed in agriculture and 9,690 in manufacturing (table 6-1). Manufacturing was mainly directed at the home market, primarily in food processing and beverages, footwear and clothing, and furniture making (table 6-2).

The dependence of Malta on British and allied military expenditures was brought out vividly in a report on the island's economic problems prepared in 1955 by the well-known Oxford economists Thomas Balogh and Dudley Seers. In the balance of payments, military purchases of Maltese goods and services in 1954 amounted to £14.7 million, whereas imports were £18.6 million. Other visible receipts of £3.2 million (which included tourism, emigrants' remittances, and investment income) and a British government grant of £3.0 million generated a modest balance of payments surplus of £1.9 million (Balogh and Seers 1955: statistical appendix table II). GNP in 1954 was about £30.9 million, of which £6.7 million consisted of the wages and salaries of Maltese defense-related workers. By comparison, manufacturing wages and salaries were only £1.0 million and farming and fishing wages accounted for £1.4 million (Balogh and Seers 1955: statistical appendix table I). The unimportance of manufacturing, in relation to income from the military base, is also reflected in the more detailed estimates of GNP and its sectoral composition from 1955 to 1962 presented in table 6-3.

Table 6-1. *Gainfully Occupied Population, by Industry, 1954–62*

Industry	1954	1955	1956	1957	1958	1959	1960	1961	1962
Agriculture and fishing	8,130	8,983	8,330	8,653	8,650	8,070	8,120	7,880	7,920
Construction and quarrying[a]	10,169	8,845	9,038	9,470	11,564	10,884	12,035	12,173	10,200
Manufacturing	9,690	8,077	8,500	8,660	9,030	14,920	14,960	15,130	15,570
Transport and communications	3,850	3,430	3,830	3,790	4,070	4,060	4,050	4,080	4,240
Wholesale and retail trade	10,830	9,650	9,710	10,610	10,700	11,610	11,320	11,510	11,500
Banking, insurance, and finance	340	320	440	510	550	600	540	530	600
Government enterprises	1,541	1,871	2,487	1,272	2,137	2,102	2,067	1,802 }	13,860
Public administration	8,860	9,474	9,795	10,748	11,139	11,444	11,538	11,825 }	
Private services[b]	6,670	5,910	7,140	7,560	8,390	8,040	8,130	8,480	8,230
Military services[c]	22,500	22,970	23,670	23,110	22,480	15,910	15,930	15,710	14,700
Total	82,580	79,530	82,950	85,383	88,710	87,640	88,690	89,220	86,820
Unemployment	—	5,650	3,100	3,250	3,460	3,180	3,730	4,370	6,360

— Not available.

a. Preliminary figures.

b. Public construction labor included.

c. The dockyard was transferred from military services to manufacturing in 1950.

Source: Malta, *Statistical Abstract of the Maltese Islands*, annual issues.

258

Table 6-2. *Number of Persons Gainfully Occupied in Manufacturing Industries (Excluding Dockyard), 1954–62*

Industry	1954	1956	1960	1961	1962
Food (excluding beverages)	1,830	1,660	1,700	1,700	1,810
Beverages	910	970	1,040	1,010	1,090
Tobacco	340	320	330	340	330
Textiles	230	310	300	340	390
Footwear and clothing	1,660	1,370	1,440	1,480	1,470
Wood and cork	50	50	80	80	70
Furniture and fittings	960	850	1,060	1,170	1,160
Paper products	—	—	20	40	30
Printing and publishing	410	440	480	500	510
Leather and products	20	70	50	60	80
Rubber products	—	30	40	110	130
Chemicals	140	120	140	140	210
Petroleum and coal products	20	10	10	10	20
Nonmetallic minerals	500	580	700	810	790
Metal products	380	190	390	450	480
Machinery	190	250	280	260	360
Electrical	30	40	50	100	100
Transport equipment	850	760	1,150[a]	1,120	1,100
Miscellaneous industries	450	380	360	350	530
Total	8,970	8,500	9,620	10,070	10,660

— Not available.

Note: The estimates in table 6-2 are not consistent with those in table 6-1 because different sources were used.

a. Estimated.

Source: Stolper, Hellberg, and Callender 1964.

The relationship between military expenditures and the island's economic fortunes is also reflected in its population movements. In the late 1940s and 1950s, for example, the military generated few jobs and outmigration absorbed more than 70 percent of the natural increase in population (Blouet 1984: ii–v). Indeed, whenever military expenditure and employment fell, there was substantial outmigration. At the end of the nineteenth century about 50,000 Maltese were living in neighboring Mediterranean countries (Blouet 1984: 171). Outmigration in lean periods continues to this day. Since World War I most of the migrants have settled in Australia and the United Kingdom.

Thus, in the mid-1950s Malta had no visible means of support except for the military. Any sudden reduction in military spending would have plunged the country into penury, and emigration seemed to offer the only escape from this prospect.

Table 6-3. GNP, by Industry, 1954–62
(millions of pounds at current prices)

Industry	1954	1955	1956	1957	1958	1959	1960	1961	1962
Agriculture and fishing	—	1.7	2.1	2.2	2.8	2.8	3.0	3.3	3.3
Construction and quarrying	—	2.6	2.9	2.9	3.5	3.0	3.4	3.0	2.6
Manufacturing	—	2.7	3.3	3.2	3.3	6.7	7.3	7.6	7.9
Transport and communications	—	1.0	1.5	1.6	1.6	1.5	1.6	1.8	1.9
Wholesale and retail trade	—	6.8	8.5	9.4	9.3	9.2	9.3	9.1	8.8
Banking, insurance, and finance	—	0.3	0.4	0.4	0.5	0.3	0.6	0.7	0.7
Government enterprises	—	1.1	1.1	1.0	1.2	1.1	1.4	1.4	1.5
Total production and trade	—	16.2	19.7	20.7	22.2	24.6	26.5	26.9	26.8
Public administration	—	2.9	3.1	3.4	3.7	4.3	4.7	5.5	5.4
Military services	—	7.6	8.1	8.5	8.6	7.0	7.7	7.6	7.3
Ownership of dwellings	—	1.8	1.8	1.9	1.9	1.9	2.0	1.9	1.8
Other property income from domestic sources	—	0.2	0.2	0.2	0.2	0.2	0.3	0.3	0.3
Private services	—	2.0	2.1	2.0	2.1	2.1	2.1	2.2	1.9
GNP at factor cost	30.0	30.6	34.9	36.7	38.8	40.1	43.2	44.4	43.5
Net income from abroad	2.2	2.4	2.5	3.0	3.6	3.3	3.4	3.2	3.2
GDP at factor cost	32.2	33.0	37.4	39.7	42.4	43.5	46.7	47.6	46.7

— Not available.
Source: Central Statistical Office.

Political Background

In the nineteenth and early twentieth centuries Malta enjoyed a considerable degree of autonomy, even though it was a colony. This autonomy was greatly extended in 1921 with the introduction of a dyarchy: local affairs came under Maltese control, while the United Kingdom remained in charge of foreign affairs and defense. The franchise was extended to all male British subjects having an income of £5 per year or more or paying a similar amount of rent.

The 1920s and 1930s brought considerable political turmoil as a number of parties joined in the struggle for power. These groups ranged from the conservative Unione Politica to the left-leaning Labour party, all of which had different ideas about Malta's political future. The Maltese Constitutional party, for example, wanted close union with the United Kingdom, whereas the Nationalists favored association with Italy. Politics also became entangled in personal rivalries and the economic problems related to low military expenditures.

During World War II the constitution was suspended and Malta was put under direct military rule. Self-government was restored on September 5, 1947. The new constitution introduced universal suffrage and a unicameral legislative assembly. The first post–World War II election, held in 1947, was contested by five parties. The Labour party, headed by Paul Boffa, having received 60 percent of the votes and twenty-four of the forty-eight seats in the Legislative Assembly, formed a cabinet; the Nationalist party, under Enrico Mizzi, won nine seats and became the main opposition party. Two years later the Labour party split over British policy toward the dismissal of redundant shipyard workers, but Boffa continued in office with a minority government until 1950.

In the September 1950 elections the Nationalists won twelve assembly seats, and Mizzi formed a minority government with the support of the Workers' party, which had been organized after the Labour party split. On his death, Mizzi was succeeded by Giorgio Borg-Olivier. Although the Workers' party lost votes in the 1951 and 1953 elections (and finally disappeared), minority Nationalist governments held sway until 1955, when Labour, under Dom Mintoff, won 57 percent of the votes and twenty-three assembly seats and formed a cabinet.

In the 1950s the Malta Labour party favored complete integration with the United Kingdom, while the Nationalists wanted to obtain Commonwealth status. The Labour government negotiated for integration, but serious objections were raised on both sides about the wisdom of applying to Malta British laws, especially those pertaining to the minimum wage and social security system. The Maltese Catholic church was concerned about losing its prominent position, and many people feared that they would lose their Maltese cultural identity. A referendum was won by prointegration forces, but a majority of voters abstained. A period of social unrest followed; the government resigned, and in 1959 self-government was suspended. During the ensuing period of colonial administration both major parties came to favor independence, although the small parties continued to raise objections. The United Kingdom, after some negotiations, agreed to most of the demands. Self-government was restored in 1961, elections were held in 1962, and independence within the Commonwealth was achieved on September 21, 1964. In December 1974 Malta became a republic, while remaining a member of the Commonwealth (Blouet 1984: 214–17).

The Politics of Independent Malta

Since independence, the island's politics have been dominated by the Nationalist and Labour parties, each of which has strongly influenced the economic and social structure of Maltese society.

The last preindependence election, held in 1962, was won by the Nationalists, who obtained twenty-six seats in the fifty-seat Legislative Assembly; Labour obtained sixteen, and the four smaller parties shared eight seats. In the 1966 elections the Nationalists increased their majority. As the 1970 election approached, it became evident that the Nationalists were losing their popularity. To prevent a possible tie, despite Labour's opposition the Nationalist-dominated assembly amended the constitution to increase the number of legislative seats to fifty-five.

The Labour party, led by Dom Mintoff, won the 1971 election by a margin of one seat and increased its majority in 1976. Although the Nationalists won 51 percent of the popular vote in 1981, Labour got thirty-four of sixty-five parliamentary seats. (The number had been increased again.) The Nationalists thought they were robbed of a victory and boycotted the assembly until March 1983. In December 1984 Dom Mintoff resigned from active politics, and Carmelo Mifsud Bonnici became prime minister.

Following the 1981 election the Nationalists demanded that the constitution be amended to guarantee that the party that won the majority of the popular vote would also win the parliamentary majority. Labour, for its part, wanted Malta to be constitutionally declared neutral and nonaligned. Each party blocked the other's proposal, but under a compromise reached in January 1987 both amendments were adopted.

Personalities, rather than policies, dominated the May 1987 election campaign. The Nationalists impressed the electorate with their call for a change and received 50.57 percent of the popular vote. Under the new rules they also obtained thirty-five parliamentary seats and, for the first time in seventeen years, formed a government.

Although both parties try to appeal to the median group of voters, the political climate is often acrimonious, sometimes verging on violence. Of the two larger parties, the Nationalists are the more conservative. In office they have initiated many dirigiste policies, but they want the state to encourage and guide private enterprise, not supplant it. They also lean toward fiscal conservatism. By contrast, the Labour party's social and economic ideas closely parallel those of the more left-wing factions of the British Labour party. The Malta Labour party displays a distrust, verging on disregard, of the market mechanism, and favors an economically active government, with public enterprise playing a major role in the economy. It is strongly egalitarian and concerned with education and social services.

The main core of Labour party support comes from the General Workers' Trade Union (GWTU), whose 31,000 members constitute 70 percent of organized labor. Historically, the GWTU has derived most of its support from the left-leaning dockyard workers, who have had a tradition of direct action. Since 1971 the secretary and the president of the GWTU have sat in on Cabinet meetings when the Labour party is in power. In 1977 the party and the union were formally united; since then five members of each body sit on the other body's Executive Council, and the two organizations have established a coordinating committee in which both have equal membership and which both take turns chairing every six months.

The remaining 18,000 organized workers are loosely affiliated with the rival Conference of Trade Unions (CTU). The CTU derives most of its support from the Movement of United Teachers and other organizations of white-collar workers. It has no formal political affiliation, but many of its members support the Nationalists. The Nationalist party also draws support from people in rural areas, the self-employed and professionals, business, and the church.

Malta is a small country in which everybody knows everybody else, and personalities count as much as, if not more than, formal party programs. The dominant personality of the 1970s was undoubtedly the Labour party leader Dom Mintoff. An engineer-architect by training and a former Rhodes scholar, Mintoff combined a brilliant intellect and a forceful personality with a confrontational approach to obtaining compensation for the British military withdrawal. His tactics not only appealed to the strong Maltese sense of nationalism but, more important, were eminently successful in extracting the maximum "rent" from the British. His negotiations resulted in a seven-year agreement under which the United Kingdom pledged to pay £14 million for the 1972–79 period. In addition some of the United Kingdom's NATO partners, notably Italy, agreed to provide bilateral economic aid.

Mintoff's aggressive style, which appeared to pay off in international negotiations, had less impressive results in the sphere of economic policy. Here he seemed inclined to make arbitrary decisions without carefully calculating the costs and benefits. The choice of investment projects and trade policy were adversely affected as a result. His successor, Mifsud Bonnici, took a more pragmatic approach.

Historically, the Catholic church played an important political role: as late as 1966 official ecclesiastical disapproval of the Labour party was said to have swung many votes to the Nationalists. By the 1971 election the church had assumed a neutral stance, which may partly explain the gain in Labour votes. The dispute that broke out between the Labour government and the church in the early 1980s over church property and church-run schools and hospitals (discussed below) probably affected the voting in the election of 1987.

During the transition to independence and in the first decade after independence, Malta concentrated on providing infrastructure and fiscal incentives for manufacturing industries and tourism and on encouraging emigration. After the 1971 election victory the Labour government assumed an active entrepreneurial role. Malta severed its remaining economic ties with the United Kingdom and adopted an independent foreign exchange policy. It also tightened its economic controls and launched a series of social reforms.

The narrow electoral victory of Mintoff and the Labour party in 1971 marked a change from the "moderate" period of the 1950s and 1960s to the more interventionist Labour regime, in power from 1971 to 1987.

The 1950s and 1960s

When, at the close of World War II, Malta's strategic importance declined, the government became concerned that the British military establishment would be phased out and the island left with a shaky economic future. High priority was therefore given to obtaining financing from foreign sources to replace the revenue from military bases; to promoting local productive activity; and to providing employment, at home or abroad, for Maltese workers. Attention also turned to the need for social services, a need made urgent by the rapid, war-triggered transformation of Malta from a traditional to an egalitarian society.[2]

Economic Policies

In 1945 the U.K. Colonial Office asked a committee headed by Sir Wilfred Woods to (a) estimate the amount of war damage Malta had suffered, which was to be compensated by the government of the United Kingdom, (b) suggest how to improve social standards in Malta, and (c) suggest how the government of Malta could increase its revenue to cover ordinary expenditure (United Kingdom 1946). The subsequent report estimated that private property had suffered war damage totaling £26.8 million. The assistance needed to repair the damage to private and public property and to improve schools, hospitals, water, and electricity was reckoned at £42.4 million, to be expended over several five-year plan periods. Sir Wilfred also recommended that Malta introduce an income tax and a private property tax and that it eliminate subsidies to public utilities. In response, the United Kingdom increased the British War Damage Fund (originally granted in 1942) from £10 million to £30 million. An income tax was introduced and subsidies were abolished in 1948.

The first Labour government, headed by Paul Boffa, in 1950 commissioned Sir George E. Schuster to report on the economic position of Malta, to suggest ways of increasing government revenue, and to propose what form eventual assistance from the United Kingdom might take (Schuster 1950). Sir George's report concluded that Malta needed to expand industry, rationalize agriculture, and promote tourism. It was also important, the report noted, to improve infrastructure; to provide industrial incentives in the form of protective duties, fiscal exoneration, and training grants; and to conduct detailed studies to determine the economic potential of various parts of the economy. The recommendations were not carried out for lack of finances.

In 1955 Dom Mintoff, as head of the Labour government, called on Balogh and Seers to devise a development strategy.[3] Their report, like Schuster's, called for infrastructural improvements and for the transfer of relatively labor-intensive industries from the United Kingdom to Malta. An industrial estate needed to be established and facilities developed for training local technicians. Unlike the two previous reports, which clearly promoted emigration, the Balogh-Seers report argued that emigration was costly to Malta. During the six fiscal years between 1948–49 and 1953–54 the government of Malta had provided £673,000 in aid to migrants. Altogether, the Maltese, British, and Australian governments had paid out £2.6 million for emigration and training grants, to which must be added the hidden costs of the brain drain—most of the migrants were young and highly skilled. The debit side far outweighed the credit side: emigrants remitted only £300,000 a year (Schuster 1950: xxiii–xxxv).

The Balogh-Seers report estimated that to put the development program into effect, Malta needed capital grants of £3 million to £3.5 million a year and a current budget support grant of £1.5 million a year. The Balogh-Seers recommendations were reflected in a five-year plan for capital spending for the period 1956–57 to 1960–61, which was never published.

Once the United Kingdom agreed to cofinance Malta's economic development (Malta Round Table Conference 1955), the island was able to launch its first development plan, covering the years 1959–64. This plan and the subsequent plans formulated by the Nationalist governments consisted of a program for improving the infrastructure (to be carried out by the government with the assistance of foreign donors), a package of investment and emigration incentives, and forecasts of likely outcomes.

The first plan envisaged a total expenditure on infrastructure amounting to £32,250,000, of which £22,000,000 was to be provided by the British government in the form of grants and loans. Infrastructural improvements were to promote industrial development and also assist agriculture and tourism. Import substitution would be encouraged through a protective tariff based on the degree of fabrication, but the planners hoped to attract export-oriented industry as well. New industrial investment would be encouraged through capital grants or loans ranging from 33.3 to 50 percent of an investment. The new industries were exempted from import duties on inputs, were granted a ten-year tax holiday, and were offered low-cost factory rentals in an industrial estate developed by the government at Marsa (Malta 1959).

In another project under the 1959–64 plan, the Royal Navy dockyard was converted to commercial use and put under private administration. It lost money, however, and in the early 1970s was taken over by the government (see Blouet 1984: 213–14).

The industrialization drive met with mixed success. A number of import-substituting industries became firmly established, and some export-oriented operations got started. At the same time, many domestic-oriented enterprises, such as an automobile assembly plant, soon found that the local market was too small to support their operations.

The biggest failure of the first plan period was the disappointing rate of job creation, which did not make up for the decline in military-connected employment. Even though accelerated emigration had caused the population to fall, the number of unemployed rose from 3,772 (3.8 percent of the labor force) at the end of 1960 to a peak of 7,900 (7.8 percent of the labor force) in 1965.

In 1962 the government of Malta asked the United Nations for assistance in formulating its second five-year plan. The UN report (known as the Stolper report; see Stolper, Hellberg, and Callender 1964) covered all aspects of development strategy, from the relative advantages of Malta's association with the United Kingdom, the European Free Trade Area (EFTA), and the EEC to an analysis of the contracting practices of government departments. The report had a strong free-market orientation, although it did endorse subsidies for technical training. Perhaps its most notable feature was its pessimism concerning the possibilities for creating employment. Massive emigration was seen as the only practical way of maintaining the current standard of living in the absence of the British military presence.

In 1964, when Malta became independent, the United Kingdom pledged to provide £51 million (75 percent in the form of a grant and 25 percent in loans) for capital improvements over a period of ten years. This aid played a vital role in financing public projects envisaged under the 1959–64 development plan.

Like the 1954–59 plan, the 1964–69 plan focused on building up infrastructure and giving fiscal incentives to industry, agriculture, and tourism. In the light of recent experience and the opinions of the Stolper mission, however, it encouraged emigration to solve the unemployment problem. The plan foresaw the creation of 5,800 jobs in industry, tourism, and the government, but it also predicted the loss of 5,000 military-related jobs. Emigration was expected to average 7,500 persons a year, which meant a decrease in population from 318,620 in 1962 to 303,644 in 1969 and a total labor force reduction of 4,138. Over the five-year period of the plan GNP was expected to fall in real terms by 3 to 4 percent.

Despite a second (and unforeseen) reduction in British forces in 1967, these projections turned out to be overpessimistic.[4] The natural population growth rate was lower than expected, 9,290 jobs were created instead of the estimated 5,800, emigration declined, and GNP rose by about 3 to 4 percent. The plan underestimated GNP growth by about 8 percent in real terms.

What explains this unexpected outcome? For one thing, job creation in industry and in tourism during the first three years of the plan surpassed the estimated five-year totals. It was construction, however, that contributed the most to the expansion. With the rebuilding of war damage virtually at an end, the plan estimated that construction employment would drop by 2,600 between 1962 and 1966–67. Instead, the number of construction workers rose by more than 3,000. The demand for labor was stimulated in part by the building of tourist accommodations, but even more by the construction of houses for British retirees attracted by the possibility of settling in a sterling-bloc, English-speaking country with a good climate. Paradoxically, the building boom, accompanied by higher real estate prices and housing costs, was one of the factors that helped defeat the Nationalists in the 1971 election—an interesting variant of the "Dutch disease."

Toward the end of the second plan period, Malta and the United Kingdom came to disagree about the magnitude and the future of British aid. Of the £51 million pledged by the United Kingdom in 1964, £28 million (mostly the grant portion) was spent in five years. Borg-Olivier, the prime minister, requested that the remaining £23 million be distributed in the form of grants, whereas the United Kingdom initially insisted on a 50-50 loan-grant split. In April 1969 the United Kingdom suspended the disbursement of these funds, and, pending the resolution of the disagreement, Malta delayed the publication of the third plan, which had already been ratified by its parliament.

Deprived of British aid, Malta started to search for alternative sources. The Federal Republic of Germany pledged £235,000, to be used on a mutually acceptable project. Of greater consequence were the overtures made by the U.S.S.R. for the use of Maltese port facilities after NATO's naval withdrawal, scheduled for 1972. In October 1970 the United Kingdom settled more or less on Malta's terms. Of the £23 million in assistance, £3 million was set aside as a grant for the development of Malta's dry docks and £1 million as a grant for the restoration of historic buildings. Of the rest, 75 percent was to be in grants and 25 percent in the form of loans. The third plan, following much the same pattern as the previous two plans, was finally published, only to be made irrelevant by the Labour victory in the 1971 election.

Institution Building

During and after the transition to independence, the government constructed the institutional framework it needed to conduct an independent monetary and trade policy.

THE MONETARY SYSTEM. As a colony, Malta used British currency until 1949, when the Currency Ordinance Bill permitted the local Currency Board to issue Maltese pounds at par with the British pound. The board notes were backed up at least 100 percent by the Sterling Note Security Fund. This link was maintained after independence, and in November 1967 the Maltese pound (later renamed the Maltese lira, or Lm) was devalued, in line with the devaluation of the British pound.

The Central Bank of Malta Act of November 1967 marks the beginning of an independent monetary policy. The Note Security Fund assets were transferred to the Central Bank as soon as it opened in April 1968. The link with sterling, however, was maintained throughout the tenure of the Nationalist government.

Under the Banking Act of April 1, 1970, selective controls were permitted to restrain bank lending either in the aggregate or for particular purposes, and the minister could prescribe purposes for which banks could not lend at all. The Nationalist government did not make use of the discretionary powers that it obtained under this act, but the Labour government did, in order to have some influence on the structure of private industry.

CONTROLS ON CAPITAL MOVEMENT. In 1939, at the outbreak of World War II, the United Kingdom instituted controls over the movement of capital out of the sterling area, which included Malta. Exchange control in Malta was given a legal framework in 1959 with the passing of the Exchange Control Ordinance, under which funds continued to move into and out of Malta from nonsterling areas.

In April 1970, as a measure to prevent the flight of capital, the exchange control system was extended to the sterling area. Traditionally, the government of Malta followed a policy of low interest rates, and in 1962 it imposed an 8 percent ceiling on all commercial loans. (This regulation is still in effect.) In the late 1960s interest rates in the sterling area rose, reaching 9 percent on U.K. government bonds, whereas time deposits in Malta bore only 2.5 to 3.5 percent. Not surprisingly, the disparity caused a drain on Maltese capital. The drain on capital intensified when, following the suspension of British aid, the government decided to finance the resulting deficit by selling 5.5 percent bonds to the Central Bank, which helped it raise Lm 21 million.

The capital drain could have been stopped if interest rates had been permitted to rise to the competitive level, but this would have pushed up the cost of future government borrowing. The government chose, therefore, to increase interest rates by only a modest amount (the discount rate went up from 5 to 5.5 percent, and the interest rate on time deposits was increased to 4.5 percent). To stem capital outflow, the government extended controls on capital movements to other sterling countries, and to reduce the attractiveness of high-yield foreign obligations, it imposed an interest equalization tax. The capital controls became a permanent feature of Malta's economy.

THE TRADE REGIME. Under the system of protection devised by the Nationalist governments in the 1960s, tariff duties are levied primarily for revenue, whereas quantitative restrictions are used for protection and balance of payments purposes. Tariff duties are determined by the Ministry of Finance, import licenses are issued by the Ministry of Trade, and there is no direct mechanism for coordinating the two types of trade restraints.

The tariff system, introduced in 1964, provided for the preferential treatment of goods imported from the Commonwealth. In 1976 the EEC replaced the Commonwealth as the favored supplier, but few other substantive changes have been made.

Under the current schedule some items, such as medical supplies and educational products, pay no tariff duty. Most foodstuffs pay 13 to 20 percent. Piece goods imported from the EEC and from other locations are charged 16 and 30 percent, respectively, clothing, 30.5 and 47 percent; wooden furniture, 60 and 75 percent; cars, 55 and 70 percent, and luxury items, 70 and 80 percent. Thus, although revenue is the main reason for levying the tariff, the system favors higher-stage manufacture of import substitutes.

The Importation Control Regulation was introduced in 1969 as a currency defense measure. Originally, Malta had an open license scheme that applied to all commodities, except for a small number of restricted items. Over the years the regulation came to be used in an increasingly selective fashion as a protective device.

PRICE CONTROLS. Following the November 1967 sterling devaluation, the government put into effect retail price controls in a (vain) attempt to stem the rise in the cost of living. As inflation subsided, the controls were removed, but they could be reimposed under existing laws.

CONCLUSION. The institutions put in place during the 1960s provided the government with powerful tools for controlling the economy. The Nationalists used the tools with restraint, whereas the Labour governments that followed applied them with great vigor. Note, however, that the difference was a matter of degree only. The Nationalists built the foundations of dirigisme, leaving Labour to put up the structure.

Economic Performance

The early 1960s were difficult for Malta. The withdrawal of the British military establishment meant less employment and lower expenditure on wages, goods, and services, but the rate of growth of the productive sectors was barely sufficient to make up for the loss. Real GNP and the total number of employed remained virtually constant, while emigration produced only a slight decrease in the total population (table 6-4).

Then, in 1965, things began to turn around. Except for the 1971 hiatus, the economy experienced rapid growth in the remaining years of the Nationalist administration (table 6-5). The boost came primarily from export-oriented manufacturing (mainly textiles), tourism (mainly British), and construction (in response to the housing demand of British retirees). Employment in manufacturing stood at 10,000 in 1961 and 13,000 in 1965; by 1971 it had reached 20,700. Employment in hotels, which barely surpassed 500 in 1961 and 800 in 1965, reached 7,900 in 1970 and remained at that level in 1971. Employment in construction rose from 9,200 in 1966 to a peak of 12,600 in 1970. It declined by 2,000 in the course of the next year, however, in part because currency restrictions had been eased and British tourists were able to travel more freely to nonsterling countries, and in part because most of the British retirees had found suitable homes by then. It was this relatively fragile nature of Malta's economic base that prompted the Labour government to turn to diversification.

In addition, Malta discovered, prosperity was breeding discontent. As land values and construction costs spiraled, ordinary Maltese families had more and more difficulty finding adequate accommodations. Since housing is greatly prized in Malta, perhaps more than in any other country, a government whose policies make housing unaffordable is

Table 6-4. Economic Indicators 1961–65

Indicator	1961	1962	1963	1964	1965
Population (thousands)	301.5	302.9	300.2	298.9	296.5
Emigration (thousands)	3.6	3.6	6.6	9.0	8.1
Gainfully employed (thousands)	84.9	84.1	83.9	84.7	85.3
Military base	15.7	14.0	13.1	11.8	11.2
Other	69.2	70.1	70.8	72.9	74.1
Unemployment (percent)	4.9	7.0	7.7	8.3	8.4
GNP at 1954 prices (millions of Maltese liri)	42.6	41.7	41.4	42.2	45.0
GNP per capita at 1954 prices (Maltese liri)	141	138	138	141	152

Source: Central Statistical Office.

Table 6-5. *Economic Indicators, 1966–71*

Indicator	1966	1967	1968	1969	1970	1971
Population (thousands)	299.8	299.9	302.0	303.4	302.8	301.7
Emigration (thousands)	4.3	4.0	3.0	2.6	2.7	2.8
Gainfully employed (thousands)	86.7	89.6	91.8	95.5	96.1	99.1
Military base	10.4	9.8	9.0	7.8	6.4	6.0
Other	76.3	79.9	82.8	87.7	98.7	93.1
Unemployment (percent)	7.1	5.7	4.4	3.8	4.9	5.6
GNP at 1954 prices (millions of Maltese liri)	49.3	54.0	58.5	61.5	69.5	71.6
GNP per capita at 1954 prices (Maltese liri)	164	180	194	203	230	237

Source: Central Statistical Office.

doomed. The general price rise that reflected the 1967 sterling devaluation also worked against the government, which, not surprisingly, found its attempts at price control to no avail. To add to its problems, the government received many complaints about the lack of social progress. Demands for higher wages, better health and educational facilities, and more generous social security allowances were spearheaded by, but by no means confined to, the dockyard workers. Purely political factors also played a role: with the continued transfer of British and NATO forces, public sentiment swung toward neutralism, a position embraced by Labour.

Labour Party Rule, 1971–87

The Labour party fought the 1971 electoral campaign on a platform of political nonalignment, government leadership of the economy, and social reform. The economic program that evolved over the next sixteen years clearly reflects this original intent, although in its application it had to take into account the changing external circumstances.

Overview

As already mentioned, Malta sought to make up for the loss associated with the phasing out of the British and NATO bases by obtaining foreign grants and concessionary loans. It resisted burdening the economy with foreign debt, however, and a law passed in 1972 prohibited the government from contracting foreign loans at interest rates higher than 3 percent. This law cut Malta off from international commercial borrowing.

Internally, the government pursued a conservative fiscal policy, keeping internal borrowing to a minimum (in most years, if foreign grants and loans are counted, the budget was balanced) and maintaining a 100 percent foreign exchange reserve as backing for the Maltese lira.

The fiscal conservatism, by itself, would have strengthened the Maltese lira, but to mitigate and, if possible, to prevent the importation of inflation, the government repeatedly revalued the currency. To maintain the high exchange rate, it imposed increasingly stringent quantitative import restrictions. The quotas were also used selectively to protect particular import-substituting enterprises.

Like the earlier regimes, the Labour government kept interest rates at a low and constant level. To prevent excessive credit expansion, the banks, under government guidance, practiced credit rationing and maintained large excess reserves; to prevent capital flight, the government introduced severe restrictions on capital. Thus, Malta became an unusual case of fiscal conservatism coexisting with financial repression and rigid controls on capital movement and trade.

To keep development under its influence, the government seized the major banks, public utilities, transport, and communications. It also started a number of enterprises in which private capital had shown no interest and took equity positions in others. Import trade was partly nationalized, ostensibly to lower import costs through bulk buying. An attempt was also made to discourage further investment in textiles and tourism through selective incentives and controls. Perhaps more important, the government discouraged the further growth of low-skill, labor-intensive activities by deliberately raising wages.

This wage policy was partly motivated by social considerations—and political ones, too, for it enabled the government to redeem its pledge to the workers. Because the high minimum wages restricted job creation, the government tried to fight unemployment by organizing a civilian job corps. Still, the situation grew worse. By 1982 the wage increases and the strong-lira policy were pricing Malta out of the world market. The government therefore decided to institute a wage and price freeze. The moment was well chosen. Given Malta's high unemployment, many workers were willing to accept the wage freeze, on condition of a price freeze. The latter, imposed at a time when world prices had stabilized, appeared to work. Business welcomed the wage stability and labor peace. Thus the government instituted far-reaching controls, to the apparent satisfaction of all.

Social reform has been one of the most important aspects of Labour's policies. During its tenure, the Labour government extended the social security and public health systems and greatly improved the housing stock through its public housing program and aid to private housing. It experimented with worker participation in management and took steps to transform and control education and to reduce the influence of the church.

To sum up, since 1971 the Labour government, relying largely on the institutions designed by earlier regimes, has transformed Malta's economy from a market-driven system into a welfare state in which the government exercises far-reaching power over economic and social affairs. The discussion now turns to the details of this transformation.

Securing Foreign Financing

As mentioned earlier, the government's first concern on entering office was to secure foreign financial support. Under existing agreements, the United Kingdom was to give Malta annual grants for the use of the naval and air base facilities. On average, these grants amounted to Lm 4.2 million during 1967–71. In 1972 Dom Mintoff negotiated a new seven-year agreement for rental of the defense facilities used by NATO forces. Under its terms, Malta was to receive an annual fee of Lm 14 million, of which the United Kingdom was to pay £5.25 million. The rental fees were vital for balancing the budget: in 1974–75 revenues and expenditures were budgeted at Lm 59 million; revenues from domestic sources amounted to Lm 44.4 million (72 percent of the total); and foreign loans and grants brought in Lm 14.6 million, of which Lm 13.7 was from NATO rental fees.

The increased NATO payments were doubtless one of the factors that helped Malta recover from the 1971 slump and that contributed to the growth in the 1972–79 period. These payments offset the oil price increase that plagued so many other countries in those years. Since the Labour party was committed to neutrality, however, the base had to be phased out by 1979, at which time payments would cease. This commitment was grounded in socialist ideology, but it also had a practical side. NATO had never clearly indicated whether it wished to maintain a large base in Malta, so the country would sooner or later have to face up to converting to a civilian economy. Another concern was that the NATO forces prevented Malta from expanding its tourist industry and from developing into the international commercial and banking service center it aspired to become.

The prime minister began negotiating intensely for other sources of foreign finance. He obtained grants and concessionary loans from Libya, Saudi Arabia, the United Arab Emirates, Italy, the EEC, and China, among others.[5] In these negotiations the prime minister made skillful use of Malta's strategic position: the countries with economic or military interests in the Mediterranean, he pointed out, could contribute what, for them, were moderate sums as insurance against having the islands come under the influence of potential foes.[6] Nonetheless, the funds did not fully compensate for the loss of rents from defense facilities, and the amounts received declined rapidly after 1984 (table 6-6).

Exchange Rate and Monetary Policies

One of the Labour government's first actions after taking office in June 1971 was to break the one-for-one link between the Maltese currency and

Table 6-6. Government Revenue, Capital Expenditures, and Foreign Aid, 1977–86
(thousands of Maltese liri)

Item	1977–78	1978–79	1980	1981	1982	1983	1984	1985	1986
A. Rents from defense facilities	13,311	13,043	—	—	—	—	—	—	—
B. Foreign grants and loans	704	4,903	10,786	18,223	9,071	20,691	—	—	1,464
C. Total, A + B	14,015	17,946	10,786	18,223	9,071	20,691	12,671	3,700	225,853
D. Total government revenue	97,350	110,260	170,152	204,662	210,724	224,523	218,558	220,548	225,853
E. Capital expenditure	22,441	30,346	32,564	31,825	38,711	37,593	40,909	40,561	45,204
C as percentage of D	14.0	16.0	6.0	9.0	4.0	9.0	6.0	2.0	0.6
C as percentage of E	62.0	59.0	33.0	57.0	23.0	55.0	31.0	9.0	3.0

— Not available.
Source: Malta, Treasury.

the pound sterling. This step paved the way for an independent monetary and exchange rate policy.

EXCHANGE RATE MANAGEMENT. Throughout the period of the Labour administration, "the overriding motivation behind exchange rate policy . . . [was] to cushion the domestic economy as much as possible from the damaging effects of imported inflation without at the same time unduly prejudicing the island's export competitiveness. In pursuance of this aim, the exchange rate of the Maltese currency [was] steered along a middle course between the hard and the soft internationally traded currencies" (Central Bank of Malta 1986: 4).

Following the delinking, the lira was allowed to float upward in relation to the depreciating sterling, and in 1972 it was linked to a trade-weighted basket of seven European currencies. As a result of the oil price increase in December 1973, the U.S. dollar became more important in Malta's trade, and the basket was revised to include the dollar. In early 1979 the basket was revised again: the weights of the U.S. dollar, the pound sterling, and the Italian lira were reduced, and the weight of the strong European currencies was raised. The change was necessary, the government explained, to reduce the rate of imported inflation and "to gain the fullest possible benefits from the relative currency stability the [European Monetary System] is intended to achieve" (Central Bank press release, 9 March 1979).

As the U.S. dollar appreciated in 1979 and in early 1980, the weight given to the dollar was increased (on March 17, 1980) "to ensure that the Malta pound is not weakened unjustifiably, thereby affecting the cost of living, which is a prime concern of the authorities" (Central Bank press release, March 17, 1980). Even with the new formula, the lira depreciated against the dollar from Lm 1 = US$2.830 on March 17, to Lm 1 = US$2.7067 on April 7, whereupon the authorities decided to restore the exchange rate that prevailed on March 17 and to further increase the weight given to the dollar. Subsequently, with a slight weakening of the dollar, the March 17 basket was once again restored. In 1985, as the dollar depreciated, its weight was drastically reduced to maintain the value of the lira in relation to that of the leading European currencies.

CONTROLS ON CAPITAL MOVEMENT. A currency can be linked to a basket of foreign currencies either by coordinating credit policy with the policies of the reference group or by resorting to capital controls. Malta chose the latter option. Throughout the period of worldwide inflation and of high nominal (and, toward the end of the period, high real) interest rates, Malta refused to raise its nominal interest rate on loans beyond the 1962 level of 8 percent. As a result, for several years real interest rates in Malta were negative. Since deposits were subject to even lower ceilings (3.5 to 4.5 percent) banks remained profitable, and depositors, having no better alternative, continued to use the bank facilities, paying, in effect, an inflation tax.

The Labour government inherited the system of capital controls from the Nationalists and over the years made them increasingly stringent. Up to 1982 every Maltese citizen had a personal foreign investment allowance of Lm 500 a year, but this was abolished when Air Malta decided to purchase three Boeing 737-200 jets. To finance the purchase, the Central Bank issued on behalf of Air Malta Lm 19 million in bonds, denominated as A-type bonds (10.5 percent repayable in eleven years) and B-type bonds (12 percent, repayable in ten years). Sale was restricted to repatriated Maltese funds held abroad and to the foreign investment allowance of Maltese citizens for the years 1982 and 1983. There was, however, no rush to repatriate capital, and, to make sure that there would be sufficient demand for the bonds, the investment allowance was suspended for two years. It has not yet been restored. In 1984, to induce Maltese citizens to repatriate funds held abroad, the government offered to pay 8.5 percent interest on repatriated funds, thus violating, for the first time, the self-imposed low-interest rule.

By moderating inflation, the government gained popularity with consumers. By controlling the banks through credit rationing, it exercised a powerful influence on business, and the favored businesses in effect became its clients. Only after worldwide inflation subsided and the nominal interest rates declined did businesses start to protest the 8 percent interest ceiling on loans. Cheaper credit has been available for encouraging certain types of investment in housing and in productive industries.

PUBLIC FINANCE. The government of Malta has an outstanding record of fiscal austerity. Under the Borg-Olivier regime, revenues matched expenditures closely in all years, with nominal levels doubling between 1960 and 1970. Despite the 50 percent increase in government expenditure at the onset of the Mintoff Labour regime, a corresponding increase in revenue after a brief lag led to a deficit of 6 percent of expenditure in 1972.

Under the Labour party, both revenues and expenditures have grown rapidly, being four to five times higher in the early 1980s than in the early 1970s. Since total government expenditure was about 39 percent of GNP in 1973 and about 45 percent in 1983, the rise, as a share of GNP, is not that significant.

The conservative thrust of fiscal and monetary policy is also evident from the growth of external reserves. Relatively small deficits in net foreign exchange earnings were more than offset by investment income and transfer payments from abroad, so that the current account of the balance of payments showed a surplus until 1983. Foreign exchange reserves grew steadily to about US$1.5 billion in 1983, which amounts to a handsome per capita figure. Balancing the budget became more difficult in the 1980s when government revenues ceased to grow. With the increase in social expenditures during the recession years, the current budget surplus began to dry up. Not wanting to abandon its major capital expenditure projects, such as the construction of a shipbuilding yard at Marsa, the government instead abandoned its policy of balancing the budget and in 1984–87 had to face a rise in deficits (table 6-7).[7]

Public Enterprise

Government investments in 1986 totaled about Lm 42 million, of which about Lm 16 million was invested directly by the government and about Lm 26 million was invested through the Malta Development Corporation (MDC). The main items in the first category are nearly Lm 6 million (equaling a 49 percent government interest) in the Libyan Arab Maltese

Table 6-7. Government Budget, 1961–87
(millions of Maltese liri)

Year	Revenue	Expenditure	Surplus (+) or deficit (−)
1961	16.4	16.7	−0.3
1962	16.8	16.6	0.2
1963	16.5	16.6	−0.1
1964	16.7	17.0	−0.3
1965	18.6	18.3	0.3
1966	19.8	9.7	0.1
1967	22.7	21.2	1.6
1968	24.4	25.5	−1.1
1969	28.8	28.1	0.1
1970	33.6	35.5	0.1
1971	47.2	49.5	−2.3
1972	45.9	51.8	−5.9
1973	49.9	42.2	7.7
1974	55.8	55.7	0.1
1975	74.5	63.8	10.7
1976	88.4	94.0	−5.6
1977	100.9	76.1	24.8
1978	97.3	93.0	4.3
1979	110.3	107.8	2.5
1980	170.2	161.6	8.6
1981	204.7	192.5	12.2
1982	210.8	216.5	−5.7
1983	224.5	221.0	3.5
1984	218.6	224.0	−5.4
1985	220.5	227.7	−7.1
1986	225.9	240.5	−14.6
1987	221.2	263.6	−42.5

Sources: Malta, *Malta Handbook*, 1985; Malta, *Quarterly Digest of Statistics*, March–June 1987.

Holding Co., Ltd.; about Lm 1.5 million in Air Malta; and about Lm 6 million in three commercial banks (Mid-Med, which is wholly state owned, and the Bank of Valetta and the Lombard Bank, which are each 60 percent state owned). Through the Libyan Arab Maltese Holding Co., Malta has undertaken a number of joint ventures with Libya in shipbuilding, the central foundry, and other engineering projects.

Investments through the MDC comprise a wide range of enterprises in food processing, textiles, engineering, transport, banking, insurance, and other fields. About half of the Lm 2.6 million invested through the MDC is accounted for by Malta Shipbuilding (Lm 12 million) and Metalfound (Lm 1.5 million), which are the main ventures of the Libyan Arab Maltese Holding Co.

Total capital invested in Malta in the productive sectors (mining, manufacturing, construction, transport, and trade) was put at Lm 163 million in 1983, according to the *Census of Industrial Production, 1983.* Thus, government investment represents about 20 to 25 percent of total investment in productive activities.

The heavy concentration of public investment in port and harbor facilities and in related industrial activities cannot be understood without considering the political economy, both national and international. First, as pointed out earlier, the political base of the Labour party was, and continues to be, the dockyard workers. The considerable upgrading and extension of the harbor facilities to increase the volume and variety of shipping services offered enlarged the membership and clout of the core group of workers, whose leader held cabinet rank in the Labour government. Second, these facilities have a long gestation period and therefore call for heavy outlays of capital, which Malta has sought on a concessionary basis from its affluent Arab ally, Libya. Third, the demand for shipbuilding services and other facilities received attention under the astute foreign policy initiated by Mintoff. The Malta Shipbuilding Company received orders for two supply vessels for China and eight timber carriers for the U.S.S.R. Despite Malta's long association with nautical matters, it is doubtful whether a purely commercial cost-benefit analysis would have led to such a concentration in investment strategy, particularly at a time when the shipping industry was so distressed throughout the world.

Public sector investments as a whole proved profitable. In 1984 the government received Lm 4.7 million, either directly or through the MDC, and earned a 10 percent return on its investment. Of this amount, 66 percent came from three government-owned commercial banks (Mid-Med, the Bank of Valetta, and Lombard), which paid a Lm 2.8 million dividend on a Lm 6.375 million investment, for a 42.8 percent return. Six categories of companies accounted for 91.8 percent of all dividends earned from the Lm 15 million investment: commercial banks, air transport and air supplies, construction, ferryboats, sea shipping, and grain trade. The investment in these six categories earned a 28.3 percent dividend. The remaining Lm 26.2 million in government investments earned 1.5 percent in dividends.[8] Recently the government has taken steps to privatize low-return enterprises in sectors that are not considered to be of great importance.

The most financially successful public enterprises earn high profits by exploiting their monopoly power. Air and sea fares are determined by international cartels and are set at levels that will ensure the profitability of Maltese transport enterprises. In 1972–73, when Sea Malta (which originally had only five or six barges) entered sea shipping on a large scale, the shipping conference raised the rates applicable to Malta by 300 percent. In banking, the Central Bank of Malta sets service charges at a level that will guarantee a high degree of profitability. Thus, although Maltese public enterprises are not a burden on the budget, they have repercussions on the private sector and hence on the economy.

Policies on Trade and Capital Movement

Quantitative import restrictions and restrictions on capital movements originated in the 1970s under the Nationalist government but were made considerably tighter by Labour. Under these restrictions, imports were divided into four categories: (a) imports that are normally freely licensed (this category includes most raw materials and machinery), (b) imports under the bulk-buying scheme, (c) imports subject to specific product quotas, and (d) items temporarily suspended. This section discusses some of these controls and other restrictions.

PROHIBITED IMPORTS AND QUOTAS. Import prohibitions or suspensions are applied to goods produced locally in a quantity deemed sufficient to satisfy the local market. For instance, there is a total ban on imports of chocolates, biscuits, soap, toothpaste, and television sets (which are assembled locally by a private firm that has a government monopoly). At one time Malta had a pig industry that satisfied local demand. When the herds were wiped out by foot-and-mouth disease, importation was permitted. Between 1983 and 1986 the herds were rebuilt with the help of government subsidies, and the importation of fresh pork was banned once again, but permits can still be obtained to import 5 to 10 percent of canned ham requirements. Larger quotas are permitted where local capacity is too small (for example, 50 percent of butter is imported), but as soon as local capacity expands, the quotas are cut down.

Quotas are also used to reduce the overall volume of imports. In times of stringency, the permitted volume of imports is cut down. The relative size of quotas, by category, is determined by the administration, an important criterion being whether the given product is or is not essential.

COUNTERTRADE. The idea behind countertrade is to provide an incentive to export by linking exports to the importation of a profitable item. In effect, countertrade acts as a subsidy on export trade carried out by an importer. In Malta the countertrade regime applies only to automobiles. In order to import a car, a dealer must generate exports equal to twice the value of the car. Tourism counts as an export.

THE BULK-BUYING SCHEME. The bulk-buying scheme was instituted in 1979 to reduce the cost of essential imported commodities. At the time, the prices of imported goods were rising rapidly, and the government hoped to achieve economies of scale by buying in bulk.

Under the scheme the Ministry of Trade acts as a purchasing agent for the importers of butter, meat, livestock for slaughter, wheat, barley, corn, potatoes, soybean oil, rice, sugar, canned milk, canned meat and fish, cheese, coffee, tea, fruit, cement, steel, and timber. In 1979 these commodities represented 15.5 percent of all imports (16.1 percent of all imports other than fuel imports, which are a government monopoly). Bulk buying covered 61.5 percent of food, 31.7 percent of crude material, 8.6 percent of vegetable oil, and 4.9 percent of semimanufactures (Malta Chamber of Commerce 1981: 5).

Purchases of each commodity or subcommodity (such as canned ham and canned beef) are handled by a board made up of not more than ten licensed private importers; if the number of licensees exceeds ten, the importers elect representatives to sit on the board . The boards meet under the auspices of the Ministry of Trade, and meetings are chaired by a senior official. The ministry keeps records of available inventories and plans and executes purchases on the basis of international tenders, the order going to the lowest bidder. Purchases are financed by the importers who sit on the boards. Import quotas are allocated to the licensed traders on the basis of past orders, with some adjustments made for changing circumstances.

The scheme gives the traders a guaranteed profit. The margins for wholesale operations, transport, storage, and retailing are fixed (they have not changed since 1979, when the scheme was instituted). Retail prices are controlled. Board members pay a notional price for the imports, which is calculated by subtracting the handling charges from the controlled retail price. If the actual c.i.f. price exceeds this notional price, the government makes up the difference; if the actual import price is less than the notional price, the government makes a profit. In the late 1980s the scheme was, on balance, profitable. Part of the profit was transferred to general revenue, and part was kept as a buffer to pay for imports should prices increase.

Retail prices are gradually adjusted to reflect world prices, but there is no one-to-one correspondence between individual import and retail prices. For instance, in 1986 the world prices of several commodities under the bulk buying scheme (especially cement) dropped markedly. Of the Lm 5 million profit made by the board, Lm 3 million was kept in reserve as a buffer against future price rises, while Lm 2 million was allocated as subsidies to reduce the retail prices of milk, fruit, and other commodities the government wishes to encourage the public to consume for health or other reasons. Occasionally, surpluses may, by decision of Parliament, be passed on to the Treasury.

The bulk-buying scheme enables the government to control and influence the business community, as well as consumers. It also appeals to the established licensed traders, since they bear no risk and receive trading margins that are apparently satisfactory; indeed, when a trader goes out of business there seems to be no lack of applicants to take up his import license. Whether the scheme serves consumers is more questionable. By buying in bulk, the authority undoubtedly manages to obtain quantity discounts unavailable to individual importers. Many special opportunities are missed when all purchases are made by tender, however, with the result that in some instances the price is lower and in others higher than it would be if purchases were made by individual importers. Consumers clearly have less product variety. Because the orders are given to the lowest bidders, the tender system also lowers the quality of imports. Perhaps as a concession to consumers, private dealers have of late been permitted to import some brands not imported under the bulk system.

PRICE CONTROLS. Peacetime price controls were first imposed in 1967 by the Nationalist government in an effort to halt the price rise provoked by the November 1967 devaluation of the British pound. A system of price controls has been in force since 1983. A general price order has fixed the margins for importer-wholesalers and retailers as a percentage of the import price, by three-digit and, in some cases, by four-digit BTN categories. Prices on domestic products are also fixed. In principle, domestic product prices cannot exceed the level that prevailed in 1982. Product prices are in fact allowed to drift, since they may reflect changes in quality.

Wage Policies

In the 1970s the Nationalist government banked on low wages to attract labor-intensive industries. By contrast, the Labour government sought to improve working conditions by imposing, and then raising, the minimum wage. This policy was not expected to discourage the hoped-for growth of high-technology industries, which were seen as a welcome alternative to tourism and to textiles because they were not as vulnerable to recessions and depended less on low-skill labor. To reduce the economy's heavy dependence on the textile and tourist industries, the government in late 1979 introduced restrictions on "bank lending to the textiles and clothing industry as well as to tourist-related activities for the expansion or acquisition of new capital assets" (Malta Chamber of Commerce 1981: 7). A minimum wage of Lm 10 a week was introduced in 1974, at which time all workers and employees also became entitled to an annual bonus. A law passed on 1 April 1976 instituted male-female wage parity and thereby deprived the textile industry of a traditional source of low-wage labor.

The minimum wage and the bonus were raised repeatedly. In 1982 the minimum wage was set at Lm 29.88 per week and the annual bonus at Lm 116. Thus, in real terms the minimum wage rose by 60 percent within eight years (see table 6-8). In 1983 the government tried to compensate for the rising unemployment through a price and wage freeze, which remained in force until 1987, when the Nationalist government reintroduced collective bargaining.

Emergency Employment

During the first two years of the Labour regime, unemployment continued to rise, jumping from a low of 3,800 persons (3.8 percent of the labor force) in 1968 to 6,300 (6.1 percent of the labor force) in 1972. As a countermeasure, the government organized a volunteer job corps to carry out public works programs. By 1974 the job corps had 4,000 members.

To help the unemployed improve their chances of obtaining jobs, the government formed a training unit for the unemployed that began

Table 6-8. *National Minimum Wage, Cost of Living Index, and Real Minimum Wage, 1974–86*
(Maltese liri per week)

Year	National minimum wage	Cost of living index (1974 = 100)	Estimated real minimum wage (1974 prices)
1974	10.00	100.0	10.00
1975	12.00	108.8	11.03
1976	13.25	109.5	12.10
1977[a]	14.75	120.5	12.24
	15.88		13.18
1978	17.38	126.0	13.79
1979[a]	18.88	135.0	13.98
	19.88		14.72
1980	22.88	156.3	14.64
	26.88		16.26
1981	26.88	174.3	15.42
1982	29.88	184.4	16.20
1983	29.88	182.8	16.36
1984	29.80	182.1[b]	16.42
1985	29.80	181.5[b]	16.45
1986	29.80	185.0[b]	16.11

a. The minimum wage was revised during the year.
b. Calculated by linking new cost of living index with base (1983 = 100).
Source: Malta, Central Statistical Office.

assisting male workers in February 1975 and female trainees in the following year. In 1976 the two programs covered about 7,800 workers (as reported by the Economist Intelligence Unit). At that time unemployment stood at 4,800, or 4.2 percent of the labor force.

In March 1976 a new volunteer corps, which was to have 1,500 members, was formed to convert reclaimed barren land into state farms. A fourth labor corps program was formed in April 1977. Together, the four groups had about 8,000 members in 1977 (table 6-9). Employment in the emergency organizations thus accounted for more than a third of public sector employment.

These employment-creating measures came at a time of decreasing emigration from Malta. Without them, emigration might have been higher, and more of those remaining in Malta might have been unemployed. In any case, the measures enabled the government to contain open unemployment, which by 1979 had been reduced to an all-time low of 3,294, or 2.7 percent of the labor force.

Following the second oil price shock and the ensuing worldwide depression, the government felt compelled to rely once again on the private sector to create employment. The emergency employment measures were deemphasized and private employment encouraged through the 1983 wage-price freeze. In the course of the next three years the number of unemployed dropped sharply, along with total benefit payments (table 6-10).

Redistributive Policies and Social Reform

Under the leadership of Dom Mintoff, the Labour government introduced a number of measures to provide social services, secularize society, foster equality, and increase government control. Some of these, such as the nationalization of medical services, met with strong opposition; others were willingly accepted by most of the population.

SOCIAL SERVICES. The first elements of a social insurance scheme were introduced in the interwar period, starting with pensions for the widows of government employees, in 1927, and the Workmen's Compensation

Table 6-9. Labor Force and Employment, 1977

Sector	Number employed
Private sector	78,000
National defense	3,000
Government service[a]	22,000
Labor corps	8,000
Unemployed	5,000

a. Excludes the four labor corps.
Source: Malta, Central Statistical Office, and Economist Intelligence Unit.

Table 6-10. Unemployment Claims and Benefit Payments, 1980–86

Year	Claims (number)	Payments (thousands of Maltese liri)
1980	8,142	291
1981	10,536	556
1982	16,889	789
1983	15,190	10,020
1984	15,581	767
1985	16,651	735
1986	12,418	510

Source: Malta, *Quarterly Digest of Statistics*, March–June 1982.

Ordinance of 1934. The ordinance introduced a contributory scheme providing compensation for injuries at work and industrial diseases and pensions for widows of victims of industrial accidents.

In 1948 the authorities introduced a noncontributory old age pension scheme, which is still in force. Subject to a means test, this scheme provides a flat-rate pension to all citizens of Malta who are sixty or older and to the blind. Since 1974–75 it has also applied to severe mental illnesses and serious handicaps.

Comprehensive national welfare schemes, however, were not introduced until the first Mintoff government took office. The first two important measures—the National Assistance Act and the National Insurance Act—were introduced in 1956. The noncontributory National Assistance Act provides financial assistance for needy households, cash benefits for the chronically ill, and special assistance for the unemployed. The contributory National Insurance Act incorporated the 1934 Workers' Compensation Ordinance and was modeled on the United Kingdom's National Insurance Scheme. This act provides cash benefits for marriage, maternity, child support, sickness, unemployment, widowhood, orphanhood, retirement, disability, and industrial accidents. Employees, employers, and the government each contribute one-twelfth of an employee's salary.

Social legislation remained unchanged between 1956 and 1971, when the Labour party took office. The new government extended the social security system and raised the benefits. Starting in 1979, it provided a retirement pension equal to two-thirds of the average of the highest wage or salary earned in any three years before retirement and gave widows five-ninths of that sum. Since 1982 self-employed persons have been entitled to two-thirds of their average earnings in the ten years prior to retirement.

The most important—and controversial—extension of welfare legislation was the socialization of medicine. In 1977 the government decreed that all doctors should serve for two years in the National Health Service, thus provoking a protracted confrontation with the medical profession. In 1978 the National Health Scheme provided free hospitalization (including any form of medical intervention) to all Maltese citizens, free outpatient service at the polyclinic, free dental health care and free vaccinations for school children, and free homes for old people. The scheme also established free community health care, making qualified nurses available for home care. In 1986 the scheme was extended to include subsidies to families who take care of the aged and the handicapped at home.

The budget for fiscal 1987 allotted Lm 54.7 million for expenditures under the 1956 National Insurance Act and Lm 17.7 million for expenditures under the National Health Act. The total, Lm 73.3 million, represents 38 percent of all recurring expenditures (Lm 192.5 million). Of the 73.3 million, Lm 36.5 million is covered by employers' and employees' contributions, and Lm 36.8 million (16 percent of the total ordinary revenue) is a burden on the budget.[9]

SECULARIZATION. To reduce the influence of the Catholic church, the government in 1978 eliminated Mass from public schools, an action that provoked a teachers' strike. In 1980 the government announced that all church-run schools would be required to admit pupils free of charge. At the time, about one-third of all children attended fee-charging parochial schools. The church complained that its funds were insufficient to offer free education, but it was reluctant to accept government subsidies for fear of losing its autonomy. Protracted negotiations led to a settlement virtually in accordance with government demands. The state also tried (unsuccessfully) to eliminate hospitals run by religious orders. The government did manage to reduce the church's considerable economic power through a 1983 law that transferred to the state any real property to which the church did not have a clear title. Since much of the land is held without clear title, the law, if enforced vigorously (which it does not appear to be), would confiscate the greater part of the church's substantial landholdings.

CONTROL OF HIGHER EDUCATION. The government seized total control of higher education. The Labour party was opposed to the Old University, founded in 1769, because of its elitist character and instead favored the recently founded College of Arts, Sciences, and Technology, which provided a modern, technical education. In 1978 the college was transformed into the New University, and the faculties of technology, medicine, and education were transferred to it from the Old University. In 1980 the Old University was closed.

The New University, unlike the old institution, does not offer degrees in the arts or sciences. Instead, it is organized along functional lines into the faculties of law, medicine and surgery, dental surgery, engineering and architecture, management studies, and education. The primary purpose of the New University is to serve the needs of the economy. All students must be sponsored by prospective employers, and periods of study alternate with periods of work. In practice, however, private sponsors are lacking, and the Malta Development Corporation is assuming the function of sponsorship.

WORKER MANAGEMENT. As one of its measures for promoting social equality, the government has encouraged workers to participate in the management of industry. To date, worker participation has been fully implemented only in the case of the dry docks, traditionally the most troubled enterprise in Malta.

Before the 1971 election, a seven-month strike occurred in the dry docks over the differences in working conditions and equity between blue-collar and white-collar workers. On assuming office, the Labour government appointed a managing board of four government and four union representatives and in 1975 instituted a system of self-management. Every two years workers elected a council, which was given a voice in management decisions. In other industries, too, a movement was initiated to put worker-directors on company boards. The dockyard workers, who make up the core of Labour party support, were satisfied with the new system, but others, especially in the private sector, regarded it with considerable skepticism.

Economic Performance, 1971–87

The long rule of the Labour party from 1971 to 1985 can be broken into two periods. In the first, from 1971 to 1980, the economy underwent remarkable expansion as a result of export-led growth. Its record even compared favorably with that of Hong Kong and Singapore over the same period. This accomplishment is particularly noteworthy in light of the tight government controls.

Over the 1970s GNP increased by 160 percent (table 6-11). Exports of goods and services grew even faster, more than tripling over the decade.

Table 6-11. Basic Economic Indicators, 1971–80
(millions of 1980 Maltese liri)

Indicator	1971	1975	1980
GNP	162.4	251.2	422.5
Private consumption	167.1	182.7	253.5
Government consumption	36.5	43.5	63.5
Gross domestic investment	63.4	57.0	96.5
Exports of goods and services	111.6	196.1	356.6
Resource balance	−117.9	−56.1	−21.4

Source: World Bank 1989.

In 1971 Malta had a real trade deficit amounting to two-thirds of GNP. By 1980 this had fallen to only about 5 percent. Because Malta was depending less on external resources, domestic absorption grew much more slowly than GNP. Hong Kong's GNP growth was significantly better than Malta's over the decade, but Singapore's was just slightly better.

Manufacturing and tourism led the expansion. Employment in manufacturing increased from 20,662 in 1971 to 34,476 in 1980; manufacturing's share of total employment rose from 20 to 30 percent, and its share of total value added from 15 to 25 percent. Real earnings per worker in manufacturing more than doubled over the decade. The export-oriented character of the manufacturing expansion can be seen in the share of output exported, which rose from 35 percent in 1971 to 60 percent in 1980. The number of tourists rose from 179,000 in 1971 to 729,000 in 1980, and hotel employment increased from 3,315 to 5,189 over the same period. Merchandise exports, mainly manufactures, grew slightly faster than tourism and other services, each contributing roughly half of total export earnings in 1980.

The improvement in living standards in the late 1970s and early 1980s is especially clear from the flow of emigration. Throughout the 1950s and up to the mid-1970s the number of emigrants exceeded the number of returning migrants by a substantial margin. Since then, however, the number of emigrants has declined, while the number of returning migrants has increased, leading to a net inflow in most years (table 6-12).

The return migration is explained by a mass exodus of Maltese from the United Kingdom, once the principal destination of emigrants (table 6-13). Malta apparently became preferable to England. The number of returnees from Canada also exceeded the number of new emigrants, while emigrants to Australia and the United States continued to outnumber those returning.

Starting in 1980 the rate of GNP growth slowed, and it turned negative in 1983 (table 6-14). The movement in GNP seems to have been driven by two exogenous components, the export of goods and services, on the one hand, and gross fixed capital formation (GFCF), on the other. Exports rose sharply during the phase of rapid GNP growth from 1978 to 1980, whereas GFCF rose only slowly. Exports declined from 1981 to 1983, pulling GNP down despite a spurt in GFCF.

This downturn in exports came about in part because of the world economic slowdown, particularly in Western Europe; the policy of maintaining the Maltese lira at an appreciated level to cheapen imports; and, possibly, the growth of wages and associated labor costs in Malta. One econometric study has suggested that the world slump and the loss of competitiveness were responsible for 13.5 and 10.5 percent, respectively, of the 24 percent decline in Maltese exports (below trend) between 1979 and 1982 (Scicluna 1984). Tourism, another important source of income, also slumped sharply; the number of arrivals decreased from 729,000 in

Table 6-12. Population, Emigration, and Return Migration, 1962–86

Year	Population	Emigration	Return migration
1961	301,487	3,580	451
1962	302,938	641	525
1963	300,162	6,579	536
1964	298,857	8,987	495
1965	296,505	8,090	520
1966	299,814	4,340	193
1967	302,218	3,971	36
1968	301,913	2,922	343
1969	301,632	2,648	282
1970	301,539	2,696	317
1971	301,453	2,798	143
1972	300,979	3,163	202
1973	299,657	4,059	230[a]
1974	299,903	4,189	535[a]
1975	303,263	1,624	2,957
1976	307,563	1,107	2,472
1977	311,580	1,237	2,261
1978	314,135	1,577	1,678
1979	318,051	1,303	2,289
1980	320,938	1,373	1,753
1981	322,993	1,966	1,644
1982	326,178	938	1,193
1983	329,189	641	1,052
1984	331 996	629	654
1985	340,907[b]	731	700
1986	343,334	737	622

a. Refers to migrants who returned within two years of emigration.
b. Census data.
Source: Malta, Central Statistical Office, Annual Abstract of Statistics, various issues.

Table 6-13. Emigration and Return Migration, by Country, 1979–85

Country	Emigration	Return migration	Balance
Australia	6,666	5,420	1,246
Canada	1,445	1,596	−151
United Kingdom	493	3,834	−3,341
United States	1,150	699	451
All others	142	48	94
Total	9,896	11,597	−1,701

Source: Malta, Central Statistical Office, Annual Abstract of Statistics, 1985.

Table 6-14. GNP *at Constant 1973 prices, 1977–84*
(millions of Maltese liri)

Indicator	1977	1978	1979	1980	1981	1982	1983	1984
Consumption	131	136	140	149	154	158	160	167
Government expenditures	31	35	38	39	42	44	44	43
Gross fixed capital formation	36	35	39	40	46	53	62	57
Inventory changes	2	5	5	9	13	26	6	7
Exports of goods and services	140	147	172	192	170	147	144	150
Imports of goods and services	141	136	149	166	153	150	140	145
GDP	200	222	245	263	271	278	276	279
Investment income from abroad	13	12	10	15	22	25	19	22
GNP	213	234	256	281	293	302	295	300

Sources: Malta, *National Accounts of the Maltese Islands*, 1983; Central Statistical Office.

1980 to 480,000 in 1984. Emigration responded with a lag, but by 1984 the number of emigrants once again exceeded the number of returnees.

In the mid-1980s the situation changed for the better. European recovery stimulated demand for Malta's exports. Tourism, encouraged by currency discounts offered to tour operators, revived; in 1988 there were 746,000 arrivals, more than at the 1980 peak. In 1985 real GDP grew by 2.5 percent, in 1986 it climbed 4 percent, and in 1987 it moved even faster. By election time the economic crisis was over.

Conclusions

During the long rule of the Labour party, Malta's economic record was one of successful export-oriented growth in manufacturing and tourism, which allowed the country to create a strong welfare state. Although statistics are meager, Malta seems to have had a remarkably equitable income distribution, with no visible signs of either luxury or poverty. In the export industries, Maltese entrepreneurs collaborated easily with international corporations.

State enterprise in Malta consists, on the one hand, of banking, transport, and public utilities that manage to be profitable because of their monopolistic position and, on the other hand, of capital-intensive projects heavily cofinanced by foreign partners, mainly Libya. As a consequence, these low-yielding ventures are a great drain on local resources, at least in the short run. Joint Maltese-Libyan companies have been formed for the express purpose of supplying the Libyan market. Libya is now Malta's fourth largest customer (after Germany, the United Kingdom, and Italy) and is the only country with which Malta has a large positive trade balance. At least up to now, Malta has been able to generate business for such ventures as shipbuilding by astutely exploiting political rivalries among world powers.

The fact remains, however, that during the years of Labour rule Malta was highly dependent on donor aid and on economic contracts granted for political reasons—as in the case of its contracts with Libya. Moreover, Malta's restrictive trade policy was a serious obstacle to a sustained increase in prosperity. Instead of attempting to make the island the Mediterranean marketplace at the crossroads between North Africa and southern Europe, Maltese citizens did as much shopping as they could in Sicily, which was also the source of much smuggling to Malta. Exports of services and higher value added manufactures were also hindered by this policy.

The Nationalist government that took office in 1987 is cautiously moving toward a freer, more open economy and plans to make Malta into a center of offshore business. New incentives to attract foreign investment have been put into place. But controls have been difficult to remove, for over the years vested interests have grown up around trade restraints and internal regulations.

Notes

1. For a brief history of Malta, see Blouet (1984).

2. Traditional society consisted of a small priestly, professional, and business class and the mass of poor peasants and workers. World War II and the years immediately after brought increased geographic mobility, greater access to jobs, and improved education. These changes generated demands for greater social opportunity and economic equality, and the democratization of political life and the universal franchise made it possible to translate these aspirations into political action.

3. The consultants were instructed to carry out a general survey of Malta's economic situation, suggest how Malta's economy could be improved and strengthened through capital development projects and other government action, indicate to what extent Malta could legitimately expect economic aid from the United Kingdom, and state what economic measures should be adopted to implement a closer union with the United Kingdom in conformity with the views of the Maltese government (see Schuster 1950: i).

4. The problems caused by the withdrawal of the armed forces led the United Kingdom and Malta to appoint a joint mission in 1967 to explore ways of promoting industrial growth and employment and to provide estimates of the number of jobs that could be created. The committee's report reiterated the need to improve infrastructure and came out strongly in favor of more and better training. The available incentives were deemed satisfactory. In the committee's opinion, 15,000 jobs could be created in the 1969–74 period, 7,000 of them in industry. See *Report of the Mission to Malta* (1967).

5. In addition to its initial contribution, Libya extended to Malta a US$28 million concessionary loan to finance a new pier at Marsa (July 1975), a US$3 million concessionary loan (1976), and a Lm 23 million grant (1979) to be spent over the next four years. Libya also participated—both through the Libyan Arab Maltese Holding Co., in which it holds a 53 percent interest, and directly—in

financing numerous investments. Under a 1972 agreement extended by a 1977 protocol, China constructed a harbor dock (nicknamed the "red dock") a highway tunnel linking Valetta and Slima, a breakwater covering a container ship terminal, and two public sector factories. In 1976 the EEC agreed to provide grants and concessionary loans amounting to 26 million European currency units over a period of five years and US$25 million in October 1983. In 1976 Saudi Arabia gave Malta a US$10 million soft loan for the construction of a new port at Marsaxlokk. Another credit, amounting to Lm 8 million, was granted in 1978, and the United Arab Emirates contributed Lm 2.8 million for port development. In 1981 Malta received a US$20 million loan from Saudi Arabia for the port of Valetta and a US$5 million grant for the Marsa shipyard. Italian contributions started modestly with a gift of turbines and transformers for Malta's Electricity Authority in 1976. In 1980, however, Italy pledged US$12 million in assistance for four years, a concessionary credit of US$15 million for development, and a US$4 million grant for projects of technical, social, economic, and cultural cooperation. This list is far from exhaustive.

6. To give one example of the intricate political maneuvers, Mintoff pursued a policy of strict neutrality from the time of his 1971 election. In 1977, however, frustrated by his inability to obtain Western European funds, he warned that neutrality "could not possibly survive indifference of the EEC" and threatened to sign a military pact with Libya. In 1980 Italy signed a treaty recognizing Malta's neutrality and pledged aid. Nevertheless, in 1984 Mintoff signed, on behalf of Malta, a five-year mutual defense pact with Libya.

7. The government counted on a grant from Italy to help finance its 1987 capital projects, but the Italian Senate delayed approval of the grant. To fill the gap, Malta issued short-term notes.

8. The data are government budget estimates. For a discussion of the rationale of government investment activities, see Grech (1986).

9. Employers, employees, and the government each contribute one-twelfth of the employees' wages. In the case of self-employed persons, the government matches the one-twelfth contribution of the earner. In addition to the budgetary contributions, the government as employer will pay Lm 5.8 million in 1987. The health scheme is noncontributory, and its burden falls entirely on the budget (see Malta 1987).

References

Balogh, Thomas, and Dudley Seers. 1955. *The Economic Problems of Malta: An Interim Report*. Malta: Government Printing Office.

Blouet, Brian. 1984. *The Story of Malta*. Malta: Progress.

Central Bank of Malta. 1986. *The Banking System in Malta*. Valetta.

Grech, John C. 1986. *Private Initiative and State Encroachment*. Malta: Chamber of Commerce.

Malta. 1985. *Malta Handbook*. Valetta.

——. Various issues. *Quarterly Digest of Statistics*. Valetta.

——. Various issues. *National Accounts of the Maltese Islands*. Valetta.

Malta, Central Statistical Office. 1983. *Census of Industrial Production*. Valetta.

——. Various issues. *Annual Abstract of Statistics*. Valetta.

——. Various issues. *Statistical Abstract of the Maltese Islands*. Valetta.

Malta, Chamber of Commerce. 1981. *The Realities of Bulk-Buying*. Valetta.

Malta, Department of Information. 1959. *Development Plan for Maltese Islands 1959–1964*. Malta.

Malta, Ministry of Finance and Customs. 1987. *Estimates 1987*. Malta.

Malta Round Table Conference. 1955. *Report*. London: Her Majesty's Stationery Office.

Report of the Mission to Malta. 1967. Command 3366. London: Her Majesty's Stationery Office.

Schuster, George E. 1950. *Interim Report on the Financial and Economic Structure of the Maltese Islands*. Malta: Government Printing Office.

Scicluna, Edward. 1984. *Export Competitiveness and the Maltese Economy*. Malta: Federation of Industries.

Stolper, Wolfgang F., Rune R. Hellberg, and Sten Ove Callender. 1964. "Economic Adaptation and Development in Malta." United Nations, Commissioner for Technical Assistance, Department of Economic and Social Affairs, New York.

United Kingdom, Colonial Office. 1946. *Report on the Finances of the Government of Malta*. London: His Majesty's Stationery Office.

World Bank. 1989. *World Tables. 1988–89 Edition*. Baltimore, Md.: Johns Hopkins University Press.

7 *The Comparative Study*

Ronald Findlay
Stanislaw Wellisz

This chapter compares the five economies in several respects, beginning with their growth performance over the period 1960 to 1985.

Growth Performance between 1960 and 1985

In 1960, at the onset of the period covered by this study, the per capita incomes of the five economies fell within a relatively narrow range, with Hong Kong at the top (US$1,737) and Mauritius at the bottom (US$1,012). The disparity between these extremes was only 70 percent. Singapore and Jamaica were close to Hong Kong, and Malta was about 20 percent above Mauritius (table 7-1).[1]

By 1985 the picture had changed drastically. Singapore, followed by Hong Kong, was well over US$9,000 per capita and was approaching the level of the industrial countries. Jamaica was at the bottom with US$1,725, having been overtaken by Mauritius, now slightly higher at US$1,869. Malta had become the median member at a level more than twice that of the laggards and slightly more than half that of the two star performers. The disparity between top and bottom, only 70 percent in 1960, had skyrocketed to 460 percent. Jamaica's per capita income had grown only 17 percent in twenty-five years, whereas that of Singapore had risen more than 500 percent. These two small, open economies represent the most dramatic extremes in growth performance experienced in the entire developing world.

Although Singapore in 1960 had the second highest per capita income among the five economies, the future looked precarious. The British naval base and entrepôt trade had been the mainstays of its existence, but the British were about to withdraw their military forces from the Far East. Although Hong Kong, too, relied on entrepôt trade—which had been seriously disrupted by the revolution on the mainland—it had already begun an impressive career as an exporter of labor-intensive manufactured exports. Malta, even more dependent than Singapore on

Table 7-1. Real GDP *Per Capita in 1980 International Prices, Selected Years,*
1960–85
(U.S. dollars)

Year	Jamaica	Mauritius	Malta	Hong Kong	Singapore
1960	1,472	1,012	1,282	1,737	1,528
1965	1,807	1,153	1,355	2,704	1,753
1970	2,422	1,025	2,068	3,555	2,869
1975	2,293	1,367	3,099	4,521	4,130
1980	1,857	1,484	4,630	7,268	5,817
1985	1,725	1,869	5,319	9,093	9,834

Source: Summers and Heston 1987, supplement.

British military expenditures, found the prospect of the withdrawal
particularly threatening. Mauritius was also in dire straits; its population
was growing more than 3 percent a year and putting extreme pressure
on the land, which at this point was devoted almost entirely to the
cultivation of sugar.

Jamaica, by contrast, seemed to have a bright future. Just five years
earlier its income per capita had been below that of Mauritius and only
slightly higher than that of Malta. But then bauxite production got under
way, bringing great prosperity to the island during the second half of the
1950s and driving per capita income up even faster than in Hong Kong.
In contrast, Mauritius suffered an absolute decline. By 1960 Jamaica was
well past the levels of Mauritius and Malta and was close to that of
Singapore. By 1965 the continuing bauxite boom had pushed Jamaica
ahead of Singapore in per capita income.

The most rapid progress, however, was made by Hong Kong, where
labor-intensive manufactured exports were beginning to fuel the engine
of growth. Malta was making only slow progress, while Mauritius was
stagnating, its income fluctuating from year to year in response to the
swings in sugar prices and climatic conditions.

In the second half of the 1960s Singapore joined Hong Kong as an
exporter of labor-intensive manufactures, after the British withdrawal
and the break with Malaysia. Starting later and with a smaller base,
Singapore found its economy growing even faster than that of Hong
Kong. Malta also did well after the British withdrawal because of its
thriving tourism and manufactured exports. Income per capita rose
sharply and the rate of emigration declined, despite the fall in revenues
from the naval base. Mauritius was still entirely dependent on sugar and
was now in the doldrums. In Jamaica the bauxite boom showed signs of
faltering, and per capita income grew only 6 percent in five years.

During the 1970s Hong Kong and Singapore continued on the path of
spectacular growth, despite the oil shocks of that decade and the associated disruptions in the world economy. Malta also made significant

progress with the help of manufactured exports and tourism. Mauritius got on the bandwagon at last when its manufactured exports enclave, in the form of the Export Processing Zone (EPZ), began to take off. It was also bolstered by the profits from the sugar boom of the first half of the decade, which improved its terms of trade from 100 in 1970 to 214 in 1975. When sugar prices fell and the second oil shock hit toward the end of the decade, the EPZ was able to weather the storm. Jamaica, however, ran into severe problems. Although it received the benefits of an increased bauxite levy in the early 1970s, the Manley regime's deficit-financed public expenditures and policies hostile to the private sector precipitated a disastrous decline.

In the first half of the 1980s, deteriorating terms of trade forced both Jamaica and Mauritius to retrench public expenditure and adopt stabilization programs sponsored by the IMF. Mauritius managed to make a good recovery spearheaded by tourism and manufactured exports from the EPZ. Jamaica, however, was unable to find any alternative to the bauxite industry, which its own policies had undermined, and recovery was slow despite the apparent market orientation of the Seaga regime. Malta performed quite impressively, while Singapore and Hong Kong continued their vigorous export-oriented growth in spite of the world economic slowdown of the early 1980s.

The table below (based on table 7-1) summarizes the performance of the five economies during the period 1960–85.

	GNP per capita, 1985 (1960 = 100)
Jamaica	117
Mauritius	185
Malta	415
Hong Kong	551
Singapore	643

On the basis of that performance, the five small economies can be grouped according to three patterns.

1. The brilliant success stories of Singapore and Hong Kong, both city-states with predominantly Chinese populations, "autonomous" governments, and liberal trading regimes, but without natural resources.

2. The poor performance of Jamaica and, to a lesser extent, Mauritius, both resource-abundant primary exporters with ethnically mixed populations, a competitive parliamentary government subject to interest group pressures, and interventionist economic policies.

3. The moderate performance of Malta, which—like Hong Kong and, to a lesser extent, Singapore—is ethnically homogeneous and has no natural resources other than a harbor and strategic location and which

is similar to Jamaica and Mauritius in having a parliamentary system and a record of intervention in economic policy.

Determinants of the Growth Patterns

The first explanation that might come to mind for the variation in growth patterns is that it has something to do with the availability of natural resources. That is simply false for these economies, since the least endowed, Singapore and Hong Kong, perform the best, whereas the best endowed, Jamaica, has the worst record.

During the 1950s, in the early days of development economics, domestic saving and capital formation were regarded as the key constraints on economic growth. It was suggested, by Arthur Lewis and others, that the main task was to raise saving and investment rates from about 5 percent of national income to about 12–15 percent. All five economies, even Jamaica, were able to do this quite easily, and Singapore has posted an unbelievable increase of savings, to more than 40 percent of GDP.

Nor do the differences in human capital formation and education account for the variation in growth outcomes. The population of Hong Kong may be more energetic and enterprising, on average, than that of Jamaica, but it is not noticeably better educated in a formal sense. In fact, when it comes to education, the multilingual Maltese and Mauritians have the most impressive record, while Jamaica also holds its own quite well in health and literacy.

Hollis Chenery would have suggested considering foreign exchange as a possible constraint, but it certainly played no role in the five economies. Hong Kong, Singapore, Malta, and Mauritius all took advantage of the opportunity to expand and open markets for manufactures in the advanced countries. Jamaica alone was not able to do so, clearly because of internal rather than external obstacles. Phases in which primary exports brought handsome returns led to successful diversification in the case of the sugar boom of the 1970s in Mauritius but generated extravagant waste in the case of the bauxite levy in Jamaica.

A prominent idea among economists in the late 1960s and 1970s was that there is a tradeoff in development between growth and equity. Accordingly, members of this school might argue that the city-states sacrificed the latter to the former, while Jamaica and Mauritius did the opposite. Here again, the reality is the reverse. Labor-intensive manufactured exports led to rapid employment growth and higher wages in Hong Kong and Singapore, whereas in Jamaica stagnation and decline have worsened the already skewed income distributions of an economy well endowed with natural resources developed by large foreign enterprises.

The last of the "suspects" usually blamed or credited for development performance is economic policy. Indeed, that is the real "culprit" in this case. The single most important factor here is that Hong Kong and

Singapore have consistently implemented market-oriented policies within a stable monetary and fiscal framework over the entire period under consideration. Similarly, Malta and Mauritius have by and large adhered to "sound" monetary and fiscal policy, although they have intervened extensively in the allocation of resources and in the distribution of income; both, however, relied more on the market once they recognized their policy mistakes. In contrast, Jamaica—particularly during the Manley regime of the 1970s—lost control over its budget and money supply and tried to squeeze more revenue out of primary exports rather than create new sources of wealth through exports. Policies that are hostile to the private sector are particularly costly in a highly open economy such as Jamaica, with its historical connections to Britain and proximity to the United States. Such policies merely encourage multinational corporations, small businessmen, and skilled professionals to leave, to the long-term detriment of the local economy.

Although policy is clearly important, it does not follow that pure laissez-faire must be the path to success. Hong Kong is the only one of the five that comes close to this state, but even there the government has intervened in land use and in the provision of public housing. Singapore's government has intervened in the labor market and in the savings decisions of households via the Central Provident Fund (CPF). It has also provided several inducements—notably a strong infrastructure—for direct foreign investment. Both Hong Kong and Singapore have been free of trade restrictions, and this fact has obviously been a primary ingredient of their success. Malta, despite its tiny size, has attempted to combine import substitution with export-oriented manufacturing, a strategy that has probably held back its growth. Mauritius only began to prosper on a sustained basis with the establishment of the EPZ.

Economic policy in any given country at any given time is influenced by what might be called the current *Zeitgeist*—a mixture of the theories in fashion and the notable successes and failures in other countries. Thus, after World War II the idea of planning was obviously in the air, perhaps because of the combined influence of the Soviet example and the Fabian doctrines associated with the British Labour party. Few believed that foreign trade could be an engine of growth, and as a result, countries throughout the developing world emphasized import substitution instead. All five economies discussed here, with the exception of Hong Kong—perhaps because of its lack of political independence—were subject to these influences in the 1950s and 1960s. In the 1970s the pendulum began to swing in the opposite direction under the influence of Ronald Reagan and Margaret Thatcher and, more important, the success of the newly industrializing economies (NIEs) of East Asia, including Hong Kong and Singapore. The World Bank and the IMF also played an important role in giving institutional expression to these ideas of what constitutes successful development policy.

The career of Michael Manley reflects these swings vividly. His first period in office during the 1970s was clearly inspired by the revolutionary example of Castro's Cuba, the success of the OPEC cartel, and the UNCTAD concept of a "new international economic order." After the bitter failure of the strategy guided by this example, Manley, in his second administration, began stressing the need for liberal market-oriented policies, although the economy still does not appear to be responding to any signals emanating from the government.

In keeping with the "new political economy" viewpoint adopted in our study, we shall attempt to account for the differences in economic policy in our five economies by looking at interest group pressures and the goals of the governing elites. The governments of both Hong Kong and Singapore are able to act with a high degree of "autonomy," relatively free of special interests. This state of affairs has enabled them to consistently pursue policies that benefit their societies as a whole over the long run, such as monetary and fiscal stability and free trade. The other three economies operate under more open and contentious political systems in which the government at times tries to transfer income from some groups to others that it wishes to favor, often to the detriment of society as a whole.

Another factor of considerable influence is the degree of ethnic homogeneity of the society. Hong Kong and Singapore are both predominantly Chinese, although the latter has significant Malay and Indian minorities. Malta is also ethnically homogeneous (which does not prevent vigorous political competition between parties on economic, social, and religious issues). In Jamaica and Mauritius class differences are accentuated by ethnic ones, a situation that makes for contentious politics.

Although these sociopolitical variables certainly command attention, they in no way suggest that economic policy can be reduced to some simple function of the variables. The influence of external economic and political events and of strong personalities has been too great in these five economies to justify any such conclusions. Things might have gone very differently in each of the economies had it not been for the impact of such leaders as Ramgoolam in Mauritius, Dom Mintoff in Malta, the two Manleys in Jamaica, and, above all, Lee Kuan Yew in Singapore.

Hong Kong and Singapore: Alternative Export-Oriented Strategies for Successful Industrialization

The remarkable success of Hong Kong, Singapore, Korea, and Taiwan (China) over the past two to three decades has generally been attributed to the outward orientation of their trade regimes and development strategies and to the Confucian basis of their cultures, as manifested in their discipline, thrift, and respect for hard work. Although all four have indeed been successful, neither of these general explanations seems entirely satisfactory. The Confucian "ethic" has been present in East Asia for the past two and a half millennia and was even regarded as an obstacle to development by such eminent social scientists as Max Weber not too long ago. As for the outward orientation of the trade regime, it is not clear why this should be responsible for a sustained increase in the *rate* of growth as opposed to a mere rise in the *level* of real income, as predicted by the conventional argument for the gains from trade and comparative advantage.

It might be argued, of course, that the natural energy and enterprise of Chinese people has taken so long to manifest itself, and then only on the periphery of the mainland, because it has been persistently held down by a dominant bureaucratic state, which has altered its form but not its substance in the transition from the imperial dynasties to the present Communist regime. There are many well-documented examples of sustained expansions of production and trade in China that were ultimately throttled by excessive taxation and regulation by the imperial bureaucracy. Such impressive outward-looking feats as the voyages to Southeast Asia and East Africa during the Ming dynasty, which preceded Columbus and da Gama but were abruptly discontinued, provide further evidence of latent expansive tendencies constrained within the stifling framework of an immense land-based empire.

The development of Hong Kong and Singapore since World War II can be seen in this light—as instances of the opportunity to pursue profit and economic opportunity within a facilitating rather than restricting political environment, provided by British civil servants in the one case and by Lee Kuan Yew's People's Action party in the other. Is this simply, however, a matter of laissez-faire generating the inevitably successful outcome, as many would have it? It is by now well understood that the four East Asian NIEs by no means uniformly and collectively illustrate this proposition.

Extensive state intervention has occurred in Korea and, to a lesser extent, in Taiwan (China). Both are different from the city-states of Hong Kong and Singapore, which are also different from each other, as chapters 2 and 3 have demonstrated. It is time now to examine more closely the differences underlying their common pattern of export-oriented industrialization.

Consider, first, Hong Kong's total exports. They grew at a steady rate of about 9.5 percent a year in the twenty years from 1965 to 1985, whereas GDP rose by 8.5 percent in 1965–80 and by only 5.9 percent in 1980–85 (table 7-2). Hong Kong is therefore clearly a case of export-led growth, at least in the limited statistical sense of exports growing faster than other components of national income. Singapore, however, appears *not* to fit this pattern. Its total exports grew by only 4.8 percent over the 1965–80 period, rising to 5.9 percent in 1980–85, in both cases well below the annual GDP growth rates of 10.2 percent for 1965–80 and 6.5 percent for 1980–85.

Table 7-2. Growth Rates of GDP and Total Exports, Hong Kong and Singapore, 1965–85
(average annual percentage change)

Year	Hong Kong		Singapore	
	GDP	Total exports	GDP	Total exports
1965–80	8.5	9.5	10.2	4.8
1980–85	5.9	9.4	6.5	5.9

Source: World Bank 1987.

What is the explanation? It must be remembered that both Hong Kong and Singapore began as entrepôt centers and that reexports must therefore be taken into account. In 1950 almost 90 percent of total exports from Hong Kong consisted of reexports. The revolution in China, however, brought considerable refugee capital and entrepreneurship to Hong Kong, as it did to Taiwan (China). As a result, the colony developed rapidly as a manufacturing center for labor-intensive exports. By 1960 reexports had fallen to only 27 percent of total exports, declining further to about 19 percent by 1970. Then the opening up of mainland China again stimulated the growth of reexports, not only directly but as an intermediary between Taiwan (China), Korea, and China. In 1980 reexports constituted 30 percent of total exports. Between 1960 and 1980, therefore, the share of domestic exports fluctuated considerably but was roughly the same as at the beginning of the period in Hong Kong.

In Singapore, however, domestic exports were only 6 percent of total exports in 1960, and 10 percent of GNP. Singapore was thus more dependent on its entrepôt role in 1960 than Hong Kong was in 1950. It was only after independence and the break from Malaysia that domestic manufactured exports took off—which they did with a vengeance. In 1982 domestic exports made up two-thirds of total exports, only slightly less than in Hong Kong, and 93 percent of GNP. In terms of *domestic* exports, then, there is no doubt that foreign trade has indeed been the engine of growth for the Singapore economy.[2]

Although both Hong Kong and Singapore have relied on exports to promote growth, their export sectors are quite different in character. Hong Kong's exports have typically been produced in small plants owned and operated by local residents using relatively little capital and unsophisticated technology. These small firms have been extremely adaptable and flexible, adept at moving into profitable lines and out of unprofitable ones very quickly. The early dependence on cheap clothing, footwear, plastic toys, and so on has been replaced by diversification into more expensive clothing with higher value added (including fashion items) and by electronics.

In Singapore multinational corporations have played an increasingly important role in exports, as well as in the economy in general. These corporations produce sophisticated components and items such as computer disk drives, semiconductors, printed circuit boards, and oil rigs. Petroleum refining also contributes substantially to Singapore's foreign exchange earnings. This pattern of exports is promoted by a conscious strategy of attracting direct foreign investment through fiscal concessions, peaceful labor relations, and physical and social infrastructure backed by heavy capital outlays by the government. The government also intervenes selectively in the pattern of production, consciously attempting to "pick winners" and to promote high-technology projects that are supposed to represent the wave of the future. The licensing process and a variety of negative and positive incentives—including wage policy—are used to keep foreign investment moving in the desired direction.

Foreign capital is important in the financial sector of Hong Kong but appears to be relatively unimportant in manufacturing, where overseas firms probably account for less than 10 percent of output, employment, and exports. Foreign firms, however, may have played a significant role in product innovation, initiating the production of digital watches and other electronic products that were quickly imitated by local firms.

In Singapore foreign investment contributed 57 percent of value added and exports in 1963 and 32 percent of employment in the manufacturing sector. By 1980 these ratios had risen to 81 percent of value added, 72 percent of employment, and 93 percent of exports. Foreign firms export about 75 percent of their output, compared with 52 percent for joint ventures and 25 percent for local establishments. Productivity growth in the different sectors varies positively with the proportion of foreign participation. The indigenous share of GDP fell to 75 percent in the early 1980s, in contrast to about 90 percent in the mid-1960s.

Despite its many limitations as an analytic concept, the incremental capital-output ratio (ICOR) is a useful indicator of the capital intensity and productivity of investment. The ICOR in Hong Kong remained at a surprisingly low level during the entire period under consideration. Between 1961 and 1973 GDP grew, on average, at a rate of 9.6 percent, whereas investment averaged 23 percent of GDP, yielding an ICOR of just 2.4. After the oil shock, the growth rate fell to 8.3 percent, the investment rate rose to 25 percent, and the ICOR moved up to 3, which is still very low.

In Singapore in 1960–65 the ICOR was also very low (table 7-3). During 1966–73, the period of export-oriented labor-intensive industrialization, the share of investment doubled, but the rate of growth more than doubled and the ICOR fell slightly. At the onset of the world recession that followed the first oil shock, Singapore's rate of GDP growth dropped to 6.4 percent a year, while the share of investment in GDP rose to 40.0 percent, and the ICOR to 6.2—that is, to twice the value of Hong Kong's ICOR. In 1978–83 GDP grew 8.8 percent a year, and although the invest-

Table 7-3. Singapore: Four Phases of Growth, 1960–83

Phase	Year	GDP growth (annual average percentage change)	Investment/GDP (percent)	Incremental capital-output ratio (ICOR)
I	1960–65	5.7	15.6	2.7
II	1966–73	12.3	32.1	2.6
III	1974–77	6.4	40.0	6.2
IV	1978–83	8.8	43.3	5.0

Source: For GDP growth rate and investment/GDP, Lee Soo Ann 1984.

ment/GDP ratio edged even higher, the ICOR fell to 5.0—still a high figure compared with Hong Kong's rate.

One explanation for the differences between Hong Kong's and Singapore's ICORs can be found in their development strategies. Hong Kong's development took place under a minimalist government that sought to limit infrastructural investments to bare essentials and to cover their cost, if possible, by user charges. The government in Singapore was much more active. It made use of the Central Provident Fund (CPF) to raise aggregate savings. It invested heavily in infrastructure and picked and promoted potential winners from among private investors. In 1960, before the economy took off, Singapore's ratio of gross domestic savings (GDS) to GDP equaled 5 percent. By 1965 it had doubled, but it was still low, at 10 percent; consumption amounted to a high 80 percent of GDP. In subsequent years, savings, spurred by the CPF legislation, rose rapidly, reaching 31 percent of GDP in 1977. By 1982 the GDS/GDP ratio had risen to 40 percent—among the highest in the world—while the ratio of private consumption to GDP had fallen to 48 percent, one of the lowest in the world. By contrast, the private consumption/GDP ratio remained virtually unchanged in Hong Kong, which was able to maintain a high growth rate with a relatively modest investment rate of 25 percent through efficient allocation of capital to labor-intensive industry. Singapore's growth was achieved through capital-intensive investment at the cost of a much greater savings effort.

In general, the East Asian NIEs are economies with free labor markets in which wages and employment are determined competitively by demand and supply, not by institutions such as activist trade unions backed up by pro-labor legislation, as in advanced industrial countries or in many developing countries. Hong Kong is close to laissez-faire, and Singapore's docile government-controlled unions negotiate wages and working conditions in a framework that is designed not to place any obstacles in the way of foreign or domestic employers, with the important exception of contributions to the CPF.

The population has grown much faster in Hong Kong than in Singapore because of intermittent massive waves of immigration from China. Between 1960 and 1980 the population of Hong Kong increased by 64 percent, whereas in Singapore it increased by 46 percent. Since the growth of GNP per capita has been higher in Singapore, employment growth would be expected to be slower than in Hong Kong and the rise in real wages to be greater. It is therefore surprising to find exactly the opposite.

Between 1961 and 1976 employment in Hong Kong rose at a rate of 3.1 percent a year, whereas in Singapore it rose by as much as 3.7 percent a year between 1957 and 1979 (Fields 1985). The explanation, in part, is that female labor force participation increased sharply in Singapore, from about 19 percent in 1957 to 42 percent in 1979. Unemployment in Singapore was also rather high in 1960, running at about 13 percent of the labor force, but by 1979 it had been eliminated.

The biggest surprise, however, is in the growth of real wages. From 1960 to 1980 average real monthly earnings rose by 140 percent in Hong Kong but by only 33 percent in Singapore. How can this be explained?

One possibility is to look at the employer's contribution to the CPF, perhaps the single most significant institution in Singapore. Labor remuneration in an economy as open to foreign investment as Singapore's must be governed by the necessity for consistency with the world rate of return. The effective incidence of any "employer's contribution" is therefore not going to be on the employer himself but on the worker. Since the inception of the CPF scheme, the employer's (and employees') compulsory contributions were raised repeatedly up to the middle of the 1980s, reaching levels of about 25 percent each. The figures reported by Fields (1985) do not include the employer's contribution, but since that contribution is in effect a wage tax, it should be added to real monthly earnings. A wage of 100 in 1960 with no employer's contribution rose to 133 in 1980, net of 25 percent contribution. After the contribution is added in, real monthly earnings, gross of tax, can be calculated at an index of 165 in 1980 in relation to 1960. This calculation in part helps explain the shortfall in relation to Hong Kong, but there is still a gap.

Fields attributes the difference to the "repressive" control of wages by the National Wages Council. This tripartite body issues annual guidelines to industry which, although they are not mandatory, receive considerable attention in the local media and in the academic literature, suggesting that they somehow influence real wages. If this view is correct, then the real wage in Singapore for much of the 1960–80 period must have been below the equilibrium, or market-clearing, level, and formal or informal labor rationing must have been necessary. There is no evidence that any such mechanisms were ever instituted or needed, although complaints continually arise about high labor turnover, or "job hopping." If wages had been significantly depressed below market-clearing levels, there would have been more direct evidence of the consequences of rationing. Since there is no evidence to this effect, it cannot be assumed that deliberate and successful repression by the government took place. What seems more likely is that the capital-intensive mix of activities and projects that the government chose, as revealed by the rising ICORs, reduced the demand for labor in comparison with the more labor-intensive mix in Hong Kong, thus slowing the rise in wages in relation to any given shift in supply.

The government has, however, significantly influenced the supply of labor through social measures: it has increased the participation of the female labor force, located housing close to industrial parks, provided childcare facilities, and so on. It has also permitted a controlled and selective influx of guest workers, particularly in the construction industry. Foreign workers constituted as much as 11 percent of the labor force in 1980.

To sum up, the government has affected the labor market in Singapore on both the demand and supply sides by influencing the composition of output and by promoting the participation of females and foreign workers in the economy. This is not the same as keeping real wages below the equilibrium level.

The best way to compare Hong Kong's laissez-faire strategy with the activist techniques of Singapore is to examine those infrastructural outlays by the government that were specifically designed to attract foreign investment, comparing them with the present discounted value of the future stream of returns brought in by the direct foreign investment, net of all remittances and subsidies paid to foreign corporations. Figure 7-1 illustrates how this might be done: the distance OA measures the income that direct foreign investment would generate for the host country in the absence of any special inducements. That is, it represents the laissez-faire return that accrues to a society such as Hong Kong.

We postulate that there is a significant discontinuity, or indivisibility, in the relationship between infrastructural outlays and the net income from the direct foreign investment that they bring in because the return curve $AB'F$ is flat from A to B'; that is, outlays below the level of OB on the horizontal axis do not bring in any additional income. Beyond OB the return is positive, but with diminishing marginal returns, as indicated by the concave segment $B'F$ of the returns function.

The 45-degree line indicates the cost on the vertical axis of the corresponding outlays on infrastructure. The optimal strategy is to choose a level of outlays OC^* at which the slope of the returns function is equal to unity; in other words, marginal return is equal to marginal cost. The point E, at which the vertical axis is intersected by the tangent to the returns function at OC^* level of outlays, indicates the "surplus" OE from the "project." Depending on the position of the returns function $AB'F$, the distance OE could be bigger or smaller than OA.

This implies that there is no a priori reason why either strategy should be preferred. The choice would depend on the circumstances in each case. The Singapore solution, as already mentioned, calls on the state and its technocrats to play a more active role than does Hong

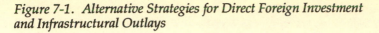

Figure 7-1. Alternative Strategies for Direct Foreign Investment and Infrastructural Outlays

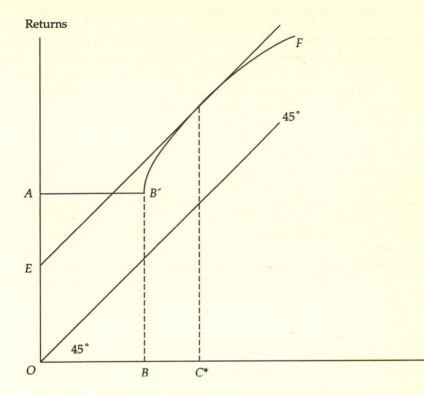

Outlays on infrastructure

Kong's decentralized solution. Thus the choice appears to be guided primarily by political factors. In Hong Kong the government acted as if it were the guardian of commercial and local business interests. In Singapore the government assumed a leadership role that consisted in part of intervening in all major aspects of the city-state's economic and social life.

The Transition in Two Primary-Exporting Economies

Jamaica and Mauritius, despite their different geographic locations, had developed along parallel lines up to World War II. Sugar was the primary export in each case and was particularly important for Mauritius. In Jamaica the labor force consisted primarily of the descendants of former African slaves; in Mauritius it was mainly composed of the descendants of indentured workers from India, both Hindu and Muslim. With the discovery of extensive bauxite deposits in Jamaica in the 1950s, the two countries' development paths began to diverge. Jamaica increased its GNP at about 8 percent a year, an extremely high rate for that period, while per capita income in Mauritius fell by almost 20 percent over the decade as a result of high population growth and diminishing returns on land, which was almost entirely devoted to sugarcane. "The Overcrowded Barracoon" was the contemptuous title of a travel piece on Mauritius by V. S. Naipaul. Jamaica, in contrast, was being hailed as a success story. Meade (1961) in a rather pessimistic appraisal of the prospects for Mauritius, suggested that it look to Hong Kong and Jamaica as examples of how to successfully overcome its difficulties. He was half right.

In a resource-based plantation economy, growth can continue as long as there is the possibility of adding to the effective quantity of land, be it through additions of cultivated area of equal productivity or through land-saving technical progress. Problems arise, however, if the population outpaces the growth of the effective quantity of land. To simplify the analysis, consider a situation in which the effective land area and the terms of trade are constant but the population continues to grow. As more labor and capital are applied, rents will rise and the marginal product of capital and of labor will fall. If wages are determined by the marginal product of labor, they fall. With a sufficiently large fall in wages, manufacturing may become profitable; labor will be absorbed by industry, and the economy will take off again.[3] But labor may resist real wage cuts and fight to appropriate a part of the rising rents, or the government may do so on labor's behalf. The higher wages reduce the international competitiveness of domestic industry. Moreover, insofar as rentiers' propensity to save is higher than that of the wage earners or of the government, the redistributive measures reduce aggregate savings and investment.

Mauritius neared the Ricardian frontier in the 1950s. In the 1960s, contrary to Meade's advice, it pursued a high-wage policy. Although GDP per capita was declining, minimum wages were repeatedly raised, and the general real wage increased. The demand for labor in the sugar industry was virtually constant. Employment opportunities in the small, capital-intensive, import-substituting manufacturing sector were strictly limited. With a stagnant demand for labor and a labor force growing at 2 percent a year, unemployment was rising rapidly and the social situation was growing more tense.

When world sugar prices rose in 1972, the terms of trade for Mauritius improved rapidly. Wages and taxes rose, as did the landlords' incomes. The sugar taxes made the sugar industry an unattractive investment, however, and, since investment abroad was prohibited, the landlords disposed of their savings through other outlets. A highly educated group, the landlords constituted a pool of potential entrepreneurs. Why these Franco-Mauritians continued to be so energetic when they enjoyed an economically and socially privileged position is an interesting question. Perhaps their position was more precarious than meets the eye— there were not many of them, and they had nowhere to go.

A boom in raw materials usually strengthens the country's currency but handicaps other export-oriented activities and favors nontradables. Because of sharp labor segmentation, Mauritius by and large escaped that fate. Labor in the sugar fields and mills is exclusively male, as is most of the labor in the import-substituting sector. Organized male labor did not oppose legislation permitting the employment of women at lower wages in export-oriented industries because the female labor force constituted a noncompeting group, and indeed, wages brought in by women were a welcome addition to family income. For capital owners, too, the industry posed no threat. The import-substituting industries stood to profit from the export-oriented sector, insofar as the latter would raise domestic incomes and hence the demand for domestic products. Thus, the export zone met with strong support and little opposition. As the zone expanded, real wages rose, the export-oriented industries attracted male workers, the same minimum wage was applied to men and to women, and the duality of the economy became less pronounced.

In contrast, Jamaica's economy in the 1950s was much more diversified. Mauritius was a monoculture in which sugarcane accounted for 22 percent of GDP and sugar manufacturing for another 12 percent. Jamaica relied on agriculture for about 30 percent of its GDP, but only half of its agricultural production was for export, and although sugar was the main commodity, it was not the only one. Manufacturing generated a smaller proportion of GDP than in Mauritius (11 percent against 18 percent), but nonsugar manufacturing was more developed in Jamaica, where it contributed 8 percent of GDP (in contrast to 6 percent in Mauritius). Jamaica also had more highly developed tourism and services industries.

Between 1955 and 1973 in Jamaica bauxite spurred economic growth in the manner of a typical natural resource boom. During the initial period, between 1952 and 1959, value added by mining and refining (consisting almost entirely of bauxite and alumina) rose, on average, more than 20 percent a year; construction and installation was the second-fastest growing sector, with 16 percent a year. Manufacturing grew somewhat faster than GDP (8.6 percent against 8.3 percent a year). Of the principal sectors, agriculture grew at the slowest pace—2.2 percent a year. In the 1960s GNP growth slowed to 5 percent a year; the expansion of the bauxite-alumina sector slackened to 8 percent a year and that of manufacturing to 5.4 percent. Administration now grew the fastest, at 8.7 percent a year. Agriculture continued to grow, albeit at a very slow pace. Between 1964 and 1972 the value of agricultural production at constant prices rose by 24 percent, but that of export-oriented agriculture *fell* by 4 percent; during the same period the value added by sugar and sugar product manufacturing fell by 20 percent. Manufacturing of other tradables suffered, too, whereas nontradables, including goods manufactured for the increasingly protected home market, expanded. Jamaica developed a typical case of "Dutch disease" (see, for example, Corden 1984).

The events of the 1973–79 period show how inappropriate policies can stem growth. The socialist experiment of Michael Manley's government discouraged private activities. The inflow of foreign capital virtually ceased, and domestic capital and managerial and technical skills fled the island. Productive activities (manufacturing, mining, agriculture, and construction) declined, whereas defense and public administration grew at an accelerated pace (see table 7-4).

By increasing public expenditure, the Manley government succeeded in raising real wages between 1973 and 1976 despite the fall in aggregate income, thereby adding to the problems of the tradable sector. The expansion of governmental activities was financed, in part, by the proceeds of the bauxite levy imposed in 1973. In the preceding ten years rents and royalties had brought in a total of US$270 million; in the next ten years the levy generated US$1.7 billion. These proceeds still could not meet the mounting expenses. Toward the end of the 1970s the budget deficit climbed to more than 20 percent of GDP. The collapse at the end of the decade was followed by a period of painful retrenchment and reorientation.

The basic difference between the experience of these two economies is that Mauritius used part of the windfall from its natural resource boom to finance the expansion of outward-oriented activities (the EPZ industries), whereas Jamaica concentrated on expanding inward-oriented activities (import substitution and public projects). No doubt, expectations concerning the possible length of the boom also differed. In Mauritius everyone seemed to recognize the limits of sugar production, but in Jamaica the bauxite-alumina boom appeared long lasting; moreover, Michael Manley's government obviously underestimated the elasticity of demand for Jamaica's production.

Table 7-4. *Contribution to GDP, Jamaica, 1972–83*
(millions of 1974 Jamaican dollars)

Year	Material production[a]	Defense and public administration
1972	983	207
1973	954	251
1974	951	251
1975	920	265
1976	830	307
1977	793	328
1978	801	344
1979	764	360
1980	693	350

a. Agriculture, mining, manufacturing, and construction.
Source: World Bank data.

Differences can also be seen in the political economy of the two states. In Mauritius, as already mentioned, labor did not oppose the establishment of a low-wage, free-trade, export-oriented industry. In Jamaica a low-wage group would pose a threat to organized labor, even if it consisted mainly of women, since most occupations, including import-substituting manufacturing, are not gender-specific.

Furthermore, in Mauritius domestic capital was captive and entrepreneurs were not outwardly mobile, but in Jamaica both capital and entrepreneurs can easily emigrate. Because of its geographic situation, Jamaica is inherently more "open" than Mauritius. Distortions are therefore more costly for those who stay behind. These distortions, which had been triggered by a policy shaped by social and political factors, turned Jamaica's economic miracle of the 1950s and 1960s into a dismal failure over the next twenty years.

Political Economy and Economic Policy

To reiterate, the main reason for the enormous disparity in performance of the five economies is the character of their economic policies and the vigor and consistency with which the regimes in power pursued them. All five had been subject to the same British colonial influences up to 1960 or thereafter and to the same trends in international opinion on the manner in which development was to be tackled. Why they took different paths is explained by economic circumstances and opportunities, as well as by the different backgrounds of the political elites.

Up to the eve of World War II the British colonial authorities pursued more or less laissez-faire policies that reflected not only their general ideology but also budgetary prudence with respect to limiting the costs of maintaining an empire. The local oligarchies of planters and traders generally had their own way in questions regarding labor relations, taxation, and other matters affecting their interests. Laissez-faire in economic policy thus came to be associated with the colonial past and its privileged relics among the local populations. Gradual democratization in the form of an extended franchise and greater administrative powers for the former subjects had taken place even before World War II, but the trend accelerated when the Labour government of Clement Attlee came to power. Attlee and the nationalist politicians in the colonies came under the same intellectual influences, emanating from the Webbs, Harold Laski, and Fabian socialism generally. A comprehensive welfare state in Great Britain, financed by progressive taxation administered by an interventionist bureaucracy, would seem appropriate for the colonies as well. The British Colonial Office became increasingly concerned with the well-being of the local populations and the installation of political, economic, and social institutions that would enable the colonies to become viable sovereign states on the model of the mother country, despite their different backgrounds and conditions.

Powerful global trends reinforced these tendencies away from laissez-faire. The Great Depression and the Keynesian revolution undermined the belief in free enterprise and free trade, while the U.S.S.R.'s role in defeating Hitler spread the myth that central planning with an emphasis on heavy industry was the best formula for the rapid development of a backward economy. The "balanced growth" and "big push" doctrines of early development theorists such as Nurkse, Lewis, and Rosenstein-Rodan reflected a similar distrust of the power of free trade and the price mechanism to promote rapid growth in the developing countries of the postwar world.[4]

One of the most prominent manifestations of the new postwar climate in the colonies was the rapid development of the trade union movement, inspired by the example of the British Trades Union Council and the Labour party. Organized labor played a leading role in Jamaica, Mauritius, Malta, and Singapore, not only through unions but also through labor-oriented political parties. When independence was achieved—in Jamaica in 1962, in Malta in 1964, in Mauritius in 1968, and in Singapore in 1959 (separation from Malaysia took place in 1965), the ruling party in all the Westminster-type parliamentary regimes that took over from the British had strong links to the labor movement.

Jamaica is unusual in having two parties linked to the trade unions and competing for workers' support. The Jamaican Labour party was organized as an offshoot of the Bustamante Trade Union, whose founder, Alexander Bustamante, became prime minister in 1944, before full independence was granted. The rival, somewhat more left-oriented, People's National party was organized by another outstanding popular leader, Norman Manley. This party created a rival labor organization, the Trades Union Congress, with the help of which it won the 1955 election. The two parties have maintained their roots in organized labor and their relative positions in the right wing–left wing spectrum, and both developed strong patronage machines.

The situation in Malta is closer to that prevailing in Great Britain. About 70 percent of organized labor belongs to the General Workers' Trade Union (GWTU), which has at its core the dockyard workers and a strong radical tradition. The GWTU backed the Labour party throughout its time in power, from 1971 to 1987. The moderate Nationalist party draws support from members of white-collar and craft unions loosely organized into a Conference of Trade Unions and from unorganized members of the middle class.

In Mauritius Dr. Ramgoolam and his Labour party, strongly backed by Hindu plantation laborers, played a key role in the independence movement. But the island's complex social mosaic and its constitutional provision of parliamentary representation for all ethnic groups made it difficult for any single party to gain control. Instead, a multiparty system emerged, with no party strong enough to form a government. Labor support, which is vital for the survival of any government, was also weak because labor itself was segmented. In fact, all Mauritian parties (even the conservative ones) are "labor," "socialist," or "militant."

In Singapore, during the early phases of the transition to independence, the moderates were represented by the Labour party (which in 1955 gave Singapore its first chief minister) and the left by the People's Action party (PAP). The latter was split into a majority anticommunist and a minority procommunist wing. By 1959 the PAP had purged itself of its procommunist elements (they formed their own party) and had established a parliamentary majority. Since then, the PAP, led by Lee Kuan Yew, has won all its elections by a wide margin and has established a firm grip on the government. To stay in power, the government has resorted to firm and even strong-arm methods. Nonetheless, it enjoys a high degree of support, perhaps as a result of what appears to be an unwritten social contract: in exchange for general support, the government delivers a rising standard of living to all the potentially important interest groups, none of which has been permitted to achieve strong independent organizations.

In contrast to the other four economies examined here, Hong Kong was left virtually unaffected by the trend toward self-rule. Moreover, organized labor barely established a foothold. Throughout the period under discussion power was concentrated in the hands of Crown appointees: the governor (who appointed his Executive Council) and the financial secretary. The Legislative Council was made up of ex officio and government-appointed unofficial members. At first the latter consisted exclusively of the colony's business leaders; after the 1966 riots an effort was made to expand representation to other parts of society. The government listened to the people, but it was under no compulsion to obey them. The administration acted responsibly toward the population's social needs (for example, by providing refugee housing), but it resisted economic pressures. Its economic policies were highly pragmatic. Laissez-faire was originally adopted because it was considered appropriate to Hong Kong's activities as a trading outpost. The same policies proved successful when Hong Kong became a manufacturing center, and they continued to be pursued.

Despite their small size, the four states that obtained political independence from Britain were pessimistic about foreign trade and emphasized industrialization for the domestic market. Even tiny Malta went in for a fairly wide range of import substitution. Pioneer industry acts granting preferences and protection to new branches of industry were adopted in all four. Singapore joined Hong Kong in pursuing an essentially free trade policy only after the break with Malaysia in 1965. Import substitution continued in all the others, modified only by the establishment of export processing zones, most successfully in Mauritius in the mid-1970s.

Although Singapore, like Hong Kong, removed all restrictions on imports and exports, it by no means practiced laissez-faire in other matters. The government controlled domestic savings (through the CPF), screened foreign investment, and regulated the labor market. Thus, the brilliant success of its development strategy cannot simply be ascribed to some inevitable triumph of free enterprise that reflects the "magic of the market." In fact, die-hard advocates of intervention often claim that in the case of Singapore, as in Korea and Taiwan (China), it is the *quality* not the *absence* of intervention that matters for successful economic development.

Singapore has not relied on domestic private business, unlike Hong Kong with its small enterprises and Korea with its giant conglomerates. Rather, it has depended on direct foreign investment and state enterprise. The ruling party, guided by Lee Kuan Yew and a small group of close associates, has offered foreign corporations a strategically located base of operations, with state-of-the-art, world-class infrastructure and a skilled and disciplined work force. In addition the party has established several highly successful state enterprises, of which Singapore Airlines is only the most prominent example. The state itself thus serves as an entrepreneur as well as the essential intermediary between the foreign corporations operating on its soil and the local work force. The mainstay of this development strategy is the political and administrative elite recruited by the PAP, which itself reflects the values and ethos of this group.

To a large extent, the PAP is the institutional embodiment of the interests and aspirations of the English-educated Chinese lawyers, academics, and other professionals of the local elite who assumed the reins of power from the British in the 1950s. Their only competitors were the communists, with whom they were briefly allied before suppressing them. Both the formal education and the political ideals of this group were inspired by the British example. The British legacy they accepted was not democracy, which had never really been adopted in the colony, but the precepts and example of a highly efficient and incorruptible civil service working, apparently selflessly, for the benefit of the loyal and obedient native masses. To a certain extent this behavior may have been reinforced by the Confucian aspects of their cultural heritage. In any case, both systems placed a high value on competence as determined by performance in examinations, which are an obsession in Singapore. The PAP still appears to treat the people of Singapore in much the same way that the enlightened "pukka sahibs" of the Indian Civil Service treated their subjects—as wards being slowly trained for the full responsibilities of citizenship, to be exercised at some distant and unspecified time in the future.[5]

The majority of the Chinese in Singapore did not possess the education and culture of this Anglicized elite and were engaged in unskilled labor or petty trade. They were given employment opportunities in the foreign-owned plants, new state enterprises, and growing nontraded sectors, such as construction and local transport services and trade. The education system offered the more talented of their children an avenue to the top of the meritocratic pyramid. With full employment, rising real wages, a generous provision of public housing, and educational opportunities for their children, it is little wonder that the working classes in Singapore seem to feel that the PAP has kept its side of the implicit social contract.

Thus, both the British civil servants in Hong Kong and the British-inspired PAP elite of Singapore have come to operate as autonomous guardians of the societies over which they rule. Their development strategies, as already mentioned, have been quite different. Singapore chose an option that would give the state a much higher profile in a capital-intensive setting that relies on direct foreign investment and state enterprises as the main engines of growth rather than on flexible and adaptable small domestic enterprises, as in Hong Kong. It is hard to argue with either strategy. Free trade and export orientation are common to both and undoubtedly serve as an essential ingredient of their success.

Jamaica, Mauritius, and Malta are among the relatively few developing countries in which the Westminster-type parliamentary institutions established at the time of independence have survived. All three countries have experienced active political competition between parties in reasonably free and honest elections, with peaceful transitions taking place. The other side of the coin, however, has been that the ruling parties have felt obliged to cater to special interests—particularly labor, but also the fledgling protected industries. Liberal trade policies have therefore been postponed, to the detriment of growth. For the labor-oriented ruling parties, the profits of the sugar estates in Mauritius, largely owned by the Franco-Mauritian minority, and the rents from bauxite extraction by foreign multinationals in Jamaica were tempting targets for redistributive policies.

It was Mauritius which first recognized that such policies can lead to a dead end and therefore established the Export Processing Zone (EPZ). This zone employed mainly female labor, and existing labor legislation, aimed at the situation of male workers on the sugar estates, did not apply to it. Together with tourism, the increasingly high value added exports of manufactures from the EPZ are bringing significant growth to the island.

Jamaica, with its rich bauxite deposits, held out the longest. When the Manley government fell, the bauxite boom was over, and the Seaga regime, under the influence of the IMF and the World Bank, switched to more market-oriented policies that were slow to take effect. Although Michael Manley and the PNP have returned to power, the old discredited policies have not been embraced again. Too much has changed since the heady days of the early 1970s.

Malta appears to be curiously out of phase. It had a liberal regime in the 1960s under the Nationalist government of Borg-Olivier, at a time when other countries were engaging in import substitution, but then it switched to intervention and import substitution under the Labour government of Dom Mintoff and his successors. For a while, Malta's strategic location enabled it to draw substantial rents in the form of foreign loans and grants, which were used to support its distortionary policies. When the Nationalists returned to power, however, Malta too joined the movement toward economic liberalization and also looked toward closer integration with Europe rather than continuing to flirt with Libya and the Eastern bloc.

Ethnicity and Society

Three of the five islands are home to genuinely multiracial communities; two—Hong Kong and Malta—are more or less ethnically homogeneous. What role does ethnicity play in determining the success or failure of economic performance? There is no simple correlation between ethnic homogeneity or diversity, on the one hand, and success or failure in economic development, on the other. Of the two star performers, Singapore and Hong Kong, one is diverse and the other homogeneous. Of the other three economies, the homogeneous one, Malta, has done better than the two diverse ones, Jamaica and Mauritius.

This lack of a simple correlation does not necessarily mean that the ethnic factor is irrelevant. The connections are there, but they are subtle and complex. Ethnic differences can intensify social conflicts based on wealth, income, and status, and society may therefore find it difficult to accept the consequences of adapting to market forces, as required for successful development performance. Increases in the world price of primary exports may not be accepted as a benefit to society as a whole—indicating the need and providing the incentive to expand production—if the increases are perceived as accruing mainly to the advantage of wealthy planters descended from former rulers, as in the case of the Franco-Mauritian owners of huge estates in that country. An ethnically different majority—for example, the Hindus in Mauritius—is more likely to tax this source of income and redistribute the proceeds in its own favor through higher wages or transfer payments. Much of the political economy of Mauritius after independence can be explained by the struggle between white planters and Hindu labor over rents from the sugar sector.

This is not to say that ethnic homogeneity is always an advantage. Many of the most enterprising and innovative groups have been small ethnic minorities in larger societies, such as the Jews in Europe, the Lebanese in Africa, and the Chinese in Southeast Asia. Such groups not only bring prosperity to themselves but can stimulate development in the larger society. The task for the state in a multiethnic community is to ensure that each ethnic group contributes to the common good and that the majority is sufficiently satisfied with its share of the national product. A strategy designed to achieve short-run gain at the expense of minority groups can destroy the incentive of those groups to be productive—to the detriment of the entire society over the long run.

Among the five cases under discussion, Jamaica is clearly a negative example of this phenomenon. The island was populated largely by labor imported by the British to work the sugar plantations. The cruelty and oppression of slavery was met with fierce revolts that were harshly put down, but some slaves escaped to form independent communities. The tradition of labor militancy established at that time continued after slavery was abolished, as is evident in the strikes, riots, and labor disputes that are common in Jamaica to this day. Such an atmosphere is hardly conducive to successful development, whether export oriented or of some other design.

The Manley regime's radical economic policy of the 1970s discouraged small businessmen and middle-class professionals, many of whom were mixed-blood descendants of the European elite or other ethnic minorities. The small but active Chinese immigrant community also felt immobilized by the interventionist measures. Jamaica's open economy gave them the option to leave, and many of them moved to Great Britain or the United States, thus depriving the home country of their talents and enterprise. Although ethnic differences have become blurred in Jamaica since independence, the bitter racial divisions of the past have affected the island's prospects for development and could be responsible to a considerable extent for the economy's disappointing performance up to now.

The multiethnic society of Mauritius has had a more positive experience, even though a more complex social pattern evolved there during British colonial rule. The local economic elite, the Franco-Mauritian planters, shared the French language and Roman Catholic religion with the mixed-blood Créoles and the poorest ethnic group, the Afro-Mauritians. Unlike Jamaica's white planters, most of whom left at independence or earlier, the Franco-Mauritians continued to look on the island as their home. In spite of the struggle over sugar rents with the Hindu Indian majority, the extent of the redistribution aimed at the planters through taxation and other means did not reach such an intolerable level as to drive them out of the country. Instead, they stayed on and invested much of their wealth in the activities of the EPZ, sometimes in collaboration with foreign partners, as well as in hotels and other tourist-related ventures. The parliamentary system in Mauritius, although dominated by the labor-oriented Hindu majority, has provided sufficient incentive for a productive minority, including a small but active community of Chinese immigrants, to contribute to the progress of the society as a whole. The descendants of the Indian settlers provide the bulk of the labor force but also dominate politics, administration, and the professions. Mauritius thus seems to have evolved into a polity with a stable equilibrium between the different ethnic groups.

The ethnic situation in Singapore differs substantially from that in the two plantation economies. The British departed without leaving behind any remnants, and the community that subsequently grew up was built by settlers from the southern provinces of China and by their descendants, who now constitute about 70 percent of the population. The rest are mainly Indians and Malays. A past history of racial tension connected with the situation in neighboring Malaysia has led the PAP regime to put a great deal of emphasis on preventing any outbreaks of conflict between the different groups in Singapore. This desire to avoid tension, conflict, and violence between the races has given the government further justification for tightly regulating any overt manifestations of cultural or religious differences and for practicing its brand of "autonomy," with respect to the "civil society" of Singapore. Like the colonial rulers before them, the English-educated Chinese elite who created the PAP believe that without intervention from the top the different ethnic and religious groups would be at each other's throats. The autonomy that the regime has thereby gained enables it to maintain the integrity and stability of its market-oriented economic policies. Whether or not such close regulation is indeed necessary to preserve racial harmony, it has helped Singapore achieve spectacular development results.

Hong Kong is more homogeneous than Singapore because it does not have an Indian and Malay component, as Singapore does, and because it is so close to the Chinese mainland. Moreover, its status as a temporary British possession has not altered its ethnic and cultural identity. The 5.5 million Chinese, many of whom are first-generation immigrants from the mainland, appear to have been grateful for the opportunity to pursue their economic advancement while leaving the tasks of government to the British civil servants. The administration has been active in urban planning, public transport, housing, health, and education, with considerable help from the private sector. The enterprise and energy of Hong Kong are matched by the success of those parts of the mainland where the regional authorities have been prepared to relax controls.

Malta, like Hong Kong, is ethnically homogeneous, but its tiny population is even more unusual in having a unique language and culture that date back to antiquity. At the same time, the people have a strong sense of being at the crossroads of the Mediterranean, with ties to southern Europe, North Africa, and the Middle East. This combined heritage has given them a strong sense of solidarity in their domestic affairs and a cosmopolitan outlook in their external affairs. As a result, the Maltese have launched both an ambitious welfare state and a diversified program of foreign aid and cooperative ventures.

Poverty and Equity

Some of the literature on development theory has suggested that there is an inevitable tradeoff between growth and equity. The more skewed the income distribution, so the argument goes, the higher the average propensity to save and therefore the higher the rate of growth for a given capital-output ratio. Differentials for skill and effort in the wage structure and in returns to capital for risk-taking were said to point in the same direction. Thus it was believed that countries such as Sri Lanka, which consciously chose a humane welfare state despite a relatively low per capita income, would pay an acceptable price in terms of a lower growth rate, whereas countries in which the economic and social structure generated high inequality, such as Brazil, would be able to grow rapidly and could perhaps alleviate poverty through "trickle-down" effects.

Comparative data on income distribution are extremely hard to find. Nevertheless, the data that are available on the five economies of interest here cast considerable doubt on the growth-versus-equity hypothesis. The cases of high growth—Hong Kong and Singapore—both started out in 1960 with *less* inequality than resource-abundant Jamaica; furthermore, they experienced small *declines* in inequality over the next two decades, whereas inequality in Jamaica rose even higher. The Gini coefficient in Hong Kong fell from 0.487 in 1966 to 0.447 in 1981; in Singapore it fell from 0.499 in 1966 to 0.455 in 1980; but in Jamaica it rose from 0.628 in 1968 to 0.655 in 1980 (Fields 1984).

In Hong Kong the proportion of households below a fixed poverty line fell from 18 percent in 1966 to 11 percent in 1971 and 7 percent in 1976. In a similar calculation for Singapore, but with a different poverty line, 37 percent were below the line in 1966, 29 percent in 1975, and 18 percent in 1980. Although this last figure seems surprisingly high, recall from chapter 3 that among the poorest 4.8 percent of households in Singapore more than 80 percent have television sets, 55 percent have telephones, and 19 percent have washing machines.

In both Hong Kong and Singapore, health indicators such as life expectancy and average caloric intake are fully comparable to the levels in industrial countries. Although poverty has certainly not been eradicated there (or in industrial countries, for that matter), it cannot be argued that the remarkable growth achieved by Hong Kong and Singapore has been at the expense of the least advantaged.

Both governments, particularly that of Singapore, have placed tremendous emphasis on providing extensive public housing. In Singapore in 1985 no less than 84 percent of the population lived in government-built or administered housing facilities and 64 percent in owner-occupied units. The PAP regime in Singapore made public housing the core of its strategy for building a new society. The massive resources channeled into the CPF were used to finance housing construction and help workers acquire ownership. At the same time, the government used its control over space and housing to further its political domination of the island and to promote the social patterns that it favored with respect to family size and the structure and ethnic composition of neighborhoods.

The experience of Hong Kong and Singapore clearly demonstrates that one of the most effective ways of improving, or at least stabilizing, income distribution over the long term is to generate employment opportunities, for they will raise real wages and help eliminate poverty.

Jamaica, which consciously tried to follow a more liberal or even radical policy, ended up making inequity and poverty worse. Unfortunately, almost no data are available on income distribution in Mauritius and Malta. The vestiges of the former plantation economy are still present in Mauritius, which also shows signs of considerable inequality. The Franco-Mauritian community lives in elegant suburbs, while many Afro-Mauritians and some Indians continue to live in shanties and substandard facilities. The EPZ, however, must have helped greatly to alleviate poverty and perhaps reduce inequality, as well.

The Role of Natural Resources

Throughout the history of civilization, growth has occurred wherever natural resources have been available, although some societies enriched themselves not through the exploitation of their own resources but through trade—Phoenicia, Venice, and the Hansa being familiar examples. In the case of the five islands discussed here, there appears to be an inverse relation between endowments of natural resources and economic success. Singapore, Hong Kong, and Malta have no resources other than their geographic location, yet all three developed at a vastly greater pace than the two resource-rich economies. Jamaica, the best endowed of the five, stagnated after a boom in raw materials that lasted some fifteen years, and Mauritius made little headway until it abandoned its resource-based strategy.

Part of the explanation for this apparent anomaly can be found in the social structure that developed around the production mode. Plantation agriculture depended on large numbers of unskilled workers—originally slaves in the case of Jamaica and indentured laborers in Mauritius. Opportunities for "middle-class" employment and for skilled labor were few. The social polarization that emerged from these historical circumstances survives to this day. Where production is not based on resources, there is more of a socioeconomic continuum. Social conflicts are less intense; and there is less distortion benefiting particular groups and more stability favoring growth.

Resource flexibility is another consideration. The capital equipment used in exploiting primary resources tends to be more specific than the capital employed in secondary production. The small light industry in Hong Kong relies, for the most part, on general equipment, and the composition of the product can respond rapidly to changes in demand. Sugarcane mills or bauxite-mining machinery, by contrast, are meant for a specific use, and plantation workers and miners have product-specific skills. It follows that an adverse trade shock is likely to have a stronger adverse effect on resource-based economies than on those based on "footloose" activities.

When political economy is taken into account, yet another reason emerges to explain why rich resources may be a curse in disguise. The rents generated by natural resources—especially if they are highly concentrated at a particular site, as in the case of a mine or a strategically located harbor—have two important consequences. First, they provide a ready source of revenue for the government. Second, the associated labor force is able to transfer some of the rent into higher wages for itself and thus behave as a kind of "labor aristocracy." The high wages may be dispensed by foreign firms amenable to displaying their goodwill in this regard, or they may be a response to the threat, implicit or otherwise, of damaging strikes or other forms of labor action. The high wages may become generalized, either through union activity or through legislation. Mauritius and Jamaica have both experienced prolonged periods of high real wages and of unemployment; unemployment, in turn, puts pressure on the government to undertake public works or other action that will redistribute income.

By itself, the revenue available for the government is not a problem, since it could help the government lighten the tax burden on the rest of the economy. If the state is regarded as a fiscal Leviathan, however, it will simply use whatever additional resources it acquires to expand further its own activities, whether or not these are socially productive at the margin. The wage levels of the privileged workers in the resource-based enclave could also have a spillover effect on other sectors, in addition to causing unemployment in the Harris-Todaro manner.

As the literature on the "Dutch disease" has stressed, expenditure out of natural resource rents diverts resources from the production of other tradable goods into the nontraded sector. This can be deleterious in the long run, insofar as the productivity of these other tradables is likely to grow faster than that of nontraded goods and services. The rent proceeds can also be used to subsidize inefficient import substitution, as was done in Jamaica and Mauritius.

The important point to note, however, is that natural resource rents allow the government and society to avoid the hard policy choices that are integral to truly viable growth strategies. In boom periods the ready rent revenues make it easy to launch social programs, but in time it usually proves impossible to maintain these programs and difficult to shrink them. Rent revenues may also be used to support real wages at an untenably high level, to refrain from devaluation, and to assuage nationalist concerns by keeping out foreigners or by getting them out if they are in already. Many examples of these tendencies can be found in the experiences of Mauritius, Malta, and, most egregiously of all, Jamaica.

By contrast, the sole reason that Hong Kong and Singapore have survived and progressed has been their drive to export competitively to the rest of the world whatever goods and services the effort, skill, and enterprise of the local population can put forth. The very scarcity of land is an advantage in that it raises the relative price of nontraded goods and diverts demand and domestic resources such as labor into the production and export of tradables—mainly manufactured goods, but also financial and other services. This relative scarcity of land seems to have been overlooked in many accounts of the success of the Far Eastern economies, including Japan and Taiwan (China), as exporters of manufactured goods.[6]

Despite their varied beginnings—as naval stations, trading centers, and sugar plantations—the key to sustained growth for our five small open economies has been their ability to emerge as exporters of manufactured goods. While Hong Kong and Singapore have had the most spectacular successes, Malta and Mauritius are both also well on the way to progress along these lines. Only Jamaica has yet to make its move.

Notes

1. Although a variety of national income data can be used to compare the five economies of interest in this volume, the discussion relies on the estimates of Summers and Heston (1987), which represent the most thorough attempt thus far to overcome the obstacles that beset all international and intertemporal comparisons of real incomes.

2. See Tan (1984) for a review of the role of foreign trade and investment in Singapore's development.

3. The transition process is formally analyzed by Hansen (1979) and Findlay (1985).

4. See Arndt (1987) for an interesting historical survey of development thought.

5. See Edwin Lee (1989) for the British colonial legacy in Singapore.

6. See Findlay (1989) for a model that stresses the role of scarcity of land in relation to the allocation of resources between nontraded and traded goods.

References

Arndt, H. W. 1987. *Economic Development: The History of an Idea.* Chicago, Ill.: University of Chicago Press.

Corden, W. M. 1984. "Booming Sector and Dutch Disease Economics: Survey and Consolidation." *Oxford Economic Papers* 36:359–80.

Fields, G. S. 1984. "Employment, Income Distribution and Economic Growth in Seven Small Open Economies" *Economic Journal* 94(March):74–83.

————. 1985. "Industrialization and Employment in Hong Kong, Korea, Singapore and Taiwan." In Walter A. Galenson, ed., *Foreign Trade and Investment: Economic Growth in the Newly Industrializing Asian Countries.* Madison: University of Wisconsin.

Findlay, Ronald. 1985. "Primary Exports, Manufacturing and Development." In Mats Lundahl, ed., *The Primary Sector in Economic Development.* London: Croom Helm.

————. 1989. "Theoretical Notes on Singapore as a Development Model." In K. S. Sandhu and Paul Wheatley, eds., *The Management of Success: The Moulding of Modern Singapore.* Singapore: Institute of South East Asian Studies.

Hansen, Bent. 1979. "Colonial Economic Development with an Unlimited Supply of Land." *Economic Development and Cultural Change* 27:611–27.

Lee, Edwin. 1989. "The Colonial Legacy." In K. S. Sandhu and P. Wheatley, eds., *The Management of Success: The Moulding of Modern Singapore*. Singapore: Institute of South East Asian Studies.

Lee, Soo Ann. 1984. "Problems of Economic Structure in Singapore." In You Poh Seng and Lim Chong Yah, eds., *Singapore: Twenty-Five Years of Development*. Singapore: Hong Leong Group.

Lim, Linda Y. C. 1989. "Social Welfare." In K. S. Sandhu and P. Wheatley, eds., *The Management of Success: The Moulding of Modern Singapore*. Singapore: Institute of South East Asian Studies.

Meade, J. E. 1961. "Mauritius: A Case Study in Malthusian Economics." *Economic Journal* 71(283):521–34.

Summers, Robert, and Alan Heston. 1987. "A New Set of International Comparisons of Real Product and Prices for 130 Countries, 1950–1985." *Review of Income and Wealth* ser. 34(1):1–26.

Tan, Augustine. 1984. "Changing Patterns of Singapore's Foreign Trade and Investment since 1960." In You Poh Seng and Lim Chong Yah, eds., *Singapore: Twenty-Five Years of Development*. Singapore: Hong Leong Group.

Index

324 *Ronald Findlay and Stanislaw Wellisz*

Singapore, 109, 123–24. *See also*
Fiscal deficits; Taxation
Bulk-buying scheme in Malta, 12,
280–81
Bureaucracy: in China, 299; in
Hong Kong, 76; in Jamaica, 159,
180, 196; in Singapore, 109, 111–
12, 132
Business community: in Jamaica,
143–44, 146–47, 160–61, 194; in
Singapore, 106–7
Business families in Jamaica, 157,
160, 193
Bustamante, Alexander, 144–45, 310
Bustamante Industrial Trade
Union, 144

Capital account. *See* Balance of pay-
ments; Debt, external; Direct for-
eign investment
Capital controls: absence in Hong
Kong of, 16; in Malta, 268, 269,
275–76, 279; in Mauritius, 241
Capital Development Fund (CDF,
Jamaica), 185, 187
Capital flight: from Jamaica, 177,
179, 188, 189, 208; from Malta, 268
Capital formation: in Hong Kong,
47–49, 55, 56, 83 n26, 84 n27; in
Malta, 287; in Singapore, 98–99,
109. *See also* Saving and invest-
ment
Capital markets in Hong Kong, 54–
56, 80, 85 n38
Caribbean Basin Initiative, 201, 205
Caribbean Economic Community
(CARICOM), 181, 187, 212 n44, 213
n51
Caribbean Free Trade Association,
212 n44
CARICOM, 181, 187, 212 n44, 213 n51
Catholic Church: in Malta, 261, 263,
285; in Singapore, 102
CDF. Capital Development Fund
(Jamaica), 185, 187
Central Bank of Malta, 268, 279
Central banks. *See specific bank*
Central Development and Welfare
Committee (Mauritius), 228

Centralization of policymaking in
Singapore, 113, 134
Central Provident Fund (Singapore),
8, 106, 109, 118–23, 132–33, 297,
302–3
Certificates of indebtedness (Hong
Kong), 81 n3
"Challenge-response" pattern of development, 97
Chamber of Commerce (Jamaica),
147
Chemical industry in Hong Kong,
48
Chenery, Hollis, 296
China: cession of Hong Kong to
United Kingdom by, 81 n1; cul-
tural influence on Hong Kong of,
40–43, 54, 75; emigration to Hong
Kong from, 17–18, 24, 30–31, 47;
emigration to Mauritius from,
220; links between Singapore
and, 94; planned reunification of
Hong Kong with, 76, 88 n59; rela-
tions between Malta and, 291 n5;
sympathies in Hong Kong to-
ward, 34, 36–37, 70; trade embar-
goes on, 17, 48
Chinese communities: in Jamaica,
142; in Mauritius, 220, 226; in
Singapore, 94, 131
Citrus Expansion Program
(Jamaica), 210 n16
City District Officer program
(Hong Kong), 70, 72
Civil service. *See* Bureaucracy
Clothing industry. *See* Textiles and
apparel industry
Comité d'Action Musulman
(Mauritius), 227
Committee on Diversification
(Hong Kong), 75
Commonwealth Sugar Agreement,
224, 252 n8
Communications and transport in
Hong Kong, 22
Communism: in Hong Kong, 32, 36,
70; in Singapore, 95, 311
Conference of Trade Unions
(Malta), 263